The Last Great American Picture Show

The Last Great American Picture Show

New Hollywood Cinema in the 1970s

edited by Thomas Elsaesser, Alexander Horwath and Noel King

Amsterdam University Press

Front and back cover illustration: Faye Dunaway in BONNIE AND CLYDE (1967, Arthur Penn)

Cover design: Kok Korpershoek, Amsterdam
Lay-out: JAPES, Amsterdam

ISBN 90 5356 493 4 (hardcover)
ISBN 90 5356 631 7 (paperback)
NUR 674

Table of Contents

Part Four Critical Debates

Part One
Introductions

The Impure Cinema: New Hollywood 1967-1976

Alexander Horwath

> So you have stumbled indeed, without the aid of LSD or other indole alkaloids,
> onto a secret richness and concealed density of dream; onto a network by which X
> number of Americans are truly communicating whilst reserving their lies, recita-
> tions of routine, arid betrayals of spiritual poverty, for the official government de-
> livery system; maybe even onto a real alternative to the exitlessness, to the
> absence of surprise to life, that harrows the head of everybody American you
> know, and you too, sweetie.[1]

The title of this book suggests a certain cultural pessimism. It talks about a
Golden Age and a closed chapter of history: *The Last Great American Picture
Show*. Generally, demarcations of this sort are hard to justify and are more of a
hindrance to an open engagement with films. They tend to originate in the romantic notion that cultural history unfolds in discrete episodes ("narratives"),
and they often reflect the formative influences of the author. If you have come
of age as a cinema-goer during the heyday of New Hollywood cinema – some-
time between BONNIE AND CLYDE and TAXI DRIVER – you've probably experienced the main brands of post-1970s American cinema by necessity as less
rich, less intelligent, less political, as retrograde.

My own first experiences of the cinema stand in contrast to this account –
even if, in the end, they led to similar conclusions. I started to go the movies
regularly at the end of the Seventies. *Star Wars*, which I saw six or seven times
during 1977/78, propelled this habit. It's a film that fairly exactly marks the
point at which public discourse and popular cinema in the United States underwent a crucial shift in emphasis. Towards the end of the Seventies, the increasingly complex narrative negotiation of (both fictional and very real) contradictions and conflicts started to recede behind the phantasms of a neo-
conservative discourse of re-mythologisation, re-evangelisation and re-milita-
risation, gradually disappearing from view altogether in the course of the
Reaganite era. So in a sense my first cinema was already "post-classical"[2] and
post-modern – a cinema of hyper-genres, often accompanied by an ironic affirmation of shop-worn myths and relying more on textures, surfaces, aural-

visual effects and on "somatic" audience responses. Films such as STAR WARS, CLOSE ENCOUNTERS OF THE THIRD KIND, SUPERMAN – THE MOVIE, ALIEN, THE EMPIRE STRIKES BACK or RAIDERS OF THE LOST ARK strove to be seen repeatedly, their exhilarating physical effects had to be felt over and over again in the cinema (it was the last pre-VCR era).

Parallel to these experiences, however, I retrospectively began to explore the cinema of the Sixties and early Seventies – propelled by my first contact with very different and irritating Hollywood movies like APOCALYPSE NOW and RAGING BULL. Around 1980/81, the "Star-Kino", a repertory house in Vienna, offered the opportunity to view within the space of a few months THE GODFATHER (both parts one after another), MEAN STREETS, ALICE DOESN'T LIVE HERE ANYMORE, TAXI DRIVER, the complete works of Sam Peckinpah, EASY RIDER, THE LONG GOODBYE, NASHVILLE, ZABRISKIE POINT, ALICE'S RESTAURANT, LITTLE BIG MAN, KLUTE, ALL THE PRESIDENT'S MEN and SHAMPOO. There was a stark and inspiring contrast between these works (and their viewing context: a small, dingy suburban repertory theatre) and, on the other hand, the new spectacular films (usually shown in the "Gartenbau-Kino", an 800-seat picture palace on the Ringstrasse in Vienna, practically designed for intoxicating "feelie" effects). This contrast has grown larger over time, so much so that it now seems reasonable to speak in terms of fundamentally different temporal and aesthetic zones.

The mixture of styles and subject matter that, for simplicity's sake, shall be called "New Hollywood" here, could of course still be located in films made after 1977 (in the early Eighties, for instance, BLADE RUNNER represented the fragile intersection of the two halves of my film world).[3] And even during the past fifteen years many of the (few) important American films still had their reference points – in terms of personnel, aesthetics, subject matter or attitude – in the culture of the Seventies: THE THIN RED LINE, SHORT CUTS, L.A. CONFIDENTIAL and BULWORTH; the work of Martin Scorsese, Paul Schrader, John Sayles and Clint Eastwood;[4] JACKIE BROWN, GEORGE WASHINGTON and MY OWN PRIVATE IDAHO; the work of Richard Linklater, Paul Thomas Anderson and Wes Anderson (as well as the much-maligned, but fascinating films of Sean Penn); DRUGSTORE COWBOY, ANOTHER DAY IN PARADISE and JESUS' SON; THE ICE STORM, VELVET GOLDMINE, ALMOST FAMOUS ... and last but not least, TEXASVILLE and THE TWO JAKES, two extremely rich – if sadly under-praised – sequels and reinterpretations of classics from the New Hollywood era (THE LAST PICTURE SHOW and CHINATOWN).

On the other hand, the American "Indie" movement of the 1980s and 1990s, widely regarded as a new alternative to the major studios' increasingly conservative production and distribution policies, seems to have exhausted itself – at least as a viable cultural-political movement – and split into multiple direc-

Ben Johnson in THE LAST PICTURE SHOW

tions. Often connected to a niche consciousness, the standard-bearers of independent cinema consequently helped to establish a niche market, which could then easily be appropriated or inhaled by the mainstream industry. The important "Indie" companies of the Eighties and Nineties are today part of or closely associated with major studios. In addition, the studios themselves have set up their own labels to cater to the (formerly) "independent" market. In Late Capitalism, the so-called alternatives almost always turn out to be mere variations of one and the same economic logic.

At a cursory glance, the process of rejuvenation that the film industry enforced after 1967-68, and which resulted in a "New Hollywood", was a product of this same logic. Perhaps the crucial difference lay in the intensity of the social movements, changes, shocks and crises, which rocked American society in the Sixties and early Seventies, and moreover, in the intensity with which popular culture registered these shocks. During the Eighties and Nineties the real crises were certainly none the less intense, but the modalities of their narrative transformation into popular discourse had entirely shifted. Mainstream and large sections of independent cinema had succumbed to the same modes of repression and displacement as indeed had public life.[5]

The symbiotic relationship which links politics and popular culture in the U.S. reached an unprecedented level with the glamorous pop-cult surrounding John F. Kennedy and his administration – and it certainly manifests itself in New Hollywood cinema, too. But in the case of these films, it is often not only a matter of themes and plots related to current events or of a transfer from political to cultural energies,[6] but essentially a matter of changing modes of perception. In mid-to-late Sixties public discourse, the discrepancy between "official" images and rhetoric and real world experiences (regarding the Vietnam War, for instance) became increasingly obvious, and this gap in turn called into question all conventional means of representation previously considered valid and true to life. As the liberal consensus in American society was coming unstuck, for a brief time the generally accepted "realism" of American television and Hollywood films seemed to be open to debate. American films had begun to acquire aesthetic means of encoding such doubts since the early 1960s, as numerous new cinematographic "movements" – in tandem with the new social movements – gained a foothold in the United States (primarily in New York):[7] "The expressive possibilities that became available – and in them semiology was always imbued with and surrounded by politics – may be summarised as being hinged between authenticity and irony."[8] Yet, when viewed in retrospect, the impression of a linear, almost logical development from a classical realist to a modernist and reflective cinema (which, at the time, was generally regarded as inevitable) is largely an illusion.

This book deals with a kind of cinema which in many ways pushed back the boundaries: politically, by raising taboo topics and views (in films ranging from MEDIUM COOL to CHINATOWN); aesthetically, by striving to replace a seemingly transparent and natural norm of realist representation with self-reflexivity (from DAVID HOLZMAN'S DIARY to THE LAST MOVIE); and lastly, in economic terms, by trying to extricate itself from the traditional industrial film production process through the formation of groups and the cultivation of auteur personalities (from John Cassavetes and Francis Ford Coppola's American Zoetrope to the BBS group which produced films like DRIVE, HE SAID or THE KING OF MARVIN GARDENS for Columbia).

At the same time, it was a cinema that could not help internalising these boundaries. It allegorically staged the defeats and set-backs of this "time of renewal" and unconsciously placed itself in an untenable position: politically, by more or less failing – much as American society did – to develop an alternative way out of the crisis (as manifest in films from EASY RIDER to ALL THE PRESIDENT'S MEN);[9] aesthetically, by generally seeking to reconcile its "modernist" objectives with the demands of a readily accessible cinema of entertainment

Dustin Hoffman and Faye Dunaway in LITTLE BIG MAN

(from BONNIE AND CLYDE to TAXI DRIVER); and economically, by entirely mis-understanding the willingness of a film industry – temporarily weakened by economic setbacks – to make concessions. There seemed to be no other way of resolving the dialectic between "autonomous" creativity and large invest-ments (= expectations of profit) than by staging quasi-liberating catastrophes (from ZABRISKIE POINT to HEAVEN'S GATE). In many films of the New Holly-wood era, these conflicts create a magnificent richness and enormous internal tensions and an incoherence, which lays bare their conditions of production and, consequently, the contradictions in American culture.[10] As Robin Wood has observed: "The films seem to crack open before our eyes."[11]

The different modes of negotiating or overcoming this untenable position can be roughly divided into two categories, as can indeed the various individ-ual career changes. The entire film industry acclimatised to the newly "liber-ated" situation for a brief period, and almost every director, producer, writer, actor fell into line. The great (and adaptable) majority of those employed in the film industry experienced this period as one phase among many, as a stage which allowed them to behave in a more "radical" or "independent" manner but which didn't adversely affect their ability to survive in the more conservative climate that lay ahead. A none too small minority, however, identified more deeply and concretely with the new opportunities of art and life; they exhausted their energies more rapidly (because the opposition was much greater, too) and had difficulty making the transition when all the "fun" was over.

If one were to name the typical actors of the New Hollywood era – apart from the obvious (male) names such as Warren Beatty, Jack Nicholson, Al Pacino, Dustin Hoffman, Gene Hackman, Robert De Niro, who emerged from this definitive phase in their careers with both bankability and credibility intact for decades to come, two "couples" spring to mind who epitomise two opposing poles of the time. Jane Fonda and Robert Redford: the "official" (and three times on-screen) couple – still popular today, firmly entrenched in the film industry and symbolically linked to the Sixties and Seventies. Karen Black and Warren Oates: an ideal but doubly "unofficial" couple (their liaison being purely based on my imagination; they did not share one moment of screen-time) virtually forgotten today with audiences as well as the film industry, but very concretely and painfully associated with the Sixties and Seventies.

Fonda and Redford, born in New York and Santa Monica, respectively, rose to prominence on the carefree side of Cold War Culture (which was belatedly memorialised in BAREFOOT IN THE PARK), came of age during the incipient crisis of the mid-Sixties (THE CHASE) and, after several detours, continued down a path of social awareness (DOWNHILL RACER, TELL THEM WILLIE BOY'S HERE, THEY SHOOT HORSES, DON'T THEY?) and antiwar protests. Acting as figureheads of the left, they enabled several analyses of social and screen stereotypes (THE CANDIDATE, KLUTE, TOUT VA BIEN), but stopped short of any decisive, radical step, mellowing into a kind of critical movie star liberalism (ALL THE PRESIDENT'S MEN, THREE DAYS OF THE CONDOR, BRUBAKER, JULIA, COMING HOME, THE CHINA SYNDROME). They fostered the re-romanticisation of outsider myths (THE ELECTRIC HORSEMAN) and finally became more occupied with preserving their youth, disciplining the body, consulting on media industry matters and such pursuits as sport, nature, and various entrepreneurial ventures (where the strange intersection between neo-conservatism and political correctness, between INDECENT PROPOSAL and QUIZ SHOW, is no longer an issue) – untouchable icons that transcend the film world.

Karen Black, born Ziegler in Park Ridge, Illinois, and Warren Oates from Depoy, Kentucky, came from different milieus. For them perfection was not the mother of all things, and they never strove to put well-rounded, triumphant characters on the screen. Instead, they played small, "marginal" types, gentle sufferers, hysterics and unpredictable psychos – never winking at the audience, feeling no need to rise above the intellectual horizon of their characters. They were content to capture the banality of the everyday that dominates most people's lives. Neither capable nor willing to acquire any kind of glamour, they were still in high demand and moderately successful for a number of years, because during these years – and the same holds for Fonda and Redford – the reality of America received as much recognition as its phantasms. They tended not to "dominate" the films they worked on but often collaborated with specific filmmakers for specific purposes. In Black's case, it was mainly for gloomy, "countercultural" purposes: EASY RIDER (Dennis Hopper), FIVE EASY PIECES (Bob Rafelson), DRIVE, HE SAID (Jack Nicholson), CISCO PIKE (Bill Norton), BORN TO WIN (Ivan Passer), NASHVILLE (Robert Altman). But even in the limp adaptation of THE DAY OF THE LOCUST her determined little Hollywood whore is the true centrepiece of the film. In the case of Oates, it was obsessed odd-balls and melancholic men of the West – in four films each for Sam Peckinpah and Monte Hellman,[12] as well as for other maverick directors like Peter Fonda (THE HIRED HAND), James Frawley (KID BLUE), Phil Kaufman (THE WHITE DAWN), Terrence Malick (BADLANDS), and Thomas McGuane (92 IN THE SHADE). After 1976 Black and Oates were barely able to find suitable employment, their qualities soon becoming an obstacle and their insistence on truthfulness a genuine risk for a newly regenerated cinema of escapism or stodgy liberalism. Oates died in 1982 and Black mainly appeared in small European and trashy American movies from then on. Most poignantly, her only film with Robert Redford (THE GREAT GATSBY) is considered to be one of the greatest disasters of the 1970s.

As should be apparent from such an account, the deep-seated contradictions in New Hollywood films still have the power to shape any critical engagement with this era, especially in Europe. There is a multitude of temptations to resolve the contradictions: by drawing strict lines between autonomous artistry and studio capitalism, or between "opportunistic" and "authentic" pairs of actors; by extricating individual films from their ambivalent contexts of production and displaying them as "pure", ideal artefacts; by distilling from films political intentions and messages which were often barely implied; by postulating a glorious age of new beginnings which was mostly experienced by those involved as a series of humiliations.

In a separate essay that follows I have put together some passages that focus on lesser known films and more muted undercurrents. They consist in large part of comments and statements culled from filmmakers, critics, together with excerpts from a written "conversation" that I conducted with Beverly Walker. Her published accounts of the era – both then and later on – were always highly stimulating. Since 1968, Walker has worked as a press agent, scriptwriter and in various production capacities on New Hollywood films – ZABRISKIE POINT, TWO-LANE BLACKTOP, AMERICAN GRAFFITI among many others. Her recollections and insights may help us appreciate and extend, rather than resolve, the multiple contradictions of this era.

In its original – and slightly different – German version, this book was part of a larger project initiated and financed by the VIENNALE, Vienna's International Film Festival. In the framework of its 1994 and 1995 editions the festival highlighted American narrative cinema of the Sixties and Seventies, staging two comprehensive retrospectives in close collaboration with the Austrian Cinematheque (Österreichisches Filmmuseum). In total, more than 160 films were screened. The first section was entitled *COOL – Pop, Politics, Hollywood 1960-68*. The second part went in search of *The Last Great American Picture Show. New Hollywood 1967-1976*. In both cases, publications were produced to join the film series.

I am indebted to many people without whom this book would not have been possible, especially of course to all the contributors for their inspiration, their commitment and their persistence; to Noel King, Thomas Elsaesser and the Amsterdam University Press who "picked it up" and facilitated its English-language edition and expansion; to Kent Jones (who, apart from his essay, supplied advice, practical help, a videotheque and good spirits in most generous doses) and to Beverly Walker (whose comments on my questions not only imparted first-hand experience but nipped in the bud any romanticisation of the topic). In addition, I am grateful for all manner of help and advice to Gerald Ayres, Margaret Bodde, Ed Dimendberg, Stefan Grissemann, Hans Hurch, Karin Jahn, Amy Kenyon, Peter Konlechner, Dagmar Küttner, Richard Linklater, Terrence Malick, Olaf Möller, Ralph Palka, Richard Pena, Arthur Penn, Reinhard Puntigam, Bert Rebhandl, Alexandra Seibel, Peter Spiegel and Alessandra Thiele. My heart goes out to Regina Schlagnitweit whose love of Warren Oates and BRING ME THE HEAD OF ALFREDO GARCIA set the avalanche in motion.

Notes

1.   Thomas Pynchon, *The Crying of Lot 49*, Philadelphia 1966, p. 128.
2.   Cf. Drehli Robnik, "Das postklassische (Hollywood-)Kino," in: *Filmkunst*, 145 (1995), Vienna.
3.   I recall similar sensations viewing WHO'LL STOP THE RAIN (1978, Karel Reisz), FINGERS (1978, James Toback), BLUE COLLAR (1978, Paul Schrader), DAYS OF HEAVEN (1976/78, Terrence Malick), SAINT JACK (1979, Peter Bogdanovich), HEAVEN'S GATE (1980, Michael Cimino), OUT OF THE BLUE (1980, Dennis Hopper), ESCAPE FROM NEW YORK (1981, John Carpenter), BLOW OUT (1981, Brian de Palma), REDS

(1981, Warren Beatty), TRUE CONFESSIONS (1981, Ulu Grosbard), THE KING OF COMEDY (1983, Martin Scorsese), BREATHLESS (1983, Jim McBride).

4. The screenplay for UNFORGIVEN had been "on the shelf" for about 15 years. It belongs more to the tradition of dirty westerns ca. 1971 than to the cinema of 1992. Richard Harris's line of dialogue: "Well, I mean, why not shoot the president?," makes much more sense in a late Sixties, early Seventies context.

5. "There is an incredible atmosphere of coercion in Hollywood. I think it starts with the banks who loan money to the studios to make films, and is presided over by the studio executives who have to answer to the banks and to stockholders. Eventually everyone joins the caravan – agents & managers & attorneys, and writers, directors, producers. Fear controls and dominates and shapes everything. (...) Today's films are pervaded by paranoia and a sense of dread far worse than those of the Sixties/Seventies. At bottom, all these so called 'action' films are about the terrible things a man has to do just to stay alive! How do you think Stallone and Willis became stars? (...) I personally believe that American films are much more reflective of the insular, Boschian, duplicitous cut-throat environment of Hollywood than of the country or world as a whole." (Beverly Walker, letter to the author)

6. "It is not entirely farfetched to speculate that the political energies of the Sixties were cathartically channelled into the arts – and particularly the popular arts – of the Seventies." (Diane Jacobs, *Hollywood Renaissance*, New York 1980, p. 1).

7. See also Jonathan Rosenbaum's essay in this volume.

8. David E. James, *Allegories of Cinema*, Princeton 1989, p. 27.

9. Cf. Robert B. Ray, *A Certain Tendency of the Hollywood Cinema, 1930-1980*, Princeton 1985, esp. p. 247-256.

10. Cf. Robin Wood, "The Incoherent Text: Narrative in the 70s," in: *Hollywood from Vietnam to Reagan*, New York 1986.

11. Ibid., p. 50. David E. James' perspective in *Allegories of Cinema* is a touch more pessimistic: "Admission into a commercial film of any social discontent that cannot be recuperated into final affirmation of the status quo, or the omission of accepted motifs (the woman-as-commodity, the Indian-as-savage, or the finally honest police system) sets that film into contradiction with the ideological and psychological preconditions of its function as entertainment, sets text against context. Marking the historically variable limits of the medium as capitalist industry, the boundary between possible and impossible industrial films is always process, constantly being readjusted to accommodate simultaneously the institutionalization of new social need and the industry's own need in each new film for that degree of transgression and novelty upon which constantly renewed consumption depends. (Indeed, one of the histories of Sixties cinema is that of Hollywood's discovery of a way of dealing profitably with contemporary politics.)", op. cit. p. 174.

12. See also Kent Jones's essay in this volume.

"The Last Good Time We Ever Had"

Remembering the New Hollywood Cinema

Noel King

> That an aesthetically experimental socially conscious *cinema d'auteur* could
> exist simultaneously with a burgeoning and rapacious blockbuster mentality
> was extraordinary, but it became the defining mark of 1970s cinema. That
> the two could co-exist for long, however, was an illusion as ephemeral
> as the notion of liberal ideological consensus.[1]

> Who the hell is talking to you like this? How OLD is he? The author is 52 and he
> loved the decade of the 1970s and its movies. We had movies then that you had to
> *watch*. Many of them had unfamiliar shapes, new narrative structures or strate-
> gies. They began late. They switched course. And they did not end well or hap-
> pily or comfortably. Sometimes they broke off in your hands, or your mind.[2]

> The economic disaster of 1970 produced a lot of official proclamations of
> change, but in the final analysis things didn't change very much. For all the
> successes of a few small films, it was finally the more predictable successes of
> big films and big stars that carried Hollywood bookkeeping back into the
> black. Now, more than ever before, Hollywood is on the lookout for the
> "presold" project, the films that come with a formula for guaranteed success:
> films based on runaway best-sellers and hit plays, or films with stars who in
> themselves are so big that they generate their own publicity.[3]

I

In *A Confederate General at Big Sur*, Richard Brautigan refers to "the last good
time this country ever had."[4] As we move into the twenty-first century, that
phrase also captures the way we are invited to remember the period of New
Hollywood Cinema, as a brief moment of cinematic aesthetic adventure that

happened between the mid-1960s and the mid to late 1970s and then vanished. In his recent history of this period, *Lost Illusions*, David Cook sees the years from 1969 to 1975 as an "aberration" (p.xvii), a "richly fruitful detour in the American cinema's march towards gigantism and global domination," (p.xvii) as the franchise triumphs over the notion of the individual film. And in his review of the most recent edition of Robert Kolker's *A Cinema of Loneliness*, Jon Lewis, one of the most prominent of contemporary historians of contemporary Hollywood, refers to "this wonderful and brief moment" of New Hollywood.[5]

Of course any notion of a "New Hollywood" will always be a discursive construction of a particular kind. Different critical accounts seek to describe changes in Hollywood filmmaking in the period from the 1960s to the present, and although these acts of criticism target an agreed period of Hollywood film history they make different claims for what is significant about that period. The result is that "New Hollywood" does not remain the same object across its different critical descriptions. We encounter a series of competing accounts of "the new" in relation to "New Hollywood".[6]

But one strong strand of criticism sees "New Hollywood" as a brief window of opportunity running from the late 1960s to the early 1970s, when an adventurous new cinema emerged, linking the traditions of classical Hollywood genre filmmaking with the stylistic innovations of European art cinema. This concept of "the new" is predicated on a new audience demographic making its aesthetic preferences felt by opting for a new kind of cinema, alliteratively described by Andrew Sarris as a cinema of "alienation, anomie, anarchy and absurdism".[7]

This account of "the new" is followed quickly by the arrival of the "movie brats," a film-school educated and/or film-critical generation who began making commercial American cinema with an élan that, for some, recalled the emergence of the "French New Wave". The 1960s saw Martin Scorsese graduate from NYU film school (as Jim Jarmusch, Susan Seidelman and Spike Lee would later), Brian De Palma attend Columbia and Sarah Lawrence while on the West Coast Francis Coppola, John Milius, Paul Schrader and George Lucas graduated from UCLA and USC. They were reading the 1960s American film criticism of Pauline Kael, Andrew Sarris and Manny Farber, absorbing the influence of *Cahiers du Cinéma* on Anglo-American film criticism, and admiring the films of Bergman, Fellini, Antonioni, Bertolucci, Truffaut and Godard. Accordingly, some accounts of New Hollywood see this moment as the explicit inscription within American filmmaking of the critical practice of auteurism, resulting in a self-consciously auteur cinema.[8]

Noel Carroll calls this period of American filmmaking a "cinema of allusion" and claims that a shared practice of allusionistic interplay is a distinguishing feature of the work of New Hollywood filmmakers.[9] By "allusion"

Randy Quaid, Jack Nicholson and Otis Young in THE LAST DETAIL

Carroll means "a mixed lot of practices including quotations, the memorialisa-
tion of past genres, homages, and the recreation of 'classic' scenes, shots, plot
motifs, lines of dialogue, themes, gestures, and so forth from film history, especially as that history was crystallized and codified in the sixties and early seventies."[10] Steve Neale's description of RAIDERS OF THE LOST ARK (1981) as a
film which "uses an idea (the signs) of classical Hollywood in order to promote, integrate and display modern effects, techniques and production values" would support Carroll's view.[11] This notion of a "cinema of allusion" generated by references to other cinematic practices, mainly classical Hollywood
cinema and European art cinema, was anticipated by Stuart Byron's claim that
John Ford's THE SEARCHERS (1956) was the ur-text of this New Hollywood, a
cult movie referred to in Scorsese's TAXI DRIVER (1976), Lucas' STAR WARS
(1977), and Schrader's HARDCORE (1978).[12] Similarly, the three films that
brought Peter Bogdanovich to prominence, THE LAST PICTURE SHOW (1971),
WHAT'S UP DOC? (1972) and PAPER MOON (1973) were loving tributes to the
cinema of Howard Hawks and John Ford (about whom he had made the AFI
documentary, DIRECTED BY JOHN FORD), and to lapsed classical Hollywood

genres such as madcap/screwball comedy. This New Hollywood practice of cinematic citation continued into the 1980s with Schrader's 1982 remake of Tourneur's 1942 horror classic, CAT PEOPLE and AMERICAN GIGOLO (1980) concluding with an homage to Bresson's PICKPOCKET (1959). Schrader also cites Bertolucci's THE CONFORMIST (1969) as a film "I've stolen from ... repeatedly," and says that Nic Roeg/Douglas Cammell's film PERFORMANCE (1970) "is very invigorating visually – if you ever need something to steal, that's a good one to check up".[13]

If we were to add TV as another element in the intertextual-nostalgia-memorialisation process, Carroll could be describing attempts in the 1990s to unify parent and child via a nostalgic cinematic recovery of TV memory: witness such films as THE FUGITIVE, THE FLINTSTONES, THE ADDAMS FAMILY, ADDAMS FAMILY VALUES, MAVERICK, THE BRADY BUNCH, THE BEVERLY HILLBILLIES, MISSION IMPOSSIBLE, THE AVENGERS and THE SAINT. Carroll also claims that this citational cinematic practice assumed a particular reading competence on the part of its cinéliterate audience, resulting in a two-tiered genre film that united a strong action through-line derived from classical Hollywood genres, with some of the more recondite, abstract aspects of European art cinema: "there was the genre film pure and simple, and there was also the art film in the genre film."[14]

Functioning alongside the "movie brat" film school and often overlapping with it was another film school: the Roger Corman exploitation world of AIP and New World Films. Corman's influence on the New Hollywood can scarcely be overestimated. From his time with AIP through to his establishing of New World Films, Corman provided opportunities for such directors as Scorsese, Coppola, Bogdanovich, Monte Hellman, James Cameron, John Sayles, Joe Dante, Jonathan Demme, Jonathan Kaplan, John Milius, Dennis Hopper, Ron Howard, Amy Jones and Stephanie Rothman; and for such actors as Jack Nicholson, Robert DeNiro, Bruce Dern, and Keith Carradine. Carroll credits Corman with having established the "two-tiered" film: "Increasingly Corman's cinema came to be built with the notion of two audiences in mind: special grace notes for insiders, appoggiatura for the cognoscenti, and a soaring, action-charged melody for the rest"[15] and a link with the "Old Hollywood" is apparent in the fact that both Carroll and Jim Hillier note that Corman's workers likened themselves to the "Hollywood professionals" of the studio era, specifically to Raoul Walsh.[16]

Writing a decade earlier than Carroll, Thomas Elsaesser had noted the emergence of a "new liberal cinema" in 1970s America and saw it as breaking away from the classical Hollywood fictional world in which the heroes were "psychologically or morally motivated: they had a case to investigate, a name to clear, a woman (or man) to love, a goal to reach", and moving towards cinematic fictions in which goal-orientation can only figure as nostalgic.[17] According to Elsaesser, 1970s American cinema saw the "affirmative-consequential model" of the classical Hollywood film replaced by a more open-ended, looser-structured narrative. As a result New Hollywood cinema displayed "a kind of malaise already frequently alluded to in relation to the European cinema – the fading confidence in being able to tell a story." But Elsaesser was also quick to say that the New Hollywood cinema achieved its innovations by "shifting and modifying traditional genres and themes, while never quite shedding their support."[18]

After the first two moments of the "New Hollywood" – the brief period of studio uncertainty that allowed experimentation in the early 1970s (under the alibi of the pursuit of the youth audience) and the time of the "movie brats" – the next distinctive moment of "New Hollywood" is one on which ALL critics agree: the period of Hollywood after 1975, after the release of Steven Spielberg's JAWS. David Denby says, "The movie business, perhaps American culture, has never recovered from that electric media weekend in June 1975 when JAWS opened all over the country and Hollywood realized a movie could gross nearly 48 million dollars in three days. Ever since, the only real prestige has come from having a runaway hit".[19] We now know that when JAWS opened at 464 cinemas and went on to become the biggest grossing film of all time (well, for two years, until George Lucas's STAR WARS came along and topped it) we entered the era of high concept and summer hits. As Hoberman puts it, JAWS's "presold property and media-blitz saturation release pattern heralded the rise of marketing men and 'high concept.'"[20] Justin Wyatt would then seem justified in claiming "high concept" as "perhaps *the* central development within post-classical cinema."[21]

Thomas Schatz sees the concentration on the blockbuster as an inglorious distinguishing feature of the New Hollywood period. In the classical Hollywood studio system, he says, "ultimately both blockbuster and B movie were ancillary to first-run feature production, which had always been the studios' strong suit and which the New Hollywood has proved utterly incapable of turning out with any quality or consistency."[22] The post-JAWS world, however, was one in which blockbuster films were conceived as "multi-purpose entertainment machines that breed music videos and soundtrack albums, TV series and videocassettes, video games and theme park rides, novelizations and comic books."[23] The media hype surrounding the theatrical release of films like BATMAN and JURASSIC PARK "creates a cultural commodity that might be regenerated in any number of media forms".[24]

The clarity of this third moment of change is conveyed by the brute commercial fact that post-1975 blockbusters have proved the most profitable films of all time. As Hoberman says, "Hollywood's ten top-grossing films have all been released since 1975. And even if one adjusts the figures to compensate for the dollar's reduced purchasing power, seven of the all-time blockbusters were still made between 1975 and 1985."[25] In *A Cinema Without Walls*, Timothy Corrigan ponders this new situation by looking back on the conglomerate take-overs of the majors in the 1960s and 1970s, the later pressures from video and cable television and the way the status of the blockbuster has come to figure in the corporate thinking of New Hollywood:

> Far more than traditional epic successes or the occasional predecessor in film history, these contemporary blockbuster movies became the central imperative in an industry that sought the promise of massive profit from large financial investments; the acceptable return on these investments (anywhere from $20 million to $70 million) required, most significantly, that these films would attract not just a large market, but *all* the markets.[26]

Many critics felt this form of cinema was achieved at the expense of a more meditative, adult cinema that had been present in the first two moments of the New Hollywood. Pauline Kael said that conglomerate control of the studios meant there was less chance for any unusual project to get financed, Andrew Sarris said "the battle was lost when Hollywood realized in 1970 that there was still a huge middle American audience for AIRPORT"[27] and, in a much-quoted phrase, James Monaco said, "Increasingly we are all going to see the same ten movies."[28] Monaco said that in 1979, and now we would have to say that the number is now far fewer than ten. The phrase that came to characterise this emphasis in Hollywood's economic-aesthetic strategy was the "film event". As William Paul explains: "At the time of the release of EARTHQUAKE, Jennings Lang, its executive producer, wrote an article for *American Cinematographer* in which he proclaimed that a movie had to be an 'event' in order to succeed in today's market".[29]

But there are other ways in which the exceptional commercial success of films like STAR WARS, ET (1982) and RAIDERS OF THE LOST ARK indicates a change from the first two moments of New Hollywood. If we set aside questions concerning saturation release and merchandising opportunities, the first two moments saw an auteurist cinema explore and stretch genres such as the western (THE WILD BUNCH, McCABE AND MS MILLER), the gangster film (THE GODFATHER and THE GODFATHER PART 2), and the detective-noir film (CHINATOWN, NIGHT MOVES, THE LONG GOODBYE). This laudable moment of thoughtful metafilmic exploration was then cast aside by the success of the late 1970s and 1980s films of Lucas and Spielberg, which marked a more calculatedly naive relation to classical genres. According to this view Lucas' AMERICAN GRAFFITI (1973) could be regarded as a transitional text. It was adventurous insofar as it took the then-unusual narrative step of basing its forty-five or so scenes around as many pop songs, achieving, through the labours of Walter Murch, an innovative sonic depth of field. But the film's great commercial success (made for less than $1 million and recouping $55 million) foreshadowed the mix of retro-nostalgia and middle-American populism that would be found in most of Lucas's and Spielberg's blockbuster films of the late 1970s and the 1980s. For Hoberman, the success of these films meant that, "as the seventies wore on, it became apparent that the overarching impulse was less an attempt to revise genres than to revive them."[30] Or, as Carroll said, "After the experimentation of the early seventies, genres have once again become Hollywood's bread and butter".[31]

II

Already by the 1990s, the New Hollywood period of 1967 to 1977 and its films had become a benchmark against which developments in contemporary Hollywood cinema could be measured, invoked either to confirm a continuing decline from a time of adventurous commercial cinema or to constitute the most appropriate analogy for any current instances of adventurous American cinema. An example of the latter position is apparent in Quentin Tarantino's 1991 linking of the two periods: "I think right now is the most exciting time in Hollywood since 1971. Because Hollywood is never more exciting than when you don't know."[32] There are many examples of the former attitude of lament for an aesthetic decline in American cinema. This has been a persistent discourse from the late 1970s to the late 1990s, in articles by William Paul, Jim Hoberman, Pauline Kael, David Denby, Richard Schickel and David Thomson.[33] The choral lament has increased over the past years as industry practitioners and insiders start to endorse the nostalgic narrative first posited by film-cultural critics.

For example, when interviewed in the "Film School Generation" episode of the *American Cinema* TV series, *Variety* editor Peter Bart identified the early 1970s as the moment when "the interior dialogue in Hollywood studios was corrupted irrevocably".[34] Ever since, each film has become "an industry unto itself" as filmmaking becomes a matter of selling the film-as-franchise in "all of its little parts". Judging by two of his recent books, Bart has not changed those opinions. *The Gross: The Hits, The Flops – The Summer that Ate Hollywood* examines the production and reception of the major studio films made for the (northern hemisphere) summer of 1998 by targeting the specific stars, directors, and writers involved in blockbuster films like GODZILLA and ARMAGEDDON and in smaller films like THE TRUMAN SHOW and SOMETHING ABOUT

MARY.[35] Bart is encouraged by the unexpected success of these last two films because it helps foster the (necessary) illusion that it is still possible for film-goers to make a hit out of a film that does not bring in big opening weekend dollars. It is always nice when film viewers do not behave as the carefully or-chestrated, obedient demographic the Hollywood marketing machine wants them to be.

In *Who Killed Hollywood ... and Put the Tarnish on Tinseltown?* – a collection of his *Variety* and *GQ* columns – Bart continues his critique of contemporary Hol-lywood by offering sardonic observations on various filmmaking personnel.[36] Across a series of short chapters on "suits," "stars," "scribes", and "filmmak-ers", *Who Killed?* laments the influence of globalisation on Hollywood filmmaking. Studios no longer are "seedbeds of popular culture" but are "mere appendages of vast multinational corporations grinding out 'content' for their global distribution mills", channelling "new product and ideas into theme-park rides, music, toys, videos, video game emporiums, and all the other ancillary goodies that enhance the revenue streams of their corporate parents."[37]

Bart contrasts the late 1990s context as seen from his position as editor of *Va-riety* to his moment as a participant in New Hollywood filmmaking in the early 1970s when he worked as a studio executive for Paramount, Lorimar, MGM/UA, and briefly as an independent producer. During this time Bart was involved with the production of such films as Coppola's THE GODFATHER, Hal Ashby's HAROLD AND MAUDE and BEING THERE, Polanski's ROSEMARY'S BABY, Ted Kotcheff's FUN WITH DICK AND JANE, Franklin Schaffner's ISLANDS IN THE STREAM. As an example of how economic-aesthetic decisions were arrived at in the New Hollywood era, Bart recalls his involvement in green-lighting HAR-OLD AND MAUDE, saying that it was discussed by a handful of executives who admitted they had no idea what it was about but felt they couldn't lose badly on a film that was costing $1. 2 million, and so approved it. The film went on to turn "a handsome profit"[38] and to have longevity as a cult object. The cult sta-tus of this film would later inspire Douglas Coupland's "Harolding in West Vancouver" chapter in his *Polaroids From the Dead*.[39]

As opposed to this form of decision-making, Bart says the contemporary situation is one in which "scores of executives" debate such things as: "will the movie play well in Europe and Asia? How strong is the video and DVD after-market? Will the subject matter attract marketing partners like McDonald's? Will there be tie-ins for toys and other merchandising opportunities? Could the story line inspire a theme-park ride? Could the narrative be captured in a brief TV commercial? Will the star be willing to travel to openings around the world? If the budget is north of $60 million, is co-financing money available?

Can the producers fund a completion guarantor who will intercede if overages occur?"[40]

Bart can see no likelihood of a return to a more economically restrained form of Hollywood filmmaking: "Given the monumental resources of the multinational corporations, the demands of stars and star filmmakers will continue to escalate."[41] His lament is supported by one of the most revered screenwriters of the New Hollywood period. In a similarly titled collection, *The Big Picture: Who Killed Hollywood? and Other Essays*, William Goldman says, "Most of the studio guys I've met are really smart, but they don't care much about movies as movies. As slots, yes. As merchandising tie-ins, – oh my – yes. As theme-park rides, you betcha! And that's the problem. They are mostly ex-agents or business school types. They care about slots and profit and product and Burger King cross-promotions."[42] In 1983 Goldman had published *Adventures in the Screen Trade: A Personal View of Hollywood and Screenwriting* to considerable critical acclaim and very healthy sales. In it he offered "nobody knows anything" as the main rule for understanding Hollywood's strange ways of going about its business.[43] In his follow-up volume, *Which Lie Did I Tell?: More Adventures in The Screen Trade*, the anecdote that gives his book its title shows how little his attitudes have changed over the years, and, accordingly, how little some of Hollywood's business practices have altered in the seventeen years between the two *Screen Trade* books. Goldman is in a Las Vegas room with a producer he doesn't like. The producer is showing off, making lots of self-important telephone calls as Goldman reads *Sports Illustrated* to indicate his lack of interest in these conversations. Suddenly the producer asks him, "*which lie did I tell?*".[44] This is presented as one form of Hollywood lying, the mendacity of the money men. On the other hand, of course, there are the beautiful lies fabricated by under-appreciated storytellers-screenwriters (who can tell us this anecdote) and any other Hollywood worker (director, cinematographer) who recognises the importance of a strong script. Goldman is nearing seventy, and *Which Lie* finds the celebrated New Hollywood screenwriter (who, after all, came to fame with his original screenplay for BUTCH CASSIDY AND THE SUNDANCE KID, a screenplay initially famous for the amount it fetched as much as for the story it told) honouring the classical scriptwriting of a man who worked a generation earlier. Ernest Lehman's eight-minute "crop-dusting" sequence for Hitchcock's NORTH BY NORTHWEST is "one of the very best pieces of action adventure" Goldman celebrates – something that wouldn't be possible in the post-MTV world of Hollywood editing, which favours a "blizzard of cuts" – while also analysing the filmmaking efforts of some of the hipper contemporary types, the brothers Coen (FARGO, THE BIG LEBOWSKI) and Farrelly (THERE'S SOMETHING ABOUT MARY).

III

Any description of the film-cultural world that came *after* the New Hollywood period discussed in this book can easily become a lament for a lapsed mode of being in the world with cinema: a time of movie-going before the predominance of malls and multiplexes, before brands and franchises, synergies, high concept and film as 'event,' a time when the act of going to see a film at a central city "movie palace" or a double-feature at a suburban cinema was the main event. The nostalgia (overt or implied) for this earlier time is implicit in the severity of the critique of a contemporary situation in which Hollywood film industry spokesman Jack Valenti can describe the release of a film as a "platform to other markets", where films are described as being more or less "toyetic" (and where "toyetic'" is regarded as a good thing to be), where watching GODZILLA is as much about "tacos and t-shirts" as it is about an imaginative encounter with a celluloid fiction in a movie theatre. It is a world in which, as Robert C. Allen so succinctly puts it, one's relation to the projecting of celluloid on a big screen jostles for space with a pyjama manufacturer's analysis of the Spielberg-produced animated film AN AMERICAN TALE: FIEVEL GOES WEST: "We think AMERICAN TALE will be strong in sizes 2-7."[45] From this perspective an earlier time in which we could conceive of the Hollywood studio film as a discrete textual object is replaced by an uglier cultural fact: the individual film as simply the first move in a wider game of media market exploitations. The more this cinematic cultural fall is noted, the more some writers worry about a decline in the standards of Hollywood storytelling as kinaesthetic affect overwhelms the earlier tradition of the 'literate script'. One description of this contemporary form of cinema comes in the script rewrite advice Renny Harlin handed to Joan Didion and John Gregory Dunne (on a film that didn't go forward with them as scriptwriters): "First act, better whammies. Second act, whammies mount up. Third act, all whammies."[46]

If many discussions of the mutations effected in Hollywood filmmaking in the 1970s exhibit a strong strain of romanticism and nostalgia, the question remains whether this nostalgia is historically justified. The David Thomson quotation which appears as my second epigraph openly admits to a nostalgic attitude, and Thomson repeats this position in a 1996 piece for *Esquire* by saying of the New Hollywood films: "I look back on the time of first seeing them as one of wonder, excitement, and passion. It was bracing to face such candid, eloquent dismay; enlightenment does not have to be optimistic or uplifting".[47] Citing the ending of Spielberg's THE SUGARLAND EXPRESS (in which the father is shot) he says, "that was the proper ending; in 1974 that's how American films ended. But Spielberg has never risked that tough an ending again ...."[48]

For Thomson, Rafelson's Five Easy Pieces (1970) and King Of Marvin Gardens (1972), Ashby's The Last Detail (1973) and Polanski's Chinatown (1974) – all with Nicholson – constitute a major cinematic achievement in the history of post-1960s Hollywood cinema, representing a time when "the movies mattered" in a way they haven't since. This early 1970s moment becomes the aesthetic "path not taken". Thomson regrets the passing of that brief half-decade period of productive, innovative uncertainty that enabled a more philosophical, risky, and countercultural cinema. This exciting cultural moment is lost as mainstream genre filmmaking is re-established, often by the very young Turks who supposedly were moving away from traditional forms of cinema towards more "personal" films. In one of the paradoxes of the decade, the already existing practice of "blockbuster cinema" is taken by the movie brats to new levels of profitability.

As we consider changes in modes of distributing and encountering movies from the 1970s to now, it would be hard to better some of Allen's descriptions of this immense cultural shift: "The Happy Meal toy our kids demand *before* the film is released derives its value through its strange metonymic connection (in which the part *precedes* the whole) to a movie that commands our attention as a cinema event because it's already been figured as the inedible part of a Happy Meal."[49] Or, as Jonathan Rosenbaum says in his provocative book, *Movie Wars: How Hollywood and the Media Conspire to Limit What Films We Can See*, "When Disney holds all-day 'seminars' about Native American culture and animation techniques for grade school children in shopping malls as part of its campaign to promote Pocahontas, the point at which advertising ends and education begins (or vice-versa) is difficult to pinpoint."[50] Rosenbaum is discussing a cultural context in which it is no longer clear whether in watching a theatrical release of a film one is meant to think of the film as "a viewing experience" or "the central object in a marketing campaign".[51] Of course it is both – as he well knows since he reviews films for the *Chicago Reader* – but Rosenbaum, like many commentators, wants to claim that the latter fact deforms the former experience.

In one sense Rosenbaum's *Movie Wars* pursues a point Jean-Luc Godard made in 1982 when he and Pauline Kael debated "the economics of film criticism" (an encounter organised by and subsequently published in the Californian feminist film journal, *Camera Obscura*,): namely, that there is an obligation on the film critic to practise a form of cultural analysis that distances itself from the many circuits of publicity and advertising masquerading as cultural commentary (eg *Details* magazine, *Vanity Fair*'s "Hollywood issue").[52] Godard was referring to "Why are Movies so Bad?, or, the Numbers," an article Kael published in *The New Yorker* (June 23, 1980) which now seems one of the most influential formulations of the position that argues for a continuing decline in

American cinema from the late 1970s.[53] Kael took a five-month break from writing her *New Yorker* column on movies to work for Warren Beatty and Paramount as an "executive consultant".[54] She then wrote a piece informed by her insider-knowledge of Hollywood studio film production practices of the late 1970s. Her article reveals its polemical opinion at the outset: "The movies have been so rank the last couple of years that when I see people lining up to buy tickets I sometimes think that the movies aren't drawing an audience – they're inheriting an audience." Kael delivers a familiar lapsarian narrative in which an earlier, foundational era of cinema was presided over by "vulgarian moguls" who were genuinely in touch with a notion of popular entertainment and were ready to face risks that those who replaced them – ex-agents, former TV executives, business school graduates – weren't prepared to take. As a result the quality of the standard studio product goes down. Kael found that the real power in the new, conglomerate Hollywood rested with the advertising and marketing people "who not only determine which movies get financed but which movies they are going to sell".[55] She has a nice description of how a script's status is evaluated in that early 1980s Hollywood: "To put it simply: A good script is a script to which Robert Redford will commit himself. A bad script is a script which Redford has turned down. A script that 'needs work' is a script about which Redford has yet to make up his mind."[56] It's a tribute to Redford's longevity as a star and to the unchanging ways of Hollywood's packaging of films that Kael's comment still stands; we would only have to add a few other names to go along with Redford's.

For Kael the two main enemies of good American cinema are television – the more cinema "televisionises" itself, the more it squanders its aesthetic obligation to perform specifically cinematic work on and with the image – and conglomeratisation: "Part of what has deranged American life in this past decade is the change in book publishing and in magazines and newspapers and in the movies as they have passed out of the control of those whose lives were bound up in them and into the control of conglomerates, financiers, and managers who treat them as ordinary commodities. This isn't a reversible process..." Indeed not. The recent memoirs contained in Andre Schiffrin's *The Business of Books: How the Conglomerates took Over Publishing and Changed the Way We Read* and some sections of Jason Epstein's *The Book Business* flesh out the consequences right now of the situation Kael is describing twenty years ago, and Rosenbaum's chapter, "Some Vagaries of Distribution" in *Movie Wars* updates the cinema situation in the US.[57]

For later critics, writing in the 1990s, the decline in quality of American cinema is also the result of the success of the VCR and levels of video rental and purchase. As Janet Wasko says, by 1990 this area of business outgrossed Hollywood theatrical release revenues by 10 billion dollars.[58] By 1996 that figure had risen to almost 12 billion. Writing in 1999, Robert C Allen encountered an even more intensified version of this situation. Allen notes that in 1992 Disney's Buena Vista Division became the largest and most profitable "film" studio in Hollywood, and points out that Christmas 1998 was the first time the launching of a "video game drew more consumers than the highest grossing feature film. In the last six weeks of 1998 Nintendo's 'The Legend of Zelda: Ocarina of Time' produced $150 million in retail sales, compared with Disney's A BUG's LIFE, the highest grossing film of the season, which did $114 million."[59]

Hence the crisis for some ways of thinking about the privileged or simply preferred status of Hollywood celluloid and of a lapsed period of movie-going. Since the 1980s Hollywood films have made far more money from the so-called "ancillary" (syndicated TV, cable, pay per view, etc.) markets than from their social circulation as theatrically released celluloid. Consequently we encounter a slight strangeness of relation between the term "ancillary" and its referent in the world of New Hollywood economics. For of course these ancillary markets are primary and central. Likewise, it seems perverse to refer to the merchandising/franchising elements of a film as an "aftermarket" when they determine much of the structure the film takes in the first place and when they are usually made available to film viewers before the theatrical release of the film.

Allen pushes the issues bound up with different modes of circulation and consumption of films to some kind of philosophical edge when he says, "The shift that occurs[...] – from audience to markets, from film as celluloid experienced in a theatre to film as [film] plus so many other manifestations over so long a period of time – not only alters the logics by which films are made and marketed but alters what the film 'is' in an economic sense, and by extension, in both an ontological and epistemological sense as well." And since it is now the case that theatre owners make more money on "concessions" (the sales at the "candy bar," or "drinks and lollies" as some cultures would say) than on ticket sales, then, as Allen observes, "to theatre owners and managers the most important innovation in recent film exhibition history is not surround-sound or wide-screen but the cup holder."[60]

In the Kael-Godard "economics of film criticism" exchange, Godard said he had prepared for their conversation by reading an article by Kael called "Why is the movie so bad?" Godard then says it should be "the movies" – which in fact it is. He goes on to make many funny, perverse comments, and one of his main points is that, as a film critic, Kael must take responsibility for the state of US cinema. Kael tries to say that critics have little power against advertisers – much as Robert Hughes once responded to the claim that he was a powerful and influential art critic by saying that one might as readily speak of a "powerful beekeeper". If in the short-term Kael's article had the unusual outcome of setting the terms for a debate with one of the greatest of filmmakers, in the longer term it has generated a series of considerations of the health of American cinema. Every five or ten years a prominent film critic takes a sounding and finds that Kael's criticisms still have pertinence. So, when David Denby asked, in 1986, "Can the Movies be Saved?" he was repeating Kael's polemic, and he too attacked conglomerate control by saying, "they want the smash, they're not interested in the modest profit".[61]

IV

In apparent deference to the notion of a "New Hollywood cinema", post 1970s American film sometimes is described as "New New Hollywood." The phrase was used as early as 1978 by David Colker and Jack Virrell in their article on "The *New* New Hollywood," in the Canadian journal, *Take One*.[62] In order to set the ground for their series of interviews with Badham, Kagan, Kleiser, Landis, Weill and Zemeckis/Gale, they said that Coppola "might as well be George Cukor, or Otto Preminger, for that matter." The durability of the category is shown by the fact that an account of contemporary Hollywood filmmaking in October 1995 in *GQ* magazine retains the phrase, "the 'new' Hollywood".[63]

The difficulty in deciding how to remember the period of New Hollywood cinema is indicated by the fact that David Thomson can recall 1970s American cinema as "the decade when movies mattered" while also seeing that decade of film production as one which ushered in "a terrifying spiral ... whereby fewer films were made, most of them cost more, and a fraction were profitable."[64] Bernardo Bertolucci said of post New Hollywood cinema, "how can an audience desire films if the films themselves do not desire an audience?"[65] In the current context of this collection of writing on New Hollywood cinema we could rephrase Bertolucci's point to say that the film that wants to attract *every* viewer is not the kind of film that is being written about favourably in this book. In a recent piece, Jon Lewis points out that, "as the importance of foreign markets increased, Japanese, French, Australian, Canadian and Italian companies, at one time or another during the decade (the 1990s) took control of a major 'American' film studio. By decade's end the term 'American film' had become relative, perhaps even obsolete."[66] Perhaps this can help (this reader, at least) focus what I am saying which must to some extent be an exercise in nostalgia. The New Hollywood period might be the last good predominantly *American* time American cinema had. Of course Hollywood has always imported international talent, but the New Hollywood fictions, as Elsaesser's article makes clear, touch on deeply American themes and visions. In the wake of the current crop of internationally financed globalised narratives New Hollywood of the 1970s might represent the last time American cinema was a distinctive, national entity. And as we read the following contributions to our understanding of New Hollywood cinema, we can see that this golden period of filmmaking also challenged film criticism to find a critical language appropriate to New Hollywood's cinematic achievements. This collection of criticism abundantly and inventively meets that challenge. And so the nostalgia is doubled, and also shown to be both real and justified.

Notes

1. David A. Cook, *Lost Illusions: American Cinema in the Shadow of Watergate and Vietnam 1970-1979* (Berkeley: Univ. of California Press, 2002): xvii.
2. David Thomson "The Decade When Movies Mattered," originally *Movieline* (August 1993): 43, in this volume.
3. William Paul "Hollywood Harakiri," *Film Comment* 13, 2 (1977): 62.
4. Richard Brautigan, *A Confederate General at Big Sur* (New York: Grove/Castle, 1964): 147.
5. Jon Lewis, review of Robert Kolker, *A Cinema of Loneliness: Penn, Stone, Kubrick, Scorsese, Spielberg, Altman (Third Edition)*, in *Scope: An Online Journal of Film Studies* (August 2002) at http://www.nottingham.ac.uk/film/journal/bookrev/books-august-02.htm
6. The following argument condenses points made in Noel King, "New Hollywood," in Pam Cook and Mieke Bernink, ed., *The Cinema Book 2nd Edition* (London: BFI, 1999): 98-106.
7. Andrew Sarris, "After THE GRADUATE," *American Film* 3, 9 (1978): 37.
8. James Bernardoni, *The New Hollywood: What the Movies Did with the New Freedom of the Seventies* (Jefferson, N.C.: McFarland and Co, 1991): 8.
9. Noel Carroll, "The Future of Allusion: Hollywood in the Seventies (and Beyond)," *October* 20 (1982): 51-78.
10. Ibid. 56.
11. Steve Neale, "Hollywood Corner," *Framework* 18 (1981): 32.
12. Stuart Byron, "*The Searchers*: Cult Movie of the New Hollywood," *New York Magazine* (March 5, 1979): 45-48.
13. Paul Schrader, in Kevin Jackson, ed., *Schrader on Schrader & Other Writings* (London: Faber and Faber, 1990): 210-211.
14. Carroll, 56.
15. Carroll, 74.
16. Jim Hillier, *The New Hollywood* (London: Studio Vista, 1992): 47.
17. Thomas Elsaesser, "The Pathos of Failure," originally published in *Monogram* 6 (1975): 13-19, in this volume.
18. Elsaesser, 14.

19. David Denby, "Can the Movies Be Saved?," *New York Magazine* 19, 28 (1986): 30.
20. J. Hoberman, "Ten Years that Shook the World," *American Film* 10, 8 (1985): 36.
21. Justin Wyatt, *High Concept: Movies and Marketing in Hollywood* (Austin: Univ. of Texas Press, 1994): 8.
22. Thomas Schatz, *The Genius of the System: Hollywood Filmmaking in the Studio Era* (New York: Pantheon, 1988): 492.
23. Schatz, "The New Hollywood," in Jim Collins, et al. (eds.), *Film Theory Goes to the Movies* (London: Routledge, 1993): 9-10. For more recent writing on the blockbuster, see Larry Gross, "Big and Loud," *Sight and Sound* 5, 8 (August, 1995): 6 -10; Thomas Elsaesser, "The Blockbuster: Everything Connects, but Not Everything Goes," in Jon Lewis, ed., *The End of Cinema As We Know It: American Cinema in the Nineties* (New York: NYU Press, 2001): 11-22; Sheldon Hall, "Tall Features: The Genealogy of the Modern Blockbuster," in Steve Neale, ed., *Genre and Contemporary Hollywood* (London: BFI, 2002): 11-26.
24. Schatz, "The New Hollywood", 29.
25. Hoberman, "Ten Years", 58.
26. Timothy Corrigan, *A Cinema Without Walls: Movies and Culture After Vietnam* (London: Routledge, 1991): 12.
27. Sarris, "After THE GRADUATE", 37.
28. James Monaco, *American Film Now: The People, The Power, The Money, The Movies* (New York: OUP, 1979): 393
29. Paul, "Hollywood Harakiri", 59.
30. Hoberman, "Ten Years", 38.
31. Carroll, 56.
32. Quentin Tarantino, in Mim Udovich, "Tarantino and Juliette," *Details* (February, 1996): 117.
33. Apart from the articles already cited in this essay, see Richard Schickel, "The Crisis in Movie Narrative," *Gannett Center Journal* 3 (1989): 1-15; David Denby, "The Moviegoers," *The New Yorker* (April 6, 1998): 94-101; David Thomson, "Who Killed the Movies?." *Esquire* (December 1996): 56-63.
34. Bart is interviewed in the "The Film School Generation" episode of the *American Cinema* TV series (Annenberg/CPB Project: 1995: 60 mins).
35. Peter Bart, *The Gross: The Hits, The Flops – The Summer that Ate Hollywood* (New York: St Martin's Press, 1999).
36. Peter Bart, *Who Killed Hollywood? ... And Put the Tarnish on Tinseltown?* (Los Angeles: Renaissance Books, 1999).
37. Ibid., 17.
38. Ibid., 19.
39. Douglas Coupland, "Harolding in West Vancouver," in his *Polaroids From the Dead* (London: Flamingo, 1996): 101-106.
40. Bart, *Who Killed Hollywood?*: 19-20.
41. Ibid., 22.
42. William Goldman, *The Big Picture: Who Killed Hollywood? and Other Essays* (New York: Applause, 2000): 210-211.
43. Goldman, *Adventures in the Screen Trade: A Personal View of Hollywood and Screenwriting* (New York: Warner Books, 1983).

44. *Which Lie Did I Tell?: More Adventures in The Screen Trade* (New York: Vintage, 2001): x.

45. Robert C. Allen, "The Movie on the Lunch-Box." Abbreviated version available as "Home Alone Together: Hollywood and the 'Family Film'," in Melvyn Stokes and Richard Maltby, ed., *Identifying Hollywood's Audiences: Cultural Identity and the Movies* (London: BFI, 1999): 109-131

46. John Gregory Dunne, *Monster: Living Off the Big Screen* (New York: Vintage, 1997): 37.

47. David Thomson, "Who Killed the Movies?," *Esquire* (December, 1996): 56-63.

48. Ibid., 60.

49. Robert C. Allen, "The Movies on the Lunch Box" (unpublished manuscript, 21).

50. Jonathan Rosenbaum, *Movie Wars: How Hollywood and the Media Conspire to Limit What Films We Can See* (Chicago: A Cappella, 2001): 10.

51. Ibid., 67.

52. Jean-Luc Godard and Pauline Kael, "The Economics of Film Criticism: A Debate," *Camera Obscura* 8-9-10 (1982): 174-175.

53. Pauline Kael, "Why Are Movies So Bad? or, The Numbers," in Kael, *Taking It All In* (New York: Holt, Rinehart and Winston, 1984): 8-20. The article originally appeared in *The New Yorker* (June 23 1980).

54. See Pat Aufderheide, "Pauline Kael on the New Hollywood," *In These Times* (7-13 May 1980): 12, 23. Reprinted in *Conversations with Pauline Kael*, 41-49.

55. Jean-Luc Godard and Pauline Kael, "The Economics of Film Criticism: A Debate," *Camera Obscura* 8-9-10 (1982): 174-175. Also available in Will Brantley, ed., *Conversations with Pauline Kael* (Jackson: Univ. of Mississippi, 1995): 55-74.

56. Kael, "Why Are Movies So Bad? or, The Numbers": 16.

57. Andre Schiffrin, *The Business of Books: How the Conglomerates took Over Publishing and Changed the Way We Read* (London: Verso, 2001); Jason Epstein, *Book Business: Publishing: Past, Present, and Future* (new York: W. W. Norton & Co, 2001). Jonathan Rosenbaum, "Some Vagaries of Distribution," in his *Movie Wars: How Hollywood and the Media Conspire to Limit What Films We Can See* (Chicago: A Cappella, 2001): 39-48.

58. Janet Wasko, *Hollywood in the Information Age* (London: Polity Press, 1994): 114.

59. Robert C Allen, "The Movies on the Lunch Box": 5, 11.

60. Ibid., 12. See also Thomas Elsaesser, "The Blockbuster: Everything Connects, but not Everything Goes": 14.

61. David Denby, "Can the Movies be Saved": 34.

62. See Axel Madsen, *The New Hollywood: American Movies in the 70s* (New York: Thomas Y. Crowell Co, 1975); Diane Jacobs, *Hollywood Renaissance: the New Generation of Filmmakers and Their Works* (New York: Delta, 1977/1980); Michael Pye and Lynda Myles, *The Movie Brats: How the Film Generation Took Over Hollywood* (New York: Holt, Rinehart and Winston, 1979); Thomas Schatz, *Old Hollywood/New Hollywood* (UMI Research Press, 1983); *Wide-Angle* 5, 4 (1983) is a special issue on "The New Hollywood"; Jon Lewis, *Whom God Wishes to Destroy: Francis Coppola and the New Hollywood* (Durham and London: Duke UP, 1995), pp 143-164; David Colker and Jack Virrell,"The *New* New Hollywood," *Take One* 6, 10 (August 1978): 19-23.

63. See GQ (October 1995), special issue called "The 'New' Hollywood."

64. David Thomson, "The Decade when Movies Mattered," *Movieline* (August 1993) 43-47, 90; David Thomson, *Overexposures: the Crisis in American Filmmaking* (New York: William Morrow & Co, 1981) 27.

65. Bernardo Bertolucci in Enzo Ungari, with Don Ranvaud, BERTOLUCCI ON BERTOLUCCI (London, Plexus, 1987) 181.

66. Jon Lewis, "Introduction," to Jon Lewis, ed, *The End of Cinema as We Know It: American Film in the Nineties* (New York: NYU Press, 2001) 2-3.

American Auteur Cinema

The Last – or First – Picture Show?

Thomas Elsaesser

For many critics writing in the 1980s, when Hollywood once more began to conquer the world's screens with its blockbusters, the American cinema they loved and admired – the cinema of the great studio directors as well as that of independent-minded auteurs – had entered its terminal decline. Not only was the industry that produced these new event movies different: so were the people who made them, the shoot-them-up plots that obsessed them, the special effects that enhanced them, and the money that drove them. Article after article mourned the 'death of cinema' and poured scorn on those who had 'killed Hollywood'.[']

The retrospective vanishing point from which these critical obituaries were written was located in the early 1970s. Especially the years between 1967 and 1975 became the Golden Age of the 'New Hollywood', beginning with BONNIE AND CLYDE (Arthur Penn, 1967), THE GRADUATE (Mike Nichols 1967), EASY RIDER (Dennis Hopper/Peter Fonda, 1968) and ending with Roman Polanski's CHINATOWN (1974), Martin Scorsese's TAXI DRIVER (1975) and Robert Altman's NASHVILLE (1975). Coincidentally or not, these were also the years of the most violent social and political upheavals the United States had experienced for at least a generation, and probably not since the Depression in the mid-1930s. Between the assassination of Martin Luther King in April 1968, and Richard Nixon's resignation in August 1974, America underwent a period of intense collective soul-searching, fuelled by open generational conflict, and no less bitter struggles around what came to be known as 'race' and 'gender'. The protests against the Vietnam War, the Civil Rights movement and the emergence of feminism gave birth to an entirely different political culture, acutely reflected in a spate of movies that often enough were as unsuccessful with the mass public as they were audacious, creative and offbeat, according to the critics. The paradox of the New Hollywood was that the loss of confidence of the nation, its self-doubt about 'liberty and justice for all' in those years, did little to stifle the energies of several groups of young filmmakers. They registered the moral malaise, but it did not blunt their appetite for stylistic or formal experiment. They put aimless, depressive or (self-)destructive characters on the screen, but the subject matter was often bold and unconventional, in settings that were strikingly beautiful, even – especially – in their unglamorous everydayness. A whole new America came into view, thanks to the work of Monte Hellman, Bob Rafelson, Hal Ashby, Joseph McBride, Peter Bogdanovich, Jerry Schatzberg, Terrence Malick, James Toback, Dennis Hopper: there, one came across rural backwaters, motels, rust-belt towns and Bible-belt communities, out-of-season resorts and other places of Americana, whose desolation or poignancy had rarely been conveyed with such visual poetry, enriched by oddball characters, a love of landscape and a delicacy of mood and sensibility, even in scenes of violence or torpor.

The Last Great Picture Show brings together essays that cross-reference the diversity, as well as documenting the changing evaluations of this American cinema of the 1970s, sometimes referred to as the decade of the lost generation, at other times recognised as the first of at least two New Hollywoods, though perhaps the one without which the other – the 1980s cinema of Francis Coppola, Steven Spielberg, Robert Zemeckis, Tim Burton – could not have come into being. Such an assertion, however, risks provoking immediate protest, because where the historian detects continuities, the critic sees unbridgeable gaps of talent and integrity. The challenge for the present collection of essays therefore was to convey a tone and flavour that is faithful to the commitment of those whose formative years as critics were shaped by these polemics, while also putting across the views of those whose passion for the period's films has come by way of the pleasures of rediscovery. In other words, this neither pretends to be a comprehensive history of 1970s filmmaking, nor do the essays aim for scholarly detachment, giving an even-handed account of the controversies and positions. Such accounts do exist, or are being written.[2] We wanted instead to feature chapters that take a generous look back, or celebrate a 'forgotten masterpiece', in combination with other contributions that re-situate the 1970s New Hollywood from a 'post-Fordist' (John and Henry) perspective. We have chosen essays that are personal homages to people, to films, and to places; essays that have a more theoretical approach to stylistic aspects of 1970s film culture; and essays that take a genre or a theme as their point of departure.

This book is, in a sense, both timely and anachronistic. Timely, in that an understanding of the phenomenal – and in light of the 'death of cinema' predictions, also unexpected – box-office revival of Hollywood in the 1980s and 1990s requires a revision of how we see the American cinema of the 1970s. No longer (only) as the endpoint of the classical studio epoch and the all-too brief flourishing of an American auteur cinema in the European mould, but as the period that allowed an astonishing array of talent, of contending and often even contradictory forces within US movie-making to come to the fore. The late 1960s and early 1970s deserve a fresh appraisal, because they are a genuine period of transition, as momentous in some ways as that in the late 1920s and early 1930s, when the coming of sound changed the structure of the film industry even faster than the film forms could follow, breaking open genres and styles, and in the process producing hybrids or, unexpectedly, a new prototype or cycle. Similarly in the 1970s: one can see several forks in the road, leading in directions (regrettably) not taken, and too many talents gave up in frustration, or were sidelined and subsequently fell silent. But the historical distance also makes evident the sheer scope of what was possible, by trial and error, by happenstance or unsuspected affinity: the unlikely blend, for instance, of avant-garde and exploitation, or the fusion of rock music and movies, both of which changed the traditional genres, just before new technologies of sound and image also began to have an equally great impact, and once more altered the course of the Hollywood revival.

Digital technologies did mark a watershed in the mid-1980s, but they were certainly not the only and maybe not even the decisive forces. Other – economic, managerial, demographic and 'global' – factors that subsequently turned the Hollywood cinema into the gigantic world-wide entertainment machine of blockbusters it is today, also began to make themselves felt in the 1970s, often in the same places, and occasionally even promoted by the same people that were at the forefront of what was then hailed as the New Hollywood. Whether one regards their crossover as compromise, opportunism or even betrayal, it is undeniable that Francis Coppola, Martin Scorsese, Steven Spielberg, George Lucas, Jack Nicholson, Warren Beatty or Robert de Niro (among others) have so stamped the public image of American cinema over several decades, that their choices, moves and gambles set an agenda of sorts which at least in part determined the dynamics behind the shifts from one New Hollywood to the next. In other words, their presence in the early 1970s also prepared what was to follow, for good or ill, which suggests that there is reason to reassess the 1970s in the light of the 1990s, and to provide, whatever one's aesthetics and cinephile preferences, also a 'revisionist' account next to the retrospective one: both serving, when taken together, as part of the archaeology of the present.

Such revisionism might, admittedly, be itself regarded as anachronistic. First, in that the changes that have taken place in American cinema between the 1960s and the 1980s are now so apparently well understood that there exists a 'canonical' story of these transformations. In this canonical story, spanning the late 1940s to the late 1980s, the directors and the films we are concerned with here – the emergence of an American auteur cinema, the early years of the so-called movie brats, the many talents that perhaps shone too brightly and hence too briefly – mark at best the exception. At worst, they are merely the blip in that otherwise logical and largely unproblematic history of the continuities of the American cinema almost since its beginnings. *The Last Great Picture Show*, on the other hand, implicitly assumes that these few years were a very special and unique period, unjustly subsumed under the broad sweep from the Paramount decree in 1948 and the rise of television, via the changes in the rating system in 1968, to the Time Warner merger in 1990. Apart from claiming special status for the decade, it is also a matter of re-claiming elements of this exceptionality, at the risk of appearing backward-looking, nostalgic and occasionally even as if caught in a time-warp.

The essays are ana-chronistic, too, in the way they set out to record distinct moments in time that overlap, run parallel or are contiguous, rather than continuous. The histories of the New York avant-garde and of (New) Hollywood barely touched, but once in a while made sudden contact, in the person of Dennis Hopper, for instance, as Jonathan Rosenbaum points out, or in the brief encounter that J. Hoberman once staged for Don Siegel and Clint Eastwood with Andy Warhol and Joe Dalessandro, when he compared Coogan's Bluff with Lonesome Cowboys (both 1968).[3] There is the blend of generations, where directors Robert Aldrich (b. 1918), Robert Altman (b. 1925), Arthur Penn (b. 1922) and Sam Peckinpah (b. 1925) all made films that count as New Hollywood. Their careers overlap with those of a younger generation (Martin Scorsese, b. 1942, Brian de Palma, b. 1940, George Lucas, b. 1944, Paul Scharder b. 1946), whose own role in this auteur cinema is both crucial and ambiguous. Equally typical for the 1970s is the role of godfathers like Orson Welles (for Bogdanovich, Jaglom, arguably Malick and more indirectly, Coppola), Hitchcock (for de Palma and Spielberg), Michael Powell (for Scorsese) and Roger Corman (for just about everybody else). Many temporalities are thus present simultaneously in the apparently single chronology of 1967 to 1975, tracing the different timelines, and also showing where they break off or suddenly resurface.

A diversity of voices comment on the period, names and titles repeat themselves and return, but in different contexts that add colour and give texture to the narratives. Owning up to feelings of regret and rekindled expectation, mixing nostalgia with protest and polemic, all the essays offer keen analyses that balance the commemorative gesture against exasperated impatience. The several cinematic genres and topographies mentioned throughout – avant-garde, mainstream, art cinema, exploitation – map themselves across (without converging with) geographical divides, such as New York and Los Angeles, Paris and New York, with an occasional detour via London. More broadly speaking, Europe and/versus America are, from the critical point of view, the tectonic plates and poles of mutual attraction in the seismic shifts that shook the American cinema during that period, before the transfers and crossovers became global (Asian cinema, Australian cinema) in the 1980s, and the transformations pushed by certain commercial and technological innovations (video re-corder and video-store, special effects and digital imaging) began to favour multinational and corporate players.

Finally, the book is ana-chronistic, in that most of the articles were written some time ago, around 1994-1995, on the occasion of what in effect was quite explicitly a retrospective, a look back. Alexander Horwath's book, which in ti-tle and content forms the primary basis of the present volume, accompanied a season of films he programmed at the Vienna Film Festival in 1995. Since the book consisted mainly of essays translated from English into German, the original *Last Great American Picture Show* gave Noel King – whose enyclo-paedic curiosity the book did not escape even in German – the idea of, so to speak, linguistically re-territorializing the authors into English, by geographi-cally de-territorializing them to Australia. I in turn became involved in the project when, a few years later, Noel asked me whether he could add to the col-lection the reprint of an article of mine that went back even further, to 1975. The request not only confronted me with a past I had assumed that film history had left behind. It also revived a latent split between myself as the (then) critic and the (now) historian. Another year or so later, I was called upon in yet an-other capacity, as the (general) editor of a publication series called 'film culture in transition', an appropriate enough name also for this venture. Taking on the project as co-editor, along with Alex and Noel, it seemed to me important to in-volve and invoke another temporality, again, that of a generational change, so that the final section of the book as it now appears has essays by young schol-ars and critics who, familiar with the 'heroic' account of the New Hollywood as well as with the canonical-critical story, give yet another take on the period and its key films. They are more philosophically inclined, in both senses of that word, namely more dispassionate and less polemical, and more influenced by the philosophical turn in film studies, at least as represented by the writings of Gilles Deleuze. Christian Keathley and Drehli Robnik, for instance, see in this New American cinema an aspect that, in retrospect, was more or less coinci-dentally and contiguously also present in my essay from 1975, namely Deleuze's famous 'crisis of the movement image'. In Deleuze this crisis ush-ered in modern cinema, that is to say, a cinema of different temporalities. In this modern cinema, time appears to be neither linear nor chronological, it en-velops the character and the landscape, or layers the image like a memory and a thought, rather than leading to action, with its calculable consequences, its exact 'timing' and purposeful bodily motor-coordination. A similar Deleuzian observation underlies Dana Polan's assessment of Terrence Malick's war-film *The Thin Red Line*, made, of course, at the end of the 1990s, by a director still crucially associated with the auteurism of the 1970s, and thus participating in yet another anachronicity.

The Canonical Story

In another sense, several essays emulate the films and their makers, by also re-fusing to smooth out the creases, or tuck in the corners, preferring double ex-posures, time loops and superimpositions to a tightly knit chain of cause and effect and final narrative closure. Such closure one finds, however, in what I have called the canonical story. Earlier, I suggested that for many film histori-ans, the first New Hollywood now appears as an interesting, but otherwise in-termediate episode: a happy accident to some, a symptomatic aberration to others, but at any rate, a moment of hesitation, while the juggernaut of the cor-porate entertainment business changed gears, taking a few years to get back on track, during which Europe could foster (and finance) its various New Waves, while America afforded itself (by panicky studio heads briefly bank-rolling television upstarts and industry outsiders) the New Hollywood. It was Tom Schatz who summarised most concisely what was to become the canoni-cal story: '[The] movie industry underwent three fairly distinct decade-long phases after the War – from 1946 to 1955, from 1956 to 1965, and from 1966 to 1975. These phases were distinguished by various developments both inside and outside the industry, and four in particular: the shift to independent mo-tion picture production, the changing role of the studios, the emergence of commercial television, and changes in American lifestyle and patterns of media consumption.'[4]

In line with the more economic emphasis of such a perspective, the canoni-cal narrative tends to give space to the film industry version and underline the institutional factors, rather than tell the story from the directors' point of view, which favours a Portrait of the Artist. Or the journalist, who develops a wider analysis around an individual film and spots significant social trends in genres and cycles. Although contrasting with the often polemical tone of the critics, whether partisan or participating observers, the canonical account nonethe-less contains many elements that were first proposed by critics.[5] For instance, Pauline Kael had already identified some of the crucial shifts in her review of BONNIE AND CLYDE in 1967, still considered the first full-blown manifestations of the New Hollywood, with its triple agenda of self-obsessed youth, aestheticised violence, and a distrust or contempt for all forms of established authority. The December 1967 issue of *Time Magazine* officially announced a 'renaissance' of American cinema, and identified complex narratives, hybrid plots, stylistic flourishes and taboo subject matter as its hallmarks. Beverly Walker (a participant and observer also in Alexander Horwath's essay below), writing in 1971, flags several other components. In an article entitled 'Go West Young Man' she takes that other landmark film, EASY RIDER, as her point of departure for a discussion of the changes within the film industry.[6] Apart from also mentioning subject matter with youth appeal and a low budget, she points out that established actors became engaged in moviemaking; that record companies and other American media industries began investing in films; and that finally, new production companies, such as BBS, smaller and more flexible, were set up to produce these movies.

Walker also notes that by 1971 the brief renaissance was already over, with producers and studios retrenching. She pointed to the resurgence of genre-filmmaking, with new directors having to "go the porn-horror-violence route" if they were to secure the (low budget) financing which the EASY RIDER formula had pioneered. The directors of the first New Hollywood in fact faced some of the same problems as their European counterparts, even if on a different scale: there too, getting finance for a second film was contingent on box-office (or festival success) of the first. And even where the first film had been a critical success, if the second found little or no distribution, it often terminated a promising talent's career. In Hollywood, the old industry norms were quickly re-established, with control over distribution and exhibition outlets becoming once more the factors that counted, not the director's artistic control: he or she had to do-it-yourself, as in the case of Tom Laughlin's four-wall exhibition methods for his BILLY JACK (1971), or claw back control by becoming producers, as in the case of Coppola, Spielberg or Lucas, three of the leading names of the second New Hollywood.

The film historians who since the late 1980s have studied the American cinema of the 1970s – besides Tom Schatz, I am thinking of Janet Staiger, Kristin Thompson and David Bordwell, Douglas Gomery, Robert C Allen, Janet Wasko, Tino Balio, Tim Corrigan, Jon Lewis and David Cook – have put the salient features of the New Hollywood already named by Kael, Walker and others in a broader historical framework, usually combining economic, industrial, demographic and institutional factors. The result is a composite, but there is general agreement on the outlines, and often even the particulars, of the story of Hollywood's fall and rise between the late 1950s and the early 1980s. Some historians give more prominence to the agents-turned-producers (Lew Wasserman, David Geffen) and to the rise of the package and the deal-makers (Barry Diller, Steve Ross, Sumner Redstone) than to actors, writers or directors; they discuss the shifts in media ownership and the business management practices brought in after the several waves of take-overs and mergers affecting the (assets of the) major studios (Kirk Kerkorian, Ted Turner, Rupert Murdoch); and they underline the changes in the institutional-legal frameworks under which the American cinema operated, the dates of which I already mentioned: the disinvestiture imposed on the studios by the Paramount decree of 1948, changes in the industry's self-censorship (abandonment of the

Hays Code, the revision(s) of the rating system) in the late 1960s, the relaxation of the anti-trust laws during the Reagan presidency, culminating in the abandonment of the Treasury's case against the Time Warner merger in the early 1990s. The net result of focusing on these developments is to argue that by the mid-to-late 1980s, Hollywood had effectively undone the consequences of the post-war decartelisation, and had – in somewhat different forms, and in a quite different media environment – de facto re-established the business practices once known generically as vertical integration, i.e. the controlling ownership of the sites (studios) and means (stars, personnel) of production, (access to) all the relevant systems of delivery and distribution, and (programming power over) the premier exhibition outlets.

Closure in the canonical story of the renaissance of American cinema is thus provided by a return to the beginnings, the re-establishment of the status quo ante, in good classical Hollywood narrative terms. In many ways the canonical story claims that, by the end of the 1980s, it was business as usual. Hollywood had once more demonstrated its deeply conservative character, where the fundamental forces at work confirm that the American cinema is a remarkably (or infuriatingly) stable, self-regulating organism, whose strength, or indeed, whose 'genius of the system', in André Bazin's famous words, 'lies in the richness of its ever vigorous tradition, and its fertility when it comes into contact with new elements' (Bazin 1985: 257-258). This may be too blithely optimistic an account for those who think the American cinema died around 1980, and too coarse-grained for those, who – noting some of the more subtle, but nonetheless substantial changes – think it justified to use the terms 'post-classical'. However, adaptability, the absorption of foreign elements, the appropriation of talent and incorporation of innovative techniques were already part of Bazin's definition of the classical.[7]

Crossover Auteurism

The question, in relation to the present book, is whether the non-classical, romantic, European, baroque aesthetics, as well as the antagonistic, critical, and countercultural energies manifest in the first New Hollywood were a genuine, if short-lived and aborted alternative, or whether the misfits, rebels and outsiders were necessary for the 'system' to first adjust and then renew itself. This application of the push-pull model, too, may be too neat – or cynical – an opposition, but as I shall argue, it is an option worth thinking about. What the reference to the industrial, managerial and legal frameworks of the American mainstream movie business in any case does provide is to put in place a foil against which the essays that follow can be read. Sometimes they flesh out in-dividual case studies around directors, certain genres or historical moments, but they also bring to the fore quite other parts of the picture, which are not ex-plained by economic factors, and which show up the limits of an institutional analysis. Most authors do address, albeit obliquely, aspects of the canonical story, but they also contradict and modify it, or they explore quite different connections. To signal a few of these connections: the New Hollywood links with European art cinema (Rosenbaum, Horwath); the contacts with the (New York) avantgarde (Rosenbaum, Hoberman, Reynaud); the hybridisation of genres (Hoberman, Hampton, Jameson); the Godfathers of New Hollywood and the impact of Roger Corman (King, McDonaugh, Jones); the political di-mension of Vietnam and the Nixon years (Thomson, Hoberman, Keathley); the macho codes and troubled gender relations (Jones, Martin, Reynaud); the implications for narrative structure and story motivation (Elsaesser, Martin), and finally, the philosophical-phenomenological dimension (Robnik, Polan, Keathley).

I shall not comment on each of these features in detail. Instead, I want to thematise one recurring aspect, namely the different 'crossovers' involved in defining not the essence of 1970s American cinema, but its several moments of transfer, transition and backtrack. Crossover also in the directors' many filiations to distinct traditions within American filmmaking, including those to the generation that preceded them. Crossover, finally, in the meaning we at-tribute to the various levels of analysis (historical, political, institutional) usu-ally invoked in order to explain the moves and manoeuvres from Old Holly-wood to New Hollywood, and from New to New New or Contemporary Hollywood.

The European Crossover and the French Connection. Given the emphasis on di-rectors in this collection, what cannot be stressed often enough is just how cru-cial, but also contradictory the idea of an auteur cinema was, and why it should establish itself in America at this point in time. Some explanations are well known: first of all, there is the influence of European cinema of the 1950s and 1960s, and especially the combined impact of the French nouvelle vague and their reassessment of (classical) Hollywood cinema, via *Cahiers du cinéma* and its *politique des auteurs*. Emblematically this link is preserved in the now quasi-mythical story of Robert Benton and David Newman's script of BONNIE AND CLYDE having been written for François Truffaut, and then offered to Jean-Luc Godard. Other explanations stress the role played by the newly founded film departments at NYU, UCLA and USC, where future directors were trained not only in filmmaking, but took classes in cinema studies. They read Bazin, rediscovered Ford, Hawks, Walsh, Lang, and emulated Hitchcock or Welles, once primed by Manny Farber's writings and Andrew Sarris' *The*

American Cinema: Directors and Directions, before publishing essays on *film noir*, or Master's Theses on *Transcendental Style in Film: Ozu, Bresson, Dreyer* (Paul Schrader). Then, there are style features and filmic techniques with a specifically 'expressive' charge, such as freeze frame, the zoom or slow motion. Whether these are 'European' imports in films such as THE GRADUATE, THE WILD BUNCH or BUTCH CASSIDY is debatable (they could also be seen as a technology transfer and a crossover from television), but in the cinema such devices were initially felt to be un-classical (and maybe even un-American), since they drew too much attention to themselves, allegedly lacking story-motivation and blocking transparency and therefore spectatorial identification: major sins in the classical Hollywood rule-book that have since become, if not virtues, then certainly well-understood conventions.

Taken together, European influence, film school training, a re-evaluation of American directors, and expressive style give body to the idea of the *auteur*, understood as the personality manifesting itself in a film or oeuvre through the singular, authentic 'voice'. Peter Bogdanovich, for instance, appropriating the idea for his own generation, projected it back on the grand old masters of the classical American cinema, whom he interviewed in the late 1960s and early 1970s: "in all the films I really liked, there was a definite sense of one artist's vision, a feeling of the director's virtual presence within and outside the frames we watched: often you could recognise the personality from picture to picture, as you could various paintings from the same hand." And in support, he quotes Howard Hawks, who provides him with the title of his book: "I liked almost anybody [in Hollywood] that made you realise who in the devil was making the picture .... Because the director's the storyteller and should have his own method of telling it."[8] What is perhaps elided is the difference between the romantic conception of the artist-auteur (of the New Hollywood) and the classical artist-auteur: where the latter makes his voice heard within the system and its many constraints, the former sets himself off against the system.

Other important aspects of the Europe-Hollywood story are discussed in Jonathan Rosenbaum's essay, who was himself a participant, in that he played a prominent role in the 1970s as mediator of French film culture for English-speaking viewers and readers, making the journey from America to Europe, and from Paris to New York (via London) several times and in both directions. But he adds to our picture by also pointing to literary influences: that of Rudolf Wurlitzer's neo-Beckettian novel *Nog* on the script for TWO-LANE BLACKTOP (also mentioned by Kent Jones, for instance), as well as Schrader's obsession with Dostoevsky, Sartre and Camus. Literary adaptations and the collaboration between writers and filmmakers is again associated with European cinema, when one thinks of Alain Resnais (Jean Cayrol, Marguerite Duras, Alain

Robbe-Grillet), Wim Wenders (Peter Handke) or Americans in Europe, such as Joseph Losey (Harold Pinter).

The European connection also features in Alexander Horwath's essay, who reminds the reader of just how many European directors actually went to the United States from the late 1960s onwards, often on the strength of the reputation they had built up in the meantime among New York cinephiles, but also because Hollywood, in a well-known practice, was keen to put under contract foreign talent with box office potential. Working for the American market, their names could also be exploited overseas. Not everyone, however, had the staying power of a Roman Polanski, a Milos Forman or, a little later, Louis Malle. Michelangelo Antonioni's ZABRISKIE POINT (1968) has remained the classic case study of all that can go wrong for both parties in this marriage of European auteur and Hollywood studio, but as Horwath points out, the brief sojourn of the French *nouvelle vague* in America also produced two highly reflexive, quasi-documentary films about the mutual attractions and misunderstandings between Paris, New York and Los Angeles: the self-ironic and sharply observed LION'S LOVE by Agnes Varda, and her husband's, Jacques Demy's, more playful, melancholy MODEL SHOP (both 1969). Not until the 1980s, when Wenders, an equally sensitive and cinephile soul, briefly left Germany for his Zoetrope adventure in San Francisco (HAMMETT, 1983), would there be such a hopeful if ultimately unhappy encounter between European auteurism and the New Hollywood.

The Crossovers with the Avant-garde. As well as tracing the influence on the mainstream of the European nouvelle vague – the key films are LAST YEAR IN MARIENBAD, SHOOT THE PIANO PLAYER and BAND OF OUTSIDERS – Rosenbaum also alludes to the links between New York avant-garde and mainstream movies. But for him the impact of the films of Kenneth Anger and Andy Warhol, for instance, had more to do with subject matter – homoeroticism, sex, drugs – than style, so that these films, like similar ones from Europe, mostly prepared the general public for changes which were then reflected in the new rating systems. Not even TAXI DRIVER qualifies in this respect: instead of welcoming the ingenious echoes of avantgarde techniques and the many references to European models, as Horwath does, Rosenbaum intimates that all three auteurs of TAXI DRIVER – Scorsese, Schrader and de Niro – exhibited a good deal of moral irresponsibility, paving the way for a sanitised version of counter-cultural elements to enter the mainstream, rather than creatively transforming the legacy of the New York avant-garde. In all of Rosenbaum's case studies (from THE GRADUATE to TAXI DRIVER, via BONNIE AND CLYDE, THE MANCHURIAN CANDIDATE, EASY RIDER, THE LAST MOVIE and TWO LANE BLACKTOP), he demonstrates, however, that the cinematic lineage is more complicated and subtle than is sometimes realised, and he salutes the veteran critics of whatever persuasion – Manny Farber, Andrew Sarris, Pauline Kael – for recognising the cross-fertilisations quite clearly, and appreciates them quite undogmatically.

The Exhibition Crossover. Rosenbaum's other objective is to underline the capital importance of exhibition – in line with his books, *Moving Places* and *Midnight Movies* (with J. Hoberman). Noting how many films from the 1970s which we now consider the period's artistic highlights never had an American release, he argues that the so-called art houses in Europe in the 1970s began to promote the blending of hitherto distinct film cultures. Retrospectives of mainstream directors elevated to auteur status, avant-garde films, art-cinema, or independent directors' work were all shown in the same venues. In the US, such spaces did not exist, so that the films either ended up in what Rosenbaum aptly calls a 'rather specialised no-man's land,' or they had to wait until retrieved from limbo by the classroom of the academia, a place Rosenbaum is not too fond of for movies of any kind. He finds it especially inappropriate for experimental films, since 'it tended to remove [them] from the social spaces of ordinary or makeshift movie theatres and relegate them to safer confines of various institutional venues.'

What here justifies the tone of regret is the value placed on the actual experience of cinema. The base note is the recollection of films as they came alive in a particular location, the sensation of the images projected onto a screen, viewed alone or with someone special across a possibly vast and darkened auditorium. But almost as relevant is the outside: the built site, the movie front or façade, the location on a particular block or street. The preference was for the neighbourhood or small-town movie house (as in Bogdanovich's THE LAST PICTURE SHOW, 1971), frequented during the years of their slow decline into seediness, or their rebirth as art houses (as described in Rosenbaum's autobiographical *Moving Places*). A picture show still meant – and in our title recalls – the big screen, and maybe even, as in Bogdanovich's first film TARGETS (1986), the drive-in cinemas.[9] That the New Hollywood, which for its makers just as much as for its admirers so definitely belongs in the cinemas, often found little or no distribution, and eventually happened on late-night television or in film classes, is one of the great tragedies or ironies that hover around some of the essays. It makes them, in the best possible sense, manifestos of what used to be called cinephilia, the love of cinema, and not just of films.

Crossovers between the different sites, where spectators now encounter movies, and even more so, crossover between different storage media and media-platforms are one of the major features of the second New Hollywood. This is why exhibition is often the key change that is tracked in the canonical story.[10] The forced separation of the studios from their prime exhibition outlets through the Paramount decree, which also made block-booking illegal, initiated the experiments with roadshowing, four-walling and other attempts at

Tim O'Kelly in Targets

attracting special attention for what became a film-by-film business.[11] But beginning in the mid-1970s (with the marketing of Jaws as the breakthrough
case), distribution-exhibition started once more to take the lead over production, so much so that the system eventually stabilised itself around saturation
booking, coordinated release dates, and the targeting of public holiday week-
ends. A further consequence (or is it cause?) of the new type of event-movie
(commonly referred to by the curiously anachronistic and in the meantime
oxymoronic term blockbuster) was that secondary exploitation now happened
in the ancillary markets: television, toy-shops, video game arcades, clothing
and fashion outlets, consumer electronics, theme-parks and, since the 1980s
and 1990s, video-cassettes and DVDs. Not only does exhibition wag the dog
production (and thus also the auteur), the primary exhibition outlet – the cinema (movie palace or multiplex) – is itself wagged by the secondary markets of
the broader entertainment industries and the experience economy, by becoming their advertising billboard.

In these changes from production towards marketing, the first New Hollywood occupied perhaps a more ambiguous place than the lament over lack of

exhibition suggests. Besides Spielberg's and Lucas's well-ventilated role as crossover figures in the mid-1970s, there is the case of EASY RIDER. It made industry history by its highly favourable ratio of production cost to box office earnings, as well as by establishing once and for all the youth appeal that motion picture mass entertainment henceforth had to have, and which included the sound-track as an integral marketing tool. Another case study was Tom Laughlin's campaign for getting his BILLY JACK to carefully targeted audiences, which also showed the industry the way towards advertising-led, media-blitz promotion techniques. These marketing and exhibition practices, in other words, supported by new delivery systems and the digital technologies of sound and image reproduction turned the big screen picture into something that superficially seems the same and that has yet changed utterly. As David Thomson reminds us, if we call the 1970s the decade when movies mattered, or the years of 'the last great American Picture Show', then this is also because it was the last decade without the video-recorder. Since the 1980s, there are still big screens – in fact, they are now often even bigger than they used to be in the 1960s and 1970s – but their function has doubled: site of an intensified experience, they are also a blockbuster's 'screen test', first inflating the images, before they shrink and disperse, percolating through a multitude of media outlets, all the way down to the video-rental store, at once the morgue, the supermarket and the permanent museum of our film culture.

The Generational Crossover. It (almost) goes without saying that these auteur-directors – the old ones whom Bogdanovich was interviewing, as well as the new ones he introduces alongside himself in the opening pages – Henry Jaglom and Warren Beatty – are *male*. This is true also of the ones featured in our collection: Peckinpah, Penn, Altman, and Hellman, Rafelson, Scorsese. The one exception is Barbara Loden, who proves the rule when we read Berenice Reynaud's heart-wrenching account of Loden's struggle to get her film WANDA (1970) made, and then – after its successful launch at the Venice Film Festival – to shape for herself an identity as a director, by among other things, trying to escape from under the shadow of Elia Kazan, her mentor, ex-husband and puppet-master. The male values on display are, however, suitably multiple and ambivalent. The auteur concepts presented here leave room for the rugged individualist, but also for the anxious loner, for the compulsive womanizer, the hard drugs user, as well as the flamboyantly gay avantgardist. There are long-haired heroes of the counter-cultures and inner city losers, caught in cycles of self-destructive violence. In some cases, the directors also played the leads in their films (Dennis Hopper, Peter Fonda, Tom Laughlin, Jack Nicholson), and in others, a handful of male actors (Warren Oates, Jack Nicholson, Robert de Niro, Harvey Keitel) are fictionalised stand-ins or ironically idealized alter egos (for Hellman, Rafelson, Scorsese). That there is another male dimension to this auteurism should also be mentioned: the generational 'thing', the typically oedipal mix of admiration, emulation and rebellion, which Richard Jameson briefly discusses in 'Dinosaurs in the Age of the Cinemobile', To some of the 'Dinosaurs' the label Godfathers of the New Hollywood might equally apply.[12]

These (oedipal) Godfathers can be understood within the template of auterism European style, when we think of how Eric Rohmer, Jacques Rivette and Claude Chabrol called themselves Hitchcoco-Hawksians, how Godard stylized himself as Fritz Lang's assistant in LE MEPRIS (1963) and as 'son' of Roberto Rossellini, and how Truffaut balanced his need for father-figures between the somewhat antithetical figures of André Bazin and Alfred Hitchcock, Jean Renoir and Orson Welles. As already hinted, Coppola, Scorsese, Schrader, de Palma and others also picked elective paternities, including Spielberg when – repaying the compliment, as it were – he asked Truffaut to play the fatherly French scientist in CLOSE ENCOUNTERS OF THE THIRD KIND (1977). Coppola, in turn, could be said to have become Godfather to a subsequent generation, including European directors, when he distributed in the US the films of Werner Herzog and Hans Jürgen Syberberg, or invited Wenders to direct a movie for his Zoetrope company. I already mentioned how unhappy an experience this proved to be for the German director, so much so that he felt impelled to make a movie about it. THE STATE OF THINGS (1982) is a film about filmmaking made back-to-back with Raoul Ruiz's THE TERRITORY (1981) in Lisbon, for Portugese-French producer Paolo Branco, featuring another adopted Godfather-auteur, the veteran Hollywood maverick Sam Fuller, making a film-within-the-film. But a truly inspired piece of casting on the part of Wenders was to give the (fictionalised) role of Francis Coppola to Roger Corman, since Corman might be said to have played for Coppola himself the Godfather part that Coppola played for Wenders (not forgetting that Paolo Branco was a European Corman to both Wenders and Ruiz).

The Corman Connection

The historical crux here is the one brought out by several contributors of the present volume who highlight the role of Corman in the story of the New Hollywood. The Corman legend and legacy, discussed in detail by McDonagh (and touched on by King and Horwath) fits the Godfather paradigm, but nonetheless opens up another genealogy. In plotting for the reader the convoluted undergrowth of 'exploitation' filmmaking, with its mixture of grindhouse, sweatshop and the various archipelagos of creative freedom, experiment and even exuberance that existed in this domain, her essay soon tracks down this most improbable source of the New Hollywood, geographically much closer to hand, and aesthetically more subterranean than that of European art cinema. At the centre is not an auteur-artist, but an entrepreneur, not a single masterpiece, but a stream of low-budget B-pictures, made at the margins of the studio system, but nevertheless mimicking it; made not on the expensive, labour-intensive real-estate of Culver City or Burbank, but on abandoned industrial terrain and disused railroad property behind Venice Beach.

Corman's production companies AIP (American International Pictures, owned by Samuel Z Arkoff) and New World Pictures (co-owned by Corman and his brother Gene) made biker movies and women prison movies, jungle movies and monster movies. Most of them may have been forgotten, but he is respectfully remembered by the whole generation of young ex-film graduates, the movie brats, whom he gave a chance as cinematographers, script-writers, sound technicians, editors, actors, and even as second unit directors. As McDonagh shows, the names of the people who worked for Corman, indeed were often 'exploited' by him, reads like a Who's Who of New Hollywood: among the directors, Martin Scorsese, Francis Ford Coppola, George Lucas, Peter Bogdanovich, Bob Rafelson and Monte Hellman, and among the actors-directors Denis Hopper, Peter Fonda and Jack Nicholson, among the actors Bruce Dern and Warren Oates, and among the writers Robert Towne and John Milius.

But Corman and his lurid adaptations of Edgar Allen Poe stories, his cheap horror films or youth movies had another function relevant to our argument. If in the late 1960s, it was he who supplied the dying neighbourhood flea-pits, the drive-in cinemas, the bottom half of double-bills in the disreputable end of the teen-market, he was also, in the 1970s, the American distributor of Ingmar Bergman, Federico Fellini, Francois Truffaut, Joseph Losey, Volker Schloendorff and Alain Resnais. Thus, thinking through the issue of exhibition sites as raised by Rosenbaum, one is led to another form of crossover. For Corman provides also a link between the declining second-run cinemas and their (occasional) re-emergence as art houses. Already mentioned in the passage cited from Beverly Walker about the 'porn-horror-violence route', but also implied by Rosenbaum, and demonstrated by McDonagh: the US notion of the art house was of strategic importance for the 1970s auteur sector not least because of a fruitful confusion between different kinds of transgression, taboo-breaking and deviancy. With their reputation for 'adult movies' (in the years prior to the abandonment of the Hays Code and changes in local censorship and the industry's own rating system), the art houses were home to some of the strangest encounters between European auteur cinema and commercial productions, whether from the maverick mainstream, from off-Hollywood B-picture genres, or from the sex- and blaxploitation sector. By providing both stage and outlet for New Hollywood, European auteur films, as well as exploitation movies, New World Pictures and the art house circuits invented the idea of the cult film or the 'cult classic', labels later taken over by the successors of all second-run movie houses: the inner-city basement, commercial strip, or suburban shopping mall video store, mythical home of Quentin Tarantino's mercurial talent.

In other words, even though Corman did not exactly embody the European concept of the *auteur*, any more than he was an avant-garde artist, his operation was such a vibrant and improbable hybrid that the Corman connection may be the closest the 1970s came to supplying an authentically American pedigree for the auteur theory as it 'went West' and found itself practically and unselfconsciously applied in a volatile industry situation. His version of autonomy-within-the-system even provides a clue to how the second New Hollywood evolved out of the first: if one re-centres American auteurism from New York and Paris to Los Angeles and San Francisco, then – leaving aside for a moment differences of scale, as well as ambition – it may not be altogether fanciful to see the Godfather Corman pass the baton to the Godfather Coppola, before the Zoetrope enterprise overreached itself and had to be 'rescued' by the bankers and the corporate suits, a lesson not lost on some of Coppola's fellow-alumni from the Corman Academy, UCLA and USC, who met the suits halfway.[13] Spielberg, Lucas, Milius could be more circumspect and prudent, not least because of the combined example of Corman and Coppola. In different ways, they blended the auteur with the entrepreneur, when they began making common cause with the new studio managers, the deal-strikers, talent agents, advertising executives and marketing men. If this may be no recommendation for their artistic integrity, it nevertheless, I would suggest, opens up an intriguing perspective when examining the shifts from one New Hollywood to the next.

Crossovers in the Modes of Production. Another defining feature of (the second) New Hollywood in the canonical story is the debate over the mode of production which characterises the 'renaissance' and its aftermath. If one argues from an auteurist perspective, there seems to be a clear opposition: the old Hollywood studio-system worked according to a recognizably industrial model, which – so the 1960s eventually ruinous overproduction seemed to prove – collapsed under its own weight and inflexibility. It was superseded by the more nimble, small-is-beautiful, artisanal mode of American independent film production, for which the producer-writer-director, negotiating with the studios on a film-by-film basis, or a production company dedicated to its creative talent seemed to be the pragmatic mode of organisation. The ideal(ised) model, in the 1970s, was BBS (founded by Bert Schneider, Bob Rafelson and

Steve Blauner) which produced EASY RIDER and TWO-LANE BLACKTOP. The exact relation of the one-man independents to the studios, and to distribution awaits examination in more detail,[14] but it has been noted that several major studios themselves took risks and hired considerably younger and sometimes untested heads of production, most famously perhaps Robert ('the kid stays on the picture') Evans at Paramount (producing Coppola's GODFATHER films [1972-74], Polanski's ROSEMARY'S BABY [1968] and then the same director's CHINATOWN [1975]).

Despite elements of crossover between Old and New Hollywood, the gap between New and New New, with regard to production seemed to become wider and wider as the decade wore on. In most directors' biographies (Penn, Peckinpah, Rafelson, Ashby, Hellman, Bogdanovich) the pattern of rapid decline or of patchy alternation between so-called commercial and more personal projects is by and large remarkably similar, however different their biographical circumstances. It even includes the more mainstream figures such as William Friedkin, Alan J Pakula and Bob Fosse, whose films could also be considered harbingers of the genre-based blockbusters of the 1980s. The exceptions among the generation born before 1940 are Robert Altman, whose production company Lion's Gate might fit the BBS model, and Stanley Kubrick, who moved to England and even more than Altman became a one-man studio. Despite ups and down at the box-office, their work remained very consistently 'auteurist', and above all, they were 'survivors' with a steady output of films (though this is more true of Altman, protected by Alan Ladd Jr. at Fox, than of Kubrick who required much bigger budgets). Kubrick, however, is remarkable in another sense, in that, belonging to the auteurs, he nonetheless had an inordinate influence not so much on the first New Hollywood as on the second, insofar as each of his films from DR STRANGELOVE (1964) and 2001: A SPACE ODYSSEY (1968) onwards was a kind of prototype (of the science fiction film, of ultraviolence, of the costume film, the horror film) that others could adapt into a blockbuster formula. That Spielberg should be the one to direct and produce the long-nursed, but in the event posthumous Kubrick project A.I. (2001) emblematically pays tribute to this fact.

For the canonical story, the typical feature of the New New is the package deal, put together by agents-turned-powerbrokers, or the star-turned-producer, rather than a project initiated by either the director or by a producer working closely with the director (BBS, Robert Evans). The package deal thus not only superseded the studio-system's way of making movies, with their fixed production facilities, personnel under contract, and pre-planned release schedules. It was also inimical to the auteur cinema, since the director may very well not have been the key element of the package, although in the case of Kubrick, and later Spielberg (or briefly, Quentin Tarantino), a 'director as superstar' did represent a production value in his own right. In this respect, the director in the New New Hollywood is part of the marketing, which means that he is neither unrecognised, as might have been the case in the darker days of the studio-system, nor the admired auteur of the 1960s, but instead figures as an entrepreneurial brand name, who very often has to become a celebrity and media star, on a par with his leading actors, in order to maintain his box-office value.

In Praise of Pilot Fish

There is, however, another way of looking at the changes in the modes of production that took place around the mid-1970s, which modifies somewhat the oppositions just sketched. Taking a broader view, one can think of the classical Hollywood studio system with its vertical integration as following the Fordist principles of industrial production, centred on a fixed production site, an in-house division of labour (the assembly-line) and producer-units. In such an environment, the product's outlets (the first run cinemas) and the final consumers (the family audience) are relatively stable and known quantities, while competition among different producers is regulated in the form of a cartel or trust. By contrast, the New New Hollywood mode of production, based (at the production end) on the package deal and driven (at the exhibition end) by more market-oriented, targeted campaigns to capture the fickle tastes, the unpredictable behaviour and the floating age-and-gender balance of the ever more youthful cinema audiences, would qualify as an essentially post-Fordist model of industrial production. Its economic and managerial organisation is that of conglomerate ownership, as it evolved across the two major waves of mergers and takeovers, the first in the early 1970s (by companies seeking diversification), and the second in the late 1980s (by companies seeking synergies). The diversified nature of conglomerate ownership necessarily leads to decentralisation, sub-contracting and outsourcing, which would be a more technical description of the package deal. Murray Smith, referring himself to an article by Michael Storper, identifies the blockbuster era thus as post-Fordist and attempts to integrate what happened in the film industry into the bigger picture of post-industrial trends in the developed world towards service-industries, when manufacturing became more responsive to new patterns of consumption that split the mass-market into fluctuating cycles of demand, 'boutique' tastes and niche markets. Smith, however, also adds a proviso, namely that the analogy may not be entirely appropriate, if one concedes that the classical cinema was less Fordist in the 1940s and 1950s than other industries, while also allowing for the possibility that Hollywood of the 1980s and 1990s is less post-Fordist than it appears, since production has always been a function of distribution, which has remained very centralised, both prior to and since the Paramount decree.[15]

It is this glass half-full/glass half-empty argument over the degrees of Fordist or post-Fordist organisation in the film industry between 1950 and 1990 that give the cinema of the 1970s its proper place: as a distinct moment, and nevertheless, part of several ongoing but contradictory processes. The West Coast genealogy of American auteurism I have sketched above (where, at the limit, Corman's family/academy/factory mirrors not only the studio-system but also parallels and inverts the East Coast family/academy/factory of Andy Warhol), as well as the production methods of post-Fordist outsourcing as practised by Corman's New World Pictures and Coppola's Zoetrope point to elements of the New Hollywood that the New New Hollywood would learn from (with Lucas' Industrial Light and Magic or John Lassiter's Pixar becoming rich and famous as highly specialised suppliers). Corman and Coppola were research-and-development units for – inadvertent or intentional – prototypes, but they were also do-it-yourself mini-versions (low-tech in Corman's, high-tech in Coppola's case) of various kinds of industrial post-Fordism. The same could be said, in different degrees, about Altman, Kubrick, Scorsese who, as it were, outsourced themselves in relation to the Hollywood studios' newly consolidated function as world-wide distributors. They developed prototypes for movie or television mass-production (the television series spin-off like M*A*S*H, Happy Days [after Lucas AMERICAN GRAFFITI] or Alice [after Scorsese's ALICE DOESN'T LIVE HERE ANYMORE], and the systematic planning of sequels and prequels in the wake of STAR WARS). In this version, Corman would not so much be the Godfather within the oedipal paradigm of surrogate family and elective paternity. Rather, his production methods would be an ad-hoc version of post-Fordism, with sub-contracting and the exploitation of non-Union labour power both assuring his relative economic success as well as confirming his outsider status and pariah role within the Hollywood establishment.[16]

As an alternative (or sub-category) of post-Fordism, economists like Storper and neo-Marxists like Asu Aksoi and Kevin Robins have identified a two-tier industrial dualism, where the independents or small-scale entrepreneurs act as both 'shock absorbers' and 'pilot fish',[17] which corresponds roughly to the push-pull model I mentioned earlier and is reminiscent of the relation between the hackers in the earlier years of the computer industry, whose attacks on IBM accidentally or strategically helped 'debug' the corporate giant's software. Applied to the film industry of the late 1960s and 1970s, the pilot fish model would specify that the old studios/new corporate con-

'Bruce' in JAWS

glomerates sought to renew themselves by 'attracting risk capital and creative talent which [they could] then exploit through their control of distribution',[18] or in the hacker analogy, the auteurs would have been the ones whose proto-types (but also failures) helped debug the Hollywood production system, as it slowly but inevitably moved from Fordist to post-Fordist modes of financing, marketing and asset management (notably studio-libraries of films, brands and various other types of intellectual property rights).

However, the transitions between the Old, the New and the New New Hollywood, according to this model, were not simply gradual or a matter of degree. The twists and turns would preserve their element of struggle, of antagonism and irreconcilable difference. The push-pull analogy (i.e. the mutual dependence between antagonistic forces) allows for the possibility that the protagonists involved in this story were often not in control of the parts they played (William Goldman's famous adage about Hollywood: 'nobody knows anything', or the drug excesses chronicled by Peter Biskind), and that events followed the law of unintended consequences. It also helps explain how and why there were so many crossovers from margin to centre and slippages in both directions: on the one side so many talents wasted, and on the other, so many talents 'sleeping with the enemy'. Put differently, but again, hopefully not too cynically, the auteurs drew their self-understanding from identifying with the ideology of the European artist (or the freewheeling spirit of the Corman operation and the various counter-cultures), while at another level they also played the role of the pilot fish: helping the white whales (or, more appropriately, sharks) of the blockbuster-era navigate the beach area safely and profitably. So, in a sense, both factions could agree: long live the pilot fish.

Counter-Cultural Agendas

The 'cynical' part of the argument would be its implications for the idealism of the period, the aesthetics of the films, and the politics of their makers. For if there is one theme that informs most of the essays, it is the value placed on the socially critical impact of the films, as well as the counter-cultural engagement of the directors and writers. This does not mean that the American auteurs had to belong to the left in the European sense of the term, or even liberal in the U.S. sense (though many were). They could flaunt their love for the wide open spaces of the American West and indulge in anti-modernist sentiments about cities, which Middle America might also have endorsed. But the landscapes and settings of New Hollywood show the ravages of an exploitative civilisation, at the same time as they still hold out the promise of an unspoilt nature, glimpsed, as it were, out of the corner of the eye. Above all, there is the notable bias for the underdog, the outsider, the outlaw, the working man or disaffected middle class protagonist, whose ideas of happiness and freedom imply emotional bonds that are lived outside the nuclear family, and for whom the romantic, heterosexual couple is not the end-point of the narrative, but doomed from the start, as in the many criminal couple films made in the wake of Bonnie and Clyde, such as Thieves Like Us or Badlands. Given that individualism and freedom are, in the American context, values prized in the vocabulary of the right as well as the left, the ideological makeup of New Hollywood has several dimensions, and the parties to the debate are not infrequently at cross-purposes when it comes to politics.

For instance, the counter-cultural crossover, staged between the law and the outlaw changing places or confusing the sides they are on, in Easy Rider, Sugarland Express, The Wild Bunch or McCabe and Mrs Miller, sometimes also forms the bridge between high-culture and popular culture. This encounter as well as clash is encapsulated in Jack Nicholson's Bobby Eroica Dupea, the protagonist of Five Easy Pieces, who leaves behind his middle-class home and college education, to do shift work as an oil-rigger, and who leaves Beethoven's piano sonatas behind for improvised jazz and blues. That he gets caught up with a waitress, whose elocution may be faulty and table-manners leave something to be desired, but whose emotional intelligence and sheer humanity knocks spots off his blasé nihilism, is more than the usual attraction of opposites: it completes the hero's political, as well as his sentimental education. Generally, however, it is the twin strands of movies and rock music that braid the ideological texture of the protest movement and its sense of promise as well as pride, and thus define a major element of the period's political authenticity. As Howard Hampton shows in his chapter on 'Uneasy Riders': auteurist cinema and rock each had their distinct voice during the 1970s, but as never before or since, they entered into an exchange, a contest and occasionally even into a dialogue about what it meant to be American when one has reason to be ashamed for what is being done in its name, or when anger and despair about one's country were the only honest ways of being a patriot – the Bruce Springsteen way. Hampton is hard on the missed opportunities, and sees even the New Hollywood as not having done right by rock, which is reminiscent of Wim Wenders, who in his mind's eye saw a John Ford Western when he listened to Creedence Clearwater Revival, but who thought the only music appropriate to 1960s old Hollywood was Ennio Morricone's, as played by Charles Bronson on his harmonica.[19]

If the political event that inaugurated the protest movement was the Vietnam War, on which BONNIE AND CLYDE offers only oblique comment, there is general agreement that it was the election of Ronald Reagan as president in November 1980 that brought the New Hollywood along with the counter-culture to a close. Such a perspective is implied in David Thomson's recollections from the decade where movies mattered. Highlighting the cinéphile moments in his choice films, the underlying (mock-?) bitterness seems also motivated by the sense of a political frontier having been closed since, at least as much as an aesthetic one. More recently, David Cook in *Lost Illusions* makes Reagan's election explicitly the terminal event of his account of the decade: 'In fact, the election [...] marked the loss of two illusions fabricated during the decade that preceded it. First was the illusion of a liberal political consensus created by the antiwar movement, the Watergate scandal and the subsequent resignation of Richard Nixon [...]. The second illusion, intermingled with the first, was that mainstream American movies might aspire to the sort of serious social or political content described above on a permanent basis. This prospect was seriously challenged when the blockbuster mentality took hold in Hollywood in the wake of JAWS and STAR WARS.'[20] Thomson and Cook were preceded by Robin Wood's *Hollywood from Vietnam to Reagan* and Andrew Britton's article for *Movie* 'Blissing Out', which probably coined the term 'Reaganite entertainment', subsequently invoked by several commentators (and alluded to also at end of Horwath's essay below).[21] According to this version, the counter-cultural, 'progressive' politics of the first New Hollywood were replaced in the 1980s by films and cycles whose primary function was 'reactionary', defined as a cunning mixture of repression and reassurance, with story-lines that were not only politically conservative and flag-wavingly patriotic. They also unapologetically affirmed the virtue of being dumb. As characterisation became simplistic, conflicts puerile and psychology pared down to a minimum, the movies gave more and more space to spectacle, muscle-bound action and mindless destruction.

Without going into the polemical value of this periodisation, there are two aspects relevant to my general argument. First, the issue of spectacle hints at another major so-called innovation of the second New Hollywood, besides financial management and exhibition practices: the increasing role played by technology and new kinds of special effects, as well as genres that put these special effects dramatically on display: the monster film (JAWS), the horror film (THE EXORCIST), and the sci-fi epic (STAR WARS). American cinema in the 1980s became identified with certain genres and their crossover blends: besides the sci-fi fantasy, the body horror film and the action-adventure, it was the neo-noir porno-thriller and the time-travel nostalgia film which caught the critics' attention. This return to genre filmmaking, and especially to the big screen treatment given to formerly B-picture, exploitation and television genres was in contrast to the New Hollywood's quite troubled and even, some would say, tormented relation to genre, where the road movie, the anti-Western, and the cops-and-robbers stories gone horribly wrong predominated. The critical, counter-cultural stance was manifest in the preference for unconventional story-material and for apparently incoherent or meandering narratives that contest or simply ignore the goal-oriented, affirmative, plot-driven movies with their neat resolutions and sense of closure. Genre mutations have always been regarded as among the hallmarks of the 1970s, and in a sense, this aspect of American cinema – so apparently hostile to the auteur-ethos – confirms the permanence and cohesion of Hollywood across social changes and industry transformation. But genres and their capacious adaptability are also an index of how open mainstream filmmaking has always been to the national moods, or to the permeable political meanings given to the myths and typically American themes that genres are said to encode or transport.

To say that New Hollywood films skirted some of the traditional genres, or brought to the fore the twilight elements in the Western, for instance, is thus merely to underline that its oppositional energies still worked within the system rather than in outright opposition to it. The mutations have inspired critics to offer strong, political readings of certain movies or even whole cycles.

Horwath gives such an assessment, and one could cite Robin Wood's analysis from 1976 of the horror film, which correlates the rebirth of the genre to profound changes in the American family.[22] The most sustained political reading of the decade under the heading of genre in our collection is provided by Jim Hoberman's essay 'Nashville contra Jaws' – contrasting two ways of dealing with American political history in the 1970s, one by a quintessentially New Hollywood director, and the other 'working through' the national malaise in an equally typical New New Hollywood manner. Hoberman astutely notes the asymmetrical convergence of these two films, once one sees them generically, as variations on the themes of the disaster movie. If Nashville is clearly about the complete loss of faith in the political establishment after Watergate and the Nixon resignation, to have it analysed as a disaster movie comes as an illuminating surprise. Jaws, on the other hand, can easily be seen as a disaster movie in the tradition of B-films about monsters, invading aliens or inexplicably malevolent calamities befalling a community, as a consequence of human tampering with nature. Hoberman's close mapping, however, of the politics of the *unmaking* of both Richard Nixon (Watergate) and Edward Kennedy (Chappaquiddick), while cross-referencing it to the politics of the *making* of the film, provides a powerful reading of the Hollywood mainstream in respect of the nation's agenda at any given point in time. That the blockbuster serves this agenda by seemingly dealing with something altogether different and timeless (in the case of Jaws, primordial fear of 'the deep') underlines what might be called the collusion or 'conspiracy' (Fred Jameson) that exists between Hollywood and American reality. All it requires is to see the U.S. under the dual aspect of a politics of shared myths and of shared mass media, in the push-pull of mutual dependency, even under antagonistic conditions, such as activist dissent or generational conflict, in order to validate the correspondences.

It is this trade-off between the spectacle of politics and the politics of spectacle that was one of the hardest lessons Europeans had to learn about America during the 1980s. As a consequence, whereas US film critics blamed Reagan(omics) for the (death of the) movies, the rest of the world tended to blame the movies for Reagan's populist simplifications. Especially Europeans looked at the actor-turned-president Ronald Reagan and his myth-mongering across the lens of an ultra-conformist film industry. So much so that the perception of the United States was shaped by a White House whose political agenda – with its 'Evil Empire' and 'Star Wars' initiative – was set by the season's blockbusters. Besides Star Wars, Hollywood provided feel-good movies about the American Dream (Rocky), and revisionist historical memories that turned even the war in Vietnam into a successful rescue mission (Rambo). It was partly these growing polarities between Europe and America that also intimated a widening breach within America itself, between the values of the counter-culture and those of the neo-conservative US government. So irreconcilably different did the Hollywood of STAR WARS, Stallone or Schwarzenegger appear from NASHVILLE, Nicholson or even Paul Newman that the first New Hollywood suddenly discovered greater affinities with the old, classical Hollywood than it had with the second New Hollywood. Not only did the latter supersede it; it appeared to have wiped the slate clean, by being either 'in denial' of what had gone before or deliberately misunderstanding the virtues of the classical.[23] But if critics like Wood and Britton offered among the bleakest visions of the movies of the 1980s, the better to let the films of the 1970s shine brightly, there was also the danger that the 1970s would become a sort of fetish period, the 'last' permitted site of pleasure, before the American cinema turned (once more) into the no-go area for politically committed intellectuals which it used to be prior to the French-inspired auteur theory. In the changing estimation of Hollywood, too, the continuities are almost as conspicuous as the breaks.

The Action Hero in Trouble, or The Child is Father to the Man

So far, there is one antinomy which characterised the period that has hardly been mentioned. The 1970s were the beginnings of feminism, or rather they intensely prepared the revolutions in male-female relationships. But here, too, the oppositions may not be as stark as usually argued, when pointing an accusatory finger at the relentlessly male, if not outright 'macho' flavour of the New Hollywood, both in the films, and among the community that made them.[24] The contributions in the last part of the book offer a possibly more productive way of looking at the gender issue, as well as at the fate of the countercultural energies, in the wider context of the post-Fordist economic changes alluded to above. Some of these aspects can be put under the heading of 'action image', and the male action hero, whose apparent 'return' in the 1980s in the shape of Stallone and Schwarzenegger should be seen also as the symptom of a crisis, and not merely as the affirmation of a new virility. If one adds the ambiguous protagonists played by Burt Reynolds, Bruce Willis and especially Clint Eastwood (for each DIRTY HARRY there is a PLAY MISTY FOR ME), the male action hero may not be diametrically opposed to psychopaths like Travis Bickle in TAXI DRIVER, testosterone time-bombs like Jimmy Angelelli in FINGERS, or Hamlet figures like Bobby Dupea in FIVE EASY PIECES. However, whereas the latter enact the politics of male identity mainly across the symptoms of imminent disaster and disarray, the former boldly or brutally overcompensate, repressing the knowledge that somewhere on the way to annihilating the enemy, they, too, had lost the plot. In the essay from 1975 reprinted here, I tried to suggest how the 'symptom' and the 'cure' were mutually dependent on each other, around what I called the 'pathos of failure', i.e. the inability of the New Hollywood protagonist to take on the symbolic mandate that classical Hollywood narrative addressed to its heroes: to pursue a goal or respond to a challenge. Paul Schrader once aligned this shift with the America-Europe divide when he remarked that in American movies people solved a problem, while in European films they probed a dilemma. The incapacity for purposive action is clearly related to the counter-culture's distrust of authority, which in turn sets free anarchic energies that are as destructive as they are creative. Implicit in this view of the New Hollywood is the possibility that its malaise about traditional American public institutions was matched by an appetite for self-exploration and personal experiment that, paradoxically, helped to 'modernise' Hollywood from within as much as changes in ownership structures and distribution practice modernised it from without. Thus, if the private hang-ups, drug-abuse and predatory sexual behaviour of the Movie Brats are graphically documented in Peter Biskind's account, the upside to the downside should also be recorded. Their general willingness to take risks, to follow hunches and intuitions, even the brinkmanship should be booked as assets, and not merely seen as morally irresponsible behaviour that deservedly provoked a conservative backlash on the part of the new industry bosses.

This, at least, is what is suggested to me by the essays by Martin, Keathley and Robnik. The new behavioural norms of males in the films they discuss – the mix of sensitivity and cock(iness), highlighted for instance by Adrian Martin in James Toback's FINGERS, or the tactical virtues of 'dirtiness' and 'indiscipline' identified by Drehli Robnik – show the masculinist ethic in crisis: at once excessive and deeply troubled, but also potentially 'useful' as a set of adaptive strategies in a new kind of social and psychic economy. At the same time, we can look at these ragged patterns of response as a 'working through' of the dislocations caused by the Vietnam war, and recognise in them the traumatic after-shocks to self-image and self-esteem. For Keathley, for instance, the films of the cycle he identifies as 'post-traumatic' cut across the straight left-right, countercultural-conservative ideological schema usually invoked for plotting the fault-lines of the American cinema in the 1970s and 1980s. In this sense, these male obsessions are also the concave mirror, in which one detects in often distorted form the changing role of women and the rise of feminism, so infrequently represented in the 1970s movies and thus also virtually absent in this collection. A closer, retrospective look at the male-female relations and at the macho mores of the 1970s films could provide a better appreciation of the ambiguous role that this late flowering of anarcho-individualism played, in the sphere of consumption and life-style, and as an aspect of speculative and high-risk capitalism. It is therefore to be regretted that such an essay is missing in the present collection; it might also have highlighted the enduring qualities of female leads, above all Karen Black and Cybill Shepherd, but also Sissy Spacek, Julie Christie and Shelley Duvall. The notable inarticulacy and non-communication among the men and women in 1970s films, where there is little shared intimacy and where the formation of a family-founding heterosexual couple (mandatory in classical Hollywood narratives) is nowhere in sight, gives a clue to the turmoil in gender-relations to come. But the damaged or hysterical machismo might also have to be read against that other feature of Hollywood in the 1980s, namely the growing importance of women in industry positions, as producers and in public relations, besides their more traditional roles as screenwriters and editors.[25] The broader shifts taking place not only brought in agents and deal-makers, it also re-targeted marketing to the new audience segments, among which women, and especially young women, began to figure as a core group of spectators.

Another feature of 1980s Hollywood thus gains extra political significance – even if its analysis is open to different kinds of explanation – namely, the resurgence of mainstream movies featuring children as protagonists. The popularity of STAR WARS, E.T., CLOSE ENCOUNTERS OF THE THIRD KIND, GREMLINS, HOME ALONE, BACK TO THE FUTURE showed that more was at stake than the prolonged adolescence of one or two directors, or even the demographics of a younger audience. The films that were to come to dominate the 1980s and 1990s, such as the many fairy tale or adventure stories even outside the Disney orbit featuring young boys, show a marked tendency to endow them with a deeper knowledge than the adults. They are also entrusted with cosmic missions and communicate with non-human powers, as if they were being groomed for 'inheriting' the universe, albeit that of fantasy and of self enclosed worlds. Following the different manifestations of non-normative masculinity in Hollywood, one arrives at a somewhat confusing profile of options. Besides the 'unmotivated hero' of the 1970s, there is the action hero of the 'combat films' as his obliquely communicating alter ego; next to the 'outlaw couple' films are the 'buddy movies' (prototypically Robert Redford and Paul Newman in BUTCH CASSIDY AND THE SUNDANCE KID, THE STING) with their flipside, the 'male rampage' cycle of LETHAL WEAPONS (Mel Gibson and Danny Glover). Likewise, there may be a subterranean connection between the psychopathic protagonists of the 1970s and the child heroes of the 1980s, insofar as the anti-authoritarian impulse within the counter-culture fostered and actually produced these different kinds of masculinity in crisis, rather than 'reflected' them. The crises act not only as a protective defence, projected onto feminism's purported demands, but play through so many possible responses to what one must call the post-Fordist phase of patriarchal masculinity. Post-Fordism requires a degree of deterritorialisation of the male body and a disarticulation of its traditional training for single-minded goal-directed action, in order to become a 'rapid reaction' body, full of paranoid and hysterical energies, easily mobilised and even more easily deployed against self and others. In other words, action as reaction, and agency uncoupled from choice. Kubrick has traced this new kind of unstable but effective psychotic mobility in FULL METAL JACKET, camouflaging it somewhat by confining it to the (anti-)Vietnam genre, but there are many other examples one could cite, all the way to FORREST GUMP, where hyperactivity and catatonia appear as the two sides of the same medal, readying the male for new kinds of multi-tasking.

Such a line of analysis complements Gilles Deleuze's more formal distinctions between different types of images. Notably his idea of a 'crisis of the action image' can in the present context of the New Hollywood be associated with these crises of masculinity, whether 'post-traumatic' and tied to the aftermath of Vietnam (as in Keathley's essay), or as a change in the culture's demands on the male body in a post-industrial, post-manual labour economy, as discussed above. Conversely, by seeing such crises through Deleuze's deliberately non-gendered taxonomy of different kinds of action, affection and perception images, the topics of race, gender, body so prevalent in debates about contemporary Hollywood would be extended to include another horizon of reflection. A wider field of investigation opens up which brings the non-coordination of the motor-sensory system highlighted by Deleuze and the disintegration in the post-Fordist labour and organisational hierarchies under a similar heading, offering another clue to the 'identity' of 1970s Hollywood. The triple beat of action, perception, affection image would allow us to track – in a way that is not binary but still preserves an element of conflict – the consecutive stages of Old, New and New New Hollywood, with the films of the 1970s perhaps especially sensitive to the disarticulation of action, the disorientation of perception, and the modulations of affect.

Action, perception, affection: The Deleuzian schema, applied to Hollywood of the 1970s, brings us back to the purported European influence, but now mediated by specifically American crises – the war in Vietnam, the corruption of the offices of state, the changing nature of post-industrial society – which would then correspond to the no less or even more traumatic experience of Europe after WW II and the Holocaust, reverberating, according to Deleuze, in neo-realism (Rossellini, Antonioni), the nouvelle vague (Godard, Rivette) and the New German cinema (Wenders, Fassbinder). The 'traumatic' consciousness, so often posited as the exclusive concern of European art cinema, reappears as also a dimension of the American cinema, though not necessarily folded into an inner void of ungraspable personal experience, but projected outward onto a hyperkinetic surface, turned into percussive sound, or exteriorised, self-voiding as in Martin's account of FINGERS. Likewise, politics becomes not a question of being committed to particular goals, values or ideological positions, but of bodies subject to degrees of intensity and affect that colour their actions and give contours to gestures, irrespective of whether they lack motivation, in conventional terms, or are driven by its obverse, a paranoia which suspects plots everywhere, in a vain attempt to get at 'the inner workings of power' (Fred Jameson). Vain, perhaps, because power, if we follow Foucault and Deleuze, does not manifest itself in the form of top-down hierarchies or conspiracies, capable of being pictured as concentrically organised around an inner core (as in ALL THE PRESIDENTS' MEN, and nostalgically invoked by Oliver Stone in JFK). Instead power is dispersed, transversal, interstitial: the correlative in the political realm of the affection image in the somatic realm. There, according to Keathley, the protagonists of the post-traumatic cycle, from MIDNIGHT COWBOY and MEAN STREETS, to THE CONVERSATION and SHAMPOO are 'trapped' – the inability to act being the first condition of the body having access to a different organisation of the senses. Or is it the other way round: the affection image as the first condition of the body *being accessed* by a different 'organisation' – of the military, the state?

New Hollywood – Home of Flexible Pathologies?

This more dystopian conclusion offers itself from a reading of Drehli Robnik's reinterpretation of the counter-cultural war films from the 1970s, such as M*A*S*H, KELLY'S HEROES and THE DIRTY DOZEN. Such films take a high level of systemic breakdown for granted, apparently in order to draw from dysfunctionality new energies of ad-hoc alliance and informal 'teamworking', needed for unconventional tasks or missions. It would demonstrate the push-pull model (the mutual dependence of antagonistic forces) in the sphere of affective labour, by giving, for instance, the psychopath (as well as other marginalised, pathologised or criminalised existences, including 'hippies') a potentially valuable function in periods of transition, or in emergency situations. The key to this function might be that these protagonists display or can be mobilised to display not only rapid reaction, but *random reaction* behaviour. Capable of sustaining periods or phases of randomisation, they are not hampered by an outmoded motor-sensory body-schema, and thus correspond to what Robnik sees as the ideal prototype of somatic organisation in post-industrial society generally: 'flexibilised affect' as the motor of societal change at the micro-level of power, fantasy and desire. "It is not about making the misfits fit,

but of making them refit the machinery", in other words, harvesting and harnessing the counter-cultural energies (including their anti-social excesses) for
new kinds of work, especially in those sectors where, according to Hardt and
Negri, economic and cultural phenomena can no longer be distinguished. The
randomised networks and informal teams would then be the mirror-image –
or the cold light-of-day materialisations – of those once hoped-for idealised
communities of non-hierarchical communication and cooperative participation dreamed up by hippies and flower-power activists. These, of course,
foundered not only because of state repression and capitalist exploitation, but
also on the issue of gender (the couple and the 'impossible' sexual relation representing the last bastion of resistance to randomisation), and on the nature of
power in complex social systems.

Perhaps we can now return to our initial question with a revived sense of its
paradox: why are the 1970s seen by some critics as the unique and special
highpoint of the American cinema, and by others as more like a brief interlude
in an overall development of self-regulation and self-renewal which has allowed Hollywood not only to survive but to reassert its hegemony in the
global business of mass-entertainment? At one level the answer is, of course,
that 'art' and 'commerce' once more appear to confront each other in implacable incompatibility. At another level, the present collection also challenges the
very terms of this opposition and tries to sketch a model for a third possibility:
that art and commerce are always in communication with each other. What
makes the cinema unique is that it is an art form owing its existence to the particular interplay of capitalism and the state, at any given point in time. Perhaps
more than any other creative practice, then, the cinema's potential and performance, its identity and vitality are closely aligned with the changing relations
between these forces, as the capitalist economy and the bourgeois state are
continually competing with each other over legitimacy and sovereignty in the
public realm (one possible definition of 'modernisation'). The task falling to
the cinema – as site of the economy's symbolic realm in the sphere of consumption, and as site of the state's symbolic realm in the sphere of discipline and
control (censorship, self-regulation) – would be to keep open another site of in-
vestment in change and in 'modernisation'- that of bodies and the senses.
Hence the suggestion that one way to understand the American cinema of the
1970s is to see it finally not so much as a period either of radical innovation or
of mere transition, but of crossovers, which is to say, shifts that mix the meaning of signs in order to make all kinds of slippages (or reversals of direction
from margin to centre) both possible and functional. Hence also the insistence
on asking what post-Fordism or post-industrialism might mean in and for the
American film industry, and what the equivalent of such a post-Fordism might
be in the auteur's self-image, his (re-action) hero and the male psyche. By im-

plication, this tends to re-locate the 1970s American cinema from the East Coast to California, and attributes to the diverse but unique community which is 'Hollywood' (including, since the 1970s, the Bay Area, Silicon Valley and the high-tech military establishments of Orange County) the perverse status of an art-and-commerce avant-garde. Like all avant-gardes, this one may well have been at war with itself, but it also formed a tribal entity of mutual self-interest. Evidence for both the tribal cohesion and the movie wars may be the shattered individual biographies. Evidence, however, can also be found in the films themselves, many of which now seem surprisingly legible as allegories of the very 'modernisation' processes and 'flexible' psychopathologies of which the movie community appears to have been both agent and victim. But to expand on this in more detail will have to be the subject of another collection.

Notes

1. David Thomson, 'Who Killed the Movies', *Esquire* (December 1996), 56-63; William Goldman, *The Big Picture: Who killed Hollywood* (New York: Applause 2000) and Peter Bart, *Who killed Hollywood ... and Put the Tarnish on Tinseltown?* (Los Angeles: Renaissance Books, 1999). See also Noel King's Introduction, above.

2. For a very useful overview, see Peter Krämer, 'Post-classical Hollywood', in John Hill, Pamela Church Gibson (eds.), *The Oxford Guide to Film Studies* (Oxford: Oxford University Press, 1996), 289-309.

3. See Jonathan Rosenbaum's essay below. For J. Hoberman, see 'How the Western Was Lost,' in J. Hoberman, *The Magic Hour* (Philadelphia: Temple UP, 2003), 128. Roy Grundmann has researched a similar encounter in 'Subtext, Context, Intertext: Andy Warhol's Midnight Movie Hustlers and Hollywood's MIDNIGHT COWBOY'(unpublished manuscript, 2003).

4. Tom Schatz, 'The New Hollywood', in J. Collins, H. Radner, A. Preacher Collins (eds.), *Film Theory goes to the Movies* (New York and London: Routledge, 1993), 10.

5. For a journalist's account, based on interviews conducted twenty years later, see Peter Biskind, *Easy Riders Raging Bulls – How the Sex 'n' Drugs 'n' Rock 'n' Roll Generation Saved Hollywood* (New York: Simon & Schuster, 1998).

6. Beverly Walker, 'Go West Young Man', *Sight & Sound*, vol 41/4 (Winter 71/72), 22-25.

7. See the introduction by Steve Neale and Murray Smith in their *Contemporary Hollywood Cinema* (London: Routledge, 1998), xiv-xxii, and my chapter 'Classical/Post-classical Narrative (DIE HARD)' in Thomas Elsaesser, Warren Buckland, *Studying Contemporary American Film* (London: Arnold, 2002), 26-79.

8. Peter Bogdanovich, *Who The Devil Made It* (New York: Alfred A. Knopf, 1997), 8.

9. See Dennis Giles, 'The Outdoor Economy: A Study of the Contemporary Drive-In', *Journal of the University Film and Video Association* vol 35, no 2, Spring 1983, 66-76.

10. Douglas Gomery, *Shared Pleasures: A History of Movie Presentation in the United States* (London: BFI 1992) and Tino Balio, '"A major presence in all of the world's important markets": The globalization of Hollywood in the 1990s' in Steve Neale and Murray Smith, *Contemporary Hollywood Cinema*, 58-73.

11. Justin Wyatt, *High Concept: Movies and Marketing in Hollywood* (Austin: University of Texas Press, 1994).

12. Peter Bogdanovich talks about the change of generations as a baton relay race (p. 13). He is candid about the mother and father substitutes, i.e. the generation paradigm, especially when filling in his own background in theatre and acting, in order to counter the myth that he was just a writer switching to directing, like the French critics-turned-directors of the *nouvelle vague* (*Who the Devil Made It*, 12-16).

13. Jon Lewis, *Whom God Wishes to Destroy: Francis Coppola and the New Hollywood* (Durham, N.C: Duke University Press, 1995).

14. See the sections devoted to the individual directors in David Cook's *Lost Illusions. American Cinema in the Shadow of Watergate and Vietnam 1970-1979* (New York: Charles Scribner's Sons, 2000).

15. Murray Smith, 'Theses on the Philosphy of Hollywood History', in S. Neale and M. Smith (eds.), *Contemporary Hollywood Cinema* (London: Routledge, 1998) 14-15.

16. See Corman's ghosted, boastfully titled autobiography: Roger Corman (with Jim Jerome), *How I made a Hundred Movies in Hollywood and Never Lost a Dime* (New York: Delta Books, 1990).

17. Michael Storper, 'Flexible Specialisation in Hollywood: A Response to Aksoy and Robins', Cambridge Journal of Economics 17 (1993), 479-84, also quoted in Smith, in *Contemporary Hollywood Cinema*, 9.

18. Smith, quoting Nicholas Garnham, in *Contemporary Hollywood Cinema*, 9.

19. 'Three American LPs', in Wim Wenders, *Emotion Pictures* (London: Faber and Faber, 1992)

20. David Cook, *Lost Illusions: American Cinema in the Shadow of Watergate and Vietnam 1970-1979* (New York: Charles Scribner's Sons, 2000), xv-xvi.

21. For reflections on 1980s movies by notable cultural critics, see Fred Jameson, 'Nostalgia for the Present', *South Atlantic Quarterly*, 88: 2, Spring 1989, and Fred Pfeil, 'Plot and Patriarchy in the Age of Reagan', *Another Tale to Tell*, (New York: Verso, 1990), 227-242.

22. Robin Wood, 'An Introduction to the American Horror Film', in Bill Nichols (ed.), *Movies and Methods II* (California University Press, 1985), 196-220.

23. See James Bernardoni, *The New Hollywood: What the Movies did with the New Freedoms of the Seventies* (Jefferson, N.C.: McFarland Press, 1991).

24. See Peter Biskind, *Easy Riders Raging Bulls* for a very full account of the sexual mores of the 1970s auteur-film community.

25. See, for instance, Julia Phillips, *You'll Never Eat Lunch In This Town Again* (New York: Signet, 1991)

Part Two

Histories

The Decade When Movies Mattered

David Thomson

I had a dream about 1970s movies. There was that image from the end of DE-
LIVERANCE (1972), of the hand coming up out of the water – the corpse that refuses to go away. One hand. Where's the other hand? I wondered. Zinger! It
erupted from beneath the cinders on the grave of CARRIE (1976), a hand to drag
us down into the darkness.

But perhaps you were only in elementary school in the 1970s, and thus, in a
country with contradictory impulses about sheltering its young, you did not
attend to what was going on then. After all, it's a fundamental right in the saga
of psychic shelter that no one really has to notice things. The most up-to-date
new frontier is knowing how to look the other way.

Who the hell is talking to you like this? How old is he? The author is 52, and
he loved the decade of the 1970s and its movies. It was a time of travail and upheaval when the world took it for granted that grownups were born to take notice. We had movies then that you had to watch. The age gave us plots as intri-
cate and unrelenting as THE STING (1973) and CHINATOWN (1974). Sitting in the
dark watching the show kept you as wired as an air-traffic controller. If you
weren't awake you would miss some sudden glimpse or murmur:

- In TAXI DRIVER (1976), Travis Bickle is guiding his yellow steel church
  through the scum when, just like a scrap of paper, a pale face scutters across
  his view; it's a kid, a girl, Iris, Jodie Foster. Bickle is riveted by the second or
  so of that face and the scent of need. He's seen a soul to rescue, and so the
  dementia of the plot begins.
- In THE LONG GOODBYE (1973), whenever anything remotely musical plays
  —not just the movie's theme, but a piano idling in a bar, a funeral procession
  in a small Mexican town, a doorbell in Malibu: it's always a variant of the
  song "The Long Goodbye," by Johnny Mercer and John Williams. The me-
  lodic phrase hangs in the air, like haze or the trade of lies in L.A. – it's the
  sound of a game, and the click of fate closing. It tells you that so much in
  L.A. is set up, scripted, produced. There's so little 'there' left – just lines,
  shots and locations.
- In SHAMPOO (1975), an unruly symphony of unease comes out of George
  Roundy (Warren Beatty), sounds that are not words, but which say so much
  about the despair of ever making sense. There are groans, grunts, moans
  and sighs, as if to say, what the hell? You could close your eyes in SHAMPOO
  and just absorb the wealth of indecisiveness that Beatty brings to George's
  hesitation.

The 1970s were full of such things: the way Al Pacino, in THE GODFATHER (1972), notices that he is not shaking when he holds a cigarette lighter outside the hospital. It is the moment he recognizes his authority; Sissy Spacek's narration in BADLANDS (1973), so affectless the whole story seems overheard on a night bus going from Amarillo to Memphis; that aimless first hour of THE DEER HUNTER (1978), filled with the day of the wedding so we grow more and more uneasy: where is this film going, and why are we going with it? And the end of FINGERS (1978), with Harvey Keitel crouched naked in the corner and we're saying, that's how a movie ends?

It was not just in moments that we had to pay attention to these movies. Many of them had unfamiliar shapes, new narrative structures or strategies. They began late. They switched course. They didn't say this guy is reliably good and that one write-off bad. They didn't stick to the rules. And they did not end well, or happily, or comfortably. Sometimes they broke off in your hands or your mind. People you had come to like took it in the head, or turned traitor. The world of the films was as complex and as frightening as anything you'd come into the theatre to escape from. And you were left there when the lights came up, having to work it all out.

In this pre-emptive culture of ours, decades get an early start, or perhaps a pre-game show. It seemed to me at the time that something new and dangerous touched the movies in... well, I'd say 1966, with BLOW UP and with a movie called THE CHASE, which I'd nominate as the first American film of the 1970s. (In the same spirit, I'd call BLUE VELVET the last film of the decade.) Directed by Arthur Penn, THE CHASE was one of the most disturbing views of America I'd ever seen on a screen. It's set in Texas, in a town dominated by a business tycoon (E.G. Marshall) but under the legal authority of a sheriff (Marlon Brando). A prisoner escapes from the penitentiary, Bubber Reeves (Robert Redford), and everyone guesses he's coming home to see his wife (Jane Fonda). Bubber doesn't know she's having an affair with the tycoon's son (James Fox). In cast and credits, THE CHASE was a prestige venture. Yet its self-appointed task was to uncover an America racked by greed, lust, paranoia, mob recklessness and a passion for violence. At the film's climax, the sheriff has rescued Bubber from the mob, but someone manages to leap up and shoot him at point-blank range. As the movie ends, the sheriff and his wife abandon the town to its dark frenzy.

There was no consolation in THE CHASE, and no escaping Penn's direction of the final murder. You felt for sure when you saw the film that this was Lee Harvey Oswald getting killed by Jack Ruby in the garage of the Dallas police station. Had real life ever been "quoted" like that in a Hollywood picture? The implication of what that moment in Dallas really meant was naked on the screen. You see, Ruby killing Oswald was a worse nightmare than the assassination that preceded it. The death of JFK had been so unexpected that it seemed like a spasm, an aberration. But when Ruby fired the bullets into Oswald, the possibility that JFK's murder had been just an irrational act was gone. Ruby made it clear there was a pattern, either of conspiracy or – as seemed more persuasive in November 1963 – of an infectious disease in America, not just violence, but wilful melodrama, an uncontrollable urge to act things out. An age had dawned in which so much 'happened' on TV. The movies were crosscut with the footage of war in Vietnam, of the Ervin Committee, of planes exploding in the desert as terrorists kept their promise, of Neil Armstrong stepping onto a wedding cake called the Moon. The real images fed into the movies, and America seemed to burn most brightly 'on camera'.

Arthur Penn's next film, BONNIE AND CLYDE, overcame mixed reviews to be a box-office sensation. Nothing matched its influence or its perilous balance of comedy and slaughter. The Barrow gang ran wild in the early 1930s, but that past drained down into 1967. Those lovely kids were robbing banks, searching for sex and living on a fatal spree because their society was depressed, dishonest and boring. A lethal young energy was being courted, and provoked. Of course, the outlaws were shot to fragments, but that slow-motion orgasm was an insolent way of honoring the humbug that miscreants must not escape.

THE CHASE and BONNIE AND CLYDE were just two of a number of late 1960s films- POINT BLANK and THE GRADUATE are two others – that assumed the moral bankruptcy of established order. All of a sudden, thank God, Hollywood had found a taste for un-American pictures. In films of the 1970s, the curtain called "happy ending" was ripped away by the life force of the people, and by the actual conditions of America. So many kinds of dismay and disenchantment made for the short-lived but still beguiling honesty of the 1970s. There was a recognition of what violence meant in the age of assassinations. No matter the enactment of so much civil rights legislation, and the determination to enforce it, we began to see how much harder it would be to dislodge racism from our imaginations. Vietnam exposed the limits of American power, the brittleness of its morale, and the helplessness of its leadership. The disasters of war were a focus for intergenerational antagonisms that flared out in Chicago at the 1968 Democratic Convention, at Kent State, and in so many other smaller communities, Americans were beginning to see how thoroughly and intelligently they were despised in other parts of the world.

Not that every blow fell on conservative attitudes. Many naive liberal and revolutionary notions were confounded by actual experiences in the late 1960s and early 1970s – the idea that love could be 'free', that drugs were good, that education could be carried out according to curricula designed by students, that what any kid wanted to say was worth listening to, that the world of rock music was a paradise, that "all you need is love". Commune philosophy led so easily to the Manson gang.

Then came Watergate. We do not have to regard that commonplace fuckup as monumental. It is just as dispiriting to accept the glum complaints of those indicted that such dirty tricks had long been the currency of American government. Richard Nixon elected to handle his own corruption the way Joan Crawford responded to age lines. His denial was vital to what became a national melodrama, a prolonged TV watch-in, and absolute confirmation for every conspiracy theory. The state was a wretched, crooked mess; there really was a 'them' planning ways to get 'us' and do dirt on the ideal of the Republic. Nixon was our real-life Michael Corleone; withdrawn, chilly, paranoid, an actor desperate for power and control.

The playing out of Watergate inspired, justified and deepened movies in which beleaguered men and women feared the worst about authority and slowly came to appreciate the steady, lapping ocean of intrigue all around them. Alan Pakula – a key director of the 1970s, and never as good since – would do a very adroit job in handling the labyrinthine plot of ALL THE PRESIDENTS MEN (1976). Who can forget that moment when, alone in the underground parking garage, Bob Woodward (Robert Redford) feels an infinite, pervasive threat to himself, to truth and to democracy. Pakula had already made two films that predicted the unease of Watergate: KLUTE (1971) and THE PARALLAX VIEW (1974). Hardly a person in KLUTE is quite whole or wholesome – everyone walks in some kind of anxiety. THE PARALLAX VIEW ends with the best people gone: disappeared, killed, frightened back into the shadows of anonymity.

ALL THE PRESIDENT'S MEN did offer comfort: two young reporters could uncover the scheme of evil. That gives the picture an old-fashioned exhilaration (especially since the reporters are impersonated by stars), the cleansing of having a mystery solved. It is also why ALL THE PRESIDENTS MEN did better than KLUTE or THE PARALLAX VIEW, and it is the white lie of Bernstein and Woodward. Twenty years later, government has learned to obscure its tracks better, while too many journalists have been tamed by the prospect of becoming celebrities like "Woodstein". The greater achievement of PRESIDENTS MEN lay in its supporting roles, a gallery of uneasy consciences and hustling ambitions – the soldiers of Washington. Among the supporting players one saw the compromise and the insecurity that knows how idealism is trapped by muddle, gridlock and the tranquil ambivalence of graft and disorder. It was in the 1970s that we recognized how compelling villains could be – Nixon, Dean, Mitchell, Liddy... The line could include the Corleones. Martin Sheen's casual killer in BADLANDS and Travis Bickle. By now it numbers such 'stars' as John Gotti, Claus van Bulow and Ted Bundy-so wicked we can hardly take our eyes off them.

Consider Noah Cross, the character played by John Huston in CHINATOWN (1974), maybe the best film of this troubled age. Cross possesses great power.

Jack Nicholson in CHINATOWN

He finessed the water deal that made Los Angeles a great city. He raped his daughter and had another daughter by her. He has all the crisp eloquence and brave, Western positivism that Huston could give him. He also has the wisest lines in CHINATOWN, as when he tells the detective Jake Gittes (Jack Nicholson), "You see, Mr. Gittes, most people never have to face the fact that at the right time and the right place, they're capable of anything." (In THE GODFATHER, PART II, Michael Corleone observes with the innocence of common sense, "If history has taught us anything, it says you can kill anyone.")

CHINATOWN was written by Robert Towne, an important figure for the 1970s, if most often in the background. Towne did a lot of rewriting on BONNIE AND CLYDE; he wrote the final scene between Brando and Pacino in THE GODFATHER – the most touching moment in the history of the Corleones; and he wrote THE LAST DETAIL (1973) and SHAMPOO. His script for the story of water in L.A. grew out of a life-time in the city and a deep regret at how much it had changed for the worse as it spread. But the script had had a hopeful ending: Gittes was to have been reunited with Evelyn Mulwray (Faye Dunaway) and her daughter; Noah Cross was killed. Then the director of CHINATOWN, Roman Polanski, began to argue, and the battle is characteristic of the 1970s.

Towne wanted to be optimistic: he wanted to believe in humanity, and he had been raised in the culture of happy endings. Polanski is Polish. Some of his relatives had died in concentration camps. He came from an Eastern Europe of repression, hardship and bureaucratic brutality. He allowed himself few illusions. His wife, Sharon Tate, had been one of those slaughtered by the Manson gang at the house on Cielo Drive. Some instinct told Polanski that Towne's ending was too 'soft', too benign. Look at the real Los Angeles! Feel how power really worked! So Polanski went for unmitigated tragedy: Evelyn is killed, shot through the eye; Cross has sinister care of his daughter/ granddaughter; and Gittes is shattered, led away by his partner who can only tell him: "Forget it Jake. It's Chinatown." In CHINATOWN, the law was different: the cops made deals, they did as they liked. It was the metaphor of the age—1930s? 1970s? 1990s'? CHINATOWN was maybe as somber a picture as has ever been a great hit. Its closing fatalism seemed to capture a public mood as well as Norman Mailer's warning from the late 1960s – "The shits are killing us." Only now we had to appreciate that we might be the shits ourselves.

I have looked at a dozen or so films which end in degrees of bleakness (and don't forget the abyss of ambiguity in the two GODFATHER films, where personal evil helps consolidate family power and a sense of civic purpose!). You may be sufficiently of another generation to be depressed by so many 'downers'. Weren't there optimistic pictures in the 1970s? Of course STAR WARS (1977); ROCKY (1976); even COMING HOME (1978), in which a decent woman and a paraplegic seem likely to make a good marriage; NORMA RAE (1979), where Sally Field unionizes the plant and slaps a smile on her face; JAWS (1975), in which the shark is defeated (so long as you've never heard of sequels); and don't forget the smirking camaraderie of THE STING (so rigged a film that it now looks like a closet gay story).

I don't want to depress you. I'm only trying to illuminate a passage in our history. So it's right and proper, in passing, to mention some other defeats for positive thinking: APOCALYPSE NOW (1919), in which the military code doesn't match up to unusual conditions in the field; A CLOCKWORK ORANGE (1971), where everything is unspeakable in the future; THE CONVERSATION (1974), in which being a solitary bugger is removed from the list of suitable careers for a boy; DIRTY HARRY (1971), in which a freelance and laconic Clint Eastwood throws away his cop badge in disgust; DON'T LOOK NOW (1973), in which losing a child is foreplay for having your husband murdered near the canals of Venice; SAVE THE TIGER (1973), in which we see so breathtaking a survey of Middle-American disenchantment that Jack Lemmon actually works as a heel; STRAW DOGS (1971), in which Dustin Hoffman may have his slut wife all to himself so long as he kills every other man around; LOOKING FOR MR. GOODBAR (1977), in which the pursuit of the orgasm goes a few screams too far;

and NIGHT MOVES (1975), another Arthur Penn movie, where the private eye (Gene Hackman) brings about the death and disaster he hoped to avoid. It's always dangerous to say that films like that would not be made now – so many films are made for reasons that defy sense. But times have changed. Where in TAXI DRIVER we had to argue with ourselves whether Travis was a killer or a hero, and in any case whether he should go free, in THE SILENCE OF THE LAMBS Lecter becomes just a sick joke. And if you want a demonstration of how a mood was lost over the course of 16 years, look at that travesty THE TWO JAKES (1990), the belated sequel to CHINATOWN.

There was commercial daring in the 1970s. It came from instability and the smell of success; the structure of the business was coming undone, but American domestic rentals tripled. The code of censorship that had lasted over 30 years broke down in the mid-1960s. In 1963, THE SERVANT only suggested sexual depravity; in 1966, there was a clear glimpse of pubic hair in BLOWUP; by the time of MIDNIGHT COWBOY (1969) and EASY RIDER (1969), there was wholesale nudity, unmistakable evidence of fucking, orgies, drugs and language. In THE WILD BUNCH (1969), Sam Peckinpah made violence and bloodletting things of dreamy, lyrical beauty. Within the space of a few years, a whole range of recently forbidden behaviours could be seen and enjoyed. Such liberty might earn an X-rating – MIDNIGHT COWBOY and LAST TANGO IN PARIS had that alleged mark of shame – but audiences were not daunted. A whole generation found instruction in how to make love by going to the movies, which is not the healthiest way perhaps, but that's another story. Naked women doing it was as great a boost to the medium as sound had been in the late 1920s.

A chasm opened up between movies and TV in terms of what the two media would allow. In the time it took Jane Fonda to turn a trick in KLUTE, TV was established as the soporific entertainment of the tired, the cautious, the prudish – the enemy. Movies were for young bold people – all of which was rather flattering if you were young, as well as subtle encouragement not to listen to parents. (By now, of course, it is clear that we are as afraid of sex as ever our parents may have been.) This young audience went into frenzy with EASY RIDER. There is no need now to make any pretense about the film being better than rubbish, but in 1969 it was a sensational unbuttoning and turn on. And it ensured that movie contracts were thrown at newcomers. Fortunately, many of these new people would prove more talented than Peter Fonda or Dennis Hopper.

EASY RIDER relied on a production company. Raybert, made up of Bert Schneider and Bob Rafelson. With Steve Blauner, they formed BBS Productions, and on the cash flow of EASY RIDER they did a deal with Columbia for a series of low-budget features that would draw on new talent. BBS made FIVE EASY PIECES (1970), directed by Rafelson, and starring Jack Nicholson as a refined pianist who has dropped out and become a wanderer; THE LAST PICTURE

SHOW (1971), the third movie by Peter Bogdanovich; DRIVE, HE SAID (1972), Nicholson's directorial debut, an anarchic study of college and basketball; A SAFE PLACE (1971), the debut of Henry Jaglom, staring Orson Welles, Nicholson and that moody goddess of the 1970s, Tuesday Weld (in the same decade she gave wonderful performances in I WALK THE LINE, PLAY IT AS IT LAYS and WHO'LL STOP THE RAIN); and THE KING OF MARVIN GARDENS (1972), directed by Rafelson again, with Nicholson and Bruce Dern as brothers, the depressive and the manic halves of the American soul.

At least two of the BBS films were hits – FIVE EASY PIECES and THE LAST PICTURE SHOW. Nicholson was set on course as one of our great actors (and a case can be made that he has not surpassed the two 1970s films with Rafelson). Bogdanovich showed his versatility with WHAT'S UP, DOC? (1972) and PAPER MOON (1973). And, everywhere, 'kids' were in demand. Francis Ford Coppola was trusted with THE GODFATHER – not without misgivings at Paramount – and his triumph made him a don to his generation. Martin Scorsese got his chance with BOXCAR BERTHA (1972) and MEAN STREETS (1973), William Friedkin made a huge splash with THE FRENCH CONNECTION (1971), which let us know that modern cops might be as devious and as violent as those they hunted, and THE EXORCIST (1973). Aged 27, Steven Spielberg made a clever road film – half-comic, half-desperate – out of SUGARLAND EXPRESS (1974). A year later, he delivered the summer wallop, the beach-clearing JAWS (1975). George Lucas introduced a team of fine young actors in AMERICAN GRAFFITI (1973) and then did all he could in his modest way to persuade dull heads at Fox that STAR WARS might do well.

There was exuberance as these young men – many of them friends, some since film school – got their break, scored hits, had actresses on their arms, and saw the world opening up. Strangely enough, the happier they felt, the freer they were to be gloomy in their work. These guys had come of age in the era of Kennedy and Nixon, civil rights, Vietnam, campus riots and drug experimentation. They witnessed an America with more self-inflicted wounds than Hollywood had ever cared to admit. They proposed tough new material – it was a new age of *film noir*, albeit in colour. They had their own actors and actresses: Nicholson, Beatty, De Niro, Pacino, Duvall, Hackman, Harrison Ford, Donald Sutherland; Jane Fonda, Julie Christie, Ellen Burstyn, Faye Dunaway, Sissy Spacek, Diane Keaton, Meryl Streep. And studio money competed for their dark visions.

Robert Altman was 15 years older than these directors, yet he was doing his best work, too. In THE LONG GOODBYE, he took Philip Marlowe – once Bogart's role – and turned the sardonic private eye into an amiable stooge who is used and deceived by a more ruthless world. At the end, beyond the law, he can only walk away to the mocking sounds of "Hooray for Hollywood!" Then in

Sterling Hayden and Nina Van Pallandt in THE LONG GOODBYE

NASHVILLE (1975), on the eve of the bicentennial, Altman made a gentle satire not just of country music, but of all American hopes and dreams. Here was a film that took in the whole untidy crowd, hinted at the profusion of stories going on all together, heard the protestations of honour and sincerity, and recorded the endless lies. It had an assassination and a political candidate (eerily like Ross Perot). It saw the chaos and loved the stupid energy that kept everything in motion.

Altman is from Kansas City, but NASHVILLE had some traces of European sensibility. It had no heroes or villains: it seemed to drift and circle; it was so alert to life that it neglected story. There were intriguing influences from Europe in the 1970s. Luis Bunuel's THE DISCREET CHARM OF THE BOURGEOISIE won the Oscar for best foreign film in 1972. Its surreal, absurdist view of wealthy people denied a meal was debated at dinner parties in Manhattan and Beverly Hills. No foreign film was more emulated than Bernardo Bertolucci's THE CONFORMIST (1971), a story about betrayal – that favourite topic – so richly realized that some Americans copied its look and ended up hiring its crew-photographer Vittorio Storaro (who would film APOCALYPSE NOW and REDS);

designer Fernando Scarfiotti (who was a visual consultant on AMERICAN GIG-
OLO) and composer Georges Delerue (THE DAY OF THE DOLPHIN and JULIA).

Brando would accept Bertolucci's offer to make LAST TANGO, and by the
end of the decade Jill Clayburgh had followed for LUNA (1979). Michelangelo
Antonioni had nearly ruined MGM with ZABRISKIE POINT (1970), but there
were filmmakers in America who knew he was a genius. Later on, Nicholson
went to Africa to star in Antonioni's THE PASSENGER (1975), an inspired alliance of *film noir* with the tone of Albert Camus, Jorge-Luis Borges and Paul
Bowles. Louis Malle came to America to do PRETTY BABY (1978) and ATLANTIC
CITY (1980). A refugee from Czechoslovakia, Milos Forman, added an Iron
Curtain edge to the institution in ONE FLEW OVER THE CUCKOO'S NEST (1975).
When I saw the film in New York, there were people on their feet, roaring in
anger and loathing at Nurse Ratched.

By now, this is a long article, somewhere between a list and a generaliza-
tion. Yet there is so much I have left out – THE HOSPITAL (1971) and NETWORK
(1976), two scathing films written by Paddy Chayefsky, full of gallows humour
about American institutions. John Cassavetes was the leading figure in American independent pictures: A WOMAN UNDER THE INFLUENCE (1974) was one of
the first movies to treat the virtual imprisonment of ordinary wives. The Andy
Warhol factory broke onto the art-house circuit with TRASH (1970) and HEAT
(1972). Who had ever before seen the representation of ingrained poverty as it
appeared in John Huston's FAT CITY (1972) and who has seen it since? The
Western came alive again, only now the events of the late 19th century were
seen as precursors of modern American materialism – LITTLE BIG MAN (1970)
MCCABE AND MRS. MILLER (1971) and PAT GARRETT AND BILLY THE KID (1973).
So many of these films are from 1971, 1972 or 1973. Did Nixon watch a lot of
movies? Is that why he was jittery?

In the 1970s, for a few years at least, our movies spoke to us with unaccus-
tomed candour. For that moment, not just the audience, but the business responded. There was so much noticing going on, with coffee-shop talk about
numbered frames in the Zapruder film or delicacies of evasion in John Dean's
testimony. So many kids wanted to put everything on film; so many people
reckoned anything could work there. For a few years it was all one could do to
wait for the next startling picture. In colleges, people studied film history and
foreign films. In bookstores, film was a new section. Pauline Kael and Andrew
Sarris were at their best. Repertory theatres were thriving – this was, let it be
noted, the last time audiences had no choice but to sit in the dark and be overwhelmed by the image on the big screen. Video was in by the end of the decade, and pictures got smaller – just as Norma Desmond had lamented in SUN-
SET BOULEVARD.

A Walking Contradiction (Partly Truth and Partly Fiction)

Alexander Horwath

Usually, the tale of a New Hollywood is founded on two genealogies. The mainstream version begins with THE GRADUATE, POINT BLANK and BONNIE AND CLYDE (all 1967) and their acknowledged debt to European art cinema. The parallel – and slightly more "cultish" – genealogy opens with Roger Corman's 1960s productions at AIP, where filmmakers like Dennis Hopper, Monte Hellman, Jack Nicholson, Francis Ford Coppola, Peter Fonda, Peter Bogdanovich or Henry Jaglom were able to assume multiple functions, mainly for economic reasons, in a flexible working climate. The Corman Factory allowed them to learn the tools of the trade and to develop a less constrained, more personal filmmaking practice. They were part of a "low" culture, but for them the motto "film as art" was still free of derogatory connotations.[1] Works such as Hellman's THE SHOOTING (1966) and Bogdanovich's TARGETS (1968) bear witness to a happy marriage of genre and modernist elements. AIP also produced films such as THE TRIP (1967) and WILD IN THE STREETS (1968) which explicitly addressed the counter-culture and topical political events. The cycle of biker films commencing with Corman's THE WILD ANGELS (1966) gave expression to a fundamentally nihilistic outlook and to a confusing mixture of "leftist" and "right-wing" elements.[2] Hopper's EASY RIDER (1969), the major studio release which – in terms of characters, themes and personnel – merged all of these elements, became a huge commercial success.

In this narrative of New Hollywood, causality and linearity reign supreme, and the setting is always Los Angeles. The fact that the film industry and seemingly all wisdom about movie economy are LA-based tends to obscure other settings and sub-plots of the main story. In Martin Scorsese's MEAN STREETS (1973) there is a scene in which Harvey Keitel and Robert de Niro go to the movies and watch one of Corman's Poe adaptions starring Vincent Price. In the foyer of the theatre we can see three film posters: POINT BLANK by John Boorman, Corman's X – THE MAN WITH THE X-RAY EYES and HUSBANDS by John Cassavetes. In a sense, this is Scorsese's understanding of how the bastard-child New Hollywood (exemplified by MEAN STREETS itself) came into being: It was conceived from the union of the Americanized art film (POINT BLANK), homegrown independent exploitation films (X) and New York based "outsider cinema" (HUSBANDS).

In the context of such a troika, Cassavetes represents a decidedly non-Californian film culture which had fostered a New American Cinema since the end of the Fifties, mainly in the form of avantgarde and documentary films. New York had become the focal point for creative energies which were to leave their mark on Hollywood only much later and in much more hesitant form (Arthur Penn and Mike Nichols, the directors of BONNIE AND CLYDE and THE GRADUATE, respectively, lived and still live in New York).

Beverly Walker recalls: "My perspective had begun to change in the mid-Sixties when I began working at the NY Film Festival – for Amos Vogel and Richard Roud who were teachers as well as bosses. Within a brief period I was exposed to an incredible array of films unlike anything I'd ever even imagined. Ray, Ichikawa, Kurosawa, Dreyer, Wajda, not to mention the deities of the Nouvelle Vague, as well as American experimentalists like Stan Brakhage and Andy Warhol, and independents such as Shirley Clarke and Jonas Mekas blew me away. Almost overnight, I changed from a sporadically employed stage actress and civil rights activist to someone who regarded film as a medium of social change and comment as well as an art form of infinite plasticity and possibility."

Between 1967 and 1970 several feature films were made in New York, which in varying ways paid tribute to Godard and American underground cinema. They took up the themes of political violence and radicalisation in the U.S., discussed the social role of cinema and played "documentary" and "fiction" off against each other. Norman Mailer's book about the antiwar march to the Pentagon, *The Armies of the Night* (1968), offered two perspectives: "History as a Novel" and "The Novel as History", and blurred the boundaries between observer, narrator and actor. In pseudo-documentary style, Jim McBride's marvellously ironic film DAVID HOLZMAN'S DIARY (1967) shares this idea; DAVID HOLZMAN'S DIARY portrays the sufferings of a filmmaker who decides to record his own life. Following Godard's example, his creed is to film the truth 24 times per second, but the first second of the film already contains 24 times the lie. McBride and his co-writer and lead actor, L. M. Kit Carson, plunge the audience into a downward spiral of false expectations, philosophical traps and debates on film theory which are not only not resolved but increasingly question the existential conditions of David Holzman's diary – as well as those of DAVID HOLZMAN'S DIARY.

McBride has this to say about his film school beginnings at NYU: "What surprised me most, apart from the films, was the fact that all the students were actually planning to have a life and career in film – and not just hanging around like I did. Regular people were making movies; I found that really amazing at the time. [...] Marty Scorsese was in my class, as was Lewis Teague, and a year later Michael Wadleigh came in. Later he made WOODSTOCK and worked with me on my first two films. When Marty made his first movie, WHO'S THAT KNOCKING AT MY DOOR [1963-69], we were sitting in two editing rooms next to each other. I was working on DAVID HOLZMAN'S DIARY; and Michael had shot both films. (...) There were no real directors teaching us at film school. It was mostly people who loved movies and could tell us a lot about film history. Their names may be lost to history, but they were good people. One of them, Marty's mentor, was named Haig Manoogian."

About his influences, McBride says: "In American literature, there is a highly respected tradition of writing in the First Person Singular. I guess Norman Mailer is one of the most famous and best examples of this tradition. In my case, it was also a film, Stanton Kaye's GEORG [1964], a kind of diary that ends with the suicide of the protagonist. But there was another, maybe slightly bigger influence, even if it might not be as visible in my film: Michael Powell's PEEPING TOM."[3]

In his introduction to the script for DAVID HOLZMAN'S DIARY, published in 1970, L.M. Kit Carson reflects further on these beginnings and fills in the cultural background to the film: "About three years ago, late winter 1967, Jim McBride and I sat in a coffee shop on West 45th Street off Broadway. Jim was eating, as usual, a cheeseburger. At that time we were researching a book on *cinéma-vérité* for the New York Museum of Modern Art: *The Truth on Film*. We had just taped three- and six-hour interviews with Richard Leacock, the Maysles Brothers, Andy Warhol, D.A. Pennebaker, Andrew Noren, other *cinéma-veritistes* – all of them stumbling around the basic (endless) question in cinéma-vérité, that of filming-the-Real: *Can* you get It, the Real, the Truth, on film? (...). McBride [then] handed me an outline he'd written for a movie about a filmmaker named David (no last name): a sane man and loser like most, who'd finally lost his life. My life ... haunts me,' Jim wrote David as saying: My life ... haunts me.' To stop This, David starts filming and taping the days and nights of his existence – he figures to get his life down on plastic; then It can't get away any more. (...)

It's all there, the Facts right on frames 312 through 316 of Mr. Abraham Zapruder's 8mm *cinéma-vérité* truthmovie. Have you seen It all?

Do you want DHD aesthetically to fake people out?

Someone asks this question every time. There are several answers.

FIRST All art's a decoy. Not Real. Not Fact. Not The Truth; but lures you to The Real, The Truth.

SECOND However, from the beginning, The Real and DAVID HOLZMAN'S DIARY began to rush together, mix, twist, join more than usual for a movie. (...)

THIRD Truth and Life merge, Jim McBride always steps up to the microphone and says in answer to this question. And smiles. And that's all.

A year later, walking out after a DIARY *screening, Pennebaker said to me (funny smile):'You killed cinéma-vérité. No more truthmovies.'*
No. Truthmovies are just beginning."[4]

From this East Coast milieu, other relevant feature films emerged in the late Sixties: THE EDGE (1968) and ICE (1969) by Robert Kramer probe the alternatives of political struggle versus political use of the media and generally reach pessimistic conclusions about either option. GREETINGS (1968) and HI, MOM! (1970) by Brian De Palma (who worked together with McBride at Huntington Hartford Film Center in the early Sixties) are playful satires on current politics and the mainstream media. Shirley Clarke's PORTRAIT OF JASON (1967) and Robert Frank's ME AND MY BROTHER (1968) initially present themselves to the viewer as documentary outsider portraits, but gradually start to articulate the extent to which entire lives can "invent" themselves in front of the camera. COMING APART (1969) by Milton Moses Ginsberg, another "fake documentary", chronicles the emotional crack-up of a New York psychiatrist who films himself and his various sexual encounters with a hidden camera in his apartment (Ginsberg acknowledged DAVID HOLZMAN'S DIARY as the most influential film for him at the time). Norman Mailer directed three highly personal films: WILD 90 (1967/68), BEYOND THE LAW (1968) and MAIDSTONE (1968/70), produced in close collaboration with the masters of *cinéma vérité*, Richard Leacock, D. A. Pennebaker and Nick Proferes (who was also to become Barbara Loden's most important partner in the production of WANDA in 1970).[5] And finally, there is MEDIUM COOL (1969), the first feature directed by the renowned cinematographer and documentarist Haskell Wexler. In the context of the 1968 Democratic Convention in Chicago, Wexler raises the question if and how an observer/journalist/narrator/filmmaker should take the stage, "enter the real" and become a political actor.[6] Although it weaves a complex cinematic tapestry around the themes of truth and representation, MEDIUM COOL was the only film of this group to be distributed by a major studio (due perhaps to Wexler's ties with the industry). It provoked considerable critical debate but failed to make any lasting impact on film culture. The other films mentioned above were barely noticed by the mainstream media, and neither were the regional activities of George A. Romero in Pittsburgh and John Waters in Baltimore, who only became known years later via the phenomenon of midnight movie cults.

Despite this, or perhaps because of this, many exponents of New York filmmaking were drawn to Los Angeles in 1969/70, among them McBride, Carson, De Palma, Scorsese and Jonathan Demme, a press agent at the time. Los Angeles appeared to offer a fortuitous combination of large production capital and a burgeoning new cinema. Beverly Walker left for LA in late 1968.

She was hired by MGM to shield Michelangelo Antonioni from the hostile press during the shooting of ZABRISKIE POINT and to control the flow of information from the set to the public. Walker recalls:

> Remember, there are about 2500 miles between NY and LA. Back in the Sixties that meant more than it does today. Eventually the critical positions developed in New York, based on André Bazin and other Europeans, impacted Hollywood – but it took a long time. This schism may account more than any other single factor for the early snuffing out of the movement. For instance, I don't think there was any awareness of filmmakers like McBride, Mailer or Kramer in mainstream LA film circles. McBride drove a taxi for the first several years he lived in LA – and he has never been able to create a real place for himself. (...) I and many of my friends and associates migrated to Los Angeles with the intention of entering the film industry. However, the assumptions we acted upon – of New York in the Sixties – turned out to be perilous. 'Hollywood' is not part of any regional or cultural tradition except its own. Bacon's painting of a dog chasing its own tail is a perfect iconographic image of Hollywood for me.

Apart from the New York "emigrés" Hollywood also received an influx of filmmakers from Europe. This movement is not comparable to the two waves of "Europeanisation" in the 1920s (when the film industry raided the "old world" in search of important directors, actors and cinematographers) and in the late 1930s and early 1940s (when Hollywood became the most attractive as well as treacherous place of exile). Nonetheless this new wave of emigration was significant mainly because of the high standing and influence that European cinema enjoyed, at least in New York. Directors such as Michelangelo Antonioni, Milos Forman, Roman Polanski, Krzysztof Zanussi, Karel Reisz, Bo Widerberg, Jan Troell, Jan Kadar, Ivan Passer, Agnès Varda or Jacques Demy came to Hollywood to make one or more films at the end of the Sixties and the beginning of the Seventies. At the same time, young American directors tried to incorporate the strengths and fashions of European cinema into their work, not only by means of stylistic reference but also by actually transferring their European idols to glamour land itself. Robert Benton's and David Newman's attempts to talk their gods, Truffaut and Godard, into directing their BONNIE AND CLYDE script are now the stuff of legend. In THE CHRISTIAN LICORICE STORE (1970), James Frawley's ambitious debut film, Jean Renoir plays himself – the wise old Frenchman of the movies.

The most extensive, albeit gently ironic, example of this is Paul Mazursky's second directorial work: ALEX IN WONDERLAND, an adaptation of Fellini's OTTO E MEZZO. Mazursky's alter ego (Donald Sutherland) is also working on his second film, enjoying the success of his debut (just as Mazursky enjoyed the success of BOB & CAROL & TED & ALICE) and the opportunities which have suddenly opened up to him. The film switches back and forth between Alex's increasingly obvious private and professional failure and his own private movie dreamscape to which he clings against all adversity. He travels to Rome, stumbles around Cinecitta like a young boy on his first holiday abroad and visits Fellini who is in the middle of editing I Clowns. The master is polite but short with him; this does not deter Alex from stammering out his adoration. When he returns to LA, Alex's fantasies get the better of him. In the middle of the street he runs across none other than Jeanne Moreau. They go walking side-by-side, and all of a sudden she breaks out into a song from Jules et Jim (accompanied by an off-screen orchestra). She rests her head on his shoulder and, in true fairytale fashion, rides around the city with him in a horse carriage.

Around 1968/69, Agnès Varda and Jacques Demy took the opposite route: Paris-LA via New York. In Lion's Love (1969), Varda's quasi-documentary essay on Los Angeles, the dominant influences and current affairs of the time converge. The film, shot in early 1969, is set in the first week of June 1968 and structured like a diary. The assassination of Robert Kennedy and Valerie Solanas's attempt on the life of Andy Warhol – conveyed over the television and telephone – form the "historical" background. The foreground is shared by Viva (as Viva), who is living in a type of commune with two men; Shirley Clarke, who has come to LA to meet up with possible financiers and producers of her next project; Carlos Clarens, film historian and critic, who talks of legendary Hollywood days; cameo appearances by Peter Bogdanovich and Eddie Constantine (as Viva's ex-lover); and Viva & Company's staging of a play by Michael McClure about Jean Harlow and Billy the Kid.

> Varda's film is not realistic to Los Angeles. There was no communal life to speak of there. All the people in Lion's Love are entrenched New Yorkers! Varda and Demy created their own, very special, environment in Hollywood, which was more like Paris in that it revolved around food and included many Europeans living in L.A. or passing through, and other displaced persons such as myself!" (Beverly Walker)

But like Mazursky's film, Lion's Love paints a telling picture of the American film industry's state at the time. Varda accompanies Shirley Clarke to her meetings with the film producers and manages to convey how these suits are desperately seeking new outsider artists and "edgy" material. Of course, they cannot agree to Clarke's demands for final cut (whereupon Clarke – in the film? in reality? – attempts suicide). Unlike Alex, Varda is not being overwhelmed by her fantasy world; she develops a discourse which brilliantly interweaves politics, current debates on violence, the alternative (in this case entirely passive) lifestyles of the counter-culture as well as the mythologies and the actual practice of cinema. Quite naturally, Varda dreams not of Fellini and

Moreau but of the ruptures between Old and New Hollywood. (In this context, it is remarkable to see how many American films of this moment are about filmmaking: DAVID HOLZMAN'S DIARY, SYMBIOPSYCHOTAXIPLASM, TARGETS, COMING APART, MAIDSTONE, ICE, MEDIUM COOL, ALEX IN WONDERLAND, LION'S LOVE, THE LAST MOVIE. Whereas these largely modernist works are told 'in the present tense', mirroring the filmmaking questions and problems of their own era, the wave of films-about-cinema which followed a few years later returned to feelings of nostalgia with a vengeance. THE DAY OF THE LO-CUST, THE GREAT WALDO PEPPER, THE LAST TYCOON, NICKELODEON, HEARTS OF THE WEST, GABLE AND LOMBARD, THE WILD PARTY and INSERTS seem to reflect a certain shift in American self-perceptions: The potentially anti-illusionist de-bate in which films-about-cinema always somehow engage is now being sealed off and displaced into a remote, mythical past: once upon a time, there was a cinema ...).

Gary Lockwood and Anouk Aimée in THE MODEL SHOP

In Jacques Demy's MODEL SHOP (1969) the French New Wave crosses the path of New Hollywood not just symbolically, by way of quotations, but quite sub-stantially. Perhaps this process was assisted by Demy's collaboration with the

American screenwriter Adrien Joyce (= Carol Eastman), who – among other things – wrote the scripts for THE SHOOTING and FIVE EASY PIECES. Anouk Aimée, who played Demy's LOLA in 1961, reappears under that name eight years later, still a French national, but working in an LA "model shop" where men can pay to photograph half-naked women in every conceivable pose. (It is typical of Demy's sensitivity that he does not show the usual forms of prostitution, and instead chooses a nice metaphor for it.) Gary Lockwood, a young drifter, falls in love with Lola and with what she represents: a smooth, dark, attractive 'old world'. The loud showbiz-blond with whom he lives starts to turn him off. Demy takes the contrast even further – without, as one would expect, simply playing off his French origins against American culture. He focuses his attention on contemporary youth culture (in particular the rock group Spirit), on long drives through the city to the accompaniment of Bach, on the hysterical exterior of Los Angeles as well as the plush interior of the model shop (a distant reminder of Fifties French cinema). He sees America through European eyes, and it becomes richer for it, revealing facets that 'native' artists often overlook. "It was as if I had never seen Los Angeles on the screen the way it appeared to me in reality. I felt the desire to show this city to my American friends."[7]

When the film mentions the Vietnam War, it stays calm and responds with melancholia rather than the usual agitation: Lockwood has received his call-up and, although there is talk of peace negotiations in Paris (!) on the radio, we sense that fate will soon take him far away from Lola's boudoir. At the end, on the day before his departure for the army, he tries to reach her once more on the phone, but she is already sitting in a plane to France (the ticket was his present to her). He smiles and, for the first time, he is afraid of dying.

MODEL SHOP is an impressive moment in the new American cinema. A moment, however, which – like the New York branch of the tree – had relatively little effect on the general development; just another seed in the spawning of what is destined to remain an imaginary parallel history of Hollywood.

* * *

After Tim Leary had escaped from Eldridge Cleaver's clutches, he was arrested by American agents and taken back to the States, then put in solitary confinement at Folsom prison, in a cell right next to [Charles] Manson's. The two 'hole-mates' couldn't see each other, but they could talk. Manson didn't understand why Leary had given people acid without trying to control them. 'They took you off the streets,' Charlie explained, 'so that I could continue with your work.'[8]

As EASY RIDER made its way into the box-office record books, the American film industry thought it had found a shining new recipe for future success. And the media encouraged this belief: "The mass media, having exploited every other youth truth, was now usurping youth's paranoia"(Paul Schrader, 1969).[9] Twelve to eighteen months later the industry was forced to sober up: none of the unofficial "sequels" to EASY RIDER had attracted much interest at the box-office; instead neo-conservative blockbusters like LOVE STORY or AIRPORT (both 1970) were topping the charts.

The studios and the filmmakers had overlooked the fact that EASY RIDER was both the culmination and the end point of a broader "dissident" rhetoric in American public life. During the Sixties, the bright veneer of American culture and politics had darkened considerably, but in 1969, when the film came out, even the *counter*-culture had begun to lose its shine. In the view of the public, it had betrayed its original values and allowed its beacons of hope (drugs, communal life and rock music) to degenerate into sources of madness, violence and paranoia. When Timothy Leary wanted to hand on the baton, Charles Manson was the first to grab it.

Therefore, the most challenging and "contemporary" American film of 1969 might not have been EASY RIDER but THE WILD BUNCH. A key work of this era, Sam Peckinpah's 'bad trip' to Mexico is able to illuminate not only the Vietnam War and the My Lai massacre,[10] but also the phenomenon of completely irrational violence which, by 1968/69, appeared to have taken hold of all areas of American culture. The film was discussed at length in the press, frequently in moral terms, and many critics considered it to be not just a masterpiece but a kind of perverse gift from the gods: "THE WILD BUNCH has an imaginative power and energy which takes it far beyond anything we have a right to expect now in American films. It is only in its violence and nihilism that it is, like a mirror image, just what we richly deserve."[11]

The splitting of New Hollywood cinema into a picaresque stream, which depicted 'unmotivated',[12] drifting, alienated (anti-)heroes on a journey through America (and its narrative), and a revisionist genre strand, which furnished the Western, the film noir and the urban thriller with darker, often politically motivated undercurrents, might have one of its origins in the 'contest' between EASY RIDER and THE WILD BUNCH. Paul Schrader, who as screenwriter and director would soon contribute important elements to the second strand, wrote critical essays on both films in 1969 and 1970. He made no attempt to conceal his antipathies and sympathies nor to hide his assessment of what American cinema needed most: "In the post-slaughter epilogue of THE WILD BUNCH Peckinpah rubs the spectator's nose in the killing he has so recently enjoyed. New killers arrive to replace the old. A way of life has died, but the dying continues. (...) A friend after seeing THE WILD BUNCH for the first time remarked 'I feel dirty all the way through.' Peckinpah wouldn't have it any other way. (...) THE WILD BUNCH is a powerful film because it comes from the gut of America, and from a man who is trying to get America out of his gut. The trauma of ex-patriotism is a common theme in American art, but nowhere is the pain quite so evident as in the life of Sam Peckinpah. THE WILD BUNCH is the agony of a Westerner who stayed too long, and it is the agony of America."[13] About EASY RIDER he wrote:

> If the mass media decides to exploit the Hopper-Fonda paranoia it will acquire something as worthless as last year's mod fashions and nude plays. Hopper and Fonda are too infatuated with the idea of themselves as pundits, Christs, martyrs, and Porky Pigs to examine their heroes, villains, or themselves – and this form of harmless paranoia is easily stolen and marketed throughout the media. But we are all too old for this kind of game, no?[14]

Apart from a sizeable number of ill-conceived, immature 'art films' by young directors this 'game' did, however, indirectly produce some works that have stood the test of time. They were driven by other motives and able to employ more complex means than were the "harmless paranoiacs", whose analysis of American society did not go beyond a simple reversal of the old good guys vs. bad guys dichotomy. Films like Hopper's THE LAST MOVIE (1971) and Monte Hellman's TWO-LANE BLACKTOP (1971), Bob Rafelson's FIVE EASY PIECES (1970) and THE KING OF MARVIN GARDENS (1972) seemed not only to have taken to heart the lesson to be learned from EASY RIDER; they also appeared to have grasped the message of THE WILD BUNCH: that there is no longer any common 'connective tissue' in American life which could serve as the bedrock for progressive, univocal moral positions. For these films, flashes of insight are only possible amidst the morass; amidst the dark territory that lies between the fleeing, failed, abstract individual and the powerful, if repeatedly battered, rock formations of traditional mythology which have shaped him (or much more rarely, her).

Along with related projects like DRIVE, HE SAID (1971) by Jack Nicholson, CISCO PIKE (1971) by Bill Norton, GLEN AND RANDA (1971) by Jim McBride or KID BLUE (1971/73) by James Frawley, these works and associated directing careers all suffered a number of setbacks (with the exception of FIVE EASY PIECES they were all flops). Their narrative styles were anti-illusionist or at least not designed to encourage ready identification with their heroes. Even more crucial was the change of climate that occurred between the planning/financing of these films and their (sometimes deliberately delayed) theatrical releases. Within the space of two years, studios, critics and audiences agreed on the common wisdom that the fostering of young talent with dissident intentions had been a huge mistake. The studios could boast of few successes and started either to shelve their smaller, more difficult films or bury them in limited release without any kind of promotion. The critics lumped together the exceptional with the banal 'youth movies' and outdid each other with cynically generalized judgements. And audiences, even those predisposed towards youth culture, waited in vain for that easy ride of 'vengeful' satisfaction to return.

Beverly Walker managed to negotiate the publication of the complete TWO-LANE BLACKTOP script in *Esquire* magazine, but the headline "The Film of the Year" (aesthetically correct from today's perspective) already represented a commercial miscalculation on the part of the magazine.

> Honestly, I didn't have to do a lot of 'selling' to get *Esquire* to publish the script of TWO-LANE BLACKTOP. I approached them about a feature story and they suggested the screenplay. Remember that *Esquire* considered itself a 'literary' magazine. They'd published screenplays twice before. It was just part of what was happening at the time – media exploitation of pop culture. [Studio boss] Lew Wasserman personally hated TWO-LANE BLACKTOP and killed it by withholding advertising. It would never have had the success of EASY RIDER – the pacing, the oblique, bleak vision, the wooden actors – but it wouldn't have been an abject failure either.

The relationship between the new auteurs of American cinema and the film industry that sought to take them under its wing was also destroyed to a certain extent by the filmmakers themselves. Their tendency to brood over their creations like 19th-century Romantic artists was bound to lead to irreconcilable conflicts in an exceptionally capital- and labour-intensive sector. THE LAST MOVIE epitomised this conflict. Dennis Hopper used the freedom he was granted on the basis of EASY RIDER in inimitable fashion: artistically - the film is the most radical, multi-layered critique of Hollywood that has ever emerged from inside the industry – as well as in Hopper's personal, presumably drug-propelled behaviour. He offered himself as the perfect fall guy to the mainstream press and went into battle with his production company, Universal. In doing so, Hopper took on such well-disposed partners as Ned Tanen who headed a special production unit at Universal. Apart from THE LAST MOVIE, Tanen was also responsible for producing TWO-LANE BLACKTOP, Peter Fonda's directorial debut THE HIRED HAND and Douglas Trumbull's ecologically minded 'space opera' SILENT RUNNING.

> Hopper went over the top in every respect and helped bury the 'new movement' (...). Today, he might agree with that. I was around Universal a lot during that period and I know that studio executives like Ned Tanen were just beside themselves over Hopper's drug-induced antics. (...) In later years, I came to believe that the old guard was just lying in wait for the inevitable mistakes of the upstarts ... and they

were plentifully obliged. (...) There were situations in which I was the effective liaison between the 'creative' forces – usually the director – and the studio executives. I was often put in the deplorable position of explaining each side to the other. And I regret to say that I was often deeply embarrassed by the behaviour of the filmmakers. They were like brats blackmailing their parents – at age 35!" (Beverly Walker)

The endeavours of the 'creative forces' to achieve relative autonomy from the studios did not only find expression in this sort of individualistic struggle. In the late 1960s and early 1970s filmmakers made several attempts to gain more control over their works by forming groups, or rather, by establishing semi-independent production outfits. Most of these ventures, which all co-operated with the studios, were to fail eventually: "American Zoetrope" (Francis Ford Coppola with Warner Bros.), "The Director's Company" (Coppola, Peter Bogdanovich and William Friedkin with Paramount) and "First Artists" (Barbra Streisand, Paul Newman, Sidney Poitier, Steve McQueen and Dustin Hoffman with various studios) were not able – or willing – to maintain a thoroughly autonomous mode of production.[15] The only group of directors and producers who developed a high degree of common responsibility and common aesthetic goals was BBS, headed by Bert Schneider, Bob Rafelson and Steve Blauner.[16] Apart from the forerunners HEAD (1968, Bob Rafelson) and EASY RIDER, which was produced by Schneider and Rafelson under the moniker Raybert, BBS produced FIVE EASY PIECES, A SAFE PLACE (1971, Henry Jaglom), DRIVE, HE SAID, THE LAST PICTURE SHOW (1971, Peter Bogdanovich), THE KING OF MARVIN GARDENS and a documentary about the Vietnam war, HEARTS AND MINDS (1974, Peter Davis).

Blessed with a favourable contract at Columbia (where Bert Schneider's brother and father held positions of influence), this small company managed for a few years to create an extremely productive environment that had its origins in long-standing friendships, stemming especially from the time of the Players Ring stage in LA and the Corman Factory. Although the economic preconditions in Hollywood for solidarity of this kind are very different from those in European film culture, this group was often referred to as the American *nouvelle vague*. It projected a sense of being involved in a common cause: intellectual outsiders who briefly had access to a wider market. Directors such as James Frawley, Monte Hellman or Terrence Malick were also associated with the group. Frawley commented: "You know, there really is a community of American directors now, and I think in the last three or four years we are all, in a way, beginning to find our style. I was thinking the other day that someone should really do a family tree. How I came into KID BLUE was that Dennis Hopper took the first draft of the script to Bob Rafelson and Bert Schneider to ask who should direct it, and they suggested me. They had produced *The*

Monkees for TV and given me my first professional directing job on that show. Then they had backed EASY RIDER, formed BBS, made all the BBS pictures. Jack Nicholson wrote Bob Rafelson's Monkee picture, HEAD, then later went on to direct DRIVE, HE SAID, was used in Jaglom's picture [A SAFE PLACE] with Tuesday Weld, and used Jaglom in his picture. And Richard Wexler, who produced FIVE EASY PIECES, is my partner now in developing projects. And then of course Jack Nicholson was in the two Monte Hellman Westerns, one of which was written by Carol Eastman, who also wrote FIVE EASY PIECES (...). Terry Malick, too, has always been involved to a certain extent on a personal level, and has gotten great support from Bob and Bert. It's a tree, good support, you feel you're not working in a total vacuum."[17]

The films produced by or in association with BBS are the culmination of a characteristic tendency in early New Hollywood to translate general dissatisfaction with the political, social and cultural climate of the time into the existential problems of specific individuals. Films about cynical drifters and alienated social misfits who are forced to or choose to remain in a state of constant motion because 'staying at home' smacks of corruption. Films with a loose, undramatic pace and open endings – because no alternative destination or 'home' can be found. Films that rediscover the wide open spaces, the street and everyday life, in search of a new realism and an open-ended production process, substituting the conventions of genre with more authentic means of experiencing time and space. And, lastly, films which allegorise their own limitations through their protagonists – independent-dependent (studio) productions about independent-dependent men who reject an oppressive system of rules without being able to even entertain the (political) notion of a less constraining system beyond the current one.

Bill Norton's CISCO PIKE, produced for Columbia under similar conditions as the BBS films, is a good example of this ambivalence. Norton, the son of a leftist screenwriter who had to fight for his survival during the McCarthy era, visited film school at UCLA and conceived of CISCO PIKE as a portrait of the drug and music scene in Los Angeles. When he came into contact with Gerald Ayres, a young producer working at Columbia, some of the emphasis of the project was altered but not altogether for the worse. The relationship between the characters, for instance, was developed more fully and tied in with a detailed description of the milieu. As a favour to his friend Ayres, Robert Towne reworked Norton's script. He created the character of the policeman (Gene Hackman), who forces the musician and ex-dealer Cisco Pike (Kris Kristofferson) back into the criminal underworld, and he rewrote large parts of the figure of Cisco's girlfriend (Karen Black). Like the story material, which is a mixture of genre and counter-cultural elements, the casting consists of 'official' components (Hackman), as well as 'semi-official' (Kristofferson, Harry

Dean Stanton) and "unofficial" (Viva) elements. Interestingly, the industry outsider Norton initially opposed employing the industry outsider Karen Black, whereas for the studio her name was a deciding factor in the process of greenlighting the project. Black's Academy Award nomination for FIVE EASY PIECES had seemingly made her a safe bet. The film was further changed both during and after shooting; new scenes were written and shot later (partly in New York), Ayres wrote some scenes himself, and the editor, Robert Jones, spent considerable time searching for the best version of the end.[18]

In retrospect, CISCO PIKE is one of the era's most beautiful films, and a powerful testimony to the patchwork-like, circuitous path of its own making. It blends a crime movie narrative with a comprehensive study of the milieu, 'authentic' scenes from the music rehearsal room with aggressive action sequences, a stark city portrait with quietly moving love scenes. The hero, torn between his previous life (drugs), his self-proclaimed future (music, Karen Black) and his present demimonde existence, mortgaged to Hackman (and the chance of making a lot of money), is elevated to almost iconical status in Kristofferson's acting and singing. His ballad "The Pilgrim Chapter 33" becomes an icon for the impure cinema circa 1970 and its impure protagonists who were determined to exhaust an untenable position until the end.

"The Pilgrim Chapter 33" is dedicated to Dennis Hopper (Kristofferson had worked on THE LAST MOVIE, and Hopper had planned to shoot a film based on "Me and Bobby McGee"). In CISCO PIKE the song passes cutting comment on the main character. And at the end of the era it re-emerges in unexpected circumstances: Betsy and Travis are drinking coffee, she smiles to herself, bemused by this strange guy who has just come on to her, and a song by Kris Kristofferson crosses her mind. He does not know who Kristofferson is (Travis is a taxi driver and not familiar with the tastes and rituals of the educated classes). She recites a few lines from the song to him. He says: "This is about me?" She says: "Only the part with the contradictions." And so it would seem that this one song encapsulates New Hollywood from beginning to end, from Dennis Hopper to TAXI DRIVER, with CISCO PIKE right in the middle.

> He has tasted good and evil in your bedrooms and your bars (...)
> Searching for a shrine he's never found (...)
> He's a poet, he's a picker
> He's a prophet, he's a pusher
> He's a pilgrim and a preacher and a problem when he's stoned
> He's a walking contradiction, partly truth and partly fiction
> Taking every wrong direction on his lonely way back home.

* * *

The economic crisis of the American film industry from 1968/69 onwards had been an important reason for the turn towards smaller, cheaper films (produced by new, enthusiastic and equally cheap labour). But the losses continued; in 1970/71 alone, the major studios lost 525 million dollars. During these two years Fox, Paramount and Warner cut back their production levels to a bare minimum. All studios restructured their organisations and dismissed thousands of employees. The relatively recent corporate take-overs (all studios had become parts of large conglomerates in the Sixties) were also felt at management level. A young generation of managers and agents took over running the studios and by and large put an end to the 'experiments' of the crisis years.[19] The BBS connection at Columbia broke down when in 1973 the old management (including Bert Schneider's father Abe) was replaced by a more 'business-oriented' team formed around Alan Hirschfield and David Begelman.

These attempts at economic consolidation had their counterpart in a 'consolidation' of narrative styles: the upturn of the industry – in regard to box-office earnings – was due to a series of largely unexpected hits which drew on classical genres and traditional narrative tropes: THE FRENCH CONNECTION (1971, William Friedkin), THE GODFATHER (1972, Francis Ford Coppola), WHAT'S UP, DOC? (1972, Peter Bogdanovich), AMERICAN GRAFFITI (1973, George Lucas), THE STING (1973, George Roy Hill), THE EXORCIST (1973, Friedkin) among others. This upswing is associated with a different notion of 'New Hollywood', with a certain shift in interest from the search for individual authenticity to working with given cultural forms. The great patron saints of this project are Arthur Penn and Sam Peckinpah. Both had changed genre cinema in the Sixties by aggressively appropriating new styles and reversing as well as politicizing the classical Hollywood forms – and they continued to do so until the mid-Seventies. Penn's NIGHT MOVES (1975) and Peckinpah's BRING ME THE HEAD OF ALFREDO GARCIA (1974) rank among the final and most extreme masterpieces produced by a culture of madness and desperation. (The directors who most enriched American cinema during this period were mature men, older than the egocentric youngsters who are often seen as synonymous with the era. Penn was 48 when LITTLE BIG MAN was released, Peckinpah 44 at the time of THE WILD BUNCH. John Cassavetes – patron saint of a more private strand of New Hollywood psychodrama – was 45 when A WOMAN UNDER THE INFLUENCE was shot, and Robert Altman, controversial patron saint of Seventies cynicism, was 50 when he made NASHVILLE.)

There is certainly some truth in Stephen Schiff's argument that New Holly-wood modernism is best articulated in genre films.[20] During the first half of the 1970s all genres – particularly the Western and the film noir – underwent a rad-ical re-orientation, which corresponded to the broader crisis that American so-ciety was undergoing.[21] This climate also extended to 'illegitimate' and more recent genre forms like the black gangster movies ('blaxploitation') or the apocalyptic horror film, although they were quickly marginalized and re-duced to stereotypes. On the threshold between genre and auteur cinema, however, some films by African-American artists like SWEET SWEETBACK'S BAADASSSSS SONG (1971, Melvin Van Peebles) or GANJA AND HESS (1973, Bill Gunn) bear witness to a political and aesthetic potential which easily rivals their innovative 'white' counterparts.[22]

Through 'neo noir' and Post-Watergate paranoia films, an image of Amer-ica emerges in the mid-Seventies which is dominated by corruption, individ-ual powerlessness, dark, inexplicable threats, topsy-turvy values and double-faced heroes.[23] The 'neo noir' group encompasses films like NIGHT MOVES, TAXI DRIVER, Altman's THE LONG GOODBYE (1973), Polanski's CHINATOWN (1974) and little gems such as THE OUTFIT (1973, John Flynn) or THE FRIENDS OF EDDIE COYLE (1973, Peter Yates). The second group, dealing with conspiracy, assassination attempts and terrorism, includes films such as THE CONVERSA-TION (1974, Coppola), THE PARALLAX VIEW (1974, Alan J. Pakula), ALL THE PRESIDENT'S MEN (1976, Pakula), GOD TOLD ME TO (1976, Larry Cohen) or AS-SAULT ON PRECINCT 13 (1976, John Carpenter).

In these works, the climate of fragmentation frequently infects genre cin-ema's language and its traditional abilities to articulate The Truth and to per-form some narrative healing. "With its grasp of the potential link between po-litical and formal fragmentation - how all one's assumptions about the way things work can be placed in jeopardy - THE PARALLAX VIEW nears the sophisti-cation of what is perhaps the ultimate modernist conspiracy thriller: Francis Ford Coppola's THE CONVERSATION. (...) Coppola started writing it in the late 1960s and its strongest influences are the European art movies of that era – most famously, Antonioni's BLOW-UP. Coppola takes a basic unit of cinema - a dialogue between a man and a woman - and subjects it to an extended, self-re-flexive meditation. The scene is 'shot' from three different points of view, and [the film's hero] Harry spends most of the movie trying to edit these together into a seamless reproduction – just like a film editor cutting together different shots into a single scene."[24] At one point in THE PARALLAX VIEW, the nervous re-porter who (with good reason) sees conspiracies everywhere is placated by his chief editor with the words: "Go home, go to a movie, relax." Which is pre-cisely what THE PARALLAX VIEW and similar films did not want to be: a cinema of diversion, consolation and escapism.

Concurrent with this kind of 'pessimistic modernism', a thoroughly 'post-modern' engagement with genre established itself among the "Coppola circle" and at USC film school (John Milius, George Lucas, Willard Huyck and Gloria Katz and, somewhat later, Steven Spielberg). Its most obvious, most impoverished manifestation would soon put a sudden end to both traditional and modernist notions of genre. As Stephen Schiff noted:

> In STAR WARS, George Lucas doesn't work *within* or even *on* genre. He *plugs in* genre, flashing its proven elements at us as though they were special effects. The genre explorations of the early Seventies depended on the audience's awareness of detective movies, westerns, and monster movies, but the recombinant-genre movies delight in the viewer's ignorance. (...) Parts of old genres replace the nuts and bolts of narrative that used to keep movies running. More and more, genre becomes a secret junkyard.[25]

Apart from the USC connection, an additional and significant nucleus of this generation of filmmakers (which was by no means as homogenous as the dominance of Spielberg-Lucas in the 1980s might suggest) can be located in the transitional period at Hollywood's major studios, circa 1970-1973. John Calley was an outstanding representative of the new breed of studio executives who rose to power in the early Seventies. He was appointed head of production at Warner Bros. and in 1971 launched a kind of screenwriters' workshop:

> Calley signed about a dozen young writers to a contract, gave them a weekly salary, a place to work and a lot of support. The median age of this group was 26; most had just rolled out of film school with a pronounced bias for the American film. They admired the likes of Ford, Hawks, Walsh and found Antonioni and Bergman hardly worth speaking about. MARCELLO, I'M SO BORED was the thesis film for John Milius, this group's superstar. It doesn't take much sleuthing to guess the Marcello to which he referred – or the directors whose films he was knocking.[26]

At Warner Bros., where BONNIE AND CLYDE and THE WILD BUNCH had been made a few years earlier, Calley picked up BADLANDS and MEAN STREETS for distribution and produced some of the most sensational genre-revisions (or genre exploitations) of the Seventies – films such as KLUTE, McCABE & MRS. MILLER, A CLOCKWORK ORANGE, THX 1138, DIRTY HARRY, DELIVERANCE, WHAT'S UP, DOC?, THE EXORCIST, NIGHT MOVES.[27] The revived interest in screenwriters and genre cinema was also discernable at other studios. It brought about a further shift in emphasis: the 'crazy hippie auteurs' gave way to 'good craftmansship' and to a stronger division of functions in the filmmaking process. The (new) screenwriters and the concept of genre also returned to the limelight in critical discourse, as the case of Pauline Kael shows particularly well.

Three of the most promising and/or highly paid writers of this time were John Milius, Paul Schrader and Terrence Malick.

> The studios were rushing like mad to make deals with, at first, hipsters like Fonda and Hopper, and later the macho types like Milius and Schrader. What they looked like and how they comported themselves was at least as important as their scripts. Of course directors and writers knew this and did what they had to do, which was acquire an acceptable persona and play-act. (...) I knew Terry Malick a little; obviously he wasn't included in my [*Film Comment*] critique of the guys with an abundance of ersatz machismo. I saw him and his first wife socially a few times, and interviewed him. He's a very special person. No one had more official, high-level studio backing than Terry. Why his career took the path we know surely is a highly personal story. Maybe he'll tell it someday.[28]

Although they represented 'the future' in 1972/73, all three have over time moved away from centre stage which became occupied by consensus-oriented filmmakers such as Lucas and Spielberg. Milius, whose proto-fascist and militaristic behaviour aroused fascination and revulsion in equal measure began a successful directing career which was only short-lived (THE WIND AND THE LION, 1975); today he is mostly working as a 'script doctor" and has disappeared from the limelight. Schrader, who was initially (and falsely, I would argue) suspected to be Milius' intellectual confrere, enjoyed a massive success with his TAXI DRIVER screenplay and switched to directing in 1978. With his increasingly complex, emotionally detached 'Europeanized' films, he managed to carve out a small, rather lonely (and less and less commercial) space for himself, turning into one of the few authentic auteurs that the film industry tolerates. Malick, who had interrupted a career as a philosophy professor at MIT and moved to LA (where he shot a short film at the American Film Institute while working on an early script version of DIRTY HARRY), took the most radical step: His films BADLANDS (1973) and DAYS OF HEAVEN (1976/78) count among the greatest accomplishments of American cinema, but by the end of the Seventies his personality was no longer compatible with Hollywood. Almost overnight, Malick withdrew from the film business (only to return twenty years later, with the equally outstanding THIN RED LINE).[29]

In an essay on BADLANDS, Scorsese's MEAN STREETS and Milius' THE WIND AND THE LION, written in 1975, Manny Farber provides us with his idea of a New Hollywood that channelled the experience of 'second-hand' lives into productive dissonances and which at the time seemed capable of reconciling its pop cultural status with a modernist mission. Farber describes BADLANDS as "the Bonnie-Clyde bloodbath done without emotions or reactions, plus a suave, painterly image (the visuals resemble postcards with the colour printed twice)" and the perspective of the film as "from the outside looking in on a milieu that may seem as askew and perverse as Alice's Wonderland. (...) BADLANDS is often into the most artist-bewitching strategy of the 1970s. Conceptual artists like John Baldessari, Yvonne Rainer in her two films, Eleanor Antin and Martha Rosler in their postcard diaries, Fred Lonidier, Phil Steinmerz and Allan Sekula in their photo-fiction narratives are all using visual images and verbal texts in which the alignment isn't exact, so there is a space or jar created by the disjunction. In that space, the irony, humour, absurdity or message resides. The electricity created by the jar between text and visuals, words and pictures, has become the favourite technique for pinning down the madness of the human condition. It's also a strategy that allows for an exhilarating freedom, opening up the film, photo, painting format formerly closed to the possibility of informational facetiousness. (...) All these artists are turning their backs on 1960s formalism in favour of a crossed-media art involved with biography, myth, history. (...) They spotlight various postures that make the New Hollywood film so different from its forerunners, i.e., a facetious attitude about history, an automatic distrust of cops-soldiers-presidents, and, along with the bent for or against bizarre Americana, a jamming on the idea that people are inextricably influenced by myths, clichés, media, postcards, diaries, home movies, letters, etc."[30]

The reactionary turn in American culture laid to rest all hopes for a continuation or expansion of such aesthetic strategies in industrial cinema. In the 'private' sectors of the film industry, feelings of group solidarity or a commonality of goals (as described above by James Frawley) gave way to career-oriented social contacts. "There was a kind of socializing among younger people which bypassed older, more traditional Hollywood during that era. I don't believe it was overly involved with sex, drugs or drinking. Not in my house or in my experience, anyway. The problem is that as soon as someone had a big success – sold a script, got a deal – they separated themselves from their confreres and started associating with those who had already 'made it'. Then they were put on certain lists which supplied invitations to parties and screenings. It quickly became something very unpleasant and competitive. As soon as Julia and Michael Phillips moved to LA, they started giving conspicuous parties for the sole purpose of making contacts.[31] They were like spies: 'Who has a good script? Who's talented? Who can get to such-and-such a star or studio executive? Bring them to our house on Sunday.' This worked very well for them because it was known they had access to money – development money anyway. But since their occasions had no foundation of shared experience, it's not surprising they quickly evolved into substance-fests." (Beverly Walker)

Around the middle of the Seventies when the first wave of escapist, neo-heroic 'feelies' such as JAWS, ROCKY or STAR WARS was on the rise, and audience surveys, marketing research and merchandizing became central aspects of film production, cynical, gloomy social satires like Altman's NASHVILLE,[32] Hal Ashby's SHAMPOO or Michael Ritchie's SMILE (all 1975) were still possible – and even successful to a moderate degree. Henry Jaglom's TRACKS (1976) however, a 'fractured' latecomer from BBS circles, already had to appear like a very Un-American object, an alien from outer space. This film about a Vietnam war veteran (Dennis Hopper), who takes a train across the U.S. to bury a dead friend in his home town, is a fascinating odyssey in the manic-depressive mode, largely improvised, peppered with dream visions and sweetly mad lines of dialogue – a film on speed. TRACKS was barely noticed by critics and audiences; the industry was probably too preoccupied celebrating Jack Nicholson – Jaglom's and Hopper's comrade-in-arms from earlier days – for his role in ONE FLEW OVER THE CUCKOO'S NEST. It was a role, which successfully reinvented and commodified Nicholson's original anti-hero character in terms of a 'positive resistance' and in accordance with new needs for identification.

***

A Harvard political scientist, William Schneider, concluded for the *Los Angeles Times* that 'the Carter protest' was a new kind of protest, 'a protest of good feelings'. That was a new kind, sure enough: a protest that wasn't a protest.[33]

I am really sick of everybody's being antichrist, anti-society, anti-government, anti-people, anti-life, anti-happiness. (...) I think that we have to bolster our way through hard times by fabricating good times.[34]

During the past twenty-five years, American cinema has contributed in no small measure to the mythological fabrication of a 'good time' in the face of ever worsening times.[35] Its tendency to hermetically seal off and homogenise cinematic form and content at all levels springs from the need to neutralise the very contradictions that are essential for any meaningful cultural representation of real – economic and social – rifts and tensions. For this reason, an engagement with American films of the Sixties and Seventies may still prove productive. Not out of nostalgia but because these films rehearse a drama between the possible and the impossible which is just as applicable today as it was then.

Dennis Hopper in TRACKS

Notes

1. As early as 1965 Dennis Hopper wrote in a manifesto: "Five years ago [in 1960] there were fifty art theatres in the United States; now there are six thousand ... 'Hey, how can we [the Europeans] get into their market? We cannot compete on their level of film. Hey! I've got an idea! Let's make art films. That's something they'll never think of!' And of course we haven't yet. Fifty theatres to six thousand in five years. No American films for six thousand theatres." Quoted in Robert B. Ray, *A certain Terdency of the Hollywood Cinema*, Princeton, 1985, p. 269.
2. Cf. Martin Rubin, "Make Love Make War: Cultural confusion and the biker film cycle," in *Film History*, Vol 6 (1994), p. 355-381.
3. Olaf Möller, "Im Schutz des Tageslichts. Jim McBride, maitre du cinéma, im Gespräch," in: *Filmwärts* 31, September 1994, p. 22. The filmmaker Stanton Kaye, whose GEORG McBride mentions here, is practically unknown today, his films have disappeared, although various authors and artists referred to him in the Sixties and Seventies. After GEORG, Kaye made BRANDY IN THE WILDERNESS (1969) at the American Film Institute in LA, which was well-received critically, but never got a regular theatrical release – a typical 'subject for further research'.

4. *David Holzman's Diary*: A Screenplay by L.M. Kit Carson from a film by Jim McBride, New York 1970, p. vii-xiii.
5. See Bérénice Reynaud's essay on WANDA in this book.
6. Journalist Richard Goldstein describes taking the opposite path, also in relation to the Chicago unrest – and he points to one aspect of the failure of the American Left in the late Sixties: "I made lists. Weeks before my first whiff of tear gas, I spent a night dissecting my motives and expectations in two neat columns. On one side, I wrote: adventure, good copy, and historical imperative. On the other side, I wrote: danger, loneliness, and cost. The word commitment didn't appear on either side. Not since college had I been able to associate that word with politics. I simply redirected my radicalism toward aesthetics." Goldstein, *Reporting the Counter-culture*, Boston/London 1989, p. 137.
7. Jacques Demy, *Stadtkino-Programm*, 153 (1989), Vienna, p. 6.
8. Paul Krassner, *Confessions of a Raving, Unconfined Nut. Misadventures in the Counter-Culture*, New York 1993, p. 194f.
9. Kevin Jackson (ed.), *Schrader on Schrader & other writings*, London 1990, p. 35.
10. The historian Richard Slotkin has written the definitive analysis on this topic. In his study of the American frontier myth, as reflected in the Western, THE WILD BUNCH assumes a prominent position. Slotkin, *Gunfighter Nation*, New York 1992, esp. pp. 591-613.
11. William Pechter, *Film Comment*, Fall 1970, New York, p. 57.
12. See Thomas Elsaesser, "The Pathos of Failure: Notes on the Unmotivated Hero," in this volume.
13. *Schrader on Schrader*, op. cit. p. 74, 80.
14. See, for instance, J. Hoberman's comments on the "last Westerns" and "Hippie Westerns" in his [italics:] The Dream Life. Movies, Media and the Mythology of the Sixties [not italics:] New York, 2003
15. Cf. Seth Cagin and Philip Dray, *Sex, Drugs, Violence, Rock'n'Roll and Politics. Hollywood Films of the Seventies*, New York 1984, p. 227f.
16. An extensive treatment and analysis of BBS can be found in Teresa Grimes, 'BBS: Auspicious beginnings, open endings', in: *Movie* 31/32, London, p. 54-66.
17. 'KID BLUE Rides Again', James Frawley interviewed by Tom Milne and Richard Combs, in: *Film Comment*, Jan-Feb 1976, New York, p. 54-58.
18. This information originates from a letter from Gerald Ayres.
19. Cf. Axel Madsen, *The New Hollywood*, New York 1975, p. 8-24.
20. Stephen Schiff, 'The Repeatable Experience', in: *Film Comment*, March 1982, New York, p. 34-36.
21. See, for instance, J. Hoberman's comments on the "last Westerns" and "Hippie Westerns" in his *The Dream Life. Movies, Media and the Mythology of the Sixties*, New York, 2003.
22. See Maitland McDonagh's essay on 'marginal' genre cinema in this book. Robin Wood has written in detail about the implications of the new American horror film: *Hollywood from Vietnam to Reagan*, op. cit., esp. p. 70, 161.
23. David Thomson has written eloquently about these cycles.
24. Adam Barker, "Cries and Whispers," in: *Sight and Sound*, February 1992, London, p. 24f.
25. Stephen Schiff, 'The Repeatable Experience', op. cit. p. 36.

26. Beverly Walker, 'Journals/L.A.', in: *Film Comment*, July 1973, New York, p. 2. Apart from Milius, this quite disparate group included Walter Hill, David Giler (who later produced ALIENS [with Hill] and other films), Brian de Palma, Paul Williams (whose directorial works THE REVOLUTIONARY, 1970, and DEALING, 1972, belong more to the counter-culture), Terrence Malick, Vernon Zimmermann (who directed DEADHEAD MILES, based on Malick's script, in 1971/72) and the actor Tony Bill (later co-producer of TAXI DRIVER and director of MY BODYGUARD among other films). Additional comments on this group can be found in: Beverly Walker, 'Journals/L.A.', in: *Film Comment*, May 1973.
27. Cf. Stuart Byron, 'John Calley Interview', in: *Film Comment*, November 1974, New York, p. 39-43.
28. Cf. Beverly Walker, op. cit.
29. See essay by Dana Polan in this volume.
30. 'Manny Farber examines BADLANDS, MEANS STREETS AND THE WIND AND THE LION', IN: *City of San Francisco*, September 23, 1975, VOL 9, ISSUE 11.
31. The married couple Phillips was the most successful producing team of the late New Hollywood phase (THE STING, TAXI DRIVER, CLOSE ENCOUNTERS OF THE THIRD KIND). Julia Phillips has documented her career and her descent into drug addiction in a controversial autobiography: *You'll Never Eat Lunch in This Town Again*, New York/Toronto 1991.
32. For the relationship between JAWS and NASHVILLE see J. Hoberman's essay in this volume.
33. Tom Wolfe, "The Me Decade and the Third Great Awakening," (1976) in: Wolfe, *The Purple Decades*, New York 1982.
34. Sylvester Stallone, 1976, quoted in: Peter Knobler, "A One-Way Ticket from Palookaville (1977)," in: *Very Seventies, A cultural history of the 70s from the pages of Crawdaddy*, ed. Peter Knobler/Greg Mitchell, New York 1995, p. 352.
35. The most outstanding analysis of 1980s cinema can be found in Andrew Britton, 'Blissing Out: The Politics of Reaganite Entertainment', in: *Movie* 31/32 London, p. 1-42.

The Exploitation Generation

Or: How Marginal Movies Came in from the Cold

Maitland McDonagh

Astonishing things seemed possible in the 1970s, the decade when the 1960s came home to roost. Buffeted by the same pressures that rocked American society overall, the movie industry underwent an unprecedented upheaval that left it permanently changed. In the space of a few crucial years, the citadel of Hollywood – then crowded with industry veterans whose tastes and technical skills were formed decades earlier – was stormed by writers, editors, directors, producers, cinematographers and actors who learned their craft not by rising through the ranks of major studio production, but on Hollywood's fringes: in television, film school and exploitation movies. They rejected the conventional ideals embraced and disseminated by Hollywood's venerable dream factory and produced a body of complex, ambitious movies characterized by ambiguous endings, cynical morals and puzzling, contradictory characters whose fortunes foundered on the world's casual cruelty. They ushered in a sea change in American mainstream filmmaking as the powerful, mandatory Production Code, in place since 1934, breathed its last gasp in 1968 and promised a wideopen future in which no topic was taboo.

No longer were filmmakers constrained by guidelines requiring that films uplift (or at least not lower) audiences' moral standards, refrain from creating sympathy for "crime, wrong-doing, evil or sin," depict "correct standards of life" and never, ever ridicule law ("divine, natural or human") or valorise those who do.[1] By the end of the decade, rude, crude, deliberately scruffy midnight movies, from Alejandro Jodorowsky's hallucinatory EL TOPO (1971) to Jim Sharman's giddily transgressive ROCKY HORROR PICTURE SHOW (1975), had found dedicated audiences with little advertising and run for months and even years. Low-budget independent productions had out-grossed lavishly bankrolled studio films, and major studios had released films about eccentric loners, hustlers, drug users, iconoclasts, thieves, drop-outs, prostitutes, losers, sexual rebels and even killers. The sympathy of moviegoers was regularly thrown to the side of criminals, wrong-doers and sinners whose standards of life were often in flagrant violation of mainstream notions of correctness. The very notion of law being above ridicule had some to seem preposterous; the

1960s mantra, question authority, is firmly ingrained in 1970s films. Francis Ford Coppola's THE GODFATHER (1974) owes its form to gangster pictures like LITTLE CAESAR (1930) and SCARFACE (1932), but only in the 1970s could the Mafia be depicted explicitly as the mirror image of American business and, by extension, capitalist democracy itself. SCARFACE's subtitle was THE SHAME OF THE NATION; THE GODFATHER's could have been 'the state of the nation'.

Filmmakers like Coppola helped turn the 1970s into what critic Pauline Kael dubbed Hollywood's real Golden Age, a brief period when films that defied time-tested narrative constructions and tortured easy genre formulas into weirdly challenging hybrids seemed the norm rather than the exception, a decade which, in retrospect, represented an extraordinary blossoming of talent in the commercial cinema. The changes Kael celebrated discomfited others who fretted about nihilism, vigilantism and cynicism, mourned the death of the family audience and the emergence of a new breed of viewer hungry for harder, sleazier thrills than those by which the previous generation had been formed and nourished. Traditional distinctions between art films, commercial entertainment and exploitation movies grew hazy, and as early as 1971, critic John Simon lashed out at the "new pretentiousness",[2] which he claimed Hollywood – by which he meant the movie business in general – was substituting for the spectacle it could no longer afford. He opined that arty movies were all very well and good when they were Michelangelo Antonioni's L'AVVENTURA (1960) or Ingmar Bergman's PERSONA (1966), but quite another thing when they were THE GO-BETWEEN or DEEP END (1970), TWO-LANE BLACKTOP, DEATH IN VENICE, MCCABE AND MRS. MILLER, THE HIRED HAND or JOHNNY GOT HIS GUN (1971). Simon had always hated Visconti ("a vulgar, campy poseur from way back"), so when you take him off the list, the preponderance of Americans becomes even more apparent: Monte Hellman, Dalton Trumbo, Joseph Losey, Robert Altman and Peter Fonda, home-grown non-conformists who dared challenge traditional narrative structure and Hollywood realist acting and abandon the seamless brilliance of Hollywood film language for "frantic cutting, crazy camera angles, weird opticals". Cloaked as a condemnation of affectation, Simon's diatribe was a thinly disguised shriek of horror at the sight of low culture making its way into the limelight. What was the world coming to when a sleazy little road movie like TWO-LANE BLACKTOP was discussed as though it were some kind of art?

In retrospect, it's clear that the filmmaking revolution that blossomed in the restless 1970s was itself paradoxical. At the same time that subversive, disquieting films like FIVE EASY PIECES and JOE (1970), THE FRENCH CONNECTION, CARNAL KNOWLEDGE, SWEET SWEETBACK'S BAADASSSSS SONG, DIRTY HARRY, THE PANIC IN NEEDLE PARK and A CLOCKWORK ORANGE (1971), THE GODFATHER, STRAW DOGS and FAT CITY (1972), THE EXORCIST, AMERICAN GRAFFITI and Last Tango in Paris (1973), The Conversation and Chinatown (1974), Jaws, Shampoo, Dog Day Afternoon and Nashville (1975), Taxi Driver (1976), Days of Heaven (1978) and Apocalypse Now (1979) challenged, infuriated and energized eager audiences, Stephen Spielberg's Jaws (1975) and George Lucas' Star Wars (1977) were ushering in the age of the all razzle-dazzle, no-substance blockbuster. The decade's legacy is equally contradictory: partial nudity, coarse language and brutal violence are now commonplace in mainstream movies, but truly dissident themes, thorny characters and ambiguous narratives are not. The exploitation generation stormed the gates of Hollywood's citadel and paved the way for filmmakers with backgrounds in media that didn't even exist in the 1970s, but their unwavering rejection of antiquated proprieties ushered in an aesthetic of knee-jerk coarseness and juvenile vulgarity divorced from ideological intent.

Until the 1960s, the major Hollywood studios – Twentieth-Century Fox, Paramount, MGM, Universal and Warner Bros – overwhelmingly controlled mainstream American moviemaking, a position solidified in the late 1920s when the transition to sound thinned the ranks of undercapitalized independent filmmakers and small production companies. The studio mandate was to make movies suitable for both adults and children – getting families to the movies en masse made good business sense – and rooted in an idealized vision of America defined by respect for the law and government, marital fidelity, gentility, hard work, patriotism, fairness, honesty, personal responsibility, devotion to principles and esteem for family and community. Hollywood's dream factories turned out hundreds of films annually, from A-pictures featuring the biggest stars and the best scripts money could buy to the inexpensive B-pictures that fill out double bills. Prestige dramas showcased the stars, problem pictures carefully tackled big issues without rocking the status quo, and genre movies delivered cheap, predictable entertainment. Hollywood style, glossy and seamless, became the standard by which all movies were judged.

Hollywood's hold over the industry was never monolithic; small companies like Republic Studios and Producer's Releasing Corporation – PRC for short and "prick pics" to disgruntled filmmakers who invariably got the short end of the financial stick – turned out inexpensive films catering to the popular hunger for horror movies, westerns and gritty thrillers. Road show exhibitors took films featuring a naughty hint of sex or nudity from town to town, showing them in grindhouses and improvised theatres. The race movie circuit served the black audiences who were all but ignored by Hollywood. But such marginal movies were cultural detritus, and the road between the studios and everything outside Hollywood's gates went one way. Directors like William Beaudine – who directed silent superstar Mary Pickford in the 1920s and wound up making Jessie James Meets Frankenstein's Daughter (1966) –

might end their careers in exploitation, but exploitation directors didn't parlay their experience into mainstream Hollywood careers. Once an outsider, always an outcast; to make films beyond the mainstream was to be tainted, slightly disreputable in a culture predicated on the image of respectability.

The traditional studio system held sway even after it had stopped working; post-WWII movie attendance dropped steadily, and 3-D novelties and wide screen spectaculars couldn't stem the out-rushing tide. Years of lawsuits, notably United States v. Paramount Pictures, Inc. et al., forced the studios to divest themselves of their theatre holdings and broke their stranglehold on distribution. By the 1960s, mainstream Hollywood was adrift. American society was changing convulsively – government was widely viewed with suspicion and hostility, families shattered or had drifted apart, the sexual morality of the past was challenged and abandoned – and the tastes of veteran studio filmmakers and younger moviegoers were increasingly out of sync. The prestige productions on which studio executives pinned their hopes – "more is more" adaptations of reputable plays or books shored up by lavish production values and rafts of stars – failed as often as they succeeded. Independent filmmakers were grabbing audiences with movies that delivered what Hollywood wouldn't – sex, violence and sensationalism – and TV was serving up, free and in the privacy of viewers' homes, the light comedy, genre entertainment and small-scale dramas they used to see in movie houses. With the major studios no longer setting standards or grooming and cultivating actors and artisans, where was the new talent to come from?

The filmmakers of the exploitation generation were steeped in the rebellious mores of the 1960s, which celebrated sex, drugs, rock music, pop art, high camp, low culture, épater le bourgeois pranks and wholesale rejection of venerable social institutions. They found inspiration in cultural detritus and sought to reclaim the motion picture past that nurtured them as youngsters, filtered through layers of nostalgia, pop-culture savvy and self-awareness. Unlike the leading lights of the preceding generation, they loved low genres – science-fiction, horror and crime pictures – shamelessly unapologetic, they systematically reworked the genre films they loved for contemporary audiences. Without the gritty Warner Bros gangster pictures of the 1930s, there would be no GODFATHER trilogy; without low-budget science-fiction serials, there would have been no STAR WARS. As a group, they came of age during the conformist 1950s and ached to poke below the blandly reassuring surface of mass culture. They revelled in sleaze and grit, experimented freely with narrative conventions, made films about marginal and unsympathetic characters and rejected the homogenizing sheen of classical style in favour of a grab bag approach to film language that borrowed equally from documentary, European art films, B-movie sensationalism and high Hollywood gloss. They came to filmmaking determined to make the movies they wanted to make – as opposed to the movies that studio moguls or production heads wanted to make – at the same time that a new breed of movie buffs invaded the ranks of mainstream film criticism, where they celebrated pictures that frankly baffled and dismayed an older generation of cineastes.

This new generation of filmmakers and critics, many with backgrounds – film school or fandom – that conceived of film as art rather than product, saw the medium as a vehicle for personal expression. Movie buff, critic and future filmmaker Francois Truffaut's hugely influential 'politique des auteurs', was published in *Cahiers du cinéma* in 1954 and colonized American thinking through Andrew Sarris' essay *Notes on the Auteur Theory* in 1962. But what took root in the American popular imagination differed significantly from Truffaut's notion of the dialectical relationship between the director and a system largely ruled by producers and studio heads. Truffaut celebrated the sly ways in which a successful studio director like Howard Hawks or John Ford transcended the system and created something uniquely his own. Up and coming filmmakers of the 1960s and 1970s embraced a romantically individualistic notion of authorship and acted accordingly, encouraged by the production code's demise and the introduction of the MPAA's new, nominally voluntary rating system, which meant that in theory, no subject was off limits and audiences could decide for themselves what they wanted to see. That promise, like so many others, fell short in practice.

Ratings became a tool with which to prod filmmakers into conforming with a variety of ill-defined and arbitrary standards exemplified by the turbulent history of the scarlet X. Designed to designate films like MIDNIGHT COWBOY (1969), whose content was inherently adult in the sense of 'mature' or 'sophisticated', it was immediately co-opted by the nascent industry dedicated to producing feature-length pornographic films. So many theatres refused to book any movie carrying an X rating and most newspapers stopped accepting their advertising. With their built-in audiences and specialized venues, pornographic films – 'adult movies' in the popular sense of the term – were in a position to weather the financial stigma of an X rating. Mainstream movies couldn't, and while having a film rated by the MPAA is a strictly voluntary process, unrated films were (and to a great degree still are) severely limited in the number of theatres they could play, which in turn curtailed their earning potential. The NC-17 rating was introduced in 1990 as a non-pejorative replacement and awarded first to Philip Kaufman's oh-so-serious HENRY & JUNE, but in practice NC-17 and X were treated as one and the same, so mainstream commercial movies are routinely edited to avoid the NC-17 designation. And in rare display of industrial nostalgia, pornographic movies – perpetually looking for the next big thing (pun entirely intended) – are still proudly labelled 'XXXtravaganzas'.

Still, before the 1970s no-one could have imagined that feature-length hard-core films would, however briefly, play neighbourhood cinemas or that the respectable press would give newly minted porn superstars Linda Lovelace, Marilyn Chambers, John Holmes and Harry Reems a venue in which to extol the virtues of the adult film industry and proclaim their conviction that sexually explicit movies would only become more generally acceptable in the years to come. A decade earlier, it would have been unthinkable that Marlon Brando, one-time Hollywood heartthrob and idol of a generation of actors, would appear naked in LAST TANGO IN PARIS (1973), whose frank portrayal of sexual congress was inextricably linked to its highbrow purpose. Even old-time smut peddlers were taken aback, if for selfish reasons – how could their no-name naughtiness compete with the appeal of big stars in the buff?

In the end, the prognostications were wrong; porno chic came and went. While A-list movie stars now regularly bare almost all (male members are still genitalia non grata in the American mainstream), explicit sex in non-pornographic films remains the province of foreign films like the French ROMANCE (1999) and BAISE-MOI (2000), and independent productions like John Cameron Mitchell's SEX FILM PROJECT (2004). As recently as 1995, professional provocateur Paul Verhoeven issued a direct, insider's challenge to prevailing norms with his defiantly vulgar SHOWGIRLS, a coarse reworking of ALL ABOUT EVE (1950) set in Las Vegas, the world capital of venality. But the much-hyped film failed to bring heretofore unimaginable explicitness to mainstream blockbusters or crack the door for Hollywood hardcore. SHOWGIRLS fizzled (though it found new life on video and DVD as a camp item), and full-frontal sex remains in the adult-movie ghetto. Adult movies all but abandoned the theatrical marketplace, seizing on emerging video technology as the perfect delivery system for movies that are, in the end, meant for private consumption.

Television, despised and feared by Hollywood from the moment lifelong movie fans started forgoing their regular Friday night movie date to watch variety programs and game shows, trained Bob Rafelson, Sam Peckinpah, William Friedkin, Robert Altman, Steven Spielberg and others. College-level film programs graduated aspiring filmmakers and, anti-intuitive though it might at first appear, the film school and TV/exploitation tracks converged early and often. Without relatives or family friends to get them into the motion picture craft unions, film school graduates often wound up working in TV and the hit-and-run netherworld of exploitation, where their degrees counted for less than their willingness to do just about anything for next to nothing. In fact, the bulk of actors, screenwriters, producers, editors and directors who came out of exploitation in the 1960s and 1970s passed through Roger Corman's sink-or-swim school of exploitation filmmaking.

A graduate of Stanford University who studied English literature at Oxford on the GI Bill, Corman entered the business in the mid-1950s, just as the studio system was crumbling. He genuinely loved movies but was a relentlessly practical producer. Corman worked fast and cheaply, seized on topical and exploitative hooks because he didn't have money to lose and knew that clever promotion – 'exploitation' in the traditional sense of the word – gave a low-budget movie a fighting chance against slicker, better publicized studio pictures. Corman was also a phenomenal judge of potential who recognized that aspiring filmmakers were terrific value for money. His legendary reputation for crassness and parsimony notwithstanding, just about everyone who worked for Corman said he offered fledgling filmmakers a deal that was almost too good to be true – as long as they brought the footage in on time and on budget, he left them alone to make their movies. UCLA graduate Francis Ford Coppola divided his school years between the campus and veteran producer/director Roger Corman's motion-picture sweatshop. Under Corman's tutelage, Coppola re-edited prestigious Russian science-fiction movies into schlock entertainment, recording sound on THE WILD RACERS (1963) and directed bits of footage that were inserted into foreign films Corman hoped to pass off as American; in return, Corman produced Coppola's first real feature, the promising DEMENTIA 13 (1963). After Martin Scorsese's first independent feature, the well-reviewed WHO'S THAT KNOCKING AT MY DOOR? (1969), failed to jump-start a career, he went back to NYU to teach (his students included Jonathan Kaplan and Oliver Stone) before tackling the Industry, finding bread-and-butter work as a film editor. Corman gave him the opportunity to direct the pulpy, populist BOXCAR BERTHA (1972), supported by the one-stop-shop producer's pit-bull commitment to getting his films into theaters and keeping them there until the last dollar had been wrung out of them.

Corman's protegés included cinematographers John A. Alonzo, Lazlo Kovacs and Nestor Almendros (Almendros was well-established in Europe by the mid-1970s, but his work for Corman, including 1974's COCKFIGHTER, introduced him in the US), as well as producers Jon Davison, Mark Damon, Gale Ann Hurd, Menachem Golan and Gary Kurtz and actor-directors Peter Fonda, Dennis Hopper and Jack Nicholson, editor-turned-director Monte Hellman (whom Sam Peckinpah called the best cutter in America) and screenwriter-directors Robert Towne and John Sayles, directors Peter Bogdanovich, Ron Howard, Jonathan Demme, Richard Rush, Allan Arkush, Joe Dante, Paul Bartel, George Armitage, Jonathan Kaplan and James Cameron. Individually and in ever-shifting combinations, they were instrumental in making many of the seminal films of the 1970s, including THE LAST PICTURE SHOW and TWO-

LANE BLACKTOP, directed by Bogdanovich and Hellman, respectively; THE GODFATHER and its sequels, directed by Coppola; CHINATOWN, scripted by Towne and starring Nicholson; MEAN STREETS (1973) and TAXI DRIVER, directed by Scorsese; SHAMPOO, shot by Kovacs; STAR WARS, written and directed by Lucas, produced by Kurtz; DAYS OF HEAVEN, shot by Almendros; and THE RETURN OF THE SECAUCUS SEVEN (shot in 1978, though not released until two years later), written and directed by Sayles. Several are counted among the best filmmakers of their generation, most made substantial careers for themselves in the Hollywood mainstream, and when they were through with it, the mainstream wasn't the same.[3]

The ascendancy of the exploitation generation went hand in hand with the rise of genre pictures and again, the roots of the 1970s lay in the 1960s. Arthur Penn's BONNIE AND CLYDE (1967) lobbed a virtual grenade into the laps of critics and viewers, dividing them instantly into the hip and the square. The hip loved it, the square squirmed about the violence and amorality of its portrait of a white trash couple on the run. BONNIE AND CLYDE was all about poor white trash who were young, in love and killed people, and expected you to like them. BONNIE AND CLYDE wasn't the first film inspired by real-life outlaws Bonnie Parker and Clyde Barrow, but Nicholas Ray's noir THEY LIVE BY NIGHT (1947) and the low-rent BONNIE PARKER STORY (1958) were fringe movies that stayed on the fringe: BONNIE AND CLYDE went to Cannes. THE GRADUATE, another effort aimed squarely at disaffected young Americans, was the bigger hit, but BONNIE AND CLYDE the greater *succes d'estime*. With THE WILD BUNCH (1969), it put the spotlight on an audience with an abiding lust for up-to-date versions of low-budget genre movies of the past – westerns, horror movies, thrillers and science-fiction pictures. A head movie in rocket man drag, Stanley Kubrick's 2001: A SPACE ODYSSEY (1968), ushered in the era of big-budget science-fiction. Critics, with the exception of *The New Yorker*'s Penelope Gilliatt, thought it was a disaster. Audiences loved it and went to see it again and again. Druggy, low-rent biker picture EASY RIDER (1969) was an equally eye-opening success whose key personnel – director/co-writer/star Dennis Hopper, producer/co-writer/star Peter Fonda and breakout supporting player Jack Nicholson – converged while making THE TRIP (1967), Corman's psychedelic paean to LSD.

Hopper made his screen acting debut in the Warners' production REBEL WITHOUT A CAUSE (1955), but his temperamental unsuitability to studio style filmmaking derailed his career before it had properly begun. Hopper so infuriated studio lifer Henry Hathaway on FROM HELL TO TEXAS (1958) that the seasoned director dedicated an entire day to breaking the young upstart. Hopper spent the next several years in low-budget films, including NIGHT TIDE (1961), QUEEN OF BLOOD (1965), THE GLORY STOMPERS (1967) and Corman's THE TRIP.

He and TRIP co-star Peter Fonda got so caught up in the excitement of making an authentic drug movie that they took it upon themselves to shoot 16mm hallucination footage on their own time, a scrap of which made it into the final cut. Born into Hollywood royalty and handsome enough for juvenile leads in the likes of TAMMY AND THE DOCTOR (1963), Fonda was living a Prince Hal fantasy, slumming in biker pictures like Corman's THE WILD ANGELS (1966). Fonda says he was listening to MPAA head Jack Valenti expound upon the motion picture industry's responsibility to produce more family pictures like the mega-flop DR. DOOLITTLE (1967) when the idea hit him: "The time was right for a really good movie about motorcycles and drugs."[4] How better to needle old-fashioned Hollywood, especially his own deeply conservative father? Fonda and Hopper tried to set up EASY RIDER at veteran indie house American International Pictures, where Corman had made THE WILD ANGELS and THE TRIP, but studio head Samuel Z. Arkoff wanted a contractual guarantee that the studio could take over if the film went over budget. Hopper and Fonda turned to Bert Schneider and Bob Rafelson; Rafelson had created TV's *The Monkees*, and he and Schneider co-produced HEAD (1968). Better still, Schneider's brother, Stanley, was head of Columbia pictures, where the deal to produce EASY RIDER was made. Like Fonda, the Schneiders were second-generation Hollywood, and by coincidence their father, a Columbia executive, had been in the room when the youthful Hopper made a memorably bad impression on studio head Harry Cohn in 1955.

EASY RIDER gave Jack Nicholson the stardom he'd been chasing for more than a decade; the actor, who co-wrote THE TRIP and HEAD, was beginning to resign himself to a career behind the camera after years of struggling in low-budget features, including several of Corman's. Nicholson took over the supporting part of small-town lawyer George Hanson at the last minute, replacing Rip Torn; Torn walked off after shooting had started, and Nicholson became one of the most sought-after leading men of the 1970s. The film was shot by Laszlo Kovacs, whose Corman credits included HELL'S ANGELS ON WHEELS (1967), PSYCH-OUT (1968) and TARGETS (1968). The authentic rock soundtrack, which owed more to cheap rock 'n' roll movies than the orchestral tradition of Hollywood scores, was tremendously influential (though to be fair, THE GRADUATE's Simon and Garfunkel predated it by two years), as was EASY RIDER's down-and-dirty aesthetic, which recalled the gritty, inartistic look of on-the-fly exploitation pictures. When the final accounting was done, the $400,000 picture had grossed at least ten times that, and Hollywood was forced to take notice.

EASY RIDER in turn begat BILLY JACK (1971), one of the most profitable independent films of the 1970s and a phenomenal compendium of timely elements. Like Hopper and Fonda, actor/writer/director Tom Laughlin first took his counterculture opus to AIP, where he got financing but ran into the kind of trouble Hopper and Fonda feared. Laughlin broke with AIP over "creative differences" and finished BILLY JACK by lining up independent financing and securing studio distribution on his own. Like Fonda, Laughlin had started his acting career playing bland young men a mother could love, but found his metier in motorcycle movies, which he both starred in and directed. Laughlin created the character of Billy Jack for the AIP-produced BORN LOSERS (1967), bringing together in one tough anti-hero a cat's cradle of zeitgeist-conscious concerns. A disillusioned veteran of the Vietnam War turned pacifist biker, part Native American Billy Jack rejects the white man's ways and uses his martial arts skills to kick establishment ass for his folks on the rez (the same mix of pop identity politics fantasy retribution that drove blaxploitation films), peace-loving hippies and innocent children.

Blaxploitation movies burned bright and briefly, quickly sublimating their ideological underpinnings into humorous bluster and compulsive displays of flash and cash. But they brought African-American audiences their first real attention since the demise of the race movie circuit, and conferred cult stardom on Pam Grier, Fred Williamson, Jim Kelly, Rosalind Cash, Richard Roundtree, Jim Brown, Isaac Julian and Ron O'Neal. From the late teens through the late 1940s, a "separate cinema" served black Americans, who were largely ignored by the Hollywood mainstream. Produced independently or by low-budget studios, race movies played in officially segregated theaters in the South and de facto segregated theatres in black neighbourhoods in the North, offering fare that for the most part mirrored Hollywood product but featured "great coloured casts." Some race movies were made by black writer-directors like Oscar Micheaux and Spencer Williams, whose early filmmaking career was overshadowed by his later notoriety for playing Andrew Hogg Brown when the long-running radio comedy *Amos 'n' Andy* was adapted for television in 1951. But most were black in front of the camera and white behind, and almost all were hampered by desperately low budgets; they regularly fell short of Hollywood's high gloss, but effectively exploited the genre conventions popularized by studio gangster pictures, romances, westerns, crime thrillers and comedies.

Whatever their deficiencies, DARK TOWN FOLLIES (1929), DAUGHTER OF THE CONGO (1930), HARLEM AFTER MIDNIGHT (1934), MURDER IN HARLEM (1935), UNDERWORLD (1937), THE BRONZE BUCKAROO, HARLEM ON THE PRAIRIE and THE BRONZE VENUS (all 1938), MOON OVER HARLEM (1939), SON OF INGAGI (1940), WHERE'S MY MAN TONIGHT (1944), GLORY ROAD and HOT SHOTS (both 1945), DIRTY GERTIE FROM HARLEM, U.S.A. (1946) and JUKE JOINT (1947) offered black audiences an alternative. They proffered entertaining clichés – wicked vamps and virtuous church girls, noble cowboys and snappy gangsters – rather than the demeaning, bit-part stereotypes of mammy, grinning tap-dancer, sassy maid and shuffling, sycophantic idiot.

Race filmmakers occasionally went outside the comfortable boundaries of genre entertainment to address pressing social issues of particular concern to African Americans. Micheaux's silent WITHIN OUR GATES (1920) includes a deeply controversial lynching sequence, while his BIRTHRIGHT (1924, remade with sound in 1939) dealt with a black Harvard graduate confronting Southern racism. Micheaux's BODY AND SOUL (1924) challenged the considerable authority of religious figures in the black community, charting the damage done by an ungodly man posing as a man of God (played by newcomer Paul Robeson). But overall entertainment was the order of the day, and race movies died quietly as 1950s Hollywood grudgingly followed larger social trends and began integrating serious black actors like Sidney Poitier, Harry Belafonte, Dorothy Dandridge, Brock Peters and Diahann Carroll into major motion pictures alongside the surprisingly resilient maids and mammies. And then came SWEETBACK.

Melvyn Van Peebles' aggressively independent SWEET SWEETBACK'S BAADASSSSS SONG (1971), an angry, violent screed about the racist persecution of a poor black everyman, gave birth to the blaxploitation era, which blazed briefly and burned out by the mid-1970s. Van Peebles made his first film, a downbeat interracial romance called THE STORY OF A THREE DAY PASS (1967), while living in France; it was financed with a $70,000 grant from the French Cinema Center. THREE DAY PASS gave Van Peebles the opportunity to direct a tepid, studio-financed comedy, WATERMELON MAN (1970), about the Kafka-esque tribulations of a white racist who wakes up to find himself black, but SWEETBACK was his *cri de coeur*. Van Peebles wrote, directed, produced, edited, composed and starred in this defiantly inflammatory attack on white America, which wore its revolutionary Black Power politics on its sleeve: It opens with a "can you dig it" declaration of principles ("this film is dedicated to all the Brothers and Sisters who had enough of the Man"), identifies the cast as "the black community" and makes hay with the stereotype of black man as super stud. Sweetback, an unrepentant hustler, scammer and cop killer – albeit one enraged by seeing policemen pummel an innocent black man, an incident that's only more resonant in the wake of 1992 Rodney King incident and the riots it incited – gets away in the end, and when the film earned an X rating for its sexual content and violence, Van Peebles defiantly plastered the phrase "Rated X by an all-white jury" on the posters. The searing SWEETBACK built a bridge between independent exploitation, experimental filmmaking and an increasingly empowered African-American audience clamouring to see movies in which black folks didn't always get the shaft. It inspired a slew of crime thrillers whose politics were less aggressively articulated, but whose generic cops and robbers plots were rooted in experiences that resonated deeply with many black Americans. SHAFT (1971) is a straightforward reworking of tough-guy detective movie conventions, but Humphrey Bogart's Sam Spade never had trouble getting a cab on a busy midtown street – Richard Roundtree's John Shaft does. SUPERFLY (1972) is a riot of pimpfabulous fashions and ghetto posturing, but its noir-inflected story of a cocaine dealer trying to get out of the business before it kills him has a surprisingly bitter sting. The message delivered again and again to entrepreneurial Youngblood Priest (Ron O'Neal) is that he needs to learn his place – the streets – and stay there.

The success of these films made it clear that black Americans would pay good money to see people like themselves on screen, and action pictures like WILLIE DYNAMITE (1973), BLACK CEASAR and its sequel, HELL UP IN HARLEM (both 1973), THREE THE HARD WAY (1974) and BUCKTOWN (1975) rushed in to give them what they wanted. In dramatic contrast to the race-movie era, major studios got into blaxploitation early – SHAFT was an MGM production and Warner Bros bankrolled SUPERFLY. But there was plenty of business to go around, and independent productions abounded, including a sometimes comical series of classic horror films reworked in blackface, including BLACULA (1972), BLACKENSTEIN (1973), DR. BLACK AND MR. WHITE (1975) and ABBY (1974), an EXORCIST knock-off so nakedly derivative that Warner Bros sued successfully to have it withdrawn from distribution.

Like the vintage race movies, the bulk of blaxploitation titles were made by white exploitation veterans like Larry Cohen and Jack Hill; SHAFT's Gordon Parks and SUPERFLY's Gordon Parks Jr. were notable exceptions. Unlike the phrase 'race movie', which was rooted in the positive notion of a race man as someone proud of and a credit to his race, 'blaxploitation' always carried a whiff of the derogatory. The term is generally attributed to bluestockings at CORE (the Congress of Racial Equality) and the NAACP who found the films' raucous appeal too lowbrow for their liking. Like race movies before them, blaxploitation movies were killed by the changing marketplace. Studio executives took note of the fact that a substantial piece of the box office for films like THE GODFATHER (1972) and THE EXORCIST (1973) was generated in black communities, and concluded that they could get black people into theatres without having to make specifically black-oriented films. Independent financing dried up, and downtown theatres did land-office business with inexpensive kung fu pictures that captivated the same audiences who had cheered THE MACK (1973). But though blaxploitation movies flowered and died quickly, they left an indelible legacy in the form of mainstream black action stars.

It couldn't last, of course. The 1980s brought a return to gloss and glamour – even when the subject matter was violent and ignoble – and a codification of at-

Al Pacino in GODFATHER II

titudes and characters that had been radically innovative only a few years be-fore. But the mainstream movie industry is no longer a closed shop. At the end of HEARTS OF DARKNESS: A FILMMAKER'S APOCALYPSE, the 1991 documentary about the making of APOCALYPSE NOW, Francis Ford Coppola blurts out an al-most melancholy wish/prophecy: "To me, the great hope is that now these little 8mm video recorders are around and people who normally wouldn't make movies are going to be making them. And suddenly, one day some little fat girl in Ohio is going to be the new Mozart and make a beautiful film with her fa-ther's camcorder (...) the so-called professionalism about movies will be de-stroyed forever and it will really become an art form." Coppola's little Mozart has yet to emerge, but digital video recording technology and computer soft-ware have brought the cost of low budget filmmaking lower than ever. Writers and directors come to mainstream filmmaking from television commercials and video games, documentaries, independent features, music video and film school. Where work in low-rent horror movies was once a stigma, it's now a calling card. Black filmmakers like Anton Fuqua (TRAINING DAY, TEARS OF THE SUN) and Paul Hunter (BULLETPROOF MONK) are judged not by the colour of their skin but on the content of their demo reels. That's the legacy of the exploi-tation generation, and they changed Hollywood forever.

Distinguished (and Not-So-Distinguished) Alumnae of Roger Corman University

Legendary low-budget entrepreneur Roger Corman gave early breaks to hundreds of actors, writers, editors, directors, producers and technicians, first at American International Pictures (AIP), later at New World Pictures, Concorde/New Horizons and New Concorde, the production and distribution company he owns and operates to this day. His primary market is now direct-to-video, and he's taken to remaking his old titles, but he's still in the game. Corman has had a hand in making few distinguished movies, but many distinguished movie makers. And though his greatest successes worked with him during the 1960s and 1970s, Corman graduates continue to emerge to this day. A comprehensive list would probably include a quarter of the names in the Los Angeles phone book, but the filmmakers listed below are a representative sampling of Corman graduates.

NESTOR ALMENDROS (cinematographer) Though a star in Europe who had worked with François Truffaut, Eric Rohmer and Barbet Schroeder, Spanish born DP Almendros was virtually unknown in the US when Roger Corman hired him to shoot Monte Hellman's COCKFIGHTER (1974). The film was shot on location in Georgia, and Corman figured it was just as easy to fly someone in from Paris as Hollywood. Four years later, Almendros won an Oscar for DAYS OF HEAVEN. Almendros died in 1992.

JOHN A. ALONZO (cinematographer) The prolific Alonzo's first credit was Jonathan Demme's CRAZY MAMA (1970), produced by Roger Corman. Alonzo quickly moved up to mainstream productions, and was nominated for an Oscar for Roman Polanski's CHINATOWN (1974), written by Robert Towne. Alonzo died in 2001.

ALLAN ARKUSH (editor/director) An NYU graduate, Arkush started out cutting trailers for Corman at New World, then taught the ropes to Joe Dante. They made their first film, HOLLYWOOD BOULEVARD (1976) together; Dante followed up with PIRANHA (1978), while Arkush got the project Dante really wanted: ROCK 'N' ROLL HIGH SCHOOL (1979). Arkush's greatest success came in directing episodic TV, from *Moonlighting to Dawson's Creek*, but he makes the occasional TV movie like *Elvis Meets Nixon* (1997).

GEORGE ARMITAGE (director) Called "a brilliant writer" by *The Village Voice*, Armitage's first screenplay credit was Corman's GAS-SS, OR, HOW IT BECAME NECESSARY TO DESTROY THE WORLD IN ORDER TO SAVE IT (1969), an audacious disaster. He also wrote Jonathan Kaplan's Corman-produced NIGHT CALL NURSES (1972) – Armitage was set to direct until disagreements with Corman intervened – and the DARKTOWN STRUTTERS (1975). Unlike many of his contemporaries, Armitage virtually vanished for 20 years, reappearing in 1990 with the much-praised MIAMI BLUES, produced by yet another Corman alumnus, Jonathan Demme, in whose CAGED HEAT (1974) Armitage had appeared. Armitage then slid back into the shadows until THE BIG BOUNCE (2003).

PAUL BARTEL (writer/director/actor) The New York-based Bartel, a UCLA graduate with a year of study at Rome's Centro Sperimentale di Cinematografia behind him, was making short, arty films when Gene Corman, Roger's less successful brother, offered to produce his first feature, PRIVATE PARTS (1973). Friendly with Joe Dante, Jon Davison and Martin Scorsese, all of whom were working for Roger Corman, Bartel soon found himself among their number, directing DEATHRACE 2000 (1975), which starred David Carradine. He followed up with CANNONBALL (1976), EATING RAOUL (1982), SCENES FROM THE CLASS STRUGGLE IN BEVERLY HILLS (1989), etc. Bartel died in 2000.

PETER BOGDANOVICH (writer/director) Former film critic Bogdanovich was hired to do an uncredited rewrite on Corman's 1966 THE WILD ANGELS ("three weeks of the greatest film school anyone could ever put me through"), and as 'Derek Thomas' patched together VOYAGE TO THE PLANET OF PREHISTORIC WOMEN (1966) from pieces of a Russian sci-fi epic and original footage shot on Carillo beach. Corman's financial backing for TARGETS (1968) came with conditions: Bogdanovich had to use 20 minutes of THE TERROR, 20 minutes of new footage featuring Boris Karloff, who still owed Corman two days of shooting, and 40 minutes of new footage. The result was a stunning debut that Bogdanovich matched with THE LAST PICTURE SHOW (1971); his subsequent films have been largely disappointing and his increasingly circumscribed career opportunities reduced him to a punchline in Woody Allen's embittered HOLLYWOOD ENDING (2002).

DEBORAH BROCK (writer/director) UCLA graduate Brock joined the editing staff at Concorde/New Horizons in 1983, then co-wrote and directed two sequels, SLUMBER PARTY MASSACRE II (1987) and ROCK 'N' ROLL HIGH SCHOOL FOREVER. She went on to cowrite and co-executive produce Randel Kleiser's HONEY, I BLEW UP THE KIDS (1992), the sequel to the smash hit HONEY, I SHRUNK THE KIDS (1990), and co-produced Vincent Gallo's BUFFALO 66 (1998).

JEFF BURR (writer/director/producer) Burr attended USC but never graduated; he dropped out and worked briefly at Corman's New World Pictures, as-
sisting Jim Wynorski in the advertising department. Burr has made a number
of stylish and successful horror sequels, including STEPFATHER II (1989),
LEATHERFACE: THE TEXAS CHAINSAW MASSACRE III (1990) and continues to direct straight-to-video titles.

JAMES CAMERON (writer/director) Blockbuster auteur Cameron's first feature, the one he never mentions, was Corman-produced PIRANHA 2: THE
SPAWNING (1982), the sequel to Joe Dante's PIRANHA. Cameron worked at New
World in the early 1980s, where his assignments included the special effects
unit of HUMANOIDS FROM THE DEEP, an ALIEN (1980)-inspired potboiler about
rapists from the ocean floor. His partnership with Gale Anne Hurd, then
Corman's assistant, produced THE TERMINATOR (1984) and ALIENS (1986), and
the blockbuster TITANIC (1997) made him the self-proclaimed "king of the
world".

CARL-JAN COLPAERT (writer/producer/director) Colpaert left his native
Belgium to study at AFI. He worked as an editor for Corman, and remained at
New World Pictures after Corman's departure; he founded his own company,
Cineville, Inc. in 1989. Colpaert executive produced Allison Anders' ac-
claimed GAS-FOOD-LODGING (1991), and produced her MI VIDA LOCA (1994),
and his executive producer credit appears on a wide variety of independent
art features. Colpaert's directing credits include the sharp genre picture DELU-
SION (1990).

FRANCIS FORD COPPOLA (director) Hired to work for Corman while still at
UCLA, Coppola did a dreadful job as sound recordist on THE YOUNG RACERS,
rewrote and created vulgar special effects for the Russian sci-fi epic NIEBO
ZOWLET (1959), which was released in the US as BATTLE BEYOND THE SUN and
made his official directing debut – having already made a couple of cut and
paste nudie pictures – with DEMENTIA 13 (all 1963). Coppola also supervised
the shooting of OPERACIJA TICIJIAN in Yugoslavia, an English-language film
with a non-English speaking director that was the result of one of Corman's
more outrageous deals. It was eventually cut up into several films. Coppola,
who launched the career of USC grad George Lucas by producing THX 1138
(1971) and AMERICAN GRAFITTI (1973), quickly conquered the mainstream,
striking gold with THE GODFATHER (1972). Freed from the constraints of low-
budget filmmaking, Coppola went wild, sinking fortunes into films ranging
from APOCALYPSE NOW (1979), which was worth the money, to THE COTTON

Club (1974), which wasn't. Coppola made Corman squirm by casting him in the senate subcommittee scene in THE GODFATHER, PART II (1974).

MARK DAMON (actor/producer) Damon turned in a wooden co-starring performance in Corman's HOUSE OF USHER (1960), soon abandoning acting for a successful career as a producer. Notorious for his collaborations with soft-core auteur Zalman King, Damon graduated to producing mainstream theatrical genre pictures like EYE OF THE BEHOLDER (1999), THE MUSKETEER (2001) and EXTREME OPS (2002), most of which give off a faint whiff of cheese.

JOE DANTE (director) Former film critic Dante went to work in the New World trailer department after Roger Corman hired friend Jon Davison to head up the promotion department. His first trailers were for Jonathan Kaplan's STUDENT TEACHERS (1973) and Jonathan Demme's CAGED HEAT (1974), and he directed his first film, HOLLYWOOD BOULEVARD (1976) with fellow trailer department inmate Allan Arkush; Paul Bartel played the director-within-the-film. Steven Spielberg, who produced Dante's hit GREMLINS (1984), reportedly considered the Corman-produced PIRANHA (1978) the best of the JAWS (1976) rip-offs. Dante gave Corman a cameo in THE HOWLING (1980) for the fun of making his mentor work for free.

JON DAVISON (producer) NYU graduate Davison worked with Jonathan Kaplan on the rewrite of NIGHT CALL NURSES (1972), and Roger Corman hired him to slave in New World's advertising and promotion department. Davison produced Joe Dante and Allan Arkush's HOLLYWOOD BOULEVARD (1976) after betting Corman that he could produce the cheapest movie in New World history, at $90,000. Davison later went on to produce such blockbusters as Paul Verhoeven's ROBOCOP (1987) and STARSHIP TROOPERS (1997).

DAVID DeCOTEAU (director/producer) Encouraged by Corman's then-assistant, Gale Anne Hurd, aspiring director DeCoteau came to LA and got a job working on GALAXY OF TERROR (1981), which Corman produced. DeCoteau went on to work in adult films, then became one of the most prolific direct-to-video exploitation producer/ directors of the 1980s and 1990s, frequently collaborating with Charles Band, who's often called "the New Roger Corman". DeCoteau's credits include CREEPAZOIDS and SORORITY BABES IN THE SLIMEBALL BOWL-A-RAMA (both 1987) and PUPPETMASTER III (1991), and recently formed Rapid Heart Pictures to producing discretely homoerotic, non-theatrical thrillers and horror pictures.

JONATHAN DEMME (writer/director) Demme worked as unit publicist on the second-to-last film Corman directed, VON RICHTOFEN AND BROWN (1971), and took him up on the challenge of writing a biker script. The result was ANGELS HARD AS THEY COME (1971), a sort of RASHOMON with motorcycles. Corman offered to produce a sluts-in-the-slammer picture for the aspiring director, but Demme took so long to come up with CAGED HEAT (1974) that Corman rescinded; Demme got it made anyway, and Corman distributed. Demme made a series of quirky low-budget pictures before striking it big with SOMETHING WILD (1986), which he confesses he always thought of as a Corman picture for the 1980s. Demme featured Corman in small but striking roles in both the multiple Academy Award-winning SILENCE OF THE LAMBS (1991) and PHILADELPHIA (1994).

BRUCE DERN (actor) Dern appeared in three Roger Corman films in a row – THE WILD ANGELS (1966), THE ST. VALENTINE'S DAY MASSACRE and THE TRIP (both 1967) – then returned in 1970 for BLOODY MAMA. Though Dern tried to broaden his horizons, much of his career has been in the same roles in which Corman cast him: psychotics, sadists and all-around troublemakers. Dern's then wife, Diane Ladd, was also in THE WILD ANGELS, pregnant with actress daughter Laura Dern.

PETER FONDA (actor/director) Knee-jerk nonconformist Fonda, second-generation scion of Hollywood royalty, started out his career playing boys next door, then decided he'd rather play bikers, junkies and criminals. Corman offered him a forum for his ambitions, casting him in THE WILD ANGELS (1966) and THE TRIP (1967) before the surprise success of Dennis Hopper's EASY RIDER (1969) carried Fonda out of Corman's range.

CARL FRANKLIN (director) Franklin's career in front of the camera ranged from supporting parts in FIVE ON THE BLACK HAND SIDE (1973) and THE LAUGHING POLICEMAN (1974) to a featured role on TV's *The A-Team*. *Tired of acting*, he enrolled at AFI and Corman hired him before graduation to direct EYE OF THE EAGLE II: INSIDE THE ENEMY (1989) and FULL FATHOM FIVE (1990). Franklin went on to make the critically acclaimed ONE FALSE MOVE (1992), and graduated to big budget films like ONE TRUE THING (1998) and HIGH CRIMES (2002) .

MENACHEM GOLAN (producer/director) The Israeli-born exploitation mogul, a USC student, was looking for a way to get home to Israel for the summer; Corman offered him a job as his assistant on THE YOUNG RACERS (1963), which was shooting in Europe. With his cousin, Yoram Globus, Golan went on to acquire The Cannon Group, one of the biggest low-budget producers/distributors of the 1980s. When their partnership dissolved, Globus stayed with Cannon, while Golan resurfaced at the helm of 21st-Century Releasing.

CHARLES B. GRIFFITH (writer/producer/director) Griffith was introduced to Corman by actor Jonathan Haze in 1954, and became an early protege, writing or co-writing the screenplays for more than a dozen Corman-produced films, including Corman's own GUNSLINGER and THE UNDEAD (1956), ROCK ALL NIGHT, NAKED PARADISE, NOT OF THIS EARTH, ATTACK OF THE CRAB MONSTERS and TEENAGE DOLL (all 1958), BUCKET OF BLOOD (1959), LITTLE SHOP OF HORRORS (1960) and THE WILD ANGELS (1966) and Paul Bartel's DEATH RACE 2000. Fast, prolific and apparently unambitious, Griffith continues to write genre pictures, and directed his most recent film – WIZARDS OF THE LOST KINGDOM II (1989) – for Concorde/New Horizons.

MONTE HELLMAN (editor/director) UCLA graduate Hellman shot his inauspicious first film, THE BEAST FROM THE HAUNTED CAVE (1959) back-to-back with Roger Corman's SKI TROOP ATTACK to save money; it was produced by Gene Corman. He followed up with two low budget westerns starring Jack Nicholson and in 1974 Roger Corman produced his bizarre pre-Piano art/exploitation picture COCKFIGHTER, whose protagonist refuses to speak until he wins the Cockfighter of the Year award. Joe Dante cut the trailer, filling it – at Corman's behest – with exciting material gleaned from other New World films in a vain bid to snare audiences. Sam Peckinpah called Hellman the best editor in America, but his offbeat promise as a director went largely unfulfilled.

JACK HILL (writer/director) Auteur-who-might-have-been Hill attended UCLA with Francis Ford Coppola; in fact, he claims that the last third of APOCALYPSE NOW (1979) is based on his thesis film, THE HOST (1962), on which Coppola worked. Hill and Coppola worked together on two nudie pictures – TONIGHT FOR SURE and THE PLAYGIRLS AND THE BELLBOY (both 1962) – and Hill shot additional footage for Coppola's official first feature, DEMENTIA 13 (1963), produced by Corman. Hill toiled in various capacities for Corman, made the quirky SPIDER BABY (1965) and had some success in Blaxploitation films. His last picture was for Corman, 1982's SORCERESS, from a screenplay by Jim Wynorski; Hill was so unhappy with the result that he removed his name.

(BET)TINA HIRSCH (editor/director) Hirsch began her career cutting Robert Downey's PUTNEY SWOPE (1969) and Michael Wadleigh's WOODSTOCK (1970), then edited several Corman productions, including BIG BAD MAMA (1974), Paul Bartel's DEATHRACE 2000 (1975) and EAT MY DUST (1976). Bigger budget credits include Joe Dante's EXPLORERS (1985) and GREMLINS (1984), Dante's PEAK (1997) and STEALING SINATRA (2003). Hirsch directed one movie, MUNCHIES (1987) for Corman.

RON HOWARD (director) Former child actor Howard grew up in public on *The Andy Griffith Show*; he directed his first film, GRAND THEFT AUTO (1977), for Roger Corman and is now a major mainstream player. He is one-third of Imagine Entertainment and has directed such middlebrow hits as SPLASH (1984), COCOON (1985), PARENTHOOD (1989), APOLLO 13 (1995), HOW THE GRINCH STOLE CHRISTMAS (2000) and A BEAUTIFUL MIND (2001).

DENNIS HOPPER (actor/director) Perennial bad boy Hopper was temperamentally unsuited to acting within the studio system, but found a home in exploitation movies and worked within the Roger Corman orbit on several films, including Curtis Harrington's NIGHT TIDE (1961) and QUEEN OF BLOOD (1966) and Corman's own THE TRIP (1967). Like Jack Nicholson and Peter Fonda, Hopper's career was revitalized by EASY RIDER (1969), which he wrote and directed.

GALE ANNE HURD (producer/writer) A Phi Beta Kappa graduate of Stanford University, Hurd toiled as Corman's assistant at New World Pictures, where she met aspiring director James Cameron while he was working on Barbara Peeters' inglorious HUMANOIDS FROM THE DEEP (1980). Hurd and Cameron were married, and she produced his hits THE TERMINATOR (1984), ALIENS (1986) and TERMINATOR 2: JUDGEMENT DAY (1991). Following their divorce, she married Brian DePalma, and produced his RAISING CAIN (1992) before they divorced, then wed prolific screenwriter Jonathan Hensleigh.

AMY (HOLDEN) JONES (writer/director/editor) 1975 AFI Film Festival award winner Jones was offered a job as a PA on TAXI DRIVER (1976) by judge Martin Scorsese, who also introduced her to Corman. She cut HOLLYWOOD BOULEVARD (1976) with Joe Dante and Allan Arkush, and later directed THE SLUMBER PARTY MASSACRE (1982) for Corman. Corman also produced her LOVE LETTERS (1983). Holden wrote INDECENT PROPOSAL (1993), and co-wrote Roger Donaldson's 1994 remake of THE GETAWAY, as well as all four installments of the BEETHOVEN kiddie dog-movie franchise.

JONATHAN KAPLAN (director) Child actor and NYU graduate Kaplan, a student film award winner, was recommended to Roger Corman by Martin Scorsese; Corman hired him to direct NIGHT CALL NURSES (1972). Kaplan, whose later credits include HEART LIKE A WHEEL (1983), Academy Award-winning THE ACCUSED (1988), UNLAWFUL ENTRY (1992), BROKEDOWN PALACE (1997) and a 1996 television remake of IN COLD BLOOD, credits Corman with giving him the most specific, practical criticism of his career after the first NIGHT CALL NURSES screening.

GARY KURTZ (producer) Former sound recordist Kurtz helped Corman divvy up footage from ill-fated Yugoslavian thriller OPERACIJA TICIJIAN (1962) – which wound up in Jack Hill's BLOOD BATH (1964) and PORTRAIT IN TERROR (1965), as well as Stephanie Rothman's TRACK OF THE VAMPIRE (1964) – whose production Francis Ford Coppola supervised, but is best known as the producer of George Lucas's original STAR WARS trilogy (1977, etc.).

JACK NICHOLSON (actor) The master of the sexy and insinuating sneer started his career with the lead in Roger Corman's THE CRY BABY KILLER (1958), but until EASY RIDER (1969) made him a star, Nicholson's career was a succession of small parts in smaller movies. He appeared in Corman's Little SHOP OF HORRORS (1960) and THE TERROR (1963) – a notorious mish-mash that included footage shot by Monte Hellman, Francis Ford Coppola, Jack Hill and even Nicholson himself – as well as Hellman's THE SHOOTING and RIDE IN THE WHIRLWIND (both 1966), and even wrote THE TRIP (1967) for Corman when his acting career was at a particularly low ebb. Nicholson went on to super stardom in films that included THE LAST DETAIL (1973) and CHINATOWN (1974), written by fellow Corman graduate Robert Towne.

TONY RANDEL (director) Randel started out in the mailroom of Corman's New World Pictures, rising through the ranks to amass such credits as special effects editor on BATTLE BEYOND THE STARS (1980), GALAXY OF TERROR (1981) and John Carpenter's ESCAPE FROM NEW YORK (1981), editor of SPACE RAIDERS (1983) and producer of the American version of GODZILLA (1985). He's gone on to direct horror films, including HELLBOUND: HELLRAISER 2 (1988), CHILDREN OF THE NIGHT (1991) and TICKS (1994).

KATT SHEA (RUBEN) (writer/director) Teacher-turned-actress Ruben studied briefly at UCLA and found minor roles in exploitation films, including a troubled Corman production called BARBARIAN QUEEN (1985). She pitched in and shot 2nd unit, then approached Corman with an idea for a feature about strippers, STRIPPED TO KILL (1987). With then-husband and still partner Andy Ruben, she made three more films for Corman before graduating to POISON IVY (1992), with Drew Barrymore, THE RAGE: CARRIE 2 (1999).

CHUCK RUSSELL (writer/producer/director) Russell started out as second assistant director on Paul Bartel's DEATH RACE 2000 (1975), which Corman produced. He went on to produce David Schmoeller's THE SEDUCTION (1982) and Joseph Ruben's DREAMSCAPE (1984), and made his directing debut with the third entry in the NIGHTMARE ON ELM STREET series before graduating to mainstream genre items like THE MASK (1994), ERASER (1996), BLESS THE CHILD (2000) and THE SCORPION KING (2002).

JOHN SAYLES (writer/director) Fiercely independent writer/director Sayles' first screenplay credits was on the Corman-produced PIRANHA (1978), directed by Joe Dante. Sayles' later work, starting with THE RETURN OF THE SECAUCUS SEVEN (1979), has been more high-minded – though he did write the splendidly entertaining SOMETHING WILD for Jonathan Demme in 1986 – and produced such complex multi-character dramas as LONE STAR (1996), LINBO (1999) and SUNSHINE STATE (2002)

MARTIN SCORSESE (writer/producer/director) NYU film school graduate-turned-teacher Scorsese had made two independent films when Roger Corman hired him to direct BOXCAR BERTHA (1972), a depression-era drama designed to cash in on the success of BONNIE AND CLYDE (1967). Corman stood up for Scorsese when higher-ups at distributor AIP, notably exploitation veteran Samuel Z. Arkoff, wanted to fire him for excessive artiness (Scorsese had already suffered that fate once, on 1970's THE HONEYMOON KILLERS, finished by and credited to one-time director Leonard Kastle). Scorsese quickly began recommending his NYU students and associates to Corman, and many careers were launched.

DERAN SARAFIAN (director) The son of director Richard Sarafian, Sarafian attended USC (though he never enrolled) and worked as a PA on two Corman productions, Allan Arkush's ROCK 'N' ROLL HIGH SCHOOL (1979) and Nick Castle's TAG: THE ASSASSINATION GAME (1982). He then moved to Italy (ostensibly to study film with Fellini), and directed his first two films. Sarafian moved steadily up the action/adventure ladder with pictures like Jean-Claude Van Damme's DEATH WARRANT (1990), BACK IN THE USSR (1991), GUNMEN (1993) and TERMINAL VELOCITY (1994). He now works primarily in episodic television.

ADAM SIMON (writer/director) Simon came out of a film studies background and directed one of the last truly theatrical films produced by Corman, the rubber-reality picture BRAIN DEAD (1990). Simons also made CARNOSAUR (1993), produced by Corman to cash in on Steven Spielberg's JURASSIC PARK (both 1993), which co-starred Laura Dern. Corman pulled off the exploitation casting coup of the summer by nabbing Dern's mother, Diane Ladd, who – already pregnant with Laura – made THE WILD ANGELS with her then-husband, Bruce Dern 25 years earlier. Simon has also made two documentaries about filmmaking: THE TYPEWRITER, THE RIFLE & THE MOVIE CAMERA (1995), about Sam Fuller, and THE AMERICAN NIGHTMARE (2000), which examines independent horror movies of the 1970s within their larger social and political contexts.

LEWIS TEAGUE (editor/director) NYU graduate and editor Teague wet his feet as director by shooting cockfights for COCKFIGHTER (1974) when the squeamish Monte Hellman refused. Teague's dailies made many viewers feel ill. He was second unit director on Paul Bartel's DEATHRACE 2000 (1975); Corman's wife, Julie, produced THE LADY IN RED (1979), another Sayles script, for him, and he went on to mainstream success with THE JEWEL OF THE NILE (1985) and now works frequently in television.

ROBERT TOWNE (writer/director) The idol of would-be screenwriters, Towne got his first script credit on Roger Corman's THE LAST WOMAN ON EARTH (1960); he also wrote Corman's THE TOMB OF LIGEIA (1965). Towne went on to bigger and better things with THE LAST DETAIL (1973) and CHINATOWN (1974), both starring fellow Corman alumnus Jack Nicholson, and more recently wrote the mega-budget MISSION: IMPOSSIBLE films.

JIM WYNORSKI (writer/producer/director) Determined to work for Roger Corman, Wynorski was offered a job in New World's publicity department, where his creative promotional strategies, which included making an eye-catching trailer for SCREAMERS (1979) that consisted entirely of footage not in the film, recall those of Joe Dante. Wynorski wrote several screenplays for Corman and directed sequels to several Corman productions, including BIG BAD MAMA II (1987) and DEATHSTALKER 2 (1988), and remade Corman's NOT OF THIS EARTH (1988), starring porn nymphet Traci Lords. In the great Corman tradition, NOT OF THIS EARTH was the result of a bet: Wynorski wagered that he could remake the film on the original shooting schedule and budget, adjusted for inflation. He won. The incredibly prolific Wynorski makes direct-to-video/DVD genre movies at a rate that would make most filmmakers slow down.

Notes

1. From *The Face on the Cutting Room Floor* (William Morrow and Company: New York, 1964), Murray Schumach's study of American movie and TV censorship, p. 280. These excerpts are from the 1956 version of the Production Code, which was revised frequently during the three decades during which it guided (or oppressed) mainstream filmmakers. Following its statement of principles, the Code goes on to discuss with great specificity the acceptable treatment of crime, brutality, sex, vulgarity, obscenity, blasphemy and profanity, religion, "special subjects" (bedroom scenes, hangings and electrocutions, liquor and drinking, surgical operations and childbirth and third degree methods), national feelings and cruelty to animals. Guidelines regarding costumes ("complete nudity, in fact or silhouette, is never permitted") and titles ("titles which are salacious, indecent, obscene, profane or vulgar" are forbidden) are also made clear.
2. 'An Appalling Plague Has Been Loosed on Our Films', *The New York Times*, September 19, 1971, p.13
3. For more on Corman's crew, see the sidebar
4. Cagin, Seth and Dray, Philip, *Hollywood Films of the Seventies*, p.47.

New Hollywood and the Sixties Melting Pot

Jonathan Rosenbaum

Let me begin with a few printed artifacts, all of them from New York in the early 1960s: two successive issues of the *NY Film Bulletin* published in early 1962, special numbers devoted to Last Year at Marienbad and François Truffaut; and three successive issues of *Film Culture*, dated winter 1962, winter 1962-63, and spring 1963. Cheaply printed but copiously illustrated, the two special numbers of the *NY Film Bulletin* are the 43rd and 44th issues of a monthly, respectively twenty and twenty-eight pages in length. The Last Year at Marienbad issue consists exclusively of interviews with Alain Resnais, Alain Robbe-Grillet, and editor Henri Colpi, all translated from French magazines, and a briefly annotated Resnais filmography. The Truffaut issue – apart from a translation of Truffaut's André Bazin obituary from *Cahiers du cinéma*, brief script extracts from Shoot the Piano Player and Jules and Jim, and a Truffaut filmography – contains all new material: articles on Shoot the Piano Player by the magazine's editors Marshall Lewis and Andrew Sarris and its publisher R.M. Franchi, and a ten-page interview with Truffaut by Franchi and Lewis. In *Film Culture* no. 26, eighty pages long, articles on Preston Sturges (by Manny Farber and others), Frank Tashlin, and Vincente Minnelli's Two Weeks in Another Town (the latter two by Peter Bogdanovich) rub shoulders with with a translation of the 'scenario' (i.e., treatment) of Jean-Luc Godard's Vivre sa Vie, P. Adams Sitney writing about Stan Brakhage's Anticipation of the Night and Prelude, two statements by experimental animator Robert Breer, an interview with Soviet director Grigori Chukhrai, and an article about L'Avventura, La Dolce Vita, and Breathless, among other pieces; on the cover is a reproduction of the opening title of Orson Welles's Mr. Arkadin. No. 27, in addition to featuring Farber again (this time on 'White Elephant Art vs. Termite Art'), includes Sarris's 'Notes on the Auteur Theory in 1962', Pauline Kael on Shoot the Piano Player, Jack Smith on 'The Perfect Filmic Appositeness of Maria Montez', Gregory Markopoulos on Ron Rice, more material on Breer, and a special section on Welles's celebrated 1938 *War of the Worlds* radio broadcast. And sixty-seven of the ninety-six pages of No. 28 are devoted to Sarris's soon-to-be-notorious and highly influential 'The American Cinema', later to be expanded into a book.

The point of these summaries is to give some notion of the kind of heady mix that was integral to American film culture during this period – a period when, for better and for worse, there was still only one film culture, however charged with controversy and disagreements that culture might have been. The rapid growth of academic film studies was still not to come for about another decade, and the even more dizzying changes brought about by the distribution of movies on videotape and the quantum leaps in promotion for big-studio product were even further away. At this stage, there was only a vast number of movies of different kinds being made, written about, and debated, often in the pages of the same magazines.

Though something resembling the same mix was evident in the UK around the same time, in the pages of such alternative film journals as 'Motion'and 'Movie' – without the American avant-garde, one might add, but with a similar kind of interfacing between Hollywood and continental art films – the most salient difference was that in the United States, at least, a multifaceted redefinition of the American cinema was fully in progress that involved not only a reconsideration of what it had been, but also a great deal of thought about what it might be.

Unlike the relatively staid pluralism of more established Anglo-American film journals during this period, such as *Film Quarterly* and *Sight and Sound* – which were also reflecting some of the changes that were taking place in film culture, but without celebrating them all in quite so partisan a fashion – these magazines were basically giving vent to minority positions, and a central aspect of those positions was a broadening of the usual definitions of what constituted art in movies. Within the mainstream press of both the UK and the U.S., Alfred Hitchcock and Howard Hawks were still regarded as frivolous entertainers and nothing more while the models of respectable American art films generally entailed solemn treatments of weighty subjects without the 'intrusions' of personal, directorial styles (Stanley Kramer's JUDGMENT AT NUREMBERG might stand as the locus classicus of this position). Meanwhile, the American underground – despite the recent splashes made by the first features of John Cassavetes (SHADOWS) and Shirley Clarke (THE CONNECTION) – was mainly regarded as marginal and parochial; Dwight Macdonald wrote sympathetically about both of these films in *Esquire*, a national mainstream publication, but was hostile to most other manifestations of the movement, such as Jonas Mekas's GUNS OF THE TREES, and he completely (and characteristically) ignored such figures as Brakhage, Markopoulos, Breer, and Rice.

Among the key revelations to be found in these magazines were Resnais's enthusiasm for such Hollywood pictures as SINGIN' IN THE RAIN and SUSPICION and Truffaut's buried references to Hitchcock, William Saroyan, Rossellini, LOLA MONTEZ, and the Marx Brothers in SHOOT THE PIANO PLAYER (as signalled by Sarris). But it was also quickly becoming apparent that the multiple references to Hollywood in so-called New Wave pictures from France

– the recreated sequence from GILDA and the life-size cutout of Hitchcock in MARIENBAD, the references to Bogart and Boetticher and Samuel Fuller's FORTY GUNS in BREATHLESS – were beginning to be matched by evocations of European art films in certain Hollywood movies as well: the parodic nods to both LA DOLCE VITA and MARIENBAD in the party scenes of TWO WEEKS IN ANOTHER TOWN, for instance, or the disorienting shifts between genres in THE MANCHURIAN CANDIDATE, which created much the same sort of critical confusion and controversy as the comparable shifts in SHOOT THE PIANO PLAYER – though, to the best of my knowledge, critics showed little if any awareness of this latter similarity at the time, including such rare champions of both films as Pauline Kael. For Kael, "the closest an American movie has come to the constantly surprising mixture in SHOOT THE PIANO PLAYER" was Robert Altman's M*A*S*H, released eight years later.

It's important to stress that the readership of such magazines as the *NY Film Bulletin* and *Film Culture* was extremely limited and, with few exceptions, local; copies could be found in a few specialised bookshops in Manhattan, but seldom anywhere else. Moreover, the foreign and experimental films that were written about in such magazines often had a circulation that was just as limited; foreign films that fared poorly at the box office in New York were unlikely to turn up in other cities, and apart from a handful of outposts in the rest of the country, most experimental films had limited screenings even in New York, and were likely to turn up elsewhere, if at all, only several months or even years later. Consequently, though some Hollywood directors would have been able to see some of the better known French New Wave movies of this period – e.g., LAST YEAR AT MARIENBAD and JULES AND JIM, but not PARIS NOUS APPARTIENT or LES BONNES FEMMES – the odds of them seeing films by Stan Brakhage or Robert Breer were relatively slim.

Consequently, in order to discuss the formal and stylistic influence of European art films and American experimental films on Hollywood filmmakers of the 1960s and early 1970s, it is difficult to postulate any direct lineages in any but a few exceptional cases. We know, for example, that Dennis Hopper, partially as a result of his connections with the world of contemporary painting, sculpture, and photography, was familiar with some of the experimental works of Bruce Connor and Andy Warhol (among others) when he was making EASY RIDER (1969) and THE LAST MOVIE (1971), and that he even made one or more (undocumented) experimental shorts himself prior to these features. Similarly, we can be fairly confident that when Martin Scorsese was directing TAXI DRIVER several years later, he had seen Michael Snow's WAVELENGTH and BACK AND FORTH and Godard's 2 OU 3 CHOSES QUE JE SAIS D'ELLE – though it is crucial to bear in mind that TAXI DRIVER was made in New York and that

Scorsese routinely sees many films that most of his Hollywood colleagues would never have even heard of.

But in order to speak of European or American avant-garde filmmaking making a dent on Hollywood – even during one of the few periods of this century when the U.S. was relatively open to outside cultural influences – it becomes necessary to postulate many intervening forces and way stations, and to acknowledge that any comprehensive account of such influences would have to draw on a detailed exhibition history that has never been written and almost certainly never will be. Indeed, before one even attempts to sketch such an account, four methodological obstacles should be cited at the outset:

1. The issue of direct or indirect influence is often much more complex than many critics prefer to believe. Direct imitation or citation tends to be acknowledged much more readily than any less obvious assimilation or application of influence, which generally shows more thoughtfulness and creativity on the part of the filmmaker. One case in point might be the example of Michael Wadleigh's WOODSTOCK (1970), arguably the greatest of all American documentaries made during the 1960s and early 1970s. On the face of it, WOODSTOCK bears no trace of any direct influence from either vanguard European or American underground filmmaking of the same period. Yet because the French New Wave inspired an international generation of filmmakers to draw more freely and widely from the pool of techniques available from film history, including the silent film – as evidenced by, say, the use of the iris in BREATHLESS and the uses of masking in SHOOT THE PIANO PLAYER and JULES AND JIM – it is certainly possible that Wadleigh could have been inspired by their example to draw liberally from the techniques of the great city films of the 1920s, works such as King Vidor's THE CROWD, Paul Fejos's LONESOME, F.W. Murnau's SUNRISE, Walter Ruttmann's BERLIN, SYMPHONY OF A GREAT CITY, and Dziga Vertov's The Man with a Movie Camera. (Significantly, Vidor himself expressed admiration for the drama and spectacle of WOODSTOCK's rainstorm sequence; and if Wadleigh's own 'city' consisted of some 400,000 young people camped out in a New York pasture, it seems entirely possible that his superimpositions, split-screen framings, and diverse forms of associative and rhythmic editing all stemmed directly or indirectly from the strategies of late silent films in dealing with the multiplicity and energy of urban crowds.)

2. An astonishing number of influential and/or pertinent American independent films of the early 1960s have been virtually forgotten and lost to history, at least if one relies on most 'standard' written accounts. To an alarming extent, contemporary academic studies of this subject in the U.S. essentially recycle the titles already found in a small number of books and

journals and make little effort to move beyond them. Thus in order to be aware of the major contemporary impact made by Peter Emanuel Goldman's New York independent feature ECHOES OF SILENCE (1965) or the fact that future Hollywood filmmakers John Milius and George Lucas made experimental short films as students at the University of Southern California during the 1960s, it virtually becomes necessary to refer to personal experiences rather than printed sources. In the case of Goldman's film, I can refer to my own experiences, having seen ECHOES OF SILENCE in New York during the mid-1960s and read about it in many New York publications at the time; in the case of Milius's and Lucas's early work – or the early experimental work of Hopper mentioned above – I have to depend on the memories of a west coast colleague and filmmaker, Thom Andersen, who was a film student at the University of Southern California at the same time as Milius and Lucas, and saw some of Hopper's early work in Los Angeles during the same period. Characteristically, neither Goldman's name nor this information about Hopper, Milius, and Lucas can be found in such supposedly 'definitive' reference works as P. Adams Sitney's *Visionary Film: The American Avant-Garde 1943 – 1978* or David E. James's more recent *Allegories of Cinema: American Film in the Sixties*, and these are only four examples of routine omissions that could undoubtedly be counted in the hundreds.

3. By and large, the cultural and geographical distances separating New York from Hollywood are too vast to allow one to consider either as a single cultural capital in the same way that Paris, London, Rome, or Vienna are, and appearances in Europe to the contrary, there are almost as many factors separating the east and west coasts of the U.S. as there are factors separating, say, New York from Paris or London.

4. The exhibition histories of films, both commercial and independent, in the U.S. and in Europe, are often quite separate and at variance with one another. Thus the dates most commonly assigned to European films in most U.S. print sources are not when they were made but when they were first released in the States, and the same problem often crops up with the dates assigned in Europe to many American films. To cite one salient example, Monte Hellman's THE SHOOTING and RIDE IN THE WHIRLWIND, two westerns that he shot back to back in the mid-1960s, were widely known in European film magazines of that period as examples of the 'New American Cinema', but not in many American film magazines because the films never received any theatrical release in the U.S.; their 'discovery' by film-conscious filmmakers such as Quentin Tarantino came only decades later. Similarly, Peter Emanuel Goldman's WHEEL OF ASHES, shot in Europe with

Pierre Clementi circa the late 1960s, was to the best of my knowledge seen only in Europe.

Based on the limited information that we do have, the principal examples of American 'underground' and experimental films that were widely seen in the 1960s were mainly shown in contexts that associated them with the burgeoning counterculture of that period: carnivalesque screenings, many of them held at midnight, that were popular precisely because they tended to defy the sexual, sociopolitical, and aesthetic taboos of more conventional film-going, and often attracted attention because of police raids and other censorship problems that resulted from this defiance. Screenings of Kenneth Anger's SCORPIO RISING, Jack Smith's FLAMING CREATURES, and Jean Genet's UN CHANT D'AMOUR all led on many occasions to arrests of exhibitors who showed them, and if one considers that Warhol's early films and Gregory Markopoulos's TWICE A MAN were first being shown during the same period (1963-64), it becomes clear that explicit homoerotic content had a great deal to do with what made these films popular as well as controversial. And although Warhol continued to direct (and later, produce or at least lend his name to) several homoerotic features during the 1960s, this emphasis in popular underground filmmaking largely became supplanted by an emphasis on other factors relating more to hallucinogenic drugs and various visual patterns associated with them.

Both the homoerotic and the hallucinogenic waves in experimental film were directly influential on commercial filmmaking in a number of ways, highlighting the degree to which their wider public impact generally had more to do with their subject matter and with some of the visual styles arising from that subject matter than with their experimental aspects. The Warhol Superstar party attended by the heroes (Jon Voight and Dustin Hoffman) in John Schlesinger's MIDNIGHT COWBOY (1969) and some of the op art images in Roger Corman's THE TRIP are two obvious examples of how quickly certain elements in underground film could find their way to the surface of mainstream productions.

The point at which major experimental films ceased to have this kind of public forum coincided with the advent of the so-called 'structural' film as exemplified by such works as Michael Snow's WAVELENGTH (1967), BACK AND FORTH (1969), and LA RÉGION CENTRALE (1971), Ken Jacobs's TOM TOM THE PIPER'S SON (1969/1971), and Hollis Frampton's NOSTALGIA (1971) – films associated with neither sexuality nor drugs in the minds of most viewers (though an intellectual minority continued to associate Snow's films with 'trips', in part because of his own interest in drugs). This turning point, moreover, corresponded closely in terms of both period and attitude to the institutionalizing of the American underground film via museums, archives, and academic film studies, which tended to remove experimental films from the social spaces of ordinary or makeshift movie theatres and relegate them to the "safer" confines of various institutional venues (mainly classrooms).

Prior to this change, the experimental film that was probably seen most widely and frequently was SCORPIO RISING, and the cultural impact it had, as suggested above, was not closely tied to its experimental aspects, having more to do with its iconography and sexuality and its use of pop records than to its unorthodox cutting and its relatively esoteric symbology. (Indeed, the important roles played in the film by clips of Marlon Brando from THE WILD ONE, a photograph of James Dean, panels from such comic strips as *Dick Tracy* and *Li'l Abner*, and a wind-up motorcycle toy all gave the film a much wider address than the mythical references of Anger's previous and subsequent films.) And the same could be said of the underground films that had the strongest commercial impact a few years later: Warhol's THE CHELSEA GIRLS (1966), Robert Downey's satirical CHAFED ELBOWS (1967), and, perhaps most significant of all, a travelling program of shorts packaged on the west coast by Mike Getz (an exhibitor who had previously been brought to trial for showing SCORPIO RISING) that played in weekend midnight slots at a circuit of theatres owned by Getz's uncle, Louis Sher. The first such program, which went out in early 1967 under the label "Psychedelic Film Trips #1", included George Kuchar's HOLD ME WHILE I'M NAKED, Storm De Hirsch's PEYOTE QUEEN, and Stan Vanderbeek's BREATHDEATH, and according to J. Hoberman – whose chapter on 'The Underground' in our co-authored book *Midnight Movies* is the chief source of this survey – this very successful enterprise peaked in 1969, when it reached twenty-two cities in the U.S., though it continued until the mid-1970s.

Though some of these underground movies exerted an effect on 1960s Hollywood by helping to loosen up the general public's sense of what was acceptable in commercial movies – in terms of subject matter, style, and even certain technical standards – their influence was considerably less pronounced than the impact of vanguard European filmmaking during the same years. But to examine more closely the effects of both strains on Hollywood during the 1960s and early 1970s, it would help to turn to a few individual cases. In some, I'll be focusing more on the films themselves, and in others I'll be discussing mainly their critical receptions. As is suggested by my examples, I think it can be argued that, with few exceptions, many of the biggest commercial successes in Hollywood can be attributed more to their popularizing of elements from European films than to their popularizing of elements from the American underground.

Exhibit #A: THE GRADUATE. Released toward the end of 1967, Mike Nichols's second feature went on to become the top Hollywood money maker of 1968, and its enormous success was – and still is – widely ascribed to the rebellious youth culture of the period. This may seem curious if one considers that Benjamin, the title hero (Dustin Hoffman in his first movie role), wears a coat and tie throughout the picture, unlike his hippie contemporaries, and that his rebellion relates exclusively to personal rather than social or political issues – his determination to marry the daughter (Katharine Ross) of his father's law partner after having an adulterous affair with her mother, Mrs. Robinson (Anne Bancroft). Indeed, one of the film's running gags in its latter section is the erroneous impression of a rooming-house landlord in Berkeley that Benjamin is some sort of campus radical when he doesn't even remotely resemble one.

In order to contextualize this anomaly, it becomes helpful to look at the other top moneymaking pictures of the 1960s that had some relationship with "rebellious" youth culture: SPLENDOR IN THE GRASS (1961, set mainly in the late 1920s), BYE BYE BIRDIE (1962), an adaptation of a stage musical about the impact of a rock-and-roll singer on a small town), A HARD DAY'S NIGHT (1964, a film about and starring the Beatles), THE WILD ANGELS (1966, an exploitation feature about a motorcycle gang), BLOW-UP (1967, Michelangelo Antonioni's art film about 'swinging London', the only foreign film in this category), 2001: A SPACE ODYSSEY (1968), and EASY RIDER (1969). None of these pictures with the possible exception of the last one can be accurately described as an expression or even representation of 1960s counterculture apart from a few passing elements; as with the Vietnam war, there was an evident lag time between what was happening in American culture and what the most commercially successful Hollywood pictures were prepared and willing to show. Significantly, when Antonioni himself dealt directly with American counterculture in ZABRISKIE POINT (1970), the film was a resounding flop with audiences and critics alike, and the same could be said of Otto Preminger's SKIDOO the previous year; perhaps only WOODSTOCK (1970) succeeded both in dealing directly with the counterculture and in reaching a wide mainstream audience.

In the case of THE GRADUATE, coming during the middle of this period, the sense of 'newness' undoubtedly came less from the film's subject matter than from its offscreen songs by Simon & Garfunkel – most of them already recorded and released before the film was made – and, above all, from the eclectic, free-wheeling, and attention-grabbing visual style. (Its comic verbal style, by contrast, could be traced in many ways back to Mike Nichols's own satiric routines with Elaine May, which began in the mid-1950s.) And much of that style had clear antecedents in some of the better-known art films of the early 1960s – work by such filmmakers as Truffaut, Godard, Antonioni, Fellini, and even, to a more debatable extent, Cassavetes.

The film's first extended sequence, for instance, is a party given for Benjamin by his well-to-do parents in Los Angeles, attended exclusively by the parents' friends, and this sequence is filmed almost exclusively in claustrophobic close-ups and hand-held camera movements. The style has a great deal in common with the style of party sequences in Cassavetes's SHADOWS (1959) as well as in his subsequent Hollywood feature TOO LATE BLUES (1962) – the release of his better-known FACES was not to come until 1968 – although Andrew Sarris, in his contemporary review of THE GRADUATE, noted that these "bobbing, tracking, lurching heads in nightmarishly mobile close-ups looks like an 'homage' to Fellini's 8 1/2", which indeed could be a likelier source. Either way, it is a sequence that looks nothing like standard Hollywood filmmaking of the 1960s and a great deal like what was then being identified with certain alternative filmmaking practices. (Pointedly, in his same review of THE GRADUATE, Sarris plausibly noted that "A rain-drenched Anne Bancroft splattered against a starkly white wall evokes images in [Antonioni's] LA NOTTE," and he also cited possible derivations in the film from Agnès Varda's LE BONHEUR and the 'landscape work' of American independent John Korty – both reference points of that period that are less likely to be cited or remembered today.)

An even more striking example of this tendency comes at the end of the protracted comic seduction of Benjamin by Mrs. Robinson, his future girlfriend's mother, who has already ordered him to drive her home from the aforementioned party and has subsequently issued a series of further commands to him when they are alone in her house – to have a drink, to accompany her upstairs, and so on – as she proceeds to remove part of her clothing. This climaxes in a brief scene in which Benjamin, alone in Mrs. Robinson's daughter's room, sees reflected in a framed portrait of the daughter the nude figure of Mrs. Robinson (the only name he or the dialogue ever assigns her) entering the room and closing the door behind her. When Benjamin spins around to face her, this single gesture is broken up by the editing into four separate dovetailing shots, each filmed from a different angle, all but the last of which is so brief that the effect is mainly subliminal. (The successive lengths of the four shots are fifteen frames, thirteen frames, one single frame, and then, as Benjamin says "Oh, God!", seventy frames.) Insofar as the early features of Godard and Truffaut can be said to have visual tropes, this is clearly one of them, though the use of it here is more pointedly and exclusively tied to the viewer's identification with the subjectivity of a single character than it would have been in the French originals.

This is followed by other shots of Benjamin's frantic responses to Mrs. Robinson, punctuated by other near-subliminal shots of her nude body – ten frames of her midriff, four frames of one of her breasts, and five frames of her navel – which effectively suggest the sources of his panic without spelling them out. In this case, it is more difficult to point to precise New Wave counterparts and more likely that the pressures of studio censorship led to some of the subliminal abridgements of shots. (THE GRADUATE, one should note, came out after the far-ranging revision of the Production Code in 1966 and prior to the launching of the rating system in 1968 – an inbetween period in more ways than one.) Still, the titillating effect of these brief inserts and their stylistic eclecticism both point to the recent inroads made by New Wave films on Hollywood thinking and practices. And the same could be said for many of the other stylistic flourishes of THE GRADUATE, ranging from sound overlaps (such as the beginning of a subsequent scene's dialogue over the end of the previous sequence) to fancy camera setups (e.g., Mrs. Robinson appearing at a hotel bar rendezvous with Benjamin as a reflection on a glass table) to extended uses of first-person camera (such as the sequence featuring Benjamin inside a deep-sea diving suit, nearly all of it seen from his vantage point).

The most significant differences between the uses of such techniques in New Wave pictures and their uses in Hollywood usually have a great deal to do with the mechanics of storytelling and the identification of the viewer. If the stylistic play of BREATHLESS and SHOOT THE PIANO PLAYER generally had the effect of making the viewer identify with the filmmakers, the stylistic play of THE GRADUATE and many comparable Hollywood movies was more generally motivated by a desire to make the viewer identify with the screen characters, and even if a greater awareness of the director's role ensued from this process, this was mainly a surplus factor rather than the central one. (By the same token, if the editing of BREATHLESS or SHOOT THE PIANO PLAYER brought the viewer 'closer' to the characters in those films, this was also largely a surplus factor.) In THE MANCHURIAN CANDIDATE, on the other hand, intermittent audience identification with Laurence Harvey's assassin and other brainwashed American soldiers in the plot might be said to bring the viewer somewhat closer to an awareness of his or her position as passive, manipulated spectator – an experience roughly comparable to the state of metaphysical free fall afforded by identifying with Delphine Seyrig's character in LAST YEAR AT MARIENBAD.

Exhibit #B: BONNIE AND CLYDE. During the same year that THE GRADUATE was released, one could cite a good many other Hollywood features that showed the direct influence of the French New Wave. Even Howard Hawks's relatively 'classic' and conventional EL DORADO included a verbal reference to SHOOT THE PIANO PLAYER, which was interpreted by some contemporary critics as Hawks's acknowledgement of the critical appreciation for his work shown by several New Wave directors (and Sarris, for one, went even further and argued that the citation of Poe in EL DORADO also alluded to French criticism). But a more direct and consequential lineage could be traced through such Hollywood pictures as John Boorman's POINT BLANK and Stanley

Donen's Two For the Road (two very different pictures that featured Resnais-like editing and a fractured treatment of chronology), Francis Ford Coppola's You're a Big Boy Now (which might be regarded as an alternative version of The Graduate that failed to enjoy the same success), and, most influentially of all, Bonnie and Clyde, a script and project that was actually offered to both Godard and Truffaut at separate stages before Arthur Penn took it over.

In terms of its impact, Bonnie and Clyde – though it wasn't commercially successful enough at first to become one of the top twenty money makers of 1967, and only subsequently was tabulated as the fifteenth top money maker of the 1960s (in contrast to The Graduate, which came in second) – probably had a stronger influence on subsequent Hollywood pictures than any of the titles cited above, including The Graduate. The pattern of relatively 'unsuccessful' pictures exerting more lasting influence than certified hits is not, of course, restricted to Hollywood; Shoot the Piano Player and Band of Outsiders, the two French films that probably had the strongest influence on Bonnie and Clyde, weren't commercial successes in either France or the U.S. And it was probably Bonnie and Clyde, out of all the Hollywood pictures released in 1967, that most decisively converted certain attitudes and stylistic devices of the French New Wave into a lasting part of the American mainstream. Along with the early Sergio Leone westerns that preceded it and The Wild Bunch, which appeared two years later, this tragicomic period thriller about the 1930s exploits of an outlaw couple was the film that made extravagant bloodletting aesthetically acceptable in the commercial cinema at large.

Interestingly enough, for Pauline Kael, who was in some ways Bonnie and Clyde's biggest and most significant American champion, the French sources were not altogether a good thing, at least in the way that Penn applied them. One paragraph in her famous, extended defence of the film deserves quoting in full: "If this way of holding more than one attitude toward life is already familiar to us – if we recognize the make-believe robbers whose toy guns produce real blood, and the Keystone cops who shoot them dead, from Truffaut's Shoot the Piano Player and Godard's gangster pictures, Breathless and Band of Outsiders – it's because the young French directors discovered the poetry of crime in American life (from our movies) and showed the Americans how to put it on the screen in a new, 'existential' way. Melodramas and gangster movies and comedies were always more our speed than 'prestigious,' 'distinguished' pictures; the French directors who grew up on American pictures found poetry in our fast action, laconic speech, plain gestures. And because they understood that you don't express your love of life by denying the comedy or the horror of it, they brought out the poetry in our tawdry subjects. Now Arthur Penn, working with a script [by Robert Benton and David Newman] heavily influenced – one might almost say inspired – by Truffaut's

SHOOT THE PIANO PLAYER, unfortunately imitates Truffaut's artistry instead of going back to its tough American sources. The French may tenderize their American material, but we shouldn't. That turns into another way of making 'prestigious', 'distinguished' pictures."

Ideologically speaking, one might argue that the most pivotal words in this polemic are all first-person plural pronouns: 'us' and 'our' in the first sentence, 'our' (used twice) in the second, and 'we' in the fourth. They all imply a fundamental cleavage between French and American sensibilities, French and American audiences, and even what might be called French and American property in terms of both life and history, including film history. Thus both French cinephiles who might have regarded certain American crime pictures as 'our movies' – not necessarily to the exclusion of Americans, but in concert with them – and Americans who might have felt the same way about certain New Wave pictures become automatically and irrevocably excluded from Kael's line of reasoning; the very notion of a shared tradition is deemed inadmissible by definition. In more ways than one, the xenophobic underpinnings of Cold War rhetoric are faintly echoed in this kind of critical discourse, and these strains were to become more rather than less pronounced – and not only in Kael's prose – in the years to come. Though one has to acknowledge that Kael was offering here a sharp social critique of the American snobbery that during this period was often valuing continental filmmaking over its American sources – a form of snobbery that has subsequently all but vanished from the American mainstream – the fact remains that this passage reeks with intimations of property rights. Nor should it be overlooked that Kael herself is far from being entirely exempt from the cultural snobbery she assigns to other Americans; a phrase such as 'the poetry in our tawdry subjects' indirectly implies that French crime – and the whole strain of French filmmaking devoted to it, which she strategically ignores – is not so tawdry.

Significantly, Kael virtually began her defence of BONNIE AND CLYDE by calling it "the most excitingly American American movie since THE MANCHURIAN CANDIDATE." This meant factoring out any recognition of the fact that, quite apart from the possibility that THE MANCHURIAN CANDIDATE may have been influenced by the French New Wave, it could – and perhaps should – also be seen as an American movie that paralleled much of what was going on in the more adventurous strains of French filmmaking at the time by mixing various genres and traditions, to the consternation and confusion of many filmgoers on both sides of the Atlantic. The degree to which Americans and Europeans shared many traditions and assumptions during the early 1960s shouldn't be overlooked, however much this complicates the usual scenarios of influence and appropriation. This is not to argue that the same pictures were always understood in the same ways wherever they showed, only that to some extent Americans and Europeans were swimming in the same waters. If some Americans (as well as some Europeans) tended to miss many of the comic and parodic aspects of MARIENBAD, released the same year (1962), it seems likely that some European (as well as some American) viewers missed many of the equivalent elements in John Frankenheimer and George Axelrod's film.

It's also worth stressing that neither MARIENBAD nor THE MANCHURIAN CANDIDATE were films that could be assimilated to the same degree that BREATHLESS, SHOOT THE PIANO PLAYER, or BAND OF OUTSIDERS were when they first appeared. As Axelrod noted in 1968 of THE MANCHURIAN CANDIDATE, "it went from failure to classic without ever passing through success," and it probably wasn't until the film's re-release in 1988 that most critics were finally able to come to terms with it. By then, of course, the critical climate for what was acceptable in Hollywood cinema was considerably different.

But in the case of MARIENBAD, which enjoyed some success and notoriety as a foreign art-house film in 1962, the film can't be said to have 'survived' at all, critically or otherwise: today the film is available in the U.S. in 16-millimeter and on video only in a 'scanned' version that eliminates about a third of the image,* and in recent years it has never been re-released or revived in theatres in any form at all; very few filmgoers under the age of twenty-five have heard of it, and few of Resnais's recent features have been released in the U.S. Properly speaking, the license extended to experimentation in American commercial movie-going in the 1980s and 1990s goes no further than Hollywood; it can embrace a NATURAL BORN KILLERS – which might be regarded as the bastard great-grandson of BONNIE AND CLYDE, if not a movie with any comprehensible relationship to the American avant-garde – but not any foreign counterparts.

Exhibit #C: EASY RIDER (1969). For all its own – and more sophisticated – derivations from the American avant-garde, Dennis Hopper's first feature surely owed most of its commercial success to elements that had relatively little to do with this relationship. Perhaps the most important of these elements was Jack Nicholson's performance as an alcoholic, small-town southern lawyer who briefly joins the two heroes, Billy (Hopper) and Captain America (Peter Fonda, the film's producer), on their cross-country motorcycle trek to New Orleans – a fresh and multi-faceted character that benefited from Terry Southern's dialogue and was undoubtedly the major factor in turning Nicholson into a star. Another such element may have been the film's striking and unconventional handling of violent deaths, which critic Manny Farber wrote about perceptively at the time.

In his *Allegories of Cinema*, David E. James interestingly argues how Hopper's appropriation of 'alternative' film practices in EASY RIDER "lit the way for a new Hollywood" at the same time – and perhaps for the same reason – that it de-radicalised those practices. Some of his specific examples of appropriation, however, seem rather contestable: "[Several] visual motifs – flash cutting between shots, an extended interlude of subjective psychedelic vision, and an overall looseness in scene construction, for instance... [all] derive from previous alternative film: the basic motif of the journey from west to east and the overall ethical structure derive from Bruce Baillie's QUIXOTE; flash frames which signify subjectivity or anticipation, or which diffuse transitions between scenes, derive from Stan Brakhage; the hand-held camera and the use of anamorphic lenses in the trip sequence are the staple motifs of countless underground films; the caressing attention to the technological sensuousness of the motorcycles derives from Kenneth Anger's KUSTOM KAR KOMMANDOS, as the use of rock music structurally and as ironic counterpoint derives from his SCORPIO RISING; the occasional 'real life' confrontations, such as that with the young man in the street in New Orleans, are borrowed from *cinéma verité*; and the documentation of the counterculture and its more or less scandalous rituals – drugs, nudity, communal habitation – is the defining function of underground film as a whole, originating in the various documentations of beatnik life in the late fifties. But since Hopper fails to assimilate the film practices of various dissenting and countercultural groups into a coherent style," James goes on to say, "the film remains a pastiche, an essentially orthodox industrial product, decorated with unamalgamated infractions."

But these appropriations, which James goes so far as to label as plagiarisms, are in some cases arguably much less specific and localized than he implies. The "caressing attention" to "technological sensuousness" – i.e, the worshipful pans across the motorcycles of Billy and Captain America – seem to have at least as much to do with the motorcycles in SCORPIO RISING as they do with the custom-made hot rods in KUSTOM KAR KOMMANDOS, and Hopper's frequent use of pop records, which includes more than just rock music, has virtually none of the wit or irony of Anger's uses of "Fools Rush In," "Blue Velvet," "Look Like an Angel," and "Point of No Return" (among other songs) in SCORPIO RISING. It's also questionable whether the so-called 'flash frames' in EASY RIDER (virtually all of which last longer than single frames) are directly attributable to the more radical and relatively non-narrative editing strategies of Brakhage, or whether a journey from the west coast to the east coast necessarily entails any "plagiarism" of Baillie's QUIXOTE. In short, unlike the so-called "homages" to well-known film sequences that pepper the postmodernist Hollywood pictures of such 1970s filmmakers as Woody Allen, Peter Bogdanovich, Brian De Palma, and Martin Scorsese, Hopper's uses of elements from 'alternative' American filmmaking practices are generally not so much plagiarisms or appropriations as popularized applications, and the same could be said for most other crossovers from underground to mainstream.

Dennis Hopper in THE LAST MOVIE

Exhibits #D, #E and #F: THE LAST MOVIE, GLEN AND RANDA, and TWO-LANE BLACKTOP (1971). The second feature of Dennis Hopper, THE LAST MOVIE, marks both the beginning and the end of another, albeit related kind of experimentation - the radical American 'underground' film that aimed for mainstream or at least art film status and was fed by the American (as well as European) avant-garde, while Monte Hellman's TWO-LANE BLACKTOP and Jim McBride's GLEN AND RANDA represent related efforts that exist in the same, rather specialized no-man's-land. One could, of course, cite a good many other productions that exhibited a few of the same superficial characteristics: Hopper's own previous EASY RIDER (1969) and James William Guercio's ELECTRA GLIDE IN BLUE (1973), both of which showed the marked influence of SCORPIO RISING; Roger Corman's THE TRIP (1967), which was partially inspired by the 'psychedelic' imagery of other American experimental films, by Anger and others. Even some of Paul Mazursky's wholesale borrowings and appropriations of Fellini and Truffaut and his evocations of hippie culture in his 1970s pictures – stretching from ALEX IN WONDERLAND (1970), which included both Frederico Fellini and Jeanne Moreau in its cast (along with the latter's song from JULES AND JIM) to the no less feeble WILLIE AND PHIL (1980), an American 'remake' of JULES AND JIM - retrospectively belong to the same overall Zeit-geist, in spite of their more middle-class inflections.

But THE LAST MOVIE, as its very title suggests, is substantially more radical in form as well as content than any of these, and David E. James rightly shows how Hopper's multifaceted critique and analysis of Hollywood imperialism in a Third World context (a western being shot in a remote Peruvian village) logically led to the film's commercial failure: "In the context of an exploitative cinema of pleasure, its own constitution as analysis amounted to its constitu-tion as negation that could be legitimized only by the absoluteness of its rejec-tion by the degraded public." Featuring such Hollywood icons as Hopper himself and Samuel Fuller, and benefiting from a substantial budget, the film's bold oscillation between various uncompleted plots and its numerous self-ref-erential devices – such as the incorporation of unedited rushes, successive takes of the same shots, and even animated, handwritten titles announcing "Scene Missing" – staged a kind of ultimate shotgun marriage between Holly-wood and the avant-garde that could only confound and alienate the expecta-tions of both constituencies. Characteristically, the most common form of criti-cal rejection that greeted the film was seeing it as a failed commercial effort rather than as a calculated provocation with a logic and form of its own. (Pau-line Kael: "Hopper may have the makings of a movie [perhaps more than one], but he blew it in the editing room. If he was deliberate in not involving the au-dience, the audience that is not involved doesn't care whether he was deliber-ate or not. That there's method in the madness doesn't help. The editing sup-plies so little in the way of pace or rhythm that this movie performs the astounding feat of dying on the screen in the first few minutes, before the cred-its come on.") By the same token, the Hollywood budget accorded to Hopper seemed to guarantee a disinclination on the part of critics associated with ex-perimental films and art films to deal with the film seriously on any level at all, and in the final analysis, the film was effectively disenfranchised by the main-stream, the underground, and the art film intelligentsia alike, with equal vehe-mence.

Virtually the same thing would happen with both GLEN AND RANDA and TWO-LANE BLACKTOP, both released during the same year, and both offering complex and considered (albeit implicit rather than explicit) critiques of Hol-lywood in form as well as content. Viewed with some hindsight, the fate of all three features was more or less determined by the absence of any media ma-chinery that could accommodate a film that wasn't protected or claimed by any predefined social constituency. Concise packaging labels were in effect necessary before a film could qualify for membership in any of the existing canons: if it wasn't a Hollywood film or an art film or an experimental film in any obvious way, and if it didn't adequately conform to a clear genre classification within or outside any of these categories, in certain respects it didn't, and couldn't, exist critically at all, because influential critics at the time usually weren't disposed to create new categories in order to account for them. Thus it wasn't enough to classify GLEN AND RANDA as a science fiction film (although its story unfolded in the future, in a clearly post-apocalyptic and post-nuclear era) or TWO-LANE BLACKTOP as a car-racing movie (although most of its own story consisted of a race between two cars) because, in each case, and wholly in keeping with the implicit critique of the Hollywood genre propounded in each picture, the genre expectations set up by each of these classifications were deliberately thwarted.

Although he didn't write the original story in either case, the contributions of avant-garde novelist Rudolph Wurlitzer to the scripts of both these films seems emblematic of a certain literary sensibility, both existentialist and absurdist, that helped to confound these genre expectations. At this point in his career, Wurlitzer had published two Beckett-influenced modernist novels with certain countercultural trappings, *Nog* (1969) and *Flats* (1970), both of which had attained some literary prestige; perhaps for this reason, the script of TWO-LANE BLACKTOP was published in its entirety in a single issue of ESQUIRE prior to the film's release. But the literary audience that supported Wurlitzer seemed to have negligible crossover with the film audience, and the persistence of Wurlitzer's themes in these two pictures – much more pronounced in the case of TWO-LANE BLACKTOP – had scant effect on their critical or popular receptions. This points to a striking contrast with the more symbiotic and interactive literary and film worlds of France, where the contributions of Marguerite Duras and Alain Robbe-Grillet to the first two features of Alain Resnais played a more noticeable role in enhancing the reputations of these films. (Similarly, the art world strategies employed by Hopper in THE LAST MOVIE couldn't be recognized as such within the critical mainstream of either art criticism or film criticism – with the result that they were often written off as the drug-induced ravings of a maverick who had finally lost all perspective on his work.)

For all their aforementioned parallels, including Wurlitzer's participation, GLEN AND RANDA and TWO-LANE BLACKTOP were quite different in other respects. The former was the first relatively large-budget feature of a director, Jim McBride, who had previously worked only in the New York underground, in DAVID HOLZMAN'S DIARY (1967) and MY GIRLFRIEND'S WEDDING (1969) – two films that were highly influenced by the French New Wave, especially in their Godardian ambiguities regarding documentary and fiction. (The first was a pseudo-documentary fiction, the second a genuine documentary that played with various attributes of fiction.) Based on a story by Lorenzo Mans, an actor in DAVID HOLZMAN'S DIARY, GLEN AND RANDA was a playful fantasy and a cultural satire couched in the form of a science-fiction parable and shot in a pseudo-ethnographic style, charting the progress on foot of an illiterate hippie couple across the American northwest wilderness, after a nuclear holocaust, as the hero searches for the city of Metropolis, which he has 'learned' about from a Wonder Woman comic book. In terms of genre expectations, the only way an audience of science-fiction fans could have been satisfied would have been if GLEN AND RANDA had actually reached this mythical city, a possibility that both the film's pseudo-documentary style and its satirical vantage point precluded. (To underline this refusal to play by the Hollywood rules, the film's original, pre-release title was GLEN AND RANDA GO TO THE CITY, despite the fact that the film ends quixotically with the couple and their newborn child sailing off in the Pacific Ocean, still in search of Metropolis.)

TWO-LANE BLACKTOP, on the other hand, came from a director, Monte Hellman, who already had some background in low-budget, Hollywood genre filmmaking – THE BEAST FROM HAUNTED CAVE (1959), BACK DOOR TO HELL and FLIGHT TO FURY (1965), THE SHOOTING and RIDE IN THE WHIRLWIND (1966) – even though the latter two westerns, undoubtedly because of their own confounding of genre expectations, had never opened in the U.S. And the putative plot of TWO-LANE BLACKTOP, involving a cross-country race between two cars, seemed to promise action and adventure to an audience that might well have tolerated picaresque digressions in relation to this simple framework, particularly after the huge success of a film like EASY RIDER. But at least two strategies worked fairly systematically to undermine these expectations: (1) At least two of the leading roles were played by non-professionals, James Taylor and Laurie Bird, while the leading actor with the most visible skills, Warren Oates, played a character so deliberately mutable and unfixable – like the hero and narrator of Wurlitzer's NOG – that he was identified in the credits only by the name of his car, GTO. Taylor and Bird were identified in the same credits only as 'the driver' and 'the girl', and the film's overall treatment of personal identity was sufficiently abstract and 'empty' to confound most conventional notions of psychological motivation and continuity. (2) The 'picaresque digressions' so steadily undermine the premise of the race itself in diverse ways that the narrative itself progressively begins to dissolve and disperse, rather like the character of Tyrone Slothrop in the final sections of Thomas Pynchon's novel *Gravity's Rainbow* – finally achieving something close to total incoherence after 'the girl' arbitrarily exits the film – and the race's conclusion is never reached; during a final digression, the film itself appears to burn up in the projector instead.

In short, the refusals of narrative and genre closure in all three of these features, despite the setting up of narrative and genre expectations in each case, wound up excluding these films from any sort of mainstream acceptance, while the setting up of those expectations wound up excluding them from any consideration as art films or experimental films. (Only within a few limited European circles were these films ever accepted as art films.) Within the canons of American film culture itself, it could even be argued that these films have virtually been written out of film history a quarter of a century later, simply because most mainstream and academic critics have still found no place or space for them in their surveys. To survive in such arenas, affiliation with 'commercial' or 'alternative' branches of cinema usually becomes necessary; to exist between these branches means in most cases not to exist at all.

Exhibit #G: Taxi Driver (1976). A film that clearly shows the influence of both American experimental filmmaking and vanguard European narrative filmmaking of the 1960s, Taxi Driver can be said to have at least three central auteurs – director Martin Scorsese, screenwriter Paul Schrader, and lead actor Robert De Niro – the first two of whom were deeply marked by both kinds of filmmaking. In what is still undoubtedly the best critical study of the film, 'The Power & the Gory' (*Film Comment*, May-June 1976), Patricia Patterson and Manny Farber do a good job of showing how such influences and others coexist with blatantly commercial Hollywood elements:

> Taxi Driver is always asserting the power of playing both sides of the box-office dollar: obeisance to the box-office provens, such as concluding on a ten-minute massacre, a sex motive, good-guys vs. bad-guys violence, and casting the obviously charismatic De Niro to play a psychotic, racist nobody.... On the other coin side, it's ravishing the auteur box of Sixties best scenes, from Hitchcock's reverse track down a staircase from the Frenzy brutality, though Godard's handwriting gig flashed across the entire screen, to several Mike Snow inventions (the slow Wavelength zoom into a close look at the graphics pinned on a beaten plaster wall, and the reprise of double and triple exposures that ends Back and Forth .... Taxi Driver is actually a Tale of Two Cities: the old Hollywood and the new Paris of Bresson-Rivette-Godard.

Early in the same essay, Patterson and Farber note "the jamming of styles: Fritz Lang expressionism, Bresson's distanced realism, and [Roger] Corman's low-budget horrifics", before going on to note specific echoes of scenes from other sources: "De Niro's cab almost collides with the two child-whores – just as Janet Leigh's fearful Psycho thief nearly overruns the man from whom she's stolen a bundle .... When De Niro stares at his Alka Seltzer glass, there is a tiny sneak zoom into the bubbling water, which adds one more shot to Godard's rapidly-spoken philosophizing [2 ou 3 choses que je sais d'elle] in which the camera frames the coffee cup from above." And Kael has separately described a scene where the camera moves away from the hero on a pay phone to an empty hallway as "an Antonioni pirouette".

These are of course only a few sources of the film among many. Schrader has noted in interviews how some lines in De Niro's narration are taken directly from Bresson's LE JOURNAL D'UN CURÉ DE CAMPAGNE and that the film's very title was suggested by PICKPOCKET. He has also said, "Before I sat down to write TAXI DRIVER, I reread Sartre's *Nausea*, because I saw the script as an attempt to take the European existential hero, that is, the man from THE STRANGER, NOTES FROM THE UNDERGROUND, PICKPOCKET, LE FEU FOLLET, and A MAN ESCAPED, and put him in an American context. In so doing, you find that he becomes more ignorant, ignorant of the nature of his problem." He has also described in some detail how certain aspects of the plot were suggested by Ford's THE SEARCHERS.

The apparent incompatibility of these various influences – Bresson, Ford, Antonioni, Godard, Hitchcock, Snow, Lang, Sartre, Camus, Dostoevsky, Malle – tend to be overcome by an overall process that seems analogous to the process noted earlier in assimilating the New Wave influences into strict identification with the central character in THE GRADUATE. The relatively socialized contexts of most of these influences become privatized into the alienation of a single individual (though in the case of Snow, it might be argued that the source was already relatively privatized and antisocial to begin with; as noted earlier, it was the 'structural' films of Snow, Jacobs, Frampton, and others that largely removed experimental film from a carnivalesque social setting and into classrooms). Perhaps the most pertinent difference in this case is that the character being identified with in TAXI DRIVER, Travis Bickle, is not a mildly rebellious middle-class youth, as in THE GRADUATE, but a working-class Vietnam veteran who is virtually a psychopath and winds up committing mass murder.

The degree to which Scorsese, Schrader, and De Niro identify with Bickle is moreover even more consequential than the degree to which the filmmakers of THE GRADUATE can be said to identify with Benjamin. And significantly, if one turns to Schrader's own accounts of his artistic intentions in interviews, the degree of moral conflict and confusion - no doubt stemming in part from Schrader's strict Calvinist upbringing - seems to border at times on the pathological, at least in relation to the film's actual impact on most audiences: "The controversial nature of the film will stem, I think, from the fact that Travis cannot be tolerated. The film tries to make a hard distinction for many people to perceive: the difference between understanding someone and tolerating him. He is to be understood, but not tolerated. I believe in capital punishment: he should be killed." ('Screenwriter: TAXI DRIVER's Paul Schrader interviewed by Richard Thompson', *Film Comment*, March-April 1976.)

> At the time I wrote [the script] I was very enamoured of guns, I was very suicidal, I
> was drinking heavily, I was obsessed with pornography in the way a lonely person
> is, and all those elements are upfront in the script. Obviously some aspects are

heightened – the racism of the character, the sexism .... In fact, in the draft of the
script that I sold, at the end all the people he kills are black. [Scorsese and the pro-
ducers] and everyone said, no, we just can't do this, it's an incitement to riot; but it
was true to the character. (SCHRADER ON SCHRADER, edited by Kevin Jackson, Lon-
don/Boston: Faber and Faber, 1990).

Indeed, Patterson and Farber persuasively argue that the final film is itself racist, sexist, and worshipful of guns while Bickle himself is romanticized and
largely excused: "The fact is that, unlike the unrelentingly presented worm in
Dostoevsky's *Underground Man*, this handsome hackie is set up as lean and independent, an appealing innocent. The extent of his sexism and racism is
hedged. While Travis stares at a night world of black pimps and whores, all the
racial slurs come from fellow whites."

In short, thanks to what might be termed the Hollywoodizing of TAXI
DRIVER's experimental and European elements – a process involving such elements as Bernard Herrmann's effectively romantic/bombastic score, the cha-
risma of De Niro, and the slickness of Michael Chapman's cinematography, as
well as the displacements noted above by Patterson and Farber – the audience
is invited to identify with a violently Calvinist, racist, sexist, and apocalyptic
wish-fulfilment fantasy, complete with an extended bloodbath, that is given all
the allure of expressionist art and involves very few moral consequences for
most members of the audience. (At the film's end, Bickle is declared a hero and
even wins the admiration of the heroine, Cybil Shepherd, who previously
spurned him – a Hollywood conclusion in more ways than one.) Because the
whole thing is taking place inside one glamorous individual's head, the social
ramifications are effectively rationalized to the point of non-existence. In more
ways than one, this is the overall direction that Hollywood at its most triumphant will follow for the next two decades in processing and refining its various transgressive legacies; even a film like SCHINDLER'S LIST will follow essentially the same tactics, arguably with many of the same results.

Note

*   2003 postscript: I can no longer remember the precise date when I wrote this – ten
        years ago would be a safe approximate guess – but it's delightful to report that it's
        now an anachronism; a letterboxed DVD of MARIENBAD is readily available in the
        U.S.

Major references

Farber, Manny and Patricia Patterson, 'The Power and the Gory', in *Negative Space: Manny Farber on the Movies*, expanded edition, New York: Da Capo, 1998.

Film Culture nos. 26 and 27, 1962.

Hoberman, J. and Jonathan Rosenbaum, 'The Underground', in *Midnight Movies*, expanded edition, New York: Da Capo, 1991.

James, David E., 'Considering the Alternatives' (Chapter 1), in *Allegories of Cinema: American Film in the Sixties*, Princeton: Princeton University Press, 1989.

Kael, Pauline, 'BONNIE AND CLYDE', in *For Keeps*, New York: Dutton, 1994.

New York Film Bulletin nos. 43 and 44, 1962.

Rosenbaum, Jonathan, 'THE MANCHURIAN CANDIDATE', in *Placing Movies: The Practice of Film Criticism*, Berkeley/Los Angeles: University of California Press, 1995.

Sarris, Andrew, 'THE GRADUATE', in *Confessions of a Cultist: On the Cinema, 1955/1969*, New York: Simon And Schuster, 1971.

Wurlitzer, Rudolph, *Nog*, New York: Pocket Books, 1970.

Part Three
People and Places

Dinosaurs in the Age of the Cinemobile

Richard T. Jameson

When Billy Wilder's THE PRIVATE LIFE OF SHERLOCK HOLMES opened at Christmastime 1970, no one would give it the time of day-literally. In my city, though a cosy relationship with United Artists forced the local theatre circuit to book the film into one of the few remaining downtown movie palaces, they had no expectation that it would attract an audience. If you called the theatre, asked "When's the next show?" and acted accordingly, you would arrive to find yourself in mid-film. Telephone lines had been juggled so that the staff could handle incoming calls for the sister theatre across the street, where LOVE STORY was doing land-office business. It never occurred to them that anyone might be interested in "the show" on their own screen, so they automatically gave out the LOVE STORY schedule.

This was an extraordinary case, even if we set aside the outré management practice (I have never heard of a comparable instance of procedural hara-kiri) and the eventual recognition of THE PRIVATE LIFE OF SHERLOCK HOLMES as at the very least an enchanting entertainment, and at best one of the summum masterworks of the cinema. (On that first weekend – the only one the film would have – I watched the evening show with seven other people in the auditorium.) Yet the film's complete failure in 1970 was, in several respects, definitive of that moment in film history.

For one thing, HOLMES was just the sort of sumptuously appointed, nostalgically couched superproduction that once would have seemed tailor-made to rule the holiday season. Only two Christmases before, Carol Reed's OLIVER! had scored a substantial hit, and gone on to win Academy Awards for itself and its director (a 'fallen idol' two decades past his prime). Yet in 1969-70, the mid-Sixties vogue for three- and four-hour roadshows – reserved-seat special attractions with souvenir programmes and intermissions – abruptly bottomed out. Indeed, after witnessing such box-office debacles (and lousy movies) as STAR and PAINT YOUR WAGON, United Artists demanded that Wilder shorten his film by nearly an hour before they would release it at all.

But for the buying public, length wasn't the issue. This was a new era, defined by the 'youth culture' and Vietnam War protests, by the X-rated urban fable MIDNIGHT COWBOY (John Schlesinger, 1969), and by the political-picaresque EASY RIDER (Dennis Hopper, 1969)- especially the latter, a road movie made entirely *on the road*, a triumph of that ministudio-on-wheels, the

Cinemobile. In such a climate, the U.S. audience couldn't have been less interested in a passionately romantic meditation on a 19th-century icon realised principally on exquisitely dressed sets of 221B Baker Street, the Diogenes Club, and a Scottish castle with a mechanical monster in the cellarage. (A year earlier, Italian maestro Sergio Leone had found U.S. audiences similarly inhospitable to his equally passionate, equally romantic meditation on the 19th-century West and also on classical Hollywood filmmaking, ONCE UPON A TIME IN THE WEST, even if its politics were at least as contemporary as those of EASY RIDER. Like HOLMES, ONCE UPON A TIME IN THE WEST would also eventually be embraced as a masterpiece.)

HOLMES fell outside the 1970 pale in yet another important aspect. Billy Wilder is, was, and always had been an obsessively *complete* screenwriter, not content to go into production until every image and every wisecrack dovetailed in a complex *gestalt* of cross-reference and mutual reflection – the well-made script ready for transliteration into the well-made film. Yet the rallying cry of the Sixties' self-proclaimed 'Film Generation' – after "Is it [socio-politically] *relevant*?" – was: "The cinema is a visual medium". This accorded with a decade-old, French New Wave-inspired reaction against the tyranny of 'literary' standards of cinematic value and, on a positive level, the championing of such dynamic 'auteurs' as Hitchcock, Fuller, and the besides – CITIZEN KANE Orson Welles. But just as the auteurist movement undervalued the writerly virtues of Wilder, John Huston, and Joseph L. Mankiewicz, turn-of-the-Seventies cinema often seemed in danger of rejecting narrative itself in preference for orgies of rack focus, jump cuts, handheld camera, and arrant razzle-dazzle. THE PRIVATE LIFE OF SHERLOCK HOLMES was not only a loving tribute to the legend-making of Arthur Conan Doyle, an appreciation of the pleasures of seeing a story come together before one's eyes (how enchanting is that moment when six missing circus midgets, tossed off as a verbal *jeu d'esprit* in the opening scene, become a flesh-and-blood presence in the film a year, and an hour and a half of screentime, later); it's a film *about* the consolations of imagination, the pain and transcendence of wresting fictive art from growth and heartbreak. But neither narrative nor growth were relevant at the cusp of the Seventies.

Neither was the generation of artists and craftsmen by whom, in a very real sense, the movies had been invented. Some of them were already out of the game, whether they knew or accepted it: Fritz Lang, John Ford, King Vidor, William Wellman, Raoul Walsh. Jean Renoir and George Stevens each made his last film in 1969 (both in France, no matter that the town in Stevens's THE ONLY GAME IN TOWN was Las Vegas). William Wyler signed his last film in 1970 (THE LIBERATION OF L.B. JONES, a study in racial inequity eclipsed in advance by the flashy 1967 Oscar-winner IN THE HEAT OF THE NIGHT). So did

Howard Hawks, though to his dying day seven years hence he was still "working on a script" for one of several projects.

Others would keep working, however problematically. Two stalwarts of MGM in its heyday, Vincente Minnelli and George Cukor, provided contrasting studies in survival in the post-studio world. Minnelli's need for a strong, sympathetic producer (a role frequently played by John Houseman or Arthur Freed) was apparent in the misproportioned On a Clear Day You Can See Forever (made in 1968, reworked and released in 1970), at the mercy of the monstrous mythology of Barbra Streisand while – more damning in retrospect – failing utterly to know what to do with an apparently bland young player named Jack Nicholson. Minnelli's swan song, the 1976 A Matter of Time, would find him hopelessly adrift in Italy, dubbed English, and Color by Movielab – a coarse and pathetic environment for a man who dreamed in boldest Technicolor.

Cukor also flailed – drawing the compromised assignment of Justine (1969) after Joseph Mankiewicz and Joseph Strick were aced out of the project, and finding himself helpless to wring a single vital note out of The Blue Bird (1976), the much-bruited, instantly forgotten first U.S.-Soviet co-production. But unlike most of his contemporaries, he also managed to stay in work, and often in good form. Travels With My Aunt (1971), underrated by most of the press, was mainstream Cukor, ravishingly visualised and superbly acted by Alec McCowen (though it would be Maggie Smith, strenuously mannered in replacement of Katharine Hepburn, who drew a token Oscar nomination). Cukor had one more great film in him, even if it had to be made for television: Love Among the Ruins (1975), an exquisite comedy-romance with Hepburn and Laurence Olivier that fulfilled a legend arcing back to his fascinating 1935 'failure' Sylvia Scarlett (also starring Hepburn). He and Hepburn likewise made The Corn Is Green for television in 1979, and at 81 Cukor became the oldest director to complete (and admirably, too) a Hollywood feature, 1981's Rich and Famous.

One old master who never lost the security of a studio home (Universal) – and rarely left it, even for 'location' sequences – was Alfred Hitchcock. In 1960 Hitchcock's Psycho had, along with Wilder's The Apartment, decisively marked the incoming decade as an epoch of new trenchancy in American filmmaking, of overturning old truths and shaking up convention, on screen and in the world at large. But Psycho was also Hitchcock's last big hit (as 1963's Irma La Douce was Wilder's). His ensuing films became increasingly abstract essays in what critic Robin Wood, in a landmark 1966 book, *Hitchcock's Films*, called 'pure cinema'. Seen directly as compositions in time and space, form and colour, cold logic and fiercely contained emotion, The Birds, Marnie, and Torn Curtain were indisputably masterworks – that is, works by a master – thrilling to auteurist critics as extensions and elaboration of a screen language and vision unparalleled in cinema history. General audiences found them less satisfying. They missed the nimble wit and elegance of NORTH BY NORTHWEST, the closing-trap suspense of REAR WINDOW and PSYCHO, the glamour and centripetal star presence of Cary Grant or Jimmy Stewart. With the likes of Rod Taylor, 'Tippi' Hedren, and the not-yet-beloved Sean Connery in the leads, the only star was Hitchcock himself. And when he did cast two stars in TORN CURTAIN, he used them only for marquee value. When Julie Andrews, realising that her lover Paul Newman has apparently betrayed not only her but his country, bows her head in sorrow, the emotional expressiveness of the moment inheres not in the actress's performance but in the virtual liquefaction of the image as softening focus translates her into a trembling yellow-and-tan blur.

The rhythms of filmmaking careers were changing in the Sixties and Seventies. Whereas in previous decades an Alfred Hitchcock or a Howard Hawks managed one, two, even three films a year, now the ratio had been reversed. TOPAZ came out at the very end of 1969, more than three years after the release of TORN CURTAIN. Like its predecessor, it was a spy film far removed from the larky multiple-destruction mode of the then-regnant James Bond series, and the working press took it as confirmation of Hitchcock's waning. Who was this Frederick Stafford, a European sub-Bond nearly as flat and metallic as his Berlitz accent or fixed expression, drafted to play a distinctly dull French intelligence agent in Washington? How was a moviegoer supposed to relate to a plot that, unlike that of NOTORIOUS or THE 39 STEPS, kept many of the characters from ever meeting? And what did the "Master of Suspense" expect to accomplish by telling a behind-the-scenes story about the Cuban missile crisis of 1962 – didn't we all know how that one turned out?

The answer to the last question is, of course, that TOPAZ isn't 'about' the Cuban missile crisis, any more than NOTORIOUS was about uranium ore in wine bottles. At a time when streets, campuses, and 'youth movies' were filled with rants against 'the Establishment', Hitchcock filmed a supremely lucid, supremely disenchanted critique of just what Establishments, Governments, Powers were up to, and how and how much it cost in individual human suffering. The last shot of the film has an anonymous citizen glance at a headline announcing the resolution of the missile crisis. Over the newspaper appears a montage of faces from earlier in the film – 'heroes' and 'villains' alike – contorted in pain: *this* is what that headline cost. And then the man nonchalantly tosses the paper aside.

Although that wasn't the first ending to be filmed (Hitchcock discarded at least two others), it fulfills the logic of the film succinctly. From the main title sequence, when grainy newsreel footage of a Soviet May Day parade focuses closer and closer in on the machinery of war to the exclusion of human beings, TOPAZ defines a world of heartless pattern. This extends to the precise framing and rhyming camera movements that link, and judge, the *dramatis personae* caught in the machinery of plot. The same visual strategy measures the moments when nominal hero Stafford (close to the camera, facing forward, in focus) takes leave of wife Dany Robin (in the background, out of focus) to rendezvous with his Cuban agent/lover, and later when that lover, Karin Dor (up front, facing forward, in focus), listens to his departure (rear of the shot, out of focus) from her Havana home and knows that she is saving him and dooming herself. Likewise, when a close-up camera tracks known double agent Philippe Noiret into the interior of a Paris hideaway, it reveals the man holding open the door for him – and tells us, before the dialogue can, that this man, Michel Piccoli, is Noiret's spy master, the leader of "Topaz". At the end of the sequence the same camera strategy brings Stafford's wife through the same door. We already know whom she will find, though the motive for their clandestine meeting is entirely different. For Hitchcock, the symmetry of betrayal is not stylistically facile but morally essential.

It was an article of faith with Hitchcock that the stronger the villain, the better the movie. The villains of TOPAZ are infinitely more appealing, and better acted, than the nominal good guys of Stafford and his CIA friend John Forsythe. (It should be noted there are also marvellously droll characterisations by Roscoe Lee Browne, as a Harlem florist-cum-secret agent, and Per-Axel Arosenius as a Soviet defector contemptuous of his U.S. saviours.) Sympathy extends beyond appreciation for these actors' *watchability*. Noiret's traitor, with a crippled right side and a deep wistfulness, is a heartbreakingly vulnerable figure; Piccoli is a boyish, solicitous lover, mortally abashed when he realises his treachery has been discovered. But the most complex and shocking vulnerability is displayed by John Vernon as the quintessential cigar-chomping, khaki-clad Fidelista with Castro beard who is Stafford's rival for Dor's affections. When Vernon hears her name whispered into his ear by a dying torture victim, Hitchcock cuts to the piercing blue of his eyes, then to his powerful hands braced against his rather too plushy thighs, to communicate not the vehemence of a totalitarian but the pain of a wounded lover. Vernon's final embrace with Dor, as he commits a murder that is equal parts act of revenge and act of mercy, culminates in one of the most perversely ecstatic images Hitchcock ever wrought: a bird's-eye vertical shot in which Dor's life bleeds away in the spreading violet pool of her dress. There was no finer political film in that turbulently politicised era.

If, as many historians have contended, the Vietnam War represented the last spasm of American frontierism, we should not be surprised that one venerable Hollywood genre enjoyed an enhanced profile as the Sixties gave way to the Seventies: the Western. The year 1969 alone brought Sam Peckinpah's THE WILD BUNCH, George Roy Hill's BUTCH CASSIDY AND THE SUNDANCE KID, the John Wayne-Henry Hathaway TRUE GRIT, the U.S. release of Leone's ONCE UPON A TIME IN THE WEST, and, at year's end, Abraham Polonsky's relentlessly revisionist TELL THEM WILLIE BOY IS HERE. Additionally, though neither was itself a Western, those bellwethers of the new era, MIDNIGHT COWBOY and EASY RIDER, each explicitly invoked the genre (in their very titles), its imagery, landscape, and simplistic heroism, as an index of a lost purity and clarity of purpose, and implicitly suggested that the old verities were in fact lies that had poisoned the American consciousness from the gitgo.

Even a cursory examination of the meanings, attitudes, and methods of these films would exceed the scope of our mission here. Suffice it to note, then, that (with the singular exception of WILLIE BOY, the first film in 21 years to be directed by blacklistee Abraham Polonsky), only one of these 1969 films was made by an Old Hollywood hand. In visual style and narrative craftsmanship, TRUE GRIT is utterly of a piece with the solid, unpretentious genre work, in and out of the Western, that Henry Hathaway had been reliably producing for nearly four decades. At a glance, its chief distinction, perhaps even its *raison d'être*, lay in the fact that its star of stars, John Wayne, had grown old, massively thick, and epically crotchety. It was cheerfully prepared to make great sport of this as a recipe for renewing the affection of his traditional audience while also inspiring a grudging tolerance among those who had dismissed or deplored him in earlier manifestations.

Come Academy Award season in 1970, Wayne was up against the epochal performances of both Jon Voight and Dustin Hoffman in MIDNIGHT COWBOY (in which the title of his 1960 labour of love, THE ALAMO, can be seen falling off the marquee of a Texas movie house), and also his personal notoriety as an apologist for the Vietnam War (he had produced and directed as well as starred in the shoddy, jingoistic THE GREEN BERETS in 1968). Still, no one was surprised at his sentimental victory. Curiously, it was his admirers who tended most to criticise it. (A quarter-century later, with two subsequent Oscar victories of his own as consolation, Dustin Hoffman would observe that the Academy had done the right thing.) They resented that, whereas Wayne had been an exemplary professional and occasionally (RED RIVER, SHE WORE A YELLOW RIBBON, RIO GRANDE, THE SEARCHERS) a superb actor, he could win widespread validation only by putting on an eyepatch and making a broad caricature of himself.

They had a point. But what both the affection for and regret over Wayne's performance tended to obscure was that TRUE GRIT is a splendid movie. With characters, situations, and above all dialogue carried over from an excellent novel by Charles Portis, the picture had a feeling for frontier life, language,

John Wayne in TRUE GRIT

and protocol that remains exemplary in the genre. Hathaway was always a re-doubtable pictorialist, serving up unostentatious, deeply gratifying composi-tions in which action and place are framed to mutual enhancement. He had the eye of a children's storyteller, neither romantic *à la* John Ford nor expressionis-tic *à la* Anthony Mann. Abetted by veteran cinematographer Lucien Ballard (whose foursquare, primary Technicolor images are as satisfying as, if radi-cally distinct from, his dynamic work for Peckinpah that same year), he creates a heart-stirring canvas of the West, from the homely town of Fort Smith – with train station, courthouse, and the gallows in the town square in civilising con-tiguity – to the trembling aspen forests, picturesque arroyos, and long, deep mountain meadows of the Indian Nation through which the quest of Marshal Rooster Cogburn (Wayne) leads.

The performances are unanimously worthy, even the advisedly stiff-limbed, exasperatingly resolute heroine of Kim Darby and the amateurish but endearing celebrity turn of singer Glen Campbell as a career-conscious Texas Ranger who "expects to marry well". There are flavourful supporting roles for Jeff Corey, John Doucette, and Strother Martin (also memorable in THE WILD BUNCH and BUTCH CASSIDY). And without chafing against the implacable classicism of Hathaway's direction, that *echt*-Seventies-star-to-be Robert Duvall (also featured that year in Francis Coppola's THE RAIN PEOPLE) takes the part of outlaw leader "Lucky Ned" Pepper and makes him one of the worthiest, most complex adversaries Wayne ever had.

TRUE GRIT is, then, like a film of the Thirties or Forties that had no trouble winning popularity at the end of the Sixties. In one respect, however, it is very much a film of its time. For all the gusto of Wayne's portrayal, Cogburn's lot is a sad one – living in a room behind a general store, drinking himself to sleep, supporting himself on the bounty for chasing down society's miscreants (and often having to terrorise the bounty posters into paying up), with only the dim memory of a wife and son who hated him. (The key, Oscar-cinching scene in the film is a midnight reverie on a lonely hill during which Wayne seems imbued with the shade of W.C. Fields.) And the movie has an extraordinary sense of pain – grotesque, horrible, matter-of-fact. Without light to see by, Darby hesitates to eat a biscuit from Wayne's pouch because it may be stained by the blood of men he has just killed; bodies being packed over horseback threaten to be jostled off along the trail. And there is one ferocious scene in a smoky cabin: Wayne is grilling trapped outlaw Dennis Hopper (veteran of a tempestuous earlier collaboration with Hathaway, FROM HELL TO TEXAS) while his partner, Jeremy Slate, hacks at the corpse of a turkey that has already been blown to pieces by Ranger Campbell's Sharps rifle ("Too much gun"). The tension mounts horrifically, and is capped by Slate's lopping off Hopper's fingers to stop him from talking, being shot by Wayne, and stabbing Hopper in the gut with his dying breath. It is more terrible than anything in THE WILD BUNCH, though few troubled to remark it at the time.

Wayne and Hollywood's other veteran HH, Howard Hawks, would fare less successfully the following year with RIO LOBO. Like Hawks's previous film, EL DORADO (made 1965, released 1967), RIO LOBO breaks rather awkwardly into two sections: a Civil War escapade pitting Union officer Wayne against some resourceful young Confederate guerrillas, and a post-war tale in which Wayne and his former enemies join forces to save a Texas town from a wealthy rancher and his corrupt sheriff. The narrative break in EL DORADO was occasioned by Hawks's decision to abandon a Greek-tragedy story line he found too grim and improvise the rest of the movie as a wry, self-reflexive reworking of his 1959 RIO BRAVO; the result was another Hawks-Wayne classic. RIO LOBO, in its final reels, plays snatch-and-grab with elements of both those noble films, but the carryovers are perfunctory in the extreme.

The Civil War section begins promisingly with the Rebels' hijacking of a gold train being guarded by Wayne's troop. Hawks shapes it as an essay in military organisation and communication, climaxing in the exuberant spectacle of a runaway railroad car tearing up a Southern pine forest by the roots (the

Confederates have lashed ropes across the track to brake it). But once Wayne becomes the Rebels' captive and the usual Hawks strategies for establishing rapport between worthy adversaries-the exchange and repetition of lines, ruses, joke insults-come into play, the gambit feels warmed over and the players just "aren't good enough."

In El Dorado Hawks had made his and Wayne's ageing the virtual subject of the film and developed the theme with humour, affection, and not a little wisdom. Here it is reduced to a running gag about Wayne's having become an unintimidating presence – "comfortable" – as far as his youthful co-players, especially the women in the Texas section, are concerned. Apart from the train robbery (largely shot, one assumes, by second-unit director Yakima Canutt), the visuals are unimpressive, even shoddy, Hawks and/or his cameraman, Harry Stradling Jr., making frequent resort to lazy zooms. Most dismayingly, Hawks's judgement about performers, once the sharpest in Hollywood, appears to have deserted him. Jorge Rivero (as the ranking ex-Confederate) and Jennifer O'Neill (the most prominent of the several young women) are not merely hopeless at romantic badinage – they're barely competent to read their lines. Victor French (the wicked rancher) and muscle-bound Mike Henry (the sheriff) are lumpen successors to John Russell, Ed Asner, and El Dorado's enigmatic gunfighter Christopher George; and Jack Elam, though he briefly brings spastic life to the proceedings, is florid and one-note as the 'crazy old coot' figure so triumphantly limned previously in the trilogy by Walter Brennan and Arthur Hunnicutt.

If Rio Lobo marks a dispiriting conclusion to one of the greatest of Western series and greatest of directorial careers, 1970 also saw the first Western directed by Joseph L. Mankiewicz. The honoured creator of some of the most civilised comedy-dramas in Hollywood history (A Letter to Three Wives, All About Eve, Five Fingers), Mankiewicz inherited a sardonic screenplay by Bonnie and Clyde writers David Newman and Robert Benton, who had originally written it under the title Hell with Donald Siegel cast as director. The match was not as incongruous as it may sound. Short on scenery, six-guns, and horses, There Was a Crooked Man... is fundamentally a study in mendacity on the part of a Mephistophelean criminal (Kirk Douglas) willing to seduce and betray not only anybody but, preferably, everybody to get what he wants. Most of the narrative takes place in a territorial prison surrounded by fifty miles of desert.

In phase with the spirit of the day, Mankiewicz and Newman-Benton hog-tie and up-end every Western convention they can throw a lasso over. Douglas robs the leading businessman of a Southwest town, then is captured only because he pauses to dally at a whorehouse frequented by his victim. (The judge frequents it as well, and hence is particularly harsh in his sentence.) A Western lawman (Henry Fonda) is so puritanically obsessed with running whores (indeed, sex) out of his town that he doesn't notice breaches of the law like a holdup on Main Street in broad daylight. When, belatedly, he braces the robber and lays down his own gun to persuade the fellow to disarm, he doesn't get respect – he gets shot in the leg. The lawman, a knowing caricature of a modern liberal (played by an actor who shared such politics), winds up as warden of the prison where Douglas is incarcerated; his attempts at reform, and at befriending the charming rogue, only increase the havoc Douglas is ultimately able to wreak.

Mankiewicz, an exemplary sophisticate who had long been frustrated by Hollywood's built-in forms of censorship, had only his innate good taste to restrain him in the new age of R ratings. A prostitute, rousted naked in her bed, attempts to sway Fonda by lowering the sheet. (A similar nude scene was a source of palpable discomfort for Henry Hathaway and actors Gregory Peck and Rita Gam in 1971's Shoot Out.) John Randolph and Hume Cronyn, two con artists sent to prison at the same time as Douglas, prove to be a sweet parody of a long married couple, and there is a wealth of homoerotic innuendo involving a prison guard, the pre-Fonda warden, a truculent loner (Warren Oates) who takes Douglas for his first and only friend, and indeed the fixation Fonda forms for Douglas. And in a quintessential Sixties gesture Newman and Benton throw in a prison lifer – Burgess Meredith as "The Missouri Kid" – who patiently tends a marijuana crop through rain and drought.

Despite the hipness of its writing team, the august reputation of its director (it was Mankiewicz's best film since Cleopatra broke his career), a solid cast, and the up-to-date-ness of its attitude and satire, There Was a Crooked Man... did not find an audience at the end of 1970. Even in that disenchanted time, it was scarcely a holiday picture, and its view of human nature was relentlessly bleak. Perhaps it was really ahead of its time; the early Seventies would bring a rash of nihilistic Westerns that got more bookings without displaying its wit, intelligence, or pedigree, and all of them did more business. But Mankiewicz's work on the film left a more enduring legacy. Enraptured by his personal style as a Hollywood elder statesman, Newman and Benton took him as the model for their wonderful outlaw creation 'Big Joe' (played by near-lookalike David Huddleston) in Benton's 1972 directorial debut Bad Company. And they gave Big Joe one of Joe L.'s oft-repeated lines: "I'm the oldest whore on the block".

"The Cylinders Were Whispering My Name"

The Films of Monte Hellman

Kent Jones

"How can you put yourself in any kind of historical perspective while you're living your life?" I wanted Monte Hellman to talk about where he thought he fitted into the American cinema of the early 1970s – not the Spielberg-De Palma-Coppola-Lucas New Hollywood but the Dennis Hopper-Bob Rafelson version, the one that got rolled over, the one of which Hellman was, in my eyes, the undisputed king. But I was approaching Hellman as a bygone figure from the past while he saw himself as very much alive, a working director. His string of failures, career disturbances, disappointments and bad distribution deals formed a Stroheim-like image of Hellman in my head that he himself could not afford to recognise. I had a self-congratulatory image of myself as a knight restoring the king to his throne, but that was a young man's folly.[1]

I did a long telephone interview with Hellman 10 years ago. I was in my early twenties and I had been transfixed by THE SHOOTING, his 1966 western, on late night commercial television a couple of years before. Even on a black and white 7-inch screen with commercial interruptions, the uniquely jagged rhythm of this film, the unusual argot of its characters and its unsettling atmosphere of dread kept me up until three o'clock in the morning. Not long after, there was a double bill of Hellman's two finest films, TWO-LANE BLACKTOP and COCKFIGHTER, at an excellent New York revival house called the Thalia. I was an intern at the *Village Voice* at the time, and the late Tom Allen, a wonderful writer with the distinction of being the only full-time film critic who was also a Jesuit monk (as well as an admirer of Bunuel and a disciple of George Romero), wrote about TWO-LANE BLACKTOP in a section called 'Revivals in Focus' (after Tom died of a heart attack in 1988, the column came to an end – it was virtually obsolete by that time anyway). Tom was complimentary towards the film ("a minimalist road movie with maximalist detail") but with a certain reticence.

For me, this double bill (the version of COCKFIGHTER I saw was called BORN TO KILL, a slightly different cut with some added tits and ass courtesy of producer and project originator Roger Corman) was a revelation. This was the beginning of the 1980s, the worst decade ever for American movies (thank God for Martin Scorsese and Alan Rudolph), and to encounter such lean, concentrated artistry, focused on such unusual sides of American life, was sheer joy. I went through old copies of the *Village Voice* and found Andrew Sarris's qualified assessment of TWO-LANE BLACKTOP – he had singled out Warren Oates and praised Hellman without being really enthusiastic about him or the film. David Thomson, in his 'Biographical Dictionary of Film,' had compared the film unfavourably to AMERICAN GRAFFITI of all things. Jonathan Rosenbaum had reviewed COCKFIGHTER favourably in *Film Comment* (special praise for the authenticity of the Southern accents) but had reservations about BLACKTOP. In each case, with the exception of Rosenbaum, Hellman was treated more like an interesting oddity than an artist. It was as though it was not right that an artist with such a quiet, reflective temperament should exist on this side of the Atlantic – he could be taken any way but on his own terms, because he did not fit into a fixed image of a bustling, lively, populist America.

One of Monte Hellman's central film experiences as a young man was Jacques Rivette's PARIS NOUS APPARTIENT, the most ambitious, rarefied and least appreciated (in America) of the groundbreaking New Wave films. "That was a very powerful film as far as affecting me and my ideas about filmmaking," Hellman told me. "What struck me about PARIS NOUS APPARTIENT was that people kept walking in and out of doors – scenes that would be cut out of most other pictures became the basis of the movie." That's a good description of Hellman's own approach to filmmaking (with the exception of SILENT NIGHT DEADLY NIGHT 3, Hellman begins each of his films in media res – we go right into action as though there was no proper way for a story to begin except to slice into ongoing life), and if there's any director that Hellman strongly resembles both temperamentally and as a storyteller, it's Rivette. Both are cerebral artists who operate at a distance from their stories and their characters, and ellipsis is an important feature of their respective arts. But Rivette is protected in France – he's never been a popular artist but then he's never had to be. The state subsidised *Avance sur recettes* program aside, there's a cultural niche created for people like Rivette and Rohmer out of respect for their artistry. But in America you're only as good as your last picture, and Hellman has to prove himself anew every time he makes a movie, which is rarely. His last completed film, SILENT NIGHT DEADLY NIGHT 3: BETTER WATCH OUT, was a straight-to-video slasher sequel. Although its material let his college intern sniff at, Hellman applied himself to that project with the same seriousness and professionalism he has brought to all his films.

Which brings me to Pauline Kael. I also looked up Hellman's films in her *5001 Nights At the Movies*. I can't provide a direct quote because I threw away my copy of that book years ago, but suffice it to say that she was not impressed. There's a tiny capsule review of THE SHOOTING that dismisses it as a quasi-existentialist exercise that doesn't merit scrutiny. Even more damning was her pan of Malick's BADLANDS with the ultimate putdown – a comparison with "some films made by Monte Hellman". This is vintage Kael – she takes one look at somebody, they rub her the wrong way, and the game's over. She skewered any hint of intellectualism in the cinema (sorry – the movies), but the great paradox of her career is that her Movies-Are-A-Popular-Art-Form-And-Have-No-Room-For-Intellectualism polemic was practised in a magazine whose readership was and remains intellectual, literary-minded Americans. And for someone who supposedly knew movies and what made them work so well, she certainly imposed a lot of restrictions on them. Just like an anxious mother, Kael was always trying to get all her ducks in a row. People often refer to her constant use of the word 'we' (as in, 'We don't feel anything for these characters because we just don't like them') as royal, but to me it sounds maternal.

For this mother hen, if you were a Hellman or a Malick, a Rafelson or a post-TAXI DRIVER Scorsese, you weren't just a black sheep – you weren't even worth discussing. The kids had strict orders to look the other way if they saw you walking down the street. Kael was once quoted as saying that the 1970s was the golden age of American movies, and I would tend to agree with her, but she was responsible for creating a tone that killed off a lot of possibilities during that era (ironically, so was Andrew Sarris, though to a far lesser extent, with his love for 'classical' cinema). It's largely because of this reactionary tone that spread throughout film criticism that the cinema of the early 1970s, meaning the post-EASY RIDER films (TWO-LANE BLACKTOP, THE LAST MOVIE, THE HIRED HAND, the films of Rafelson and Schatzberg, etc.) is still remembered as an aberrant hallucination and that the Spielbergs, the Lucases, the De Palmas represented a glorious return to form. Two brief ironies. Quentin Tarantino, perhaps the ultimate Kael-ite filmmaker (he's a huge fan of her final, improbable nomination for the pantheon, CASUALTIES OF WAR; I'm told that she was nuts about PULP FICTION), is a big Hellman fan (Hellman served as an executive producer on RESERVOIR DOGS). The second irony is that Sam Peckinpah, Kael's favourite director of the 1970s, went on the *Tonight Show* in 1973 and announced, for all the world to hear: "The best director working in America today is Monte Hellman".

So what follows, sad to say, is a defence of the work of Monte Hellman in addition to being a brief history of his career. At this late date, it should be a tribute, but the reality is that anything written about Monte Hellman in America must be a defence (the only book ever written on his work, by Charles Tatum, Jr., is in French). With Leo McCarey and Delmer Daves close seconds, Hellman gets my vote as the cinema's most under-appreciated great director.

When I re-read the interview, I was appalled by the number of "What were you intending when you did this?" questions, every one of which Hellman answered with a subtle rebuke – "You just don't *think* about those things when you're directing a film." Hellman, however, wasn't just playing the Old Pro game. "Maybe one of my tragic flaws is that, I hate to use the word but I'm a kind of an intellectual," he told me, a self-description that is impossible to imagine coming from a member of the old guard. "Now, if I wanted to emulate somebody I'd say I'd like to be Howard Hawks," he told me, and in retrospect Hellman seems more in the tradition of a Hawks than was initially plausible (it's interesting to compare him with directors like John Carpenter and Walter Hill, who ape the outward appearances, stylistic tics and world view of Hawks's films, but seem miles away from him otherwise). Hellman's storytelling instincts are like Hawks stripped down to his essence, and his sense of action and space are just as concrete and logical. Arguably, Hellman and the early Rafelson and McBride are a more natural bridge with the old Hollywood, having absorbed the (thematic) influences of the New Wave, Michelangelo Antonioni and Ingmar Bergman, than directors like Coppola and Spielberg who denied those influences and settled into genre formulas. It's ironic, too, that Hellman the "intellectual" is a less self-conscious artist than many of the 'entertainers' who made and spent fortunes throughout the 1970s and 1980s.

Monte Hellman was born in Brooklyn in 1932, but his family moved to California when he was six and he's lived there ever since. He gained some experience as a still photographer in high school, studied theatre at Stanford and went to film school at UCLA but quit after a year and a half to travel through Europe. When he returned, he joined a summer stock company based near San Francisco called the Stumptown Players and got his first experience as a director on *Night Must Fall*, *The Skin of Our Teeth* and *Of Mice and Men*, among other things. The company went under after three seasons, and he went to work at ABC cutting commercials into 16mm prints. He was promoted to Assistant Editor on the television series *Medic*, which got him his entry into the editor's union (Hellman is credited as editor on many of his own films). He became bored and moved to LA, where he started another theatre group and directed a production of *Waiting for Godot* (an important work for Hellman) with Jack Albertson and Joey Faye (this production is praised by his old friend Martin Landau in his introduction to Tatum's book). "After a year we got evicted... and [Roger] Corman said, 'This is enough playing around – it's about time you did something to get healthy'" which resulted in Hellman's first film, BEAST FROM HAUNTED CAVE.

BEAST FROM HAUNTED CAVE was the first of three times in Hellman's career when he would make one film back to back with another, in this case Corman's SKI-TROOP ATTACK (Corman often piggybacked one film onto another as a cost-saving measure). "He gave me this project and I started working with the writer, Chuck Griffith, and tried to at least transform it into something that was interesting to me. I had no interest in making a monster movie per se, but it was also a gangster movie – it was really Roger's version of KEY LARGO, which he's done about five times." Actually, the most poetic material in this movie, about a gang of hoods who heist gold ingots from a small reserve and then have a guide (Michael Forest) escort them through snow country, revolves around the beast and his victims, who are spun into cocoon-like webs and stood up like figurines. Hellman also builds up to the uninspiring first appearance of the monster by keeping him hidden or seen in fleeting cutaways, the shrewdest of B-movie ploys. "I made the best movie I could under the circumstances, for $35,000."

It is an education to compare this novice effort to the Corman film. SKI-TROOP ATTACK is an awful movie about an American reconnaissance group in Germany during World War II. Every so often a piece of archival footage is spliced into the Deadwood, South Dakota landscaping the laziest way imaginable, but even lazier is the action – randomly shot, badly blocked and not at all keyed to the landscape: the actors could just as well be milling around a tennis court. Corman was just marking time and grinding out drive-in fodder, but his young first-timer made the most of his minimal settings and mapped his action with great visual acuity (his training as an editor was probably a help in what would prove to be one of his greatest talents). It would be ridiculous to go into detail about BEAST, but as an apprentice effort it's impeccable. Hellman had an innate grasp of something that has always eluded Corman as a director, which is what Manny Farber dubbed "negative space". Simply put, it's using what's offscreen to dynamise what's onscreen, harnessing the experience and cultural background that an audience brings to a film and using it to make the onscreen material "resonate", to use Farber's term. Hellman had this in spades right from the start.

Hellman began making movies in a relaxed, no-pressure atmosphere, and it's possible that he would never have found his footing as an artist if he had not had the luxury of low expectations and the freedom to fail. "Today you've got to make a success of your first movie. It never occurred to us whether we would or wouldn't get a second shot. You know, we made these movies, and we never thought anybody would take them seriously... I remember at the premiere performance of BEAST FROM HAUNTED CAVE, a friend of Gene Corman's [Roger's brother] who was a well-known Hollywood writer at the time came out of the picture saying, 'You know, I don't think that beast was so badly burnt that he can't come back for another movie.' I think the times were different – there was a different attitude towards life."

Hellman got an agent and looked for more directing work at the big studios but had no luck. He did some "odd jobs for Corman," one of which was associate producer on a 1960 film called THE WILD RIDE directed by his friend Harvery Berman. He also knew one of the actors in that film, Jack Nicholson, and it was at this time that they became close friends (they would eventually form a business partnership). Hellman was assistant director on THE INTRUDER (one of Corman's very best films as a director) and was given the task of adding scenes to BEAST FROM HAUNTED CAVE and SKI-TROOP ATTACK as well as CREATURE FROM THE HAUNTED SEA and THE LAST WOMAN ON EARTH, for sale to television. "That was probably the most fun I've ever had, because I was the producer, writer and director, and I had absolute control over the crew and how the money was spent and everything. It was really fantastic, plus the fact that it was totally off the wall stuff – it was like 'Saturday Night Fever'." For CREATURE, Hellman shot a scene in which Robert Towne, who played the lead, has his tennis shoes polished (Towne was part of an acting group that Hellman helped to form, which also included Nicholson, Harry Dean Stanton, Shirley Knight and Rupert Crosse, who played the manager in Cassavetes' SHADOWS; the class was taught by Martin Landau). He also shot the title tune ("a *really* great song"), written by Carol Eastman (aka Adrien Joyce: she would later write Hellman's breakthrough film THE SHOOTING as well as FIVE EASY PIECES and Schatzberg's PUZZLE OF A DOWNFALL CHILD).

A year later, the pennywise Corman shot two days of Boris Karloff walking around a leftover set before it was demolished and gave a young UCLA film school graduate named Francis Coppola the chance to build a movie around the footage. There was no script, so Coppola wrote one quickly and did five weeks of work, most of which Corman threw out (according to critic and filmmaker Bill Krohn, Coppola went over budget – some things never change). Corman hired a new screenwriter, and Hellman directed all of the exteriors for what would eventually become THE TERROR (according to Hellman, he's responsible for about twenty-five minutes of the finished film, Coppola is responsible for around ten, and the rest is Corman's). THE TERROR was seen and liked by producer Fred Roos, who was developing projects for Robert Lippert. In the meantime, Hellman got a job on the editing team of BUS RILEY'S BACK IN TOWN at Universal. "He knew Francis and I had both worked on it, didn't know who had done what, so he cabled Lippert that he wanted Francis and me to direct these movies in the Philippines. They tried to find Francis and they couldn't, so they hired me. When I was speaking at the British Film Institute, I said, 'If it had gone the other way around, Francis might have become rich and famous.'"

On a small passenger ship to the Philippines, actor John Hackett reworked the script for BACK DOOR TO HELL, written by Dick Gutman, while Jack Nicholson wrote FLIGHT TO FURY based on a page-long outline by Hellman and Roos. Shooting on BACK DOOR began in July 1964, and there was only a three-week respite before the start of FLIGHT TO FURY. "Because I was doing the second picture I wasn't able to edit the first one, so somebody did a rough cut on it. I was aghast at how terrible it was. So when we were shooting FLIGHT TO FURY, I would get up at about five in the morning, have breakfast and then leave for the location at about six. We had drivers, and I would sleep from about six to seven while we got to the location. We would shoot until six at night, and get back to the house at seven. I would take a little nap and then have dinner, and then at nine o'clock Roos and I went to the cutting room to recut BACK DOOR TO HELL. And we would work until about two in the morning, and then come back and sleep from two-thirty to five and start the whole process over again."

BACK DOOR TO HELL and FLIGHT TO FURY are the kind of movies that really aren't made anymore. They are low budget-low profile films that afford their director the opportunity to practice his or her craft – Joseph H. Lewis, for instance, made dozens of them before his GUN CRAZY-SO DARK THE NIGHT period in the late forties. Neither film is ambitious, and there is nothing in either that shines beyond the creative ingenuity with which they simultaneously obscure and exploit their drive-in budgets. BACK DOOR TO HELL is a modestly tough movie on the theme of pacifism vs. viciousness in battle, about an American reconnaissance mission sent to help a group of Filipino rebels (the movie is marred by a final, ridiculously gung ho montage of American invasion stock footage that was inserted by Lippert and 20th Century-Fox after the film was cut). Hellman builds his movie around hard physical details and situations, an old B-movie virtue: the rigging of a pulley to carry a radio across a river, the shock on a Japanese private's face when he opens the door of a hut and finds Nicholson tapping out a coded message on a wireless set, a soldier with his dead buddy slung over his back as he marches (Hellman's camera fastens on the body until it registers graphically). It has a lean action sequence that's a good example of Hellman's supremely clear sense of space. The Americans join the rebels in a raid on a Japanese stronghold, an exciting criss-cross of gunplay, running and explosions within a consistently clear physical arena. This may sound like a minor virtue today, but it's a test few modern filmmakers could pass, nor would many think it worth the effort. The director makes great use of two sharp performers, the ethereal Annabelle Huggins (her delicate face and voice are used sparingly, to light parts of the movie with a soft glow) and Conrad Maga as Paco, the rebel leader. He is a solid, severe actor with a wiry body and a cheerless, determined face. Everything that Paco does is based on necessity. "His boots! His boots!!" he whispers urgently to Jimmie Rodgers' pacifist Lieutenant Craig, who has just killed a Japanese sentry. He's mystified as Paco unties the man's boots and throws them away, so that the Japanese will think he's been killed by bandits.

Despite Hellman's dissatisfaction with the finished product ("All I could really do was patch it up as best I could"), BACK DOOR TO HELL is a better movie than FLIGHT TO FURY. A Tarantino favourite, FLIGHT is once again interesting for the modest virtue of its clean action and decidedly weird structure.

Light-footed, surprising and funny (in an oddly detached way) until its assemblage of adventurers and diamond smugglers crash land in the jungle midway through, it devolves into a succession of stock situations enacted by Greenstreet/Lorre clones. Nicholson's gambler, a bizarre variation on Robert Walker's vampiric charmer Bruno in STRANGERS ON A TRAIN, meets Dewey Martin's Joe at the gaming table in a casino, and from then on he won't let him out of his sight. He follows Martin onto a plane as he flees a murder rap, and sits next to a shy young lady played by Hellman's first wife Jocelyn. "Do you know anything about death?" he asks her out of the blue. This is a very queer character whose scenes suggest an improbable hybrid – an Albert Camus comedy. The young Nicholson, thin, reedy, and faintly neurotic, gives the guy a strange pathos until both the movie and his character turn disappointingly mechanical. He represents the opposite of what Hellman intended – a light variation on BEAT THE DEVIL – but he is the most interesting thing in the movie.

BACK DOOR and FLIGHT suffer from an interesting problem that doesn't turn up too much in American cinema: they are cursed with their director's talent. Both films provide ample evidence of Hellman's gift for uniformity, which is not entirely beneficial (the closest analogy I can think of is THE BLACK BOOK, Anthony Mann's beautiful but godawful noir version of the terror in post-revolutionary France: Mann's talent for visual clarity is everywhere in evidence, and it highlights every ridiculous twist and turn of a horrendous script). Hellman is not a director of rhetorical flourishes or sudden jolts of action – he concentrates on the whole picture, and sets his action in one key. His films tend to unfold in a smooth, even fashion, the better to follow small events and large trajectories. These movies are fastidious to a fault, and Hellman never really goes for broke and digs into their possibilities the way that a less talented but more vulgar director like Corman might have (on a good week). At this point Hellman was still operating in his mentor's shadow – FLIGHT TO FURY in particular is prime Corman material, a quick knock-off of several other movies cobbled together in a few days. But Hellman had a special kind of temperament that would finally find its level with his next two films.

Before they left for the Philippines, Hellman and Nicholson had worked on a script called EPITAPH that they wanted to do with Corman (there is an extract in Tatum's book). "It was to star Jack and Millie Perkins, who was my next door neighbour. Roger had agreed to produce the picture and give us the money for it." The story was about a young actor in Hollywood and his circle of friends, and was explicitly autobiographical – they planned to incorporate footage from Nicholson's earlier films into the action, which covers a three-day period in which the actor tries to raise money for an abortion for his girlfriend. "When we came back, we went to Roger to make the picture, and he said that he had changed his mind, that he didn't want to do it anymore, that he thought it was too European a film... but he said that rather than totally renege on his deal we could make a western, you may as well do two, because you can make two pictures for the same price as one." Hellman and Nicholson rented office space in Beverly Hills, hired Carol Eastman, and a month later had two scripts, which would become THE SHOOTING and RIDE IN THE WHIRLWIND.

The joke was on Corman, since it's difficult to imagine films more "European" than this diptych. "Roger saw the scripts that we came up with and was ready to chuck the whole thing. But he'd already invested $5,000, and he realised that for a $75,000 budget, if he made the movies he couldn't get hurt. Whereas if he cancelled them he'd be out $5,000." So for the second time in a year Hellman shot two movies back to back. BACK DOOR TO HELL had started in July 1964 and RIDE IN THE WHIRLWIND wrapped in June 1965. He had three weeks between his Filipino movies, but there was only a week between the westerns. Outside of Corman himself and James Brown, Monte Hellman was the hardest working man in show business.

It was surprising to me that Hellman and Nicholson had set out to make 'classic' westerns (in preparation they watched many of their favourites, including MY DARLING CLEMENTINE, STAGECOACH, SHANE and ONE-EYED JACKS). "What we were trying to do was make an A western on a B budget. We wanted to do something that had the feeling of THE GUNFIGHTER, but we were also influenced by various European filmmakers of the time." This was a dilemma for many young directors during that period, and I think that the only one for whom the mixture of influences came easily was Hellman (one of the reasons was that his budgets were so low that he didn't feel compelled to hedge his bets the way other people did). While movies like THE GRADUATE, MICKEY ONE and POINT BLANK were selling a new hybrid model of flash filmmaking with varying degrees of success, along came two unassuming westerns that incorporated a European sensibility without any fuss. They remained virtually invisible here for years and gained their first notoriety in Paris, where they became cult hits when they were released there in 1969.

This issue of "European-ness" is always a focal point of any discussion of Hellman. Americans (or, rather, Hollywood executives) prefer their European influences to be ornamental rather than structural or thematic, and Mike Nichols' THE GRADUATE, which offers itself as a Europeanised object, is a case in point: its catalogue of borrowings from Resnais, Bergman and Fellini is central to its identity and its aesthetic (such as it is). Nichols's film, which Hellman greatly admired for the way it struck a nerve in American culture ("There are certain very strong stories or ideas for films that touch the core of the psychology of the audience so profoundly that they absolutely cannot fail. I think THE GRADUATE is not really a very good film, but it's a great film because of just what it is"), was made around the same time as the westerns and was probably the model for American cinema in years to come. It fetishised its influences in order to identify itself as classy, provocative and advanced: it came with a shiny badge of cultural approval pinned to its lapel. Hellman's films may not have jumped into the cultural fray with as much of a splash as THE GRADUATE, but thirty years later they are as fresh and as modern as the day they were made, whereas the high-profile movie that won all the awards has become a relic. These two small, unassuming westerns seem as definitively European as the Mike Nichols paste-up, but on a more vital level.

THE SHOOTING and RIDE IN THE WHIRLWIND are singularities in American cinema. The only other films that they resemble are Budd Boetticher's Randolph Scott westerns, but those films are grounded in character while Hellman's have a distanced tone that forefronts a looming sense of dread. Hellman is now in awesome control of his medium: the advance on the Filipino films is enormous. They mark the beginning of many things for Hellman. This is the first instance of his quiet, intellectual temperament in a fully sympathetic situation. Both westerns are carefully tailored to particular landscapes, which will become a Hellman trademark, and they represent the first real instances of his storytelling style, composed of regular, daily events as opposed to dramatic events coated with a patina of dailiness – this would later separate him from nearly every other American director. It is also the beginning of his collaboration with a toothy, ruminative actor named Warren Oates, an acquaintance of Nicholson's whom Hellman had seen and admired in a production of *One Flew Over the Cookoo's Nest*.

"Carol Eastman would bring me stuff every three or four days. She didn't have the story plotted out. She really worked more organically and let her creative juices carry her where they would. She didn't know where she was going to wind up, and I think that's why there's a tremendous feeling of suspense about the movie." Suspense is not exactly the right word, because we're not anticipating anything but trying to figure out the foreboding enigma on screen. The westerner, alone in the wilderness, hears a small sound and tenses – he's so tuned to the environment that he knows that something is coming. It's a moment we all know from thousands of westerns, but what makes it unusual here is that it's the very first thing we see in the movie, and it establishes a mood of paranoia and dread that does not abate until the final seconds of the film. Hellman's affinity for Beckett is at its most pronounced here: we know next to nothing about the four principal characters beyond the fact that they are travelling across the vast western American landscape (the films were shot in Utah).

Eastman loosely based her screenplay on a Jack London story (two men meet in a hotel bar, one of them looks at a painting, and it reminds him of an incident that is very close to the narrative of THE SHOOTING). Oates's Willet Gashade is a prospector who returns to the mine he operates with his brother

Coigne to find a sheepish helper named Coley (Will Hutchins) scared out of his wits, his partner Leland Drum dead and buried, and Coigne nowhere to be seen. "Now become calm and tell me so's I can understand where it's going," says Willett to Coley as they sit and talk by lamplight. Coigne and Leland went on a bender, Coigne killed a child in the street, came back to camp to take Coley's horse Shorty and fled. The next night someone came and shot Leland down as he was drinking his coffee. Coley tells his story over a terse flashback – Leland hunkered down in the dark by the campfire, teetering back and forth before he falls over from the fatal gunshot. "Is that the whole way of it, Coley?" says Willet. "My mind's all unsatisfied with it." Willet is exhausted, and he takes Coley's gun to sleep with him – someone has been tracking him, too. The sense of familiarity and the strange vernacular ("I think it was based on [Carol's] idea of Germans in Texas or something, this kind of sentence structure that was not really English") offsets the paranoia and makes it all the more invasive.

THE SHOOTING, whose plot is set in motion by a murderer in flight from the law, has a moral framework that's uncommon to the genre. The cowboy who sleeps with his gun, a familiar western trait, is a special circumstance here brought on by fear: action is brought down to a more human, less mythical level than usual as Hellman creates a very modern feeling of disrupted normalcy. "One thing that really affected both films was the shooting of Kennedy. That's the socio-political background of the films, THE SHOOTING consciously and RIDE IN THE WHIRLWIND unconsciously." The sense of immanent danger that colours THE SHOOTING capitalises on one of the most recognisable features of the western – the wide open yet dangerously close-quartered landscape. There's a moment early on where Gashade sits in the spot where Leland died, drinking coffee, while Coley is singing a song in the background on the left. "Somethin's comin'," Gashade mutters to himself and puts down his coffee. Hellman cuts to a gloved hand stroking a fallen white horse and putting a cocked pistol to its head. As the gun goes off Willet and Coley freeze, and then Coley runs like a banshee as Willet stands up: the camera tracks around Oates, keeping him as its axis, and follows Hutchins's movement as he runs up the hill for cover (unaccountably leaving a trail of flour dust as he goes). It's a mysterious shot that strobes between subjective and objective, concreteness and abstraction. And it crystallises a key thematic aspect of the movie: while Coley is scared out of his wits, Willet is magnetised by the ominous developments.

The shooter is a woman who speaks in riddles, played by Millie Perkins with a flat, toneless voice. She's killed her horse for some unknown reason, and she wants to pay Gashade a generous sum of money to lead her across the desert to a town called Kingsley. The enmity between them – he's immediately suspicious and she's disdainful – is complicated by Coley's romantic attachment ("You sure have a pretty way"), and a triangular road show of fatalism, cross-purposes, warning signs and red herrings is set in motion. They make their way through rough, varied terrain that becomes less and less inhabitable. Hellman's fluidity with landscape here is a welcome contrast to the abrupt change-ups that characterise most westerns, which tend to jump from one picturesque valley and rock formation to the next with no topographical logic.

The woman periodically fires warning shots, and we eventually learn that she is signalling her location to a mean, beady-eyed hired gun who will join them on their trek through the desert (the gunman, played by Nicholson, is introduced just like Perkins in a sudden close-up insert). The landscape gets rougher and the behaviour gets more and more threatening, as it gradually becomes clear that they are tracking someone. In the final moments of the film we realise that Coigne is the pursued man and that it's the woman's child who has been killed. The film starts to slow down in the manner of Godard's stop motion inflections in Sauve Qui Peut, and we hear Gashade shouting "Coigne!" Coigne appears from behind a rock, and Willet is staring into his own eyes – they are twins. The symbolism seems obvious, but to dwell on it would obscure the fleeting violence of the images. I asked Hellman if his inspiration was the Zapruder film, but he said it was actually the shooting of Lee Harvey Oswald by Jack Ruby. In fact, the ending of The Shooting plays out like a cross between those two cultural touchstones, and locks down the narrative that precedes it with breathtaking finality.

The most troubling aspect of the film is Willet's death drive. He knows that the journey will end in doom, and the money doesn't make much difference to him. He doesn't seem at all curious or drawn to the woman, but he is somehow compelled to join her. It's that mysterious compulsion that drives the action (I would have to disagree with the frequent label of "existentialist" that is hung on Hellman in general and this film in particular, often by Hellman himself – anarchist would be more like it. If you refuse to believe that Gashade would just pack up and follow this woman to his doom then the film won't mean much to you, but anyone who lived through the 1960s and 1970s ought to be able to understand the urge to embrace oblivion rather than risk the possibility of dullness by resisting it. This is the one film that I know of that distils that bygone tendency into a pure, recognisable form.

Ride in the Whirlwind is a different kind of story. The mood here is tired and a little sad, and its setting is green and mountainous where The Shooting's is parched and flat. Every tic of The Shooting's four principal characters is burned into your brain, but the cowboys in Ride in the Whirlwind (Nicholson, Cameron Mitchell and John Hackett) are insignificant men who seem to be receding into the landscape, which is appropriate since their lives are turned upside down by a mistake. They stop for the night at a small house occupied by a group of thieves, and before they get on their way in the morning they are caught in an ambush by vigilantes. Hackett is shot down but Nicholson and Mitchell get away, and they're hunted down like criminals and subsequently forced to act like criminals: through no fault of their own, their lives have been negated.

"There was the whole feeling of guilt by association, at the same time as there being a real feeling that, in a sense, you get what you deserve, that if you're gonna sleep with criminals and eat with them you better take the consequence." RIDE IN THE WHIRLWIND is no tirade against injustice, but there is no sense of a moral implication as Hellman suggests, either. Unlike THE SHOOTING, which is about the feeling and the fulfilment of paranoia, RIDE IN THE WHIRLWIND is a demonstration of the kind of nightmare scenario that would play out again and again in the America of J. Edgar Hoover and the impending law and order of Richard Nixon. In that sense it has a populist perspective while THE SHOOTING is closer to the luxuriant self-obliteration embodied by the music of the Velvet Underground. One works from the outside and the other from the inside, one is closer to the dilemma of poor Afro-American inner city dwellers while the other is akin to the feelings of white, alienated, affluent suburbanites.

Not that these films are in any way polemics – they are both as compactly mysterious as a Borges story but as imbued with the pleasure of physical detail as Hawks – but rather to suggest the social undercurrents that give them their power. The fact is that the seemingly modest RIDE IN THE WHIRLWIND might be the finest visualisation of the 19th century American west on film, more vividly imagined than anything in Peckinpah. Nicholson based his script on homesteaders' diaries, and the movie fixes on rhythms, rituals and silences, so that the loneliness and boredom of life in the wilderness, as well as the importance of little bands of people who stick together to brave its hardships, become palpable. After the initial hold-up of a stagecoach (a perfect scene, all about the logistics, finding the best tactical positions from a bluff overlooking the road, the waiting, a silent passenger in a suit looking dreamy and bored), we come upon the three partners. Nicholson's Wes has a carbuncle that's been bothering him, and it's nothing but complaints between these three in a lived-in, autumnal image with an austere beauty (the colour in both films is purposely dulled, flattened).

The outlaws live in a tiny cabin in a valley, and they are led by Harry Dean Stanton, in eyepatch and homburg (and looking almost exactly the same as he does thirty years later). They are friendly but taciturn and only slightly threatening, used to living alone in the wilderness. One fascinating character is played by Rupert Crosse, a lanky, imposing man and the crack shot of the group. He appears to be the authority figure but he barely says three words in the whole movie. Interestingly, there is nothing made of his being black (pretty unusual for 1966). The peculiar focus of this film allows for a very private sense of character, deeply rooted in environment, weather and circumstances.

When the vigilantes come, they smoke out the thieves after a languorous, protracted exchange of bullets. Wes and Vern climb up a rockface and bust in on a family that lives on the mountaintop, an older married couple and their daughter Abby (Millie Perkins). The father (George Mitchell), a plain, rumpled man, is outside chopping wood at the time. That's how he spends most of his life, and he expects Abby to call him before every meal and have his "wash-up" ready for him: the film is so keyed into dailiness that its pivotal moment comes when he goes to do his pre-dinner ritual and the wash basin is empty. Abby has forgotten to prepare it because she's so nervous, and her father co-mes undone, which sets the sad but inevitable denouement in motion.

Wes and Vern don't waste any time pleading their innocence. They know that there is no way they will be able to prove their essential goodness, and they don't have the time to try. Again, this is a new moral framework for west-erns and, in this case, for American movies in general. In the movie's scheme of things, since Wes and Vern have been forced to behave like criminals, for all intents and purposes they have become criminals. Nicholson and Hellman worked hard to avoid clichés on this film, and one of the most deeply rooted clichés in American cinema is the innately good man, able to prove his inno-cence sufficiently to satisfy the community of the film. In the morally frank vi-sion of RIDE IN THE WHIRLWIND, that cliché (which is perpetuated in current American cinema) is not even a possibility. When Vern shoots the enraged, stu-pid father in self-defence, the transformation is complete. At the end of the film, Vern himself has been shot, and he sits by a tree to wait for the posse to come and finish him off. He tells Vern to move on and leave him to die, like Hawthorne's Roger Malvin. The last shot of this haunting film, once thought to be a more conventional appendage of THE SHOOTING but really every bit its equal, is Nicholson riding over a hill and out of sight into a troubled future.

Back in the 1980s, it seemed natural to compare Hellman to Wim Wenders, but in retrospect he seems much closer to certain post-new wave French film-makers like Jean Eustache, Maurice Pialat, André Téchiné and Philipe Garrel. In their work, daily life is front and centre, and there is no moral formula by which people are judged – their films move side by side with their characters. It's no wonder that Hellman found his first real popularity in France, where the westerns achieved a cult status after making the rounds of the interna-tional festival circuit (AIP refused to pay Corman's asking price, and the films were never properly released in America). "I think THE SHOOTING played for 13 months and RIDE IN THE WHIRLWIND for 6 or 7 months, and they've been playing on and off ever since. Because of that and because of the influence of

Cahiers du cinéma and other European critics in Hollywood, I got a reputation just in Hollywood. At that time, there was an envy of Europe and European filmmakers, and the studio executives really were... you know, there was kind of a snob appeal about something from Europe." Then Hellman added, "I don't think that's true anymore," the understatement of the decade.

Hellman kicked around for a few years after completing the westerns (they took six months to edit). He was a dialogue director on Corman's THE ST. VAL-ENTINE'S DAY MASSACRE and edited THE WILD ANGELS, the musical sequences in Rafelson's HEAD and a film Corman directed under a pseudonym called WHAT'S IN IT FOR HARRY? During this period his long string of failed or discontinued projects began. "I had a deal with Roger to do a picture called EXPLOSION at AIP. It was about a black sheriff in the south. We developed the picture, and it was cancelled the week before we were to start shooting. Then I was hired to do a picture based on the play *Macbird*, and that fell apart, I guess, when Robert Kennedy was assassinated. Then I went to Europe to do a picture based on *The Two Faces Of January* by Patricia Highsmith." The money never materialised for that project, and Hellman returned to LA. "My agent found some people in Hollywood who had read a few French reviews, and he got me hired to do TWO-LANE BLACKTOP."

TWO-LANE BLACKTOP originated at a production company called Cinema Centre with producer Michael Laughlin (who would later make THE CHRISTIAN LICORICE STORE and DUSTY AND SWEETS MCGEE). The company put up $100,000 for an original screenplay by Will Corry, and Laughlin, a Europhile, offered the script to Hellman. According to Tatum, Hellman felt that Corry's script, about a white man and a black man racing across country, was "interesting but not fully realised". He gave me a different opinion. "It was... THE GUMBALL RALLY. Only it was a Disney version of that, if you can imagine such a thing. It was the most insipid, silly, sentimental, dumb movie you could imagine. But it was about a race. I was attracted to just the idea of a cross-country race." He and Laughlin agreed that they had to find a new writer – "When I think about it, it's absurd: they paid $100,000 for this script that we *totally* threw out" – and Hellman decided on novelist Rudy Wurlitzer, whose only previous screen credit was as a co-writer on Jim McBride's GLEN AND RANDA. "I read a novel that he had written called *Nog*. There was one scene in particular that was so absurd and so brilliant that I just couldn't resist him as a writer. These three people are camped out in the wilderness, two guys and a girl. And the hero of the story is sent off to gather firewood. He comes back to find the girl and the other guy fucking. And the hero says, 'So I started fucking her from behind.' And he said, 'First he came, and she came, and I plunged on alone.' That had so much... that was the human condition." Hellman finally tracked down Wurlitzer in San Francisco.

It's unclear whether the casting of James Taylor was the brainchild of Hellman, Laughlin or Fred Ross. "I saw a billboard on Sunset Boulevard and I just flipped over his face," Hellman told me. "James came out and did a screen test, and he had a moustache. We weren't sure whether we wanted him with or without it so in the screen test he shaves it off." Everything was all set for a May shoot when Cinema Centre suddenly dropped the project in April. Hellman and Laughlin made the studio rounds ("MGM thought it would be a boring film because it all took place in a car. One of the things I had to do when we were presenting it to them was demonstrate how many different camera angles you could get in a car. I think I came up with 24") and finally made their deal with Ned Tanen, whose independent production unit at Universal was also responsible for Frank Perry's DIARY OF A MAD HOUSEWIFE, Milos Forman's American debut TAKING OFF, Dennis Hopper's THE LAST MOVIE and Peter Fonda's THE HIRED HAND (which was, at one point offered to Hellman). They made the film for $850,000 and Hellman had final cut – a standard deal with Tanen's artists. "We realised that the reason that deal was made was because of EASY RIDER. There was no question that we appreciated its success as a ticket to a kind of freedom that wouldn't have been available to us otherwise."

Hellman shot TWO-LANE BLACKTOP in sequence, and took his crew caravan-style on a real cross country trip – from LA to Needles, California to Flagstaff, Arizona to Santa Fe and Tucumcari, New Mexico, then to Boswell, Oklahoma, Little Rock, Arkansas and Memphis and Maryville, Tennessee. This highly un-usual practice did not endear the director to his crew and his actors, who were doubly exasperated by getting their script pages only the night before their scenes. "In life you don't know what's going to happen to you next week, so I didn't feel that that was crucial to being able to play the scene today." As a re-sult his less experienced actors – Taylor, Beach Boys' drummer Dennis Wilson and newcomer Laurie Bird (a teenager with a strange history that fit her role as a drifting hitcher perfectly) – stay a little off-kilter but fresh, in a prolonged state of early morning clarity. Taylor's line readings are awkward, but his lanky physique and beady hawk face are perfect for an obsessive racer who cannot leave the protection of his 1955 Chevy.

The first rough assemblage of TWO-LANE BLACKTOP was four hours long. "We were contractually obligated to deliver a two-hour movie so we lost half the script. We lost some good scenes, for sure, that I fell in love with." It's possi-ble to go back and look at Wurlitzer's original script (the whole thing was pub-lished in Esquire before the film came out under the heading 'The Movie of the Year', one of the worst marketing decisions of all time), in which the characters are a bit more filled out than in the finished film. The influence of PARIS NOUS APPARTIENT is especially telling here. TWO-LANE BLACKTOP is made up of

James Taylor, Laurie Bird and Dennis Wilson in TWO LANE BLACKTOP

many of the alleged in-between moments that most filmmakers would automatically cut. I'm thinking of one scene in particular, in which Taylor and Wilson confront Warren Oates and decide to race him across country. Quite a bit of time is devoted to Oates leaning against a wall drinking a bottle of Coke, putting it half-finished in the bottle rack, drinking from it again, putting it back. The scene is made up of milling around, quietly delivered taunts from Taylor and Wilson at Oates in his flashy yellow GTO, and a geography of hurt feelings, needling, and insecurity is laid out around a sleepy gas station. It's a scene that defines the film and lays the groundwork for the strange mixture of tenderness and disconnection that develops between these four people. More correctly it is tenderness via disconnection, because the remoteness they all share provides a barrier that makes it safe for them to relate to each other. Everybody except Laurie Bird's petulant hitcher is magnetised to one another, and without the bond of conflict they remain undefined.

A common thread in 1970s art is the importance of landscape as connective tissue, as a touchstone, a home, a cure or a self-influenced punishment. Two classic instances: Joni Mitchell's 'Blue' and Bob Dylan's 'Blood On the Tracks', musical masterpieces of melancholy and regret intimately tied to wanderlust, names of places and people ("I looked for you in old Honolulu, San Francisco or Ashtabula" and "The last time I saw Richard was Detroit in 1968"). The phenomenon of the road movie is actually the fullest expression of a spirit that disappeared (from American culture) in the 1980s. Landscape in 1970s art and thought is important even in works where it is not immediately obvious – for instance, Joan Micklin Silver's lovely CHILLY SCENES OF WINTER, where the funk that has settled over all the characters seems intertwined with the snowy, overcast weather around Salt Lake City. Think also of the plays of Sam Shepard, or the writings of Gregory Bateson that were popular at the time and his insistence that Man be referred to properly as Man In Nature. We look back fondly on the best of 1970s cinema now, with its flux, its resistance to pinning people or places down with ready formulations, as an antidote to the current norm of easily tagged characters fastened to a spruced and polished backdrop. Around 1983 is when the shift begins – to Reaganism, new ageism, and in movies to a grid mentality that follows the Hitchcockian formula of emotion and camera distance to the letter and lowers it to the level of a business calculation. Man as the ultimate owner of his destiny returns and landscape disappears, becomes flattened out and standardised or turned into an exotic effect moulded to fit whatever drama is at hand.

TWO-LANE BLACKTOP offers an oblique tour of a wide variety of suburban, desert and rural settings that are never editorialised or offered for delectation. What is striking is the way Hellman gets the rolling rhythm of a changing landscape behind unchanging people. "For me, space is not neutral," Hellman told Michel Ciment in a 1973 *Postitif* interview, "not only in life but also in my films. New Mexico is not Oklahoma, and I never used a scene outside of its geographical context. The landscape is different and, from this point of view, everything was very precise. It's like the sound or the dialogue: I don't want to make an element of the film obvious. In a sense I'm a landscape painter, but I don't want to show a landscape only for its beauty, or to enhance its value." This is a holistic approach to filmmaking that puts Hellman in a select group whose other members include Hawks, Dreyer, Bresson, Renoir and Murnau. But Hellman is not an optimist like Hawks, or a sensualist like Renoir. Nor is his vision organised around transcendence or spiritual immanence like Murnau, Bresson and Dreyer. If this seems like an exaggerated claim, I think that there's a reason for that: along with Cassavetes and the Straubs, Hellman is one of the great materialist filmmakers – past the point of rejecting or questioning God, like Bergman and Godard, these are artists for whom the question of God doesn't even come up. This probably accounts for their lack of popularity with the critical establishment, who regard transcendence or its rejection as a necessary component of great art.

This movie about a cross country race between a car freak in a souped-up 1955 Chevy and a fantasist in a slick GTO moves at an even, gliding pace, and it's all about the racers stopping to gas up, to eat, to make money in a short local race, to pick up hitchhikers, to let the engine breathe, to share a drink. There's a poignance in Hellman's tough-minded approach, which does not highlight or build up but maintains a steady forward motion. All the fumbling attempts to reach out to another human being dissolve into the flow of film time. Hellman takes a sleepy Arkansas town on a rainy Sunday morning and works the specificity of place, time and circumstance to maximum effect. Taylor and Wilson stop to steal some local plates so they won't get pulled over, and the square Oates decides he needs some too – he's so drunk he falls asleep on the ground, leaning against the front of his car with the screwdriver in his hand. They can't leave him behind, though. They think they are in a race, but Hellman allows us to see that they really aren't. They are really players in a theatre of life.

Taylor and Oates attempt to absorb every person or place that crosses their path with their respective mindsets. Taylor is the introvert, and everything for him is swallowed up and contained by the road. For the extroverted Oates, everything becomes a part of a dream that he's spinning as he drives across America. Taylor's aquiline face may be the visual centrepiece of the movie, buoyed by Laurie Bird's pout ("I don't see anybody paying attention to *my* rear end") and Dennis Wilson's pudgy stoned softness, but Oates is its emotional centre. While it seems obvious on reflection that Hellman and Wurlitzer planned on such a mind-body bifurcation, it doesn't smack of schematising the way it's enacted.

There's not another character like Oates's in all American cinema. Fredric March's drunken manager of small loans in The Best Years Of Our Lives, Dana Andrews's melancholy regular guys in his films for Preminger, Christopher Walken's mercenary in The Dogs of War, Bogart's forlorned convict in Dark Passage – they all come close in their feeling for lonely smallness and bruised egos, but none of them are willing to recede and verge on disappearance the way Oates is here. In V-neck sweaters (they keep changing colour), driving gloves, a wet bar in the trunk, music to suit every mood, a cocky grin that looks like it's been practiced in the mirror and a different story for everyone he picks up along the road, this man without a name has bought the James Bond/Playboy ideal of the well-rounded man, and he adapts himself to every mood. Oates's weathered face and toothy grin never seemed as beautiful as they did here, and there is no other performance that I can think of that registers the slightest prick of wounded feelings with such care and sensitivity. "Why aren't you in Bakersfield?" says a downhome cracker that GTO picks up on the road, and Oates tries to band-aid the hurt on his face with a smile.

The man in the GTO never states anything directly, and a wealth of potential backstory is allowed to build in our minds. Oates gives him a strong sense of physical maladaption – he can't even lean against a building comfortably.

Plenty of American actors have tried to show the void lurking behind grandstanding bravado, but it's usually spoiled by a subliminal hogging, a fear of being plain. Only Oates has been brave enough to put the softness in the American character on display, the degree to which a personality can be a desperate invention. It's notable that the one real success GTO has in the movie – he smooth-talks a couple of rednecks out of beating up Taylor and Wilson by concocting a story about how they're singers and he's their manager – is thanks to his skill as a championship liar. He tries to lose his knowledge of his own desperation and dissatisfaction in the limitless possibility of the landscape.

Taylor's driver, on the other hand, tries to burrow into the landscape. That's why the last image of the movie, in which the film appears to catch in the projector and burn, is no late-1960s affectation à la THOMAS CROWN AFFAIR. "It was really the most intellectual, conscious manipulation of the audience that I've ever done. I thought it was a movie about speed, and I wanted to bring the audience back out of the movie and into the theatre, and to relate them to the experience of watching a film. I also wanted to relate them to, not consciously but unconsciously, the idea of film going through a camera, which is related to speed as well. I think it came to me out of a similar kind of thing that Bergman did with PERSONA." Hellman knows that the efforts of Taylor's character to disappear into speed are not just futile but a lie. What better way to draw us out of Taylor's head than to arrest the illusion and burn up the frame from its centre? If the film were made today, it would undoubtedly end with a realisation of Taylor's impossible fantasy, just as ED WOOD ends with the premiere of PLAN 9 FROM OUTER SPACE at the Pantages Theatre. This type of 'ambiguity' – really a way for the filmmaker to have his or her cake and eat it too – has no place in Hellman's bluntly realistic scheme of things.

TWO-LANE BLACKTOP is the least romantic road movie imaginable in that it confronts its subject and lays bare its illusions. Although it doesn't posit itself as a critique of America, in the end it is a much sharper and more complete comment on American dreaming than RAGTIME, NASHVILLE, THE GODFATHER or FOUR FRIENDS. Those films are panoramas of pain and deceit, but they are also banquets. Oliver Stone, for instance, makes films that attempt to transfer national traumas from the American subconscious whole onto the screen, but they are the formal equivalent of ten national holidays rolled into one. The celebration of America is supposedly irresistible, often taken as integral to any understanding of the country as a phenomenon, but films like Hellman's or Bob Rafelson's see a sombre, more pleading side. Hellman sees BLACKTOP as a romance (his principle prototypes were Minnelli's THE CLOCK, Lelouch's UN HOMME ET UNE FEMME and Wilder's THE APARTMENT), but that may be its least interesting aspect: it is really a film about self-delusion. Warren Oates's

GTO driver is every born-again Christian, every pontificating drunk or junkie, every young person who marries or has a baby or moves to another town because they think it will change their life, every sharp young tycoon in training who plans to make a killing in real estate and then rest on easy street. His most poignant moment is another tall tale, this one told to Laurie Bird, who's almost asleep in the passenger's seat. "We're gonna go to Florida, and we're gonna lie around that beach and we're just gonna get healthy. Let all the scars heal. Maybe we'll run over to Arizona. The nights are warm... and the roads are straight. And we'll build a house. Yeah, we'll build a house. 'Cause if I'm not grounded pretty soon... I'm gonna go into orbit." He's really just talking to himself.

After Two-Lane Blacktop, Hellman developed Pat Garrett and Billy The Kid with Wurlitzer, but the deal went sour, and the film eventually went to Peckinpah ("I didn't understand the difference between a development deal and a go picture. I wasn't that smart from a business point of view"). He also acted in James Frawley's The Christian Licorice Store, which features cameo appearances by Jean Renoir and his wife Dido. He went to Hong Kong to shoot In a Dream of Passion (the adaptation of La Maison Des Rendez-Vous) to be produced by Gary Kurtz. Sets were designed, and casting was in progress. Hellman wanted Sean Connery, his producer wanted Jon Finch, Finch's agent told Hellman that his client wasn't interested, and the film folded (Finch would later meet Hellman and tell him that he never even saw the script). Hellman soon returned to Hong Kong to direct a Hammer film called Shatter, only to be fired in mid-production ("I got fired basically because of a difference of opinion as far as treating racial subjects in the picture"). He returned to America, and Roger Corman offered him a project that he had been nurturing for some time, based on the Charles Willeford novel Cockfighter.

Hellman quickly became frustrated by the situation in which he had landed. "Roger already had a screenplay and I tried to do what I normally do, which is to remould it to suit my own purposes. I hired Earl Mac Rauch to do a re-write, and I guess after the first week Roger really started getting depressed, because it was really his baby and not mine, and he told me that I could have Mac for just one additional week." Hellman and Rauch were forced to concentrate on the scenes involving Frank (Oates) and his lover Mary Elizabeth (Patricia Pearcy), so that only the beginning of the film, a riverside encounter in the middle and the ending reflect their work. Hellman does not like Cockfighter for this reason, but his difficulties aren't reflected in the finished product.

Cockfighter (which also came out under the titles Gamblin' Man and Wild Drifter in addition to Born to Kill) is about Frank Mansfield out of

Decatur, Georgia, who speaks only in voiceover throughout most of the film – he's taken a vow of silence because it was his loud mouth that cost him a sot at the cockfighting championship the year before. He has asked his girlfriend to hold off marrying another man, so that he can prove himself stable enough for a long-term relationship. She has never seen the most important aspect of his life, and he invites her to the championship. The story falls far afield of many norms at once – of decency (the subject matter), of morality (no one gets their comeuppance for indulging in the evils of cockfighting), and of storytelling and movie acting (the hero doesn't speak). And what's so striking about Hellman's approach is its feeling of familiarity. We seem to light upon every scene, with delicacy and an appropriately southern sense of ease. The first thing we see is the inside of a moving trailer, the camera panning to the gentle rhythm of Michael Franks's score. The light is warm, cozy, and then we hear the weathered voice of Warren Oates in a conversational tone: "I learned to fly a plane... and I lost interest in it. Water skiin'... I lost interest in *it*. But, uh, this is somethin' you don't conquer. Anything that can fight to the death and not utter a sound, well..." The camera settles on a bird with brilliantly coloured feathers in a cage on a counter. The film never loses this intimate tone.

This is another remarkable performance from Oates, who doesn't play the driven side of Frank's personality. The determination comes through in his concentration. There is no wasted motion – depriving himself of speech has focused Frank as well as the actor who plays him, and every gesture is gracefully communicative. There's a wonderful scene where someone tells Frank a joke, and he waits a beat before taking off his hat and slapping it three times against his leg, then putting it back on: he's so focused that he can't be thrown by pleasantries. But the performance also has carefully inserted moments of wild abandon, like the flashback to Championship eve when he bounces off the walls of his tiny motel room boasting that his bird can take anybody else's. This is a whole, finished portrait, and a ridiculously unheralded performance.

The cockfight sequences are impromptu but heavily ritualised gatherings. It's easy to imagine another director cutting to close-ups of bloodthirsty yahoos swigging beer as they lay odds on unsuspecting birds. Here the crowd is spirited but respectful: they are participating in a tradition that has gone on for generations. There is no bloodlust, but there is a strict set of rules and codes of behaviour. "We went down there to Georgia and we just started living in that world, which is really a very important part of the life there, particularly the subculture [of cockfighting]. I really loved the people, and as I got into it, I was making a picture about them and about their life. That aspect of it I like a lot. The documentary aspect of it appeals to me."

Hellman shows a warmth in COCKFIGHTER that is not so abundant in his other work. These may be "appalling people" (an appalling description from

Leslie Halliwell's film guide) because of the sport they engage in, but they conduct themselves with gentlemanly politeness and communal good spirits. This is the most Rossellinian of Hellman's films, in that he demonstrates the desperate competitive drive of people without dramatising it by documenting their gatherings and cutting to the ferocity of the cockfighting (no doubt it is what Roger Corman meant when he complained that Hellman had made a "quiet" film). When Hellman does cut to the birds themselves in quick flashes, the effect is striking: in the hands of Director of Photography Nestor Almendros they become bright bursts of action painting. The game cocks are not symbols but extensions, facilitators – the birds are engaged in a struggle to survive that the people thrive on at a vicarious level filtered through rules, ceremony and decorum. In a strange way, the cockfights imbue these people with poignancy rather than ugliness – their frame of experience is small and circumscribed, their desires so ritualised, it is as if their existence depended on the framework of winning and losing in order to have meaning.

The film is filled with warm, sharply funny interactions between Frank and a circle of people who share this genteel world: his sister and her husband (Millie Perkins and Troy Donahue), his partner Omar (Richard B. Shull), his principal rival Jack Burke (Harry Dean Stanton) and a cockfighting judge who recognises Frank as the purest trainer on the circuit (author Charles Willeford). It is punctuated by eye-popping, wholly unexpected bursts of physical energy, another anomaly in his work (this is more of a Corman trademark, but Hellman handles a scene like the one where Ed Begeley, Jr.'s farm boy goes ballistic on Frank because his beloved game cock has lost a match with more tonal control than Corman could ever manage). Beneath the gentility, however, what sets everyone in motion here is a very American desire to win that is made all the more powerful because it's so subtly delineated. Frank sends his sister and brother-in-law packing and moves his entire house off his property because he wants to use it to train his birds. He wants Mary Elizabeth to see him and accept him in his world, but that's secondary.

The ending of the film is extraordinary. Frank's game cock goes round after round with Burke's, and wins just before he collapses: finally, Frank has a real emotional attachment to this bird, which gets him the cockfighting medal. This prompts Mary Elizabeth to walk out in disgust. "That bird had more heart than you do," she says, and Frank throws the bird to the ground, steps on it, rips its head off its body and shoves it into her hand. She shudders with horror, then gamely wraps the head in a handkerchief, puts it in her pocketbook and walks away. "She loves me, Omar," says Frank to his partner, his first words in the entire movie. It's a truly transcendent moment, a surging electric exchange of the life force that lifts the film to another plane: the sphere of life may be circumscribed, an endless repetition of competitive rituals, but within that world forces can transform themselves into spirited energy. Frank is right, she does love him, because she performs an act that matches his in audacity and sheer spontaneous expression.

During the three years between COCKFIGHTER and his next completed film, Hellman did post-production work on a biography of Muhammed Ali called THE GREATEST after director Tom Gries died (he would perform a similar chore a couple of years later when he did extensive post-production on the doomed AVALANCHE EXPRESS after Mark Robson died), he directed an episode of the TV cop show *Barretta* and edited the action sequences in Peckinpah's THE KILLER ELITE. At Christmas time 1976, producer Elliot Kastner called Hellman from Rome and told him to come and shoot a western – the script needed just a little work. "I got a couple of writer friends to agree to do a rewrite. 'This is terrible, we can't rewrite this,' they said, and I said, 'Well, just write me a new script.'" Kastner hated the new script and checked out, but the Italian producers loved it, and Hellman left for Spain to shoot what would become CHINA 9, LIBERTY 37.

CHINA 9, LIBERTY 37 (the title comes from a Texas road sign Hellman saw as he rode a cross-country train home after finishing COCKFIGHTER) is a lovely film, and a somewhat flawed one as well. Its tone is lonely and sad, very close to COCKFIGHTER, only lacking its bursts of energetic behaviour and its vibrant visual scheme. There is a pervasive sense of winding down that hovers over this movie – you can feel the uptake as horses gallop and as people walk. The weatherbeaten poetry may come in part from the fact that Hellman's father died during pre-production – in fact the character of Clayton Drum (Fabio Testi) was written to relate to certain experiences in his life. Drum is a hired gun, and he's pardoned from the gallows on condition that he kill another hired gun named Sebenec (Warren Oates) who won't sell his property to the railroad. But he finds that he likes Sebenec and decides not to murder him. Sebenec's young wife Catherine (Jenny Agutter) is sexually attracted to Clayton, and sleeps with him the morning that Clayton leaves. Sebenec divines the truth and attacks Catherine, who stabs him in self-defence. She runs after Clayton, who is less than pleased to have her tagging along, but they enjoy a few passionate nights together before they are caught – by Sebenec, who has survived, and his brothers.

After the blazing originality of the previous four Hellman pictures, the strict adherence to generic character ideas throughout much of CHINA 9, LIBERTY 37 is disappointing. It's arguable that the common denominators of the western genre are also present in THE SHOOTING and RIDE IN THE WHIRLWIND – the hired gun, the lonely cowpokes, the homesteading family alone in the wilderness. But in CHINA 9, behaviour is much more constricted than in any previous Hellman film, and two of the principal characters are severely limited. It's partly an acting problem – Testi is loveable in a way, and Hellman works hard to make his bulk play credibly onscreen, but he is never really animated dramatically or visually. Agutter was one of the loveliest actresses of the 1970s, but she was fatally inexpressive, and her Laura Ashley brand of demureness is miles away from a frontier wife, even a pampered one. There is also something beyond western stereotypes that hampers the script by Douglas Venturelli and Jerry Bryant (who ran the famed Z channel for movies in LA, and who would later commit suicide). The sexual politics that colour the relationship between Clayton and Catherine are typically late-1970s – "I want to be with you tonight – and I hate you for it," he tells her, and they come to terms with their lust like model pop-psychological partners. This is followed by an extended slow-motion sex scene accompanied by a maudlin Ronee Blakely song that may be the most modish thing Hellman's ever filmed. Their relationship is not really articulated and short-circuits on platitudes, although it must be said that, with the exception of COCKFIGHTER, romantic pairings have never been a strength for Hellman (the love story between James Taylor and Laurie Bird, contrary to Hellman's assessment, is probably the least developed aspect of TWO-LANE BLACKTOP). After Clayton kills one of Sebenec's brothers in self-defence, they flee, and their magical encounters with a travelling circus and a fanciful dime-novelist who wants to write Drum's story (Sam Peckinpah in a dry, detached performance – he delivers his lines in a failed high-dramatic voice) don't have very much to bounce off of in order to spark their intended poetry.

Predictably, this movie comes to life in every sequence with Warren Oates. Each Oates performance for Hellman is a fully-formed creation – the lean, paranoid Willet Gashade; the dreaming, lonely man behind the wheel in TWO-LANE BLACKTOP; the rousing but rigorously single-minded Frank Mansfield; and Matthew Sebenec, a rumpled, ageing, wary gunfighter. He's quiet, settled in, dresses in clothes that look like sacks – and he's deeply distrustful in a way that seems to be the result of years spent in an isolated setting. The dailiness that runs through all of Hellman's work is most pervasive and touching in the scenes with Oates, an actor who knows how to do dead time and put life around the edges. Oates's scene where he goes bananas after he discovers that Agutter and Testi have slept together is wonderful. Catherine comes in from outside, and Sebenec gets amorous. "I have to make breakfast," she says. "Fuck breakfast," he says, before he notices that her night gown is wet and sees Clayton riding away. "You've been with him, haven't you? I'll be damned... I'll be god*damned*!" This is a different kind of hurt from that of the GTO driver in TWO-LANE BLACKTOP – this is the hurt of a cuckold, a soft, nondescript older man with sunken shoulders whose wife has proved his worst fear: that he does not satisfy her sexually. Sebenec is more immobilised than any other

Oates/Hellman character, partly because Hellman builds the latter part of the film on parallel editing that carries an ideogrammatic force but keeps actors in a tableau stance. Sebenec's slowly evolving forgiveness of Catherine is collapsed and cunningly delineated through ellipses, and after a predictable shoot-out with Clayton, the film ends on a fine image – Sebenec and Catherine riding away as their house burns behind them, a beautiful symbol of the rebuilding of their marriage.

"We were both born in July, and we had a natural affinity for one another," Hellman said of Oates. He wouldn't talk much about his friend and most vital collaborator, perhaps because it was too painful – it had been only two years since Oates had died of a heart attack at the age of 53. But what could he add that would amplify their achievement together, which already speaks so eloquently? Monte Hellman and Warren Oates the great unrecognised actor/director partnership – they are as important as Ford/Wayne, Sternberg/Dietrich, Mann/Stewart and Scorsese/De Niro. And in modern American cinema, where every actor looks like he or she has just come from the gym, where self-promotion and self-expression have become confused and entangled, Warren Oates, the actor who was unafraid of playing small, insignificant men and who cultivated not an ounce of glamour, is missed beyond measure. He did some good work for Peckinpah, but not even ALFREDO GARCIA can compare to the poetry of his films with Hellman, who dedicated IGUANA, his next completed film, to Warren Oates.

CHINA 9 was never released in America. The Italian owners took a severely recut and re-looped version to Cannes in 1982 and were going to sell it to the world television market, but Hellman also attended the festival (he appears in Wenders' 1982 Cannes documentary CHAMBRE 666) and convinced his ex-lawyer, who was then a Lorimar executive, to buy the film and at least show it on TV in its correct form. It only had a quick theatrical run at the Thalia (a virtual Monte Hellman admiration society) in 1983. After CHINA 9, Hellman almost shot a German spy story called SECRET WARRIORS, but the company that was going to finance the project went bankrupt with Téchiné's THE BRONTE SISTERS; almost shot a film called DARK PASSION for Paramount and "they elected not to go ahead with that"; almost shot a film called KING OF WHITE LADY at Zoetrope but got stuck on the same development merry-go-round as Nicholas Roeg and Franc Roddham. In 1983, he shot a seven minute short called FRANCIS COPPOLA: A PROFILE for the Playboy channel. It would be five years before he would direct another film.

"Compared to IGUANA, all my previous work is like Walt Disney movies," Hellman told Tatum. I'm not sure if this holds water – the endings of RIDE IN THE WHIRLWIND and TWO-LANE BLACKTOP are pretty tough, but IGUANA is a different kind of film ("... the first art-essay film by Monte Hellman," wrote Bill

Krohn), and it sets itself on a more explicitly metaphysical plane. Hellman was able to bring the Alberto Vasquez-Figueroa novel to the screen (although the avowed source for the main character of Oberlus, the harpooner, is Melville's *The Encantadas*) in part because of a mistake: according to Tatum, an interpreter mistranslated a letter from an Italian producer who did *not* want to do the film and made it appear that he was giving Hellman a green light. The movie was shot in 1987, in Rome and the Canaries, which doubled for the Galapagos Islands. The action is set in the early 19th century. Oberlus (Everett McGill) jumps from a whaling ship, where he is tortured and ridiculed by his shipmates as well as his captain (Fabio Testi – the part was supposed to go to Patrick Bachau) even though he is the best harpooner on board. Half of his face is covered with a growth that makes him look like an iguana. Oberlus goes to an island and takes some sailors hostage who have been sent ashore to capture him – he makes them his slaves, and builds a small society that is based on the only thing he knows: force. When a woman named Carmen (Maru Valdivielso) comes ashore with her lover, Oberlus murders him and captures her to become his sex slave. He impregnates her, but vows that if the baby looks like him, he will drown it to save it from the tortures he's suffered.

IGUANA is a thrilling film, and a pretty odd and amazingly rarefied one as well. It's not just a question of Hellman being out of step with modern filmmaking (thank God for small favours!). The kind of film language and syntax that characterise IGUANA have all but disappeared from cinema, at least in America, and its brio is refreshing. The movie has a hard, raw physical beauty, worked so carefully that it seems to have been carved out of the landscape, and its few manmade details are exquisite, particularly a chest full of nautical effects. But it's also unbelievably brusque. It's possible that the financial constraints were so great that Hellman developed an aesthetic of poverty to cover his lack of production values, but his storytelling is pushed to its extremity here, and scenes are short and blunt with little room to breathe. Tatum writes that Hellman's customary "montage à la Rivette" is gone here, but I would say that on the contrary this begins as Hellman's most Rivettean film, with especially strong echoes of NOROIT (safe bet Hellman has never seen it, of course) because of the shared pirate milieu. The first section of IGUANA cuts back and forth between two apparently unrelated stories – Oberlus on the island and Carmen at home with her father and various lovers – and when they meet, the convergence isn't just narrative but poetic, much in the manner of Rivette.

But the thesis form of the film is very non-Rivette, and it is not especially suited to Hellman, who works best with situations that slowly evolve over expanses of space and time. Moreover, that thesis is so despairing that I have to question how much it's actually embraced by its author and how much it's a provocative dramatic conceit. The film is punctuated by horrendous acts of cruelty. Oberlus engages the most literate of his captives, Dominique (Joseph Culp), also the most eloquent spokesman on behalf of good will in the world, to teach him to read. Later, he decides to punish one of the slaves for insubordination and tells Dominique to decapitate him before the count of ten. If he doesn't, Oberlus will hand the sword to the other man and count to ten, and go back and forth all night if necessary before one of them kills the other. Dominique finally kills the other man, who is his friend, and his entire belief system is shattered.

Oberlus's stark vision of life is perpetually fulfilled. At the end of the film, he guides his slaves over the top of the island as they run from men searching for Carmen. She is ready to give birth, but Oberlus won't let her stop running, and the baby is born in a cave on the beach. Oberlus takes one look at it and pulls it out of Carmen's arms. As Carmen screams and the braying of tracking dogs becomes louder, he walks into the ocean and drowns himself and his child. The end of the film is undeniably powerful, but the extent to which that is due to the cumulative impact of the rest of the movie is doubtful. The bold-faced point-making that characterises the script is rendered potently as action, but the theme is never carefully elaborated. It is just cruelty, endlessly restated. Altogether, IGUANA is one of Hellman's most fascinating films, but it strikes me as the result of an uneasy marriage between the deeply personal and the readily available. The inevitable post-script, of course, is that IGUANA is far and away Hellman's most invisible film, seen by next to no one – the only writing I know of on this strange, one of a kind movie is by the invaluable Bill Krohn in *Cahiers du cinéma*.

What is there to say about Hellman's next film, SILENT NIGHT DEADLY NIGHT 3: BETTER WATCH OUT? First of all, it's completely singular as a slasher film, as Krohn has pointed out – it proceeds at a hypnotically slow pace, and a high percentage of its murders occur offscreen. The most striking sequences in the film involve the young heroine Laura (Samantha Scully), who is blind and has psychic powers (she's channelling into a maniacal, comatose killer), and Hellman holds his camera on her for long stretches, building an unsettling, dreamlike tone. Krohn has compared Hellman to Jacques Tourneur, and the comparison is apt: both are quietists, with a feel for mood and overall tone rather than dramatic attack. Hellman certainly applies himself to the horror genre just as conscientiously as Tourneur always did, without a trace of the slumming artist. But I think that providing shocks is somewhat alien to Hellman, and that BETTER WATCH OUT has some of the same problems as BACK DOOR TO HELL and FLIGHT TO FURY. Its tone is *so* uniformly oneiric that it isn't really scary. Tourneur's THE LEOPARD MAN, for instance, is one of the great, sustained pieces of 1940s Hollywood filmmaking, and it works from within the genre, building to terrifying set pieces. But Hellman applies himself *over* the horror genre, and his elegant tone feels a little divorced from the material. He has spoken of BETTER WATCH OUT in personal terms, as the second part of a "Beauty and the Beast" trilogy (in fact, there is a clip from THE TERROR in the film: a gas station owner who is about to be murdered is watching it on Christmas Eve), but at a recent season of his work at the BFI he would not allow it to be shown. BETTER WATCH OUT is an impressive film, but Hollywood in 1995 is a different world from Hollywood in 1942 or 1958 (the year of Tourneur's British CURSE OF THE DEMON). The second sequel to a slasher movie is now considered the bottom of the barrel by a community of pretentious, instant auteurs and business sharks, notwithstanding the fact that there is more artistry in a single sequence of BETTER WATCH OUT than in the collected works of Richard Donner.

"I think that we suffered, in a sense, from a kind of hubris," Hellman said of himself and his compatriots at the Corman factory. "We really were egocentric. We really were more concerned about feeling good about what we were doing and making films that we ourselves really liked. And not concerned with what the critics were going to say, or how many tickets we were going to sell. We just assumed that that was part of it, that you make a picture and people go to see it. It was before the time, such as now, when, if the picture doesn't have the potential to do a certain kind of box-office, they don't even run it... Somehow, the film schools got turned around in a funny way, and they're teaching people how to make money. They're teaching them how to make a success in Hollywood, and that never occurred to us or was never part of the training that we went through." The "we" here is instructive, a reminder of all the great creative teamwork that went on during that period: Corman's sweatshop, Warhol's factory, Oshima's 'gang', Bergman and Fellini's stock companies, the loose assemblages around Rivette and Rohmer. Those days are gone, and now everyone is a solitary artist.

Ned Tanen once said that TWO-LANE BLACKTOP was the finest film he ever worked on, and he has reason to be proud: after the dust has cleared, it stands, along with COCKFIGHTER, as one of the great works of the American cinema. Even a Hellman film that is not wholly satisfying, like BETTER WATCH OUT, has greatness in it. Hellman's cinema, on the whole, from BEAST FROM HAUNTED CAVE on, reflects the hypnotic side of existence, the immersion of consciousness deep within the rhythm of living. "Basically, I've never done my own movies. I've been a director for hire, and I've tried to do what I could with the projects I was assigned to." For a director for hire, Hellman has never compromised his own artistry, softened it for popular consumption or twisted it into a pretzel like Coppola. "His example is a source of the greatest strength," Martin Scorsese wrote of John Cassavetes. And so it is with the less flamboyant but equally uncompromising Monte Hellman. "I could've easily made a picture that reflected the popular taste and that people wanted to see, but that would've been boring to me. You spend three months or six months or a year or two years working on a film, and if all you're thinking about is making a lot of money... you know, it's two years of your life. If you're making a picture that's gonna bore you in the process and afterwards when you have to look at it, it doesn't seem to be worth it."

Hellman defended Coppola, that most solitary of all artists, against my assertions that he was one of the filmmakers who had pushed him into the shadows ("Whether you agree or disagree with what he does or how well or badly he does it, he's true to those demons within himself, and I don't think that that's true of a lot of filmmakers today"). Hellman may be right, but Coppola was one of the pioneers of what Noel Carroll identified in his 1981 *October* article as the "two-tiered system of filmmaking", in which the director satisfies audience demands and winks at cinephiles at the same time with references to other movies. Coppola was once a patchy director, and now he's a patchwork director, sewing together entire movies out of memories of old ones – BRAM STOKER'S DRACULA is one of the most grotesque films ever made by a supposedly major director, and its "artistry" is never sustained for more than a second at a time. But it's possible to sustain a modicum of sympathy for a megalomaniac like Coppola, because there are few alternatives left. The influence of films like his own or those of Spielberg or Lucas ("In STAR WARS, they literally put up every air battle that was ever shot and copied them. I mean, that seems to me such a dearth of imagination that I can't even conceive of it," said Hellman) coupled with rock videos and the validation of something called post-modernism bred an army of young directors with a concept of film as nothing more than an unmodulated stream of visual shocks. The artistry of a Monte Hellman seems outmoded now, which is a tragedy. The work of this ridiculously underappreciated director seems all the more precious when set against the products of the supremely silly moment in American cinema that was the 1990s, with movies like FORREST GUMP and SCHINDLER'S LIST. Which just goes to show, to quote Jean-Marie Straub on Dreyer's failure to find money to make JESUS, that "modern society isn't worth a frog's fart".

Note

1.   I'd like to thank Michael Henry Wilson, Bill Krohn, Jonathan Rosenbaum and Monte Hellman for their generous help with the preparation of this article.

NASHVILLE **Contra** JAWS

Or "The Imagination of Disaster" Revisited

J. Hoberman

> Psychology knows that he who imagines disasters in some way desires them.
> Theodor Adorno, *Minima Moralia*

I

June 1975 – six weeks after *Time* headlined the fall of Saigon as 'The Anatomy of a Debacle' and wondered 'How Should Americans Feel?' – two movies opened, each in its way a brilliant modification on the current cycle of 'disaster' films that had appeared with Nixon II and were now, at the nadir of the nation's self-esteem, parallelled by the spectacular collapse of South Vietnam and unprecedented Watergate drama.

The multi-star, mounting-doom, intersecting-narrative format of Hollywood extravaganzas like EARTHQUAKE and THE TOWERING INFERNO (both 1974) was, as Robin Wood noted at the time, elaborated on and politicized in Robert Altman's NASHVILLE.[1] But as NASHVILLE, the movie widely regarded as Altman's masterpiece, could be said to deconstruct the disaster film, so Steven Spielberg's JAWS would give the cycle a heightened intensity and, perhaps, a second lease on life.

Of course, cine-catastrophe was scarcely a new concept. It was only the movies, Susan Sontag had observed ten years earlier in 'The Imagination of Disaster', that allowed one to "participate in the fantasy of living through one's own death and more, the death of cities, the destruction of humanity itself", Sontag argued that the armageddon-minded science-fiction films that enlivened drive-in screens in the period between the Korean and Vietnam wars were not about science at all but rather the aesthetics of destruction, the beauty of wreaking havoc, the pleasure of making a mess, the pure spectacle of "melting tanks, flying bodies, crashing walls, awesome craters and fissures in the earth".[2]

In the Sixties, the aesthetic of destruction was globalised: After CLEOPATRA (1962) nearly capsized an entire studio, Arthur Penn created the doomsday gangster film and Sam Peckinpah the disaster western. NIGHT OF THE LIVING DEAD (1968), the most apocalyptic horror movie ever made in America, circulated for several years to achieve full cult status in early 1971 with a late-night run in Washington DC that inexorably spread to other cities and college towns. (In New York, the film ran continuously as a midnight attraction from May 1971 through the following February and then again for 34 weeks following Nixon's re-election to July 1973.)

Nor was NIGHT OF THE LIVING DEAD the only vivid representation of Judgment Day. Hal Lindsey's *The Late Great Planet Earth*, an interpretation of Biblical prophesy that extrapolated from current geopolitical events to predict an imminent worldwide catastrophe followed by the return of Jesus Christ, appeared as a mass market paperback in February 1973 after running through 26 printings in its original edition. Lindsey's predictions for the 1970s included an increase in crime, civil unrest, unemployment, poverty, illiteracy, mental illness, and illegitimate births, as well as the greatest famines in world history, the election of open drug-addicts to public office, and the increasing dominance of astrology, Oriental religions, and Satanic cults. By the end of the decade, his book went through another 30-odd printings and sold some 15 million copies.

So the Voice was heard again in the land, although the direct stimulus for disaster films was, of course, neither Watergate nor *When Worlds Collide*, the Book of Daniel nor the collapse of the counterculture, but rather the over-performance of two earlier movies: AIRPORT (1970), grossing over $45 million and for a time #14 on *Variety's* list of Hollywood's all-time money-makers, and THE POSEIDON ADVENTURE (1972) which, released shortly after Nixon's re-election, grossed nearly as much and proved the #1 box office attraction of 1973.

Once more, movies returned to their fairground origins by offering audiences the treat of spectacular cataclysms. But there was something else as well. "Use value in the reception of cultural commodities is replaced by exchange value," Adorno and Horkheimer had observed in *Dialectic of Enlightenment*, "The consumer becomes the ideology of the pleasure industry." There were no Events which everyone 'had to' see in order to fully participate in American life, even while supporting "a model of the huge economic machinery which has always sustained the masses, whether at work or at leisure".[3]

The disaster cycle gathered momentum along with the Watergate scandal, approaching its climax as the President resigned in August 1974. By then, *Time* had offered its readers 'A Preview of Coming Afflictions', reporting that Hollywood's "lemming-like race for the quintessential cataclysm" had spawned some 13 disasters at various stages of production.[4] EARTHQUAKE, co-written by

Mario Puzo, THE TOWERING INFERNO, Irwin Allen's spectacular follow-up to the POSEIDON ADVENTURE, and an AIRPORT sequel were scheduled to open by Christmas – to be followed by movies whose major attractions were an avalanche, a tidal wave, a volcanic eruption, the explosion of the dirigible Hindenburg, a plague of killer bees, and an earthquake permitting a horde of giant, incendiary cockroaches to exit the centre of the earth and overrun Los Angeles. (For the latter, veteran exploitation producer William Castle was "planning a floor-mounted windshield-wiper device that will softly brush across movie-goer's feet and ankles at crucial moments".)[5]

"There is absolutely no social criticism, of even the most implicit kind," Sontag had noted of her science-fiction films. But movies like EARTHQUAKE and THE TOWERING INFERNO were scarcely perceived as anything else. Indeed, the explanation of the trend arrived even before the trend itself.[6]

Why were disaster films taken so seriously? "Every couple of years the American movie public is said to crave something. Now it's calamity, and already the wave of apocalyptic movies – which aren't even here yet – is being analysed in terms of our necrophilia", wrote Pauline Kael shortly after *Time's* piece, thus staking out the counter-pundit position that disaster films were nothing more than meaningless pseudo-events.[7]

Necrophilia, however, was not the explanation offered by most commentators – although some did see the mode as appealing to a popular *Schadenfreude*. Disaster films were more often discussed as reflections of the economic crisis (perceived as 'natural' in capitalist society) precipitated by the OPEC oil embargo in late 1973 or else as manifestations of Watergate – as if Watergate were not the most entertaining disaster film of all. Vietnam may have been too painfully obvious to mention although Kael evoked it in spite of herself when she characterised the directors of disaster movies as "commanders-in-chief in an idiot war."[8]

Typically, in disaster films, calamity arrives as punishment for some manifestation of the Orgy. Both THE POSEIDON ADVENTURE and THE TOWERING INFERNO heighten the thrill by arranging for disaster to strike in the midst of gala parties; in TIDAL WAVE, the volcanic eruption which triggers the eponymous cataclysm is synchronised to the lovemaking of an unmarried couple on a targeted beach. Some disaster movies offered a populist critique by blaming the catastrophe on rapacious corporations and, in most cases, the disaster was worsened by mendacious, greedy, corrupt, and inadequate leaders. Thus, along with the TV cop shows and vigilante films of Nixon II, disaster movies questioned the competence of America's managerial elite. Kael extended that elite to include the captains of America's film industry, specifically Universal (which also had AIRPORT '75, THE HINDENBURG, and JAWS in the works):

> The people who reduced Los Angeles to rubble in EARTHQUAKE must have worked off a lot of self-hatred: you can practically feel their pleasure as the freeways shake, the skyscrapers crumble, and the Hollywood dam cracks ... EARTHQUAKE is Universal's death wish for film art: these destruction orgies are the only way it knows to make money.[9]

Still, it was the iron rule of disaster films that individuals were at fault, never the system itself, while the natural leader who emerged from the chaos was almost uniformly a white male in uniform (pilot, naval officer, policeman, fire chief, priest). Heroism under stress was practised by nearly everyone except the top public officials, who were typically upper-class and devious. Like the Senate's televised Watergate hearings, disaster films offered the spectacle of all-star casts impersonating ordinary, middle-class people coping, as a group, with a limited Armeggedon – the total breakdown of an institution hubristically imagined to be safe, and these ocean liners, airplanes, skyscrapers, theme parks, and cities, were, of course, microcosms of America.

Despite their overt fatalism, the disaster films were fundamentally reassuring. The cycle celebrated the inherent virtue of decent, everyday Middle Americans, linking their survival skills to traditional social roles and conventional moral values – a particularly Darwinian form of sociological propaganda. The notion of God's will may only be implicit that the cataclysm effectively disciplines an overly permissive social order. On an interpersonal level, the reversals wrought by the disaster were often positive. (Reviewing EARTHQUAKE in *The New York Times*, Nora Sayre experienced a "sense of ritual cleansing".[10]) As previously atomised individuals formed a community, class distinctions disappeared. Marriages were reinforced. Middle class virtue prevailed.

Disaster films were additionally comforting in that they revived the old time entertainment religion. In this sense, AIRPORT – like the same year's LOVE STORY – can be seen as the trial balloon for a return to proven, pumped-up Hollywood formulae. Disaster films featured all-star casts. They were populated largely by Nixon-supporters and Reagan-peers, filled with familiar faces from the Pax Americana: Charlton Heston, William Holden, Dean Martin, Shelley Winters, Ava Gardner, Jennifer Jones, Myrna Loy, Dana Andrews, Gloria Swanson, Helen Hayes, Fred Astaire, James Stewart, hardy showbiz survivors all!

It was the return of the Potlatch, tempting Hollywood's alienated audience with the promise of conspicuous consumption and spectacular effects. *The New York Times* whimsically deemed EARTHQUAKE an "awesome" advance towards the total cinema of *Brave New World's* feelies (in which an on-screen kiss made the "facial erogenous zones" of 6000 spectators tingle with "an almost intolerable galvanic pleasure") but unsarcastically called THE TOWERING INFERNO, "old-fashioned Hollywood make-believe at its painstaking best".[11]

Disaster films brought the Pax Americana epic up to date. Not only were they more economically produced and rationally conceived (everything centred upon a single gigantic special effect), but they were also set in the present. Using the a-historic direct address of HIGH NOON, disaster films denied that Americans had truly become permissive and jaded or that traditional values had broken down. They insisted, rather, that, when tested by catastrophe, these values proved to be intact and, contrary to the scenario illustrated by NIGHT OF THE LIVING DEAD, enabled people to help each other through the crisis to guarantee society's survival.

In short, the disaster cycle successfully recuperated the apocalyptic visions of the Sixties. Disaster films, Herbert J. Gans would note in the journal *Social Policy*, "almost suggest that the 1960s never happened".[12]

II

At the time of their release, JAWS and NASHVILLE were regarded as Watergate movies and, indeed, both were in production as the Watergate disaster played its final act during the summer of 1974.

On May 2, three days after Nixon had gone on TV to announce that he was turning over transcripts of 42 White House tapes subpoenaed by the House Judiciary Committee, the JAWS shoot opened on Martha's Vineyard with a mainly male, no-star cast.

The movie's star was the shark or, rather, the three mechanical sharks – one for each profile and another for stunt work – that, run by pneumatic engines and launchable by 65-foot catapult, were created by Robert Mattey, the former Disney special effects expert who had designed the submarine and giant squid for TWENTY THOUSAND LEAGUES UNDER THE SEA. Brought to Martha's Vineyard in pieces and cloaked in secrecy, Mattey's sharks, referred to collectively as "Bruce", took longer than expected to become fully operational, and JAWS was further delayed by poor weather conditions. Accounts of the production routinely refer to the movie itself as a catastrophe only barely avoided: "All over the picture shows signs of going down, like the Titanic...".[13]

In late June, a month when JAWS was still unable to shoot any water scenes while Nixon visited the Middle East and Soviet Union in a hapless attempt "to put the whole Watergate business into perspective",[14] Robert Altman's cast and crew arrived in Nashville, Tennessee. As they were all put up at the same hotel, with everyone expected to stick around for the entire 10-week shoot, there is a sense in which NASHVILLE represented a last bit of Sixties utopianism – the idea that a bunch of talented people might just hang out together in a colourful environment and, almost spontaneously, generate a movie.

Even by Altman's previous standards, NASHVILLE was a free-form composition. It surely helped that neophyte producer Jerry Weintraub's previous experience lay in managing tours, for Frank Sinatra and Elvis Presley among others, and in packaging TV specials. A number of key performers – including comedienne Lily Tomlin and singer Ronee Blakley – were making their movie debuts but, as a director of actors, Altman was famously permissive. His performers contributed much of their own material – including dialogue as well as songs. Altman filmed Barbara Baxley's monologue on the Kennedy assassination without reading it first; he let Ronee Blakley completely rework her character's breakdown. When Julie Christie and Elliot Gould dropped in to visit the set, the director built a scene around them. Joan Tewkesbury, too, had considerable latitude with her screenplay, although one stipulation was that she write an assassination scene in which the victim would be a "mother figure".

Most unusually, NASHVILLE featured a nearly autonomous character. The candidacy of the never-seen Hal Philip Walker was developed by Mississippi novelist Thomas Hal Phillips, who had once managed his brother's campaign for governor. Given his own budget, Phillips opened a campaign headquarters, ordered buttons and bumper stickers, and sent hired sound trucks through the streets. Altman's only requirements for this simulated politician were that he represent a third party, that he be someone whom Phillips himself would want to vote for, and that he was a candidate whom Phillips thought could actually be elected.

NASHVILLE was conceived as an open-ended quasi-documentary, JAWS as a tightly plotted thriller; yet, appropriate to JAWS's mega-fantasy elements, its transformation into a movie was also improvisational. Richard Zanuck and David Brown had paid $175,000 for the rights to the novel and a Benchley screenplay. The script went through three drafts, variously reworked by playwright Howard Sackler, John Milius, and actor/writer Carl Gottlieb. The last version was itself revised continually on location. As Spielberg told one journalist, "we have been making it up as we go along".

Of course, few environments are more self-absorbed than a movie set. Gottlieb's *Jaws Log* spoofs actor Roy Scheider and camera operator Michael Chapman for their fanatical consumption of each day's *New York Times*, but never bothers to acknowledge America's addiction to the summer's other main drama.[15] Nixon's fall goes similarly unmentioned in a less-detailed paperback quickie, *The Making of the Movie Jaws* by Martha's Vineyard resident Edith Blake, although another political scandal is alluded to. For July 18

marked the fifth anniversary of Senator Edward Kennedy's automobile accident on the tiny island of Chappaquiddick, off Martha's Vineyard, and the re-
sultant death of a young campaign worker, Mary Jo Kopechne.[16]

Chappaquiddick was PT 109 in reverse – an act of aquatic cowardice that effectively and forever sealed the remaining Kennedy's political fate. In the summer of 1969, a year after the assassination of RFK, it seemed inevitable that this
last Kennedy brother would fulfill the family destiny and run for president.
But, after ditching his car in the Atlantic (reportedly the first time in 20 years
that anyone had managed to drive off the Dike Bridge) and – without ever providing an adequate explanation either for the circumstances or his subsequent
behaviour – leaving a passenger to drown, Kennedy consigned himself to electoral purgatory.

As Vineyard summer resident James Reston would write in his *New York
Times* column that summer, "here perhaps more than anywhere else
[Kopechne's death] has remained a live and bitter controversy. On this island –
aside from everything else – leaving a body in the water is unforgivable."[17] For
Edith Blake, during the summer of 1974 "[i]t seemed that every news and
movie organisation was climbing around the satellite island collecting new
material on an old subject ... Filming crews over the Chappaquiddick dike
gave rise to new rumours that Universal was making a movie on the sly about
Kennedy at the dike and secretly flying key figures to Hollywood."[18] In fact,
Bruce was filmed gliding through the same channel into which Kennedy had
piloted his automobile.

Chappaquiddick was consistently in the news during the JAWS shoot. In
mid-May, as part of its inquiry into the possible impeachment of President
Nixon, the House Judiciary Committee requested and received legal papers
filed in the inquest into Kopechne's death (preparing for 1972, the White
House had dispatched a private investigator to Martha's Vineyard the same
day that Kopechne's corpse was pulled from the wreckage of Kennedy's car,
and subsequently tapped her room-mates' telephones) while *The New York
Times* reported that the dead woman's parents had recently visited the Dike
Road Bridge – for the second time – and had lunch with the local sheriff. Two
months later, the *Times* noted that the Kopechnes received a $150,000 settle-
ment from the Kennedy family while *The New York Times Magazine* ran a
lengthy article – subsequently described by another *Times* columnist as "a major political event" – devoted to the still unexplained circumstances of Mary
Jo's death, a subject rehashed by *Time*, *The Boston Globe*, and *60 Minutes*.

For the first half of 1974, Ted Kennedy out-polled all other Democratic possibilities – even though he was considered to be unelectable. Perhaps this
yearning for another Kennedy was more Watergate fall-out. The trauma of
Nixon's resignation was uncomfortably reminiscent of an earlier president's

'abandonment' of his people. But then, as James Reston analysed it: "when Nixon finally walked the plank, he took Kennedy over the side with him. Americans of all political persuasions are tired, sad, and ashamed of the frustrations and moral squalor of the age, and worried about the effects of all this on their children. To choose between Watergate and Chapaquiddick in a savage personal campaign during the 200th anniversary of the Declaration in 1976 seemed too much, even to many of the most enthusiastic supporters of President Kennedy and his brother Robert."[19]

Nixon was gone, and Kennedy had removed himself from the race by the time JAWS wrapped, as much over budget as it was over schedule, costing twice the $4 million originally planned. Both politicians were victims of what would, once JAWS saturated American consciousness, be known as a media 'feeding frenzy'.[20]

Like EARTHQUAKE and THE TOWERING INFERNO, both of which opened in December 1974, NASHVILLE and JAWS were positioned – and received – as Events. In a move designed to outflank every other film critic in America (not to mention the Paramount executives who had not yet seen his footage), Altman screened NASHVILLE in rough-cut for Pauline Kael. Four months before the film's eventual release, she published a pre-emptive rave in *The New Yorker* declaring NASHVILLE "an orgy for movie lovers".[21] Thus launched by so influential and notorious a review, NASHVILLE would enjoy considerable critical success.

As if to second Kael, NASHVILLE even opens with an advertisement for itself. But what was this ironic self-promotion or the ensuing critique of packaging compared to the uncanny power of JAWS's pre-sold high concept? Inhuman, unsleeping, omnivorous, a machine triggered by the scent of blood ... It with JAWS that the culture industry began to contemplate the culture industry.

The week before the JAWS shoot opened on Martha's Vineyard, *The New York Times Magazine* published a detailed analysis of the novel to illustrate "the making of a best seller."[22] On the one hand, Peter Benchley, 34 when JAWS was published, seemed born to write such a book – the son of novelist Nathaniel Benchley and the grandson of humorist Robert Benchley, a graduate of Phillips Exeter and Harvard, he acquired a literary agent at the age of 21. On the other hand, he had learned to articulate the Voice. After working briefly at *The Washington Post* and *Newsweek*, Benchley served LBJ as a speechwriter during the last beleaguered years of his reign. "I wrote proclamations like 'On Your Knees, America' for the National Day of Prayer," he recalled. In composing JAWS, he would be instructed by his editor at Doubleday, Tom Congdon, "to think of the whole country as a child that climbs up on its daddy's knee and says, 'Tell me a story'".

The *Times* tracked JAWS's development from the initial one-page description Benchley submitted to Congdon in June 1971, through the completion of
the manuscript 18 months later, the selection of a title, the choice of cover art,
and the development of a sales pitch through the wild auction for the paperback rights, a full nine months before the hardcover would appear. (One losing
editor maintained that she "never would have bid half a million dollars if it
hadn't been called JAWS".) As the film rights had also been sold before the
novel's February 1974 publication, the entire period of JAWS's bestsellerdom –
much of which coincided with the making of the movie – could be considered
a giant publicity trailer for a work-in-progress.

Released simultaneously at 460 theatres on an equally unprecedented wave
of saturation TV advertising, JAWS was everywhere at once – like a television
show. Only 78 days were needed to surpass THE GODFATHER's rentals and become the top-grossing movie of all time – or at least until 1977. The co-producer Richard Zanuck accrued more money from his share of JAWS's profits
than his father, 20th Century Fox mogul Darryl F. Zanuck, made in his entire
career.

Two kinds of filmmaking passed each other in June 1975. NASHVILLE was
intellectual, JAWS visceral; NASHVILLE looked back to the 1960s, JAWS ahead to
the 1980s. Altman was a grizzled hippie whose "favourite things", according
to his wife, were "smoking dope and having good parties". Spielberg had been
an abstinent member of the counterculture. "In my entire life I've probably
smoked three joints," he told *Rolling Stone* in 1978. Spielberg's experience of
the drug culture was largely vicarious. "I would sit in a room and watch TV
while people climbed the walls."[23]

Old enough to be the 28-year-old wunderkind's father, Robert Altman had
fought his way out of television to become the ultimate studio maverick;
Spielberg grew up with television and was a precocious industry insider, if not
a single-minded careerist. Julia Phillips, the Hollywood hipster who would co-
produce Spielberg's next project, CLOSE ENCOUNTERS OF THE THIRD KIND, considered it her duty to introduce him to a more youthful crowd: "Steven was
hanging out with men who were too old for him. Who bet and drank and
watched football games on Sunday. Who ran studios and agencies."[24]

Altman was more direct in stating his intentions, setting his narrative in the
Bicentennial Year of 1976 and calling NASHVILLE his "metaphor for America",
but JAWS, too, was perceived as essentially American: In praising Altman, Kael
evoked Fred Astaire and "the great American art of making the impossible
look easy". *Time*, meanwhile, termed JAWS a "rather old-fashioned, very
American way of making a movie".

There can be no doubt that NASHVILLE and JAWS appeared at a moment
when Americans were looking for some way to feel good about themselves.

The season's other national success story had seemed similarly old-fashioned and impossibly easy. On May 12, with the new Community states of Cambodia and Vietnam at war, the Cambodians detained the American container ship Mayaguez as it passed through the Gulf of Thailand. Coping with his first international challenge, President Gerald Ford convened the National Security Council which was informed by Secretary of State Henry Kissinger that there was a greater issue at hand than the capture of a single American merchant ship; in order to re-establish the nation's credibility, at home as well as abroad, it was necessary for the US to exercise its military might.

After a 24-hour ultimatum, American bombers strafed the boat used to transport the men of the Mayaguez to Cambodia's mainland and then sunk seven boats harboured around the island Koh Tang. The next morning, Koh Tang was stormed by US marines but, once the Americans were pinned down, Ford and Kissinger countermanded Congress's 22-month-old ban on bombing Indochina (along with the War Powers Act), by ordering air strikes on the port of Sihanoukville. After the crew's release, Cambodia was punished with further bombing of industrial installations.

The 40-man crew of the Mayaguez was saved at a cost of 41 American casualties with another 49 wounded. If some were appalled to see the US react so soon and massively against so puny an adversary, the victory nevertheless intoxicated the American media. *Time's* eight-page cover story provided a detailed day-by-day account of the victory ("THURSDAY. As Betty Ford was gently shaking her husband awake at 6.30am, an hour later than usual, the Mayaguez's crew was stoking the freighter's boilers...") that had "significantly changed the image of US power in the world" as well as that of President Ford who "had been hoping for weeks to find a dramatic way to demonstrate to the world that Communist victory in Indochina had not turned the US into a paper tiger".[25]

The Mayaguez operation was as star-spangled as NASHVILLE, as popular as JAWS, as extravagantly praised as both. "I'm very proud to be an American today," Vice-President Rockefeller declared while Senator Goldwater exulted that "it shows we've still got balls in this country", and Senators Frank Church and Jacob Javits, two sponsors of the War Powers Act, echoed their support for what *Newsweek* praised as "a daring show of nerve and steel". Explaining that "the show of force had many of the gung-ho elements of a John Wayne movie", *Time* did not neglect to describe the home front. Hugh Sidey's sidebar evoked a JFK-era thriller with a happy ending: This crisis, he explained, "was the old-fashioned variety", understandable and enjoyable for Cold War veterans – "a lovely bit of rascality – brief, definable, rightly punishable and done on the high seas, where US men and machines still reign".[26]

Sidey was among the select few journalists summoned to the White House lawn where a formal dinner for the Dutch prime minister was underway. "The White House in its spring splendour looked like a Hollywood set. With sombre visages and firm jaws, the actors hurried through the mellow night in their sleek black limousines." The diminutive Speaker of the House seemed three inches taller. Those senators to whom the President had revealed the "scenario" were besieged by reporters. Informed spokesmen hinted that "it was going to be an American kind of show". Henry Kissinger had returned.

> On the big crisis night ... back in his Washington office, [Kissinger] paced, ordering, listening, waiting. He flashed the V sign out the window once, and then, humour fully restored in the exhilaration of action, he made a lunging movement toward the window as he began to peel off his coat – Henry K into Super K. Deep laughter from the on-lookers, buoyed up by the old-style American confidence, echoed up Pennsylvania Avenue.[27]

III

NASHVILLE was played out in a city of lost souls, a metropolis of unstable idols and voracious fans, and the meretricious hustlers who prey on both – what some saw as a grotesque parody of Hollywood and Altman called a vision of "instant stars, instant music and instant politicians".

A musical disaster film, NASHVILLE is set against a backbeat of cliches and platitudes, and underscored by the search for a new national anthem. Self-righteous arias of idiotic boosterism alternate throughout with schematic hymns to survival: "I've lived through two depressions and seven dust bowl droughts..." Joan Tewkesbury's stream-of-consciousness introduction to NASHVILLE's published script frankly positions the movie as the culmination of postwar America's media history.[28]

"Perhaps the best thing about World War II was going to Sonja Henie movies," Tewkesbury begins her breathless catalogue. First came Alger Hiss, Richard Nixon, and the Cold War red scare. Then, "somewhere between President Eisenhower and my boyfriend's navy blue letterman sweater, the Rosenbergs were executed". Then, the John Birch Society, JFK ("against everyone else, he was Technicolor"), Timothy Leary, Angela Davis, Abbie Hoffman, Spiro Agnew, Kent State, George Wallace, Watergate and finally Robert Altman who "rounded out the RASHOMON of the United States".

In the American commercial cinema, NASHVILLE was the culmination of Robert Frank 'Desolation Row' aesthetic – the appreciation of the American vernacular landscape that had nostalgically informed BONNIE AND CLYDE and,

intermittently, EASY RIDER, was here programmatic. The once-exotic icons of
the nation's identity – the flag, the TV, political hooplah, chewing – gum, Dixie;
diners and honkytonks, jukeboxes and motorcycles, preachers and drifters,
waitresses and drum majorettes, cowboys and movie stars – appeared as
tawdry, discombobulated, second-hand, the open highway now a carnival
midway.

Bracketed by two spectacular crack-ups, NASHVILLE opens with a monumental traffic jam extending from downtown to the airport where the plane
carrying country music queen Barbara Jean (Ronnee Blakley) is about to land.
It climaxes at a Replacement Party rally on the steps of the imitation Parthenon
in Nashville's Centennial Park, where the warm-up act sings of Watergate and
impending food shortages, setting the stage for Barbara Jean's assassination
by the frozen-faced loner who, for most of the movie, has been orbiting the
action.

In the chaos that follows, Barbara Jean's spot is immediately filled by the
runaway wife Albuquerque (Barbara Harris) who effectively provides the new
American anthem:

> It don't worry me, it don't worry me
> You might say that I ain't free
> But it don't worry me!

The blank crowd eagerly joins in. A star is born.

Describing NASHVILLE as a "cascade of minutely detailed vulgarity, greed,
deceit, cruelty, barely contained hysteria, and the frantic lack of root and grace
into which American life has been driven by its own heedless vitality," *New
York Times* political commentator Tom Wicker would suggest that the movie
was not fundamentally 'apocalyptic', quoting Altman on the last scene: "In the
face of this disaster, they're going to go on".[29] Or, as Tewkesbury had concluded her introduction: "Whatever you think about the film is right, even if
you think the film is wrong".[30]

In fact, NASHVILLE inspired a remarkable critical unanimity – not to mention an extraordinary amount of attention from political pundits and high-profile literati. Reporting in *The Village Voice* on the glamorously, well attended advance screenings held a month prior to the movie's release, Arthur Bell noted
that "most critics and celebs who have seen NASHVILLE this past week are
feigning shellshock. Kurt Vonnegut claims it's the best film he's seen in his life.
Roz Drexler told us in the elevator she was an emotional wreck. And Mrs E.L.
Doctorow cried so hard she lost her contact lens." (That winter at the annual
New York Film Critics Circle awards where NASHVILLE was Best Picture and
Altman was Best Director, Doctorow made one presentation and Vonnegut the

other. At that time, Altman's announced future projects included an adaptation of Vonnegut's *Breakfast of Champions* and Doctorow's RAGTIME.)

Robert Mazzocco's thoughtful demural in *The New York Review of Books* was a rare exception to the general excitement. Mazzocco accused Altman of presenting "the crack-up of Middle America" as an in-joke and called NASHVILLE "an artificial high – a symptom of the disease and not a diagnosis of it", even linking it to President Ford's post-Mayaguez surge in popularity. Mazzocco also compared NASHVILLE unfavourably to THE DAY OF THE LOCUST, noting that while Nathanael West contrasted his loser world against the "dream dump" in NASHVILLE, the dream dump is all there is.[31] Greil Marcus was another dissident. Bracketting RAGTIME and NASHVILLE as the prime vehicles of what he termed a Failure-of-America fad, Marcus was struck by the enthusiasm with which these two essentially down-beat works were hailed as great fun and sure hits, and both were instantly cited as "metaphors" for the nation – attributing this phenomenon to a reigning "spirit of passivity".[32]

The consensus was such that even *The National Review* critic thought NASHVILLE might "perhaps [be] the most encompassing and revealing film ever made about what it is that defines this nation, this people, this age ... at least as American as apple pie". Perhaps in response, *Harpers* published a rare anti-NASHVILLE jeremiad by *National Review* contributor Chilton Williamson, Jr.[33] But not even Williamson argued that NASHVILLE was essentially false. To him, it was the response that seemed hypocritical; liberals were laughing at the grotesque spectacle they otherwise pretended to decry.

If anything, NASHVILLE inspired Williamson to call for a rightwing critique of American vulgarity (the "dangers of mass culture and mass living"), hoping that "conservative critics would be able to condemn the more repulsive aspects of American culture without feeling that they are betraying their fundamental stance by sharing certain articles of condemnation with people on the Left". In fact, the significance of the actual Nashville had already been appreciated by more pragmatic conservatives.

Not four months before Altman began filming, Nixon himself had attended the Grand Old Opry in its new $15 million home, located in the midst of the 369-acre Opryland theme-park. The first President to attend an Opry performance, Nixon received a standing ovation after he took the stage, sat down at the piano, and played "Happy Birthday" to his wife. According to *The New York Times*, Nixon then "pulled a yellow yo-yo from his pocket and presented it to Roy Acuff, known as the 'King of Country Music' whose act has used a whirring yo-yo."

Noting that country tunes talk about family, religion and patriotism, Mr Nixon said that "country music is America" and swung into "God Bless America" at the piano, raising his voice loudly to lead the singing.

"That's what it takes to be a real President," Mr Acuff said as the Nixons left.[34]

The movie NASHVILLE would scarcely be so warmly received by Opry partisans. Indeed, Altman and Tewkesbury could easily have scripted its gala Nashville premiere – held, after NASHVILLE had already opened in 35 other American markets, on August 8, 1975 (the first anniversary of the Nixon resignation) in the 100 Oaks Shopping Centre. Consumers dodged a country band, square dancers, and baton-twirlers, while television crews and journalists jostled fans to get to the stretch limousines bearing the Nashville elite. *The Nashville Banner*, which had previously run a front-page story on the movie's New York press screening, gave the event major play ('NASHVILLE PREMIERE CHURNS SOUR REACTION is the second headline after the lead story GRIM NATURAL GAS SHORTAGES FORECAST) in reporting that most of the country music personalities in attendance thought the movie "stunk".

NASHVILLE was lit up by themes as boomingly obvious and brilliantly insubstantial as a firework display on the Fourth of July. The rockets whiz skyward, the payloads explode, showering the spectator with flamboyant signs of national confusion, depression, exhaustion, division. As Robert Hatch would write in *The Nation*, "you could hardly hold a Bicentennial celebration without playing into Altman's hands".[35]

The synthesis of show business and politics predicted by Adorno and Horkheimer, deplored by A FACE IN THE CROWD, explicated by THE CANDIDATE, accepted by SHAMPOO, parades through NASHVILLE as stridently as a brass band auditioning for Sousa himself. "The ruthless unity in the culture industry is evidence of what will happen in politics," Adorno and Horkheimer predicted. But Hal Philip Walker's demographics were most eccentric. In addition to a new national anthem, his proposals included the banning of lawyers in government, the abolition of the Electoral College, the end of farm and oil subsidies. Walker is said to address his audiences as "fellow taxpayers and stockholders in America" and tell them that "a good man with some one syllable answers could do a lot for this country". On a more mystical note, he attracts college students with such sincere non-sequiturs as the question: "Does Christmas smell like oranges to you?" (In recounting this, TV newsman Howard K. Smith – free to invent his own commentary – remarks that for him, Christmas always has.)

Walker, a true pseudo-candidate, is only manifest in the form of his publicity and his advance man, John Triplette. Although *Newsweek* found Triplette "the epitome of Nixon's bright young men", Tom Wicker was reminded of those presidential candidates, like Lyndon Johnson in 1964 and Nixon in 1972, who refused to be "pinned down", and *The National Review's* David Brudnoy thought Walker an amalgam of Bobby Kennedy and George Wallace ("perhaps Altman and Co. have derived something very shrewd from those startling 1968 returns").[36] The vast majority of commentators looked at Walker however and just saw Wallace.

To that degree, NASHVILLE did anticipate the 1976 campaign which, at the time of the movie's release, was characterised by fear of Wallace and troubled – at least before Mayaguez – by the possibility of a conservative third party candidacy. In February 1975, members of the American Conservative Union and Young Americans for Freedom concluded a four-day Washington conference by creating a committee, chaired by Senator Jesse Helms of North Carolina, to explore the viability of launching a third party, preferably behind Ronald Reagan. (The now former-governor, introduced by Senator James Buckley as "the conservative movement's Rembrandt", declared that "Americans [were] hungry to feel once again a sense of mission and greatness" but declined to announce his candidacy.) Simultaneously, the Conservative Caucus, newly put together by Howard Phillips and Richard Viguerie, pushed the idea of a third-party candidacy for Reagan and/or Wallace. "I believe both of them are going to be denied their party's nomination," Phillips said in April, "They could come together to run for the presidency."

NASHVILLE anticipated the growth of spectacular politics during the 1976 presidential election, the first under a new campaign finance law that acted to further increase spending on television and consequently raise media consultants to the status of policy advisers; it correctly predicted that, after Watergate (and Vietnam), the campaign's major theme would be a longing for renewal. Walker's oxymoronic campaign slogan – "New Roots for the Nation" – evokes the first positioning of Gerald Ford even as his rival, Ronald Reagan, cast himself as the honest outsider come to clean up the mess on the Potomac.

Even the film's climactic shooting, which struck many as a tired cliché (although the Senate Select Committee on Intelligence chaired by Frank Church was then gathering information in preparation for hearings on the Kennedy assassination), was echoed by the public. There were two attempts made on the life of President Ford during a three-week period following NASHVILLE's run. September 5, in Sacramento, Lynette Alice "Squeaky" Fromme brandished a .45-calibre Army Colt automatic at the President in an attempt to call attention to the plight of her imprisoned guru Charles Manson; September 22, in San Francisco, Sara Jane Moore fired a shot at Ford from a .38-calibre Smith & Wesson revolver.

Two months later, at a Ramada Inn near the Miami airport, the maiden campaign appearance of Ford's newly declared challenger Ronald Reagan was plunged into a NASHVILLE-like confusion by the presence of a man wielding a toy gun. The assailant was later identified as a 20-year-old resident of Pompano Beach who had made a call from a public phone booth, and threatened the lives of the President, the Vice-President and Governor Reagan unless Lynette Fromme was freed.

In short, NASHVILLE was recognisable, and in February 1976, commentator and erstwhile Republican strategist Kevin Phillips wondered whether fiction had now become fact: NASHVILLE, Phillips wrote in *TV Guide*, may have "drawn a lot of criticism [sic], but in some ways it was prophetic. Dangerously prophetic. Such a candidate can sneak past television news with a smiling blur on sincerity and generality... Toothpaste-smooth former Georgia governor Jimmy Carter can and has."[37]

Hal Philip Walker's synthetic populism and cheerful negation of compli-cated realities anticipated the inspirational message of the smiling non-ideo-logical 'born again' outsider – handled by Gerald Rafshoon, a former 20th Century Fox publicist who'd worked on THE LONGEST DAY and CLEOPATRA be-fore relocating to Atlanta. For Carter, even more than for Walker, America was suffering a spiritual depression that might be dispelled by the regular applica-tion of the single-syllable words like 'right' and 'wrong'. Carter too reminded his audiences of the country's inherent virtue – a natural goodness only mo-mentarily besmirched by corrupt politicians like Nixon and Agnew – repeat-ing the mantra that the nation deserved "a government that is as good and honest and decent and truthful and fair and competent and idealistic and com-passionate and as filled with love as are the American people".[38]

Carter's perhaps naive insistence on refracting every issue through the prism of personal morality elevated his quest for the Democratic nomination into something resembling a spiritual crusade for instant renewal and the Great Second Chance. As the campaign progressed, the candidate was increas-ingly compared to John F. Kennedy. Some even thought there was a physical resemblance between the two.

IV

Where NASHVILLE exploded genre, JAWS imploded it. Spielberg stripped the disaster film, trimmed the flab, and turned it into a pure mechanism. Gone were the novel's adulterous wife and Mafia connection, impediments to Benchley's original concept which, as he had proposed to his publisher, was "to explore the reactions of a community that is suddenly struck by a peculiar natural disaster [that] loses its natural neutrality and begins to smack of evil".

NASHVILLE had offered a glibly pessimistic view of American life, predict-ing the rise of a politics as meretricious and authoritarian as the mass culture industry. JAWS was glibly optimistic in offering itself as a solution. Altman's complex interplay of sound and image – the overlapping mix of conversation, traffic noise, radios and soundtrack – was the precise inverse of Spielberg's total orchestration, the musical score (so close to the angst-producing theme from *The Twilight Zone*) functioning like an emotional rheostat, everything harmonised for maximum effect.

NASHVILLE was about the entertainment machine. JAWS was the entertainment machine – the very post-TV multi-media *Gesamtkunstwerk* that Horkheimer and Adorno had predicted, the total integration of "all the elements of the production, from the novel (shaped with an eye to the film) to the last sound effect", complete with a meta-narrative celebrating "the triumph of invested capital".

> The machine rotates on the same spot. While determining consumption it excludes the untried as a risk. The movie-makers distrust any manuscript which is not reassuringly backed by a best seller. Yet for this very reason there is never-ending talk of ideas, novelty, and surprise... Tempo and novelty serve this trend. Nothing remains as of old; everything has to run incessantly, to keep moving....[39]

To keep moving – just like a shark which, also omnivorous, devours whatever comes its way. Indeed, *The Jaws Log* opens by comparing producers David Brown and Richard Zanuck to sharks – *nice* sharks to be sure, hyper-alert but not predatory. "Just as the Great White Shark can sense the erratic vibrations of a swimmer in the water, so can Richard and David sense the movement of a literary property in the publishing world."[40]

NASHVILLE was supple where JAWS was rigid, but as NASHVILLE was superficial, Jaws ran deep. Was it while watching NASHVILLE or JAWS that Kurt Vonnegut was "thunderstruck" by the realisation of "how discontinuous with the rest of the world our culture is", its "pure and recent invention, inspired by random opportunities to gain money or power or fame" so that "even the past is faked". Nature, too. Travelling through the US during the summer of 1975, Umberto Eco noted that "the shark in JAWS is a hyper-realistic model in plastic, 'real' and controllable like the audio-animatronic robots of Disneyland".[41]

NASHVILLE was a party or a concert or, as Kael proposed, an "orgy without excess". JAWS was predicated on a more ruthless, experiential notion of movie as roller coaster. The build-up certainly was as long as the wait for a Disneyland ride. The monster remained invisible until 80 minutes into the movie. Then, with each appearance bigger than the last, it repeatedly violated human space, erupting into the frame from below – drawing on every primal conception of the sea as universal womb or collective unconscious, albeit here a repository of blood, monsters, and death. JAWS, said Spielberg, "is almost like I'm directing the audience with an electric cattle prod".

NASHVILLE was fragmented, without the presence of a unifying protagonist, but JAWS projected a far crueller fragmentation up front on the screen.
Spielberg, exhibiting a remarkably untroubled reading of his own motiva-
tions, explained his attraction to the material less as a career move – although
he did lobby strenuously for the assignment – but as a counterphobic reaction.
"I wanted to do JAWS for hostile reasons. I read it and felt that I had been attacked. It terrified me, and I wanted to strike back."

The shark – particularly as it was visualised on JAWS's book jacket and
movie poster – is at once monstrous phallus and vagina dentata. It coalesces a
whole nexus of submerged feelings and sadistic sexuality. In one scene, a dead
shark is referred to as "Deep Throat". Bruce, the crew's name for the mechanical shark was a name popularly associated with homosexuals – while, as several analysts noted, a homosexual slang term for woman was "fish".

Predating HALLOWEEN (1978) as a 'slasher' film, JAWS offers itself as the antidote to slasher anxiety. It concerns the protection of a vocation land (which is
to say an American utopia) with the welcoming name of Amity – it is the very
place to which an ex-New York City cop named Brody has brought his family
so that they can live somewhere safe.

JAWS was adapted from a monster bestseller, but it had a narrative that
might have been configured by computer, combining aspects of Ibsen's *An Enemy of the People*, in which a town doctor discovers that the mineral springs
which sustain his community are polluted and is pilloried for his integrity,
with the obsessive mano-a-mano Leviathan – battle of Melville's *Moby Dick*.
(At one point, Spielberg wanted to shoot a scene with Quint watching John
Huston's MOBY DICK but evidently Gregory Peck, embarrassed by his performance as Ahab, nixed it.)

Spielberg credited himself with streamlining the narrative: "I took the Mafia out of it, I took, not the sex out, but the affair out." In the novel, the young
oceanographer Hooper is sleeping with Mrs Brody – a relationship that would
certainly have complicated the eventual alliance between Brody and Hooper.
But although no one goes to bed with anyone in the movie JAWS, Spielberg was
certainly correct in acknowledging that he had not denuded the story of sex.
On the contrary – and not just because Peter Benchley had publicly complained that the alteration of his material was equivalent to a "gang rape".

JAWS begins with one of the most blatantly eroticised murders in the history
of cinema – and one which openly encourages the audience to identify with
the killer. A young woman detaches herself from a group of youths partying
on the beach, a chaste and diminished Orgy, and, shedding her clothes, runs
wantonly towards the ocean. She's followed down the beach by a less-than-
sober admirer but draws far more formidable interest once she plunges into
the surf, swims out ten yards, and gaily raises a leg to the sky. The viewer now

too is submerged in the ocean, peering at the swimmer from underneath – a point of view that not only coincides with the introduction of the shark's musical cue but is, in fact, the shark's. Above the water line, the woman jerks violently, crying "it hurts, it hurts", as she rhythmically thrashes up and down. Meanwhile, back on the beach, her drunken would-be lover has collapsed on the sand and is moaning "I'm coming, I'm definitely coming".[42]

Like the Chappaquiddick inquest, JAWS opens with the mystery of a young woman's corpse left in the water. Had Bruce's first victim been a man, JAWS would scarcely be the same movie. (Indeed, as if to reiterate the sexual nature of the crime, the novel delays a telephone report of the woman's disappearance so that the policeman on duty can finish reading an account of a woman who castrates a would-be rapist with the linoleum knife she'd hidden in her hair.) The Jack-the-Ripper joke made as the police view the murdered woman's remains is only amplified by Hooper's 'professional' excitement when he examines them. In general, JAWS has a surplus of innuendo: "I see you got your rubbers with you", the shark-hunter Quint teases Brody. Quint's toast "here's to swimming with bow-legged *wimmen*" is reinforced by his drinking song, "Ladies of Spain", in which a sailor bids farewell to the whores on shore. The misogyny is rationalised when Quint and Hooper bond by comparing their (women-related) scars.

A movie in which sex and violence are, if not indistinguishable forms of oral aggression, then certainly the source of kindred thrills, JAWS was "part of a bracing revival of high adventure films and thrillers", according to *Time's* admiring cover story. "Mercifully free of padding – cosmic, comic, cultural," (and, like Bruce, a most "efficient entertainment machine") JAWS promised "to hit right in the old collective unconscious and to draw millions irresistibly to the box office".

By late July 1975, the novel *Jaws* had sold over seven and a half million paperback units with Carl Gottlieb's *The Jaws Log* closing in on one million. Americans had already purchased two million JAWS tumblers, half a million T-shirts and tens of thousands of posters, beach towels, shark's tooth pendants, bike bags, blankets, costume jewellery, shark costumes, hosiery, hobby kits, inflatable sharks, iron-on transfers, board games, charms, pyjamas, bathing suits, water squirters.

JAWS was the greatest marketing bonanza since the 1955 Davy Crockett craze. The beach itself became a virtual-reality billboard – a beneficial side-effect of the movie's extended production schedule. (Amazingly, Universal had originally planned to release JAWS for Christmas 1974). Both *Time* and *The New York Times* ran features reporting that "formerly bold swimmers now huddle in groups a few yards offshore", while "waders are peering timorously into the water's edge". An official for the LA County department of beaches now

had to "force" himself to go into the water. Each day, lifeguards at Long Island's Jones Beach and the Cape Cod National Seashore received hundreds of
inquiries about sharks.

In *The New York Times* 'Arts and Leisure' section, Stephen Farber maintained that the only difference between JAWS and William Castle's BUG was the
degree of promotion. An insistent publicity campaign had transformed JAWS
into the entertainment 'event' of the year. But was pervasive advertising suffi-
cient to explain this orgy of participation? It was almost impossible to speak of
JAWS without reference to appetite. In a new and particularly self-conscious
way, JAWS's extraordinary, omnivorous box-office appeal further fed its appeal
– transforming a hit movie into something larger, a new form of feedback and a
new model for the movies.

Noting that "the spell seemed larger than its merchandising hype alone
could account for", *Newsweek* speculated that as "the summer spectacle of the
two years just past was the decline and fall of Richard Nixon", Americans
were starved for respite. "The palpable hunger in this vacation season was for
escape and JAWS offered it..."[43] In short, JAWS was correctly perceived was a political film. As Vonnegut had written of NASHVILLE, the movie was not just "a
spiritual inventory of America" but a spiritual salve, a fulfilment of the hope
that art could be "wonderfully useful in times of trouble".[44]

There were few American fears that were not displaced onto the shark. That
summer alone, the JAWS poster was parodied to show the Statue of Liberty
menaced by the CIA, Portugal by Communism, Uncle Sam by a Soviet Submarine Build-up, Gloria Steinem by male chauvinism (although here, the swimmer had submerged to attack the shark), American citizens by a New Tax Bite,
American wages menaced by Inflation, American drivers by the Energy Crisis,
American workers by Unemployment, and Gerald Ford by Recession, Ronald
Reagan, and a toothless Congress. Fidel Castro, meanwhile, identified the
Great White with US imperialism.

By the summer of 1975 there was no more Vietnam War, no further talk of
the space race, no new Miami or Las Vegas to construct. As the summit of
American accomplishment there was now only this... "It looked like a Nike
missile, but it was one of the [mechanical] sharks," *The Boston Phoenix* had reported from the set, having casually penetrated Spielberg's security system to
note Bruce's "inner workings of pumps, gauges, hoses, and clamps", another
daring show of nerve and steel. "JAWS should never have been made,"
Spielberg would maintain, and his description of his "impossible effort" was
elaborated by Gottlieb's *Jaws Log*: "Launching JAWS was a film production
problem analogous to NASA trying to land men on the moon and bring them
back."[45]

Roy Scheider in Jaws

"I have seen the future and it is Jaws," is how Kenneth Turan opened his review in *The Progressive*. More than a fad or a marketing ploy or psychosexual rollercoaster or a middle-class *Moby Dick*, Jaws held the promise of utopia redux.

V

NASHVILLE created such a compelling confusion that even the disgraced ex-President felt free to weigh in. According to Altman, Nixon himself wrote to the director to request a "copy" of NASHVILLE for his daughter Julie, maintaining that it was her favourite movie. (How much hatred of politics and desire for normalcy may be intuited here?) JAWS, by contrast, was more clear cut.

To the degree that both movies represented politics as a sleazy con-game and capitalism as a selfish, rapacious system, both movies articulated the populist distrust of big business and governmental leadership that peaked for Americans in 1975. But where NASHVILLE was fatalistic and cynical, suffused with what Robert Mazzocco called an "air of self-congratulatory befuddlement", JAWS – an action movie after all – proposed a solution.

As played by Murray Hamilton, Amity's mayor is the tawdriest of glad-handers, shamelessly wearing a stars-and-stripes tie like an usher for the Grand Old Opry. What would Julie Nixon Eisenhower make of him? The actor has a marked physical resemblance to her father and, no less than Nixon, the character he plays is undone by an attempt to conceal a crime – compelling the town coroner to falsely report that Chrissie died in a boating accident. (Perhaps, Julie would have been sensitive to the unfairness: In real life, on the real Martha's Vineyard, the mayor, if not the police chief, would be protecting the interests of the all-powerful Kennedys.)

Like the Watergate cover-up, the mayor's (economically motivated) attempt to fool Amity's citizens and tourists serves to divert attention away from the viewer's own implication in the original crime, to channel it into self-righteous anger – which is compounded, in JAWS, when the shark's second victim turns out to be an innocent child. The corrupt mayor's decision to open Amity's beaches on July 4th, despite the presence of the Great White lurking offshore, creates the movie's ultimate debacle. A tidal wave of panic hits the beach. It is with the July 4th collapse – the equivalent point to NASHVILLE's ending – that the final act of JAWS begins.

In *The Jaws Log*, Carl Gottlieb recalls a lengthy cocktail party – perhaps on Independence Day – at which *New York Times* political columnist and Vineyard regular James Reston buttonholed producer Richard Zanuk, a public Nixon supporter in 1972, and berated him for Hollywood's apparent lack of interest in celebrating the impending Bicentennial. What Reston couldn't know was that JAWS would be that celebration.

JAWS's characters are almost less than television stereotypes. Brody is easily imagined as the protagonist of a TV cop show. It's COOGAN's BLUFF in reverse – a former big-city policeman relocated to a picturesque HIGH NOON town where, as Brody likes to say (after John and Robert Kennedy), "one man can make a difference". Charlton Heston, the Universal saviour in EARTHQUAKE and AIRPORT 1975, wanted the role; as played by the narrow-shouldered, harried-looking, bespectacled Roy Scheider, the character is necessarily diminished. Brody may represent the Law on land, but he's powerless at sea – rendered impotent through his city-kid fear of the water.

In the novel, Brody is on-island working-class, and his wife is mainland upper-crust. In the movie, the fisherman, Quint is the blue-collar tough-guy, the would-be Dirty Harry of Shark City. Hooper, initially visualised as a scruffy hippie-type, is shown to be both privileged and educated. Throughout there's class tension between Hooper's "wealthy college boy" and Quint's "working-class hero", as each characterises the other. One has no difficulty imagining their respective stands on the Vietnam War. (*Time's* cover-story helpfully notes that Dreyfuss registered with his draft-board as a conscientious objector; true or not, Dreyfuss's character in AMERICAN GRAFFITI had been projected as a draft-dodger who took refuge in Canada during the Vietnam War.) Brody, who is outside their conflict and dependent on both, is more sympathetic to Hooper – Spielberg having thoughtfully eliminated the adulterous subplot.

Spielberg also contributed to JAWS's underlying mysticism or, at least, understood it. For it is not just business that is predatory and irresponsible. The shark is nature's revenge. Like NIGHT OF THE LIVING DEAD, JAWS is rooted in the cheap drive-in science-fiction and beach-party monster movies of the Pax Americana. The true ancestor of the Great White, as many pointed out, was the Japanese monster Godzilla who emerged from Tokyo harbour, reactivated from eternal slumber by the atomic bomb. JAWS, too, is haunted by the idea of nuclear holocaust and a fear of retribution. The movie's release coincided with the 30th anniversary of the Hiroshima and Nagasaki bombings, a subject of some media attention that implied no small desire for expiation.

The *New York Times* 'Travel' section for February 16, 1975, for example, ran a cheerful account of present-day life in the city where 78,000 were incinerated in a single blast and another 180,000 perished from the effects of radiation:

> We had come [to Hiroshima] with long faces, feelings of guilt, ready to shrivel under accusing eyes... And now my wife and I found ourselves in a Wizard of Oz city, plump with gaiety like a laughing Buddha, prosperous... There was a poll recently among the school children. "Of all the countries in the world beyond Japan who are your favourite people?" the children were asked. The majority wrote, "Americans".[46]

Oh doubly blessed relief! Out on the sea, Quint tells the true story of the battleship USS Indianapolis which, after transporting material from San Francisco to Guam for the atomic bombs that would be dropped on Japan, suffered a suitably cosmic trial. Hit by a Japanese torpedo, the boat goes down, forcing its crew to abandon ship in shark-infested waters. It is the greatest disaster of a ship at sea in the history of the US navy. Hundreds of seamen are devoured. Shaw's description of this scene, a virtual radio play in this most visual of movies, is a tribute to language and the intensity of his performance. (As this powerful subplot does not appear in the novel, one suspects it was the inspired contribution of John Milius, whose enthusiasm for military history is well known.)

Who shall live and who shall die? Which individual or alliance can best preserve Amity from the terror of the Great White Shark? Which of the three men is shark bait? The combination of Hooper and Brody – middle-class law-and-order plus youth-culture technocracy – not only suggests self-consciously hip cop shows like *Mod Squad* or the later *Miami Vice* but also the coalition that would support Jimmy Carter. The sacrifice of Quint, meanwhile, has the additional advantage of cancelling the nuclear guilt he articulates and the historical nightmare represented by his service on the Indianapolis.

Sontag wrote that the "imagery of disaster in science fiction is above all the emblem of an *inadequate response*",[47] but that is scarcely the case with JAWS. Brody is born again – literally, baptised in the sea – to be precisely the Adequate Response. He overcomes his fear of the water and single-handedly slays the dragon. (In the novel, Hooper is devoured along with Quint, and the shark mysteriously expires just as its fearsome snout reaches Brody.) Thus, the film's hero – a family man as well as a cop – triumphed over brute nature and mendacious politicians alike, defeating the Great White Shark where ivory-tower oceanographers and working-class fishermen had failed to do so.

Time ended its cover-story with the sentiment that "in JAWS, the only thing you have to fear is fear itself". This evocation of the Great Depression and Franklin Roosevelt seems hardly inappropriate to a fantasy in which the American middle-class survived the onslaught of a monster to regain control of their vacation paradise. JAWS presented a national rite of initiation. It not only reconstituted a new Hollywood, it imagined the end of an old America and the birth of a new one – even revived in New York, the day following Jimmy Carter's inauguration.[48]

VI

Once more, a year to the day before the 1980 election, JAWS would rear out of the collective unconscious and into American presidential politics. Sunday night, November 4, 1979, JAWS had its television premiere on ABC, amassing a 57% share of the TV audience to make it the second highest-rating ever achieved by a televised movie, exceeded only by the premiere telecast of GONE WITH THE WIND in November 1976.

NBC had counter-programmed the second part of MACARTHUR – which proved to be the week's least-watched network program. Only marginally better attended was the third network alternative, the *CBS Report* on another American political personality, Senator Edward M. Kennedy. Kennedy was at the apex of his popularity on the night *Teddy* was broadcast. In two days he planned to announce that he was challenging President Jimmy Carter for the Democratic nomination, and the press was already prepared to anoint a winner; polls published that weekend had Kennedy enhancing an already substantial lead over the President – whose advisers denounced the media's perceived bias in Kennedy's favour.

Teddy opened as Carter's worst nightmare with newsreel footage of the two martyred Kennedys that re-evoked the national tragedy, positioning Teddy as survivor and heir, the leading man in a public drama with a final act yet to be played. Then followed by a relaxed conversation between the Senator and newsman Roger Mudd outdoors at the Kennedy family compound in Hyannis Port. Kennedy dealt easily with questions about his own fear of assassination and his treatment by the press but seemed to freeze when Mudd asked after the "present state" of the Senator's marriage. Kennedy's barely coherent reply precipitated a public breakdown worthy of NASHVILLE's Barbara Jean. Over the next few agonising minutes, the befuddled Senator fumbled for words while Mudd broached other aspects of Kennedy's private life, including inevitably the incident at Chappaquiddick – a memory and a cover-up which the presence of JAWS, a mere zap of the channel-changer away, could only reinforce.

Kennedy proved incapable of even articulating his desire to run for president, responding to Mudd's query with a vague succession of meaningless banalities. Carter had reason to be pleased – although the night that Kennedy self-destructed and Spielberg ruled, Iranian militants occupied the American Embassy in Tehran and took the staff hostage, thus setting the stage for a teledrama that would play to an audience even larger than JAWS's estimated 80 million.

Notes

1.   Robin Wood, *Hollywood from Vietnam to Reagan* (New York: Columbia University Press, 1986) p. 29.
2.   Susan Sontag, 'The Imagination of Disaster,' *Against Interpretation and Other Essays* (New York: Dell, 1966) p. 212.
3.   Max Horkheimer and Theodor W. Adorno, *Dialectic of Enlightenment* (New York: Seabury Press, 1972) p. 158.
4.   *Time* (June 10, 1974) p. 68.
5.   Ibid. p. 68.
6.   In his influential essay 'The Me Decade and the Third Great Awakening,' published in *New York* magazine during the summer of 1976, Tom Wolfe mocked 'the current fashion of interpreting all new political phenomena in terms of recent disasters, frustration, protest, the decline of civilisation ... the Grim Slide.' See Tom Wolfe, *Mauve Gloves & Madmen, Clutter & Vine* (New York: Bantam Books, 1977) p. 119.
7.   Pauline Kael, 'On the Future of Movies,' *Reeling* (New York: Warner Books, 1977) p. 427.
8.   ibid. p. 427.
9.   Pauline Kael, 'Decadence,' *Reeling* op. cit. p. 511.
10. Nora Sayre, 'EARTHQUAKE,' *New York Times* (November 16, 1974) p. 20.
11. Vincent Canby, 'The Towering Inferno,' *The New York Times* (December 20, 1074) p. 20.
12. Herbert J. Gans, *Social Policy* (Jan./Feb. 1975) vol.5 no.5, p. 51
13. Carl Gottlieb, *The Jaws Log* (New York: Dell, 1975) p. 177.
14. Nixon's diary, cited in Len Colodny and Robert Gettlin, *Silent Coup: The Removal of a President* (New York: St. Martin's Press, 1991) p. 420.
15. Gottlieb op.cit. p. 198.
16. Edith Blake, *The Making of the Movie Jaws* (New York: Ballantine, 1975) p. 116. Altman, by contrast, was said to have been obsessed with the Watergate endgame – among other current events, such as the attempted assassination of South Korean President Park Chung Hee in mid August. The attack on Park foreshadowed the assassination which climaxes NASHVILLE. As the Korean President delivered his Liberation Day address from behind a bullet-proof podium at the new National Theater in Seoul, a husky 40-year-old man ran down the center aisle firing a snub-nosed revolver. Seated behind her husband, Mrs Park was shot in the head; as the screaming, mainly elderly audience, assembled political leaders, and high school choir scrambled for safety, security men gunned down the assailant. A high school girl was mortally wounded in the crossfire. A small boy ran crying to the fallen assassin and tried to kick him until security men pulled him away. Despite the injury to his wife, President Park finished his speech and received a standing ovation. The incident had been televised live. Afterwards the Ministry of Home Affairs declared a state of national emergency and the entire government tendered its resignation.
17. James Reston, 'Lingering Tragedy,' *New York Times* (September 25, 1974) p. 39.

18. Blake op.cit. p. 116.

19. Reston op.cit. p. 39.

20. Fittingly, the first reported usage was by former Nixon press-secretary Gerald L. Warren in March 1977.

21. Pauline Kael, 'Coming: "Nashville",'*Reeling* op. cit. p. 591.

22. Ted Morgan, 'Sharks,' *New York Times Magazine* (April 21, 1974) pp. 10-11ff.

23. Chris Hodenfield, 'The Sky is Full of Questions!!' *Rolling Stone* (1/26/78) p. 35.

24. Julia Phillips, *You'll Never Eat Lunch in This Town Again* (New York: Random House, 1991) p. 140.

25. 'A Strong but Risky Show of Force,' *Time* (May 26, 1975) p. 9.

26. Hugh Sidey, 'An Old-Fashioned Kind of Crisis,' *Time* (May 26, 1975) p. 18.

27. ibid.

28. Joan Tewksbury, 'Introduction', *Nashville* (New York: Bantam, 1976) unpaginated

29. Tom Wicker, ' "Nashville" – Dark Perceptions in a Country-Music Comedy,' *New York Times* (June 15, 1975) section 2, p. 17.

30. Tewksbury op. cit.

31. Robert Mazzocco, 'Letter from Nashville,' *New York Review of Books* (July 17, 1975) p. 18.

32. Greil Marcus, ' 'Ragtime' and 'Nashville': Failure-of-America Fad,' *Village Voice* (August 4, 1975) p. 61.

33. Chilton Williamson Jr., 'The Nashville Sound,' *Harpers* (September 1975) p. 78.

34. B. Drummond Ayres Jr., 'Nixon Plays Piano On Wife's Birthday At Grand Ole Opry,' *New York Times* (March 17, 1974) p. 52.

35. Robert Hatch, 'Films,' *The Nation* (July 5, 1975) p. 29.

36. David Brudnoy, 'Their Town,' *National Review* (August 15, 1975) p. 890.

37. Kevin Phillips, 'News Watch,' *TV Guide* (February 21-17, 1976) p. A-3.

38. Jules Witcover, *Marathon: The Pursuit of the Presidency 1972-1976* (New York: Viking, 1977) p. 198.

39. Horkheimer and Adorno op.cit. p. 134.

40. Gottlieb op.cit. p. 17.

41. Umberto Eco, *Travels in Hyperreality* (San Diego: Harcourt Brace Jovanich, 1986). p. 57. Two sequels, several re-releases, innumerable clones later, and 19 years later a JAWS ride finally opened at Universal Studios Florida – a six-minute boat trip in which a 32-foot latex and polyurethane shark, moving 20 feet per second with the thrust of a 727 jet engine surfaces approximately once a minute, spooking and spraying patrons as it circles their craft.

42. Paul Wendkos's made-for-TV INTIMATE AGONY (ABC, 3/21/83) hilariously remakes *Jaws* in more explicitly didactic sexual terms. A young doctor arrives on the vacation beach community of Paradise Island and finds a burgeoning epidemic of genital herpes – enough cases to cause 'genuine concern in a community where sexual promiscuity is generally accepted.' Informing the press and otherwise alerting residents, he discovers that the old doctor whom he is replacing has worked closely with an unscrupulous real-estate developer (Robert Vaughn, the craven Senator in TOWERING INFERNO) to keep the disease secret. 'Why not a leper colony?' the developer exclaims when the young doctor opens a special herpes clinic. Like the shark in JAWS, the disease keeps attacking: One man gives it to his pregnant wife; next, the doctor's best friend is infected (thus jeopardising his life-

style as Paradise Island's resident tennis pro), then, the doctor's love interest confesses that she too has contracted herpes; finally, the developer's 16-year-old daughter gets the disease.

43. 'Jawsmania: The Great Escape,' *Newsweek* (July 28, 1975) p. 16.

44. Kurt Vonnegut, Jr., 'Nashville,' *Vogue* (October 1975) p. 103.

45. No less remarkable than Universal Studio Florida's $45 million JAWS attraction is Landshark – an 'incredible state-of-the-art radio broadcast facility on wheels' constructed from the same 'space-age polyproplene honeycomb utilised in NASA's space shuttle vehicles' and created to whip the populace into a frenzy of JAWS consciousness.

46. Howard Whitman, 'Dynamism + Dior = Hiroshima + 30,' *New York Times* (February 16, 1979) section 10 p. 1.

47. Sontag op. cit. p. 224.

48. During the 1976 campaign, Carter's toothsome smile was used as a syntagm for the candidate himself. A mask with nothing but a set of giant red lips and bared teeth was a novelty hit at the Democratic Convention. It is tempting to view this ferocious grin as an inverted version of a shark's ghastly grimace – perhaps even its negation. The souvenir peanuts that were emblazoned only with Carter's smile have an even more suggestive resemblance to Bruce turned upside down.

49. Les Brown, ' 'Jaws' Played to 80 Million on ABC,' *New York Times* (November 7, 1979) p. C29.

For Wanda

Bérénice Reynaud

A small, forgotten masterpiece

Winner of the Critics Prize in Venice in 1970, Barbara Loden's WANDA (1970) was, as the *New York Times* meekly puts it, "a critical hit but failed to create excitement at the box-office".[1]

Shot in cinema-verité style on grainy 16mm film stock, WANDA tells the story of the unlikely partnership between a coal-mining wife from Pennsylvania (played with sensitivity and brio by the filmmaker herself), dumped by her husband and the men she met while drifting, and a petty crook on the rebound, Mr Dennis (Michael Higgins), who convinces her to pull a major "bank job" with him. The film was released in one theatre in New York, Cinema II, and never shown in the rest of the country.[2] Ten years later, WANDA was "already forgotten in the United States", but "much admired in Europe".[3] It was screened in the 'Women and Film' event at the 1979 Edinburgh Film Festival and in Deauville in 1980. Loden died of cancer on September 5, 1980, "the day [she was] booked to fly to Paris-Deauville. Her death was announced from the stage of the Festival."[4]

So there would not be another film by Barbara Loden. As in the case of Rimbaud, the tragic scandal was not only that a talented artist had died too young (Loden was 48) but that such a promising career had been reduced to silence. Yet, unlike that of the much-remembered *poète maudit*, Loden's voice seemed doomed to historical erasure. Indeed WANDA was a "critical hit" – but only in the New York daily papers. At the time of its brief commercial release, Vincent Canby stressed "the absolute accuracy of its effects, the decency of its point of view and the kind of purity of technique that can only be the result of conscious discipline".[5] Roger Greenspun added: "It would be hard to imagine better or more tactful or more decently difficult work for a first film. I suppose it is significantly a woman's film in that it never sensationalises or patronises its heroine, and yet finds her interesting."[6] This was followed by Marion Meade's feature article on two films "written and directed by women who also play the leading roles", Elaine May's A NEW LEAF (1970) and WANDA. While praising this "remarkable development [that gives us] an unusual slant on the realities of women's existence and feelings", Meade seems uneasy about the "message" she reads in WANDA: "But now Barbara Loden arrives at the crux of the problem, which is, where do you go after you reject the only life society permits? And once a woman gains her freedom, what can she do with it? The answer: nowhere and nothing."[7]

The process of historical erasure may have started then. The meeting between WANDA and "serious" criticism did not happen, at least not in the United States.[8] The *Critical Index* has a single entry on WANDA: an interview with Loden published in the now-defunct *Film Journal* in the summer of 1971.[9] In *From Reverence to Rape*, Molly Haskell mentions Loden briefly, including her in lists of "American women known to have directed films" and of "remarkable women's performances". Opposing "the less compliant zombiism of Barbara Loden in WANDA" to the "zombie-like beauty of Dominique Sanda or Candice Bergen",[10] Haskell adds: "Then comes Barbara Loden's WANDA to tell us that country bumpkins are no better off than city slickers... [and] just as susceptible of anomie as the big-city heroines."[11] And when the editors of a feminist anthology invited Andrew Sarris to write a correction to his contemptuous treatment of women in *The American Cinema* [12], he only mentioned Loden once.[13]

This was followed by 20-odd years of silence, sometimes broken by Raymond Carney, who, in his two books on John Cassavetes,[14] mentions Loden as a director working along similar lines – "exploring realities available to him or her".[15] Like Cassavetes or Robert Kramer, she was appreciated more in Europe than in the US, which Carney attributes to "the American critical tradition... [taking] for granted that art is essentially a Faustian enterprise – a display of power, control and understanding".[16]

As Hollywood was changing during the 1970s and B-grade movies were virtually disappearing, "non-virtuosic cinema", or cinema of imperfection, was somehow pushed to the margins, and while mainstream cinema continued to explore the undersides of the American experience, its approach also changed: it became slicker, and its conception of the outsider evolved from dark pulp fiction to candy-coloured pop culture. While *film noirs* of the 1930s and 1940s had produced a most alienated kind of urban outsider, the "New Hollywood", from the late 1960s on, set to glamorise the outsider or sensationalise violence. The stage was set by Arthur Penn's 1967 version of the Bonnie Parker and Clyde Barrow story,[17] resplendent with box-office stars Warren Beatty and Faye Dunaway.[18] So, when WANDA was released, Loden had to contend with comparisons with the film. For Canby, Wanda "has shared something approximating an adventure with a petty crook, Mr Dennis, who has tried, without success, to transform her into a Bonnie for his Clyde". Ruby Melton's first question to Loden was if Penn's film had influenced her. "I wrote the script about ten years before Arthur Penn made BONNIE AND CLYDE," replied Loden. "I didn't care for [it] because it was unrealistic and it glamorised the characters... People like that would never get into those situations or lead that kind of life – they were too beautiful... WANDA is anti-BONNIE AND Clyde."[19]

So, in emphasising WANDA's "non-Faustian aesthetic",[20] in praising it as a "neglected small masterpiece",[21] Carney stood alone. The eradication of Loden's work in film history is such that the most recent edition of *Halliwell's Film Guide* does not have a "WANDA" entry, even though the film is occasionally aired on cable channels such as the now-defunct Channel Z, Bravo or The Independent Channel[22]. Even the feminist *Women in Film: An International Guide* mentions the film *only* when describing the Amsterdam-based distribution company Cinemien: "With other 350 titles currently in distribution... Cinemien's work in feminist distribution... is unparalleled... About 10 percent of the collection is distributed nowhere else in the world – often not even in the films' own countries of origin, [such as] WANDA."[23] This neglect is all the more surprising in that the main editor of the book, British feminist Annette Kuhn, wrote extensively about "the new women's cinema" of the 1970s, in which "the central characters are women, and often women who are not attractive and glamorous in the conventional sense. Narratives, moreover, are frequently organised around the process of a woman's self-discovery and growing independence."[24] The films she praises are, in Hollywood, Claudia Weill's GIRL-FRIENDS (1977) and Fred Zinnemann's JULIA (1977), and, in experimental cinema, Sally Potter's THRILLER (1979), Yvonne Rainer's LIVES OF PERFORMERS (1972), Michelle Citron's DAUGHTER RITE (1978) and Chantal Akerman's JEANNE DIELMAN, 32 QUAI DU COMMERCE, 1080 BRUXELLES (1975) – films that "hold out the possibility of a 'feminine language' for cinema".[25] While WANDA has been ignored by every major text of feminist film theory published in English over the last 20 years, Akerman, Potter and Rainer have become household names. Granted, Akerman is a more assured filmmaker than Loden, but the alienation of her Belgian housewife-cum-hooker may be read as the reverse of that of Loden's Pennsylvania housewife-turned-drifter: one was *too good* at keeping house, the other not good enough. The "market value" of both women depended on how good housewives they were, and how they could please men. Both found the equation unbearable and devised various strategies to ward off their anxiety. One locked herself in her apartment and her routine, making sure there wouldn't be any speck of dust on her table nor any hole in her schedule; the other started to drift in the sea of her own insignificance, clinging to unworthy men as a way to avoid drowning. Both showed unexpected moments of resilience, hidden reserves of strength that failed to save them, because the dice were loaded. Yet, there is a major, poignant difference between the two films, one that may explain why Jeanne became a feminist

heroine *par défaut* and Wanda easily forgotten. In Akerman's film, men are pe-
ripheral; they are mouths to be fed, cocks to be satisfied, but the film hints at
the possibility of a utopian space structured by women's desires, stories, needs
and anxieties. Jeanne would never address any of her tricks as "Mister", and
Akerman didn't make her film under the terrifying gaze of one of Hollywood's
sacred monsters. In WANDA's narrative space, however, men cast a giant
shadow.

The story of the lump

> "Woman is symptom to man."
>
> Jacques Lacan

Barbara Loden appears in the last third of Elia Kazan's bulky autobiography,
and is mentioned again and again, in ways that defeat the reader's efforts to
picture the real woman behind Kazan's self-centred prose: "I'd met a young
actress who, many years later, was to be my second wife... Conceived in a field
of daisies, Barbara Loden was born anti-respectable... [She] was feisty with
men, fearless on the streets, dubious of all ethical principles...."[26] It may sound
familiar and indeed it is: a successful man of 44, happily married, suffers a
mid-life crisis and draws inspiration from a younger woman. Later, Kazan reworked and fictionalised his on-and-off affair with Loden in his best-selling
novel, *The Arrangement* (1967), and then turned it into a movie in 1969. Yet,
Kazan doesn't say much about Loden's background, her needs and desires,
even her work as an artist. Again, one has the eerie feeling of a life being slowly
erased under the ornate carving of official history. Kazan often calls Loden "a
bitch", and saw her as bold, fearless, a sexual adventuress, maybe a gold-
digger – while her close collaborators, Nicholas (Nick) T. Proferes who shot
and edited the film, and Michael Higgins who played Mr. Dennis to her
Wanda, perceived her as "insecure" and "sensitive".

The second time Loden appears in Kazan's book may be considered a genuine instance of the Freudian *uncanny*. A few years later, at 48, Kazan went to a
psychoanalyst, Dr Kelman, and then started discussing an area of pain under
his rib cage. "What you have in you," said the analyst, "is a great lump of
unreleased anger."[27] Alone, Kazan thought of Barbara: "She'd physically attacked a film casting director on an open street, slapped him around until he'd
stopped denying what he'd said that got Barbara so mad (slurs on her charac-

ter as well as her talent)... That was what I admired about the girl... *Barbara had no lump*... I envied [her]; she made me understand what Kelman meant."[28]

No matter how insightful Kelman might have been in Kazan's case,[29] he left him with a blind spot concerning the relationship between signifiers and the unconscious, for Kazan is unaware of the meaning of his own repetition of the word "lump". "One day she stood naked before me, took my hand, and put it on her left breast. 'Do you feel it?' she asked. I found a lump there. It was January of 1978. She died in September 1980, on the fifth."[30] *She was 48, Kazan's age when he first consulted Dr Kelman* (another structuring signifier). If Kazan had listened, he might have realised that Loden's anger was not always released in the fearless, spontaneous and spectacular way he once envied. She had said: "I have a lot of pain and suppressed anger in me, just like Wanda,"[31] and explained the apparent "apathy" of her character as a way to conceal an inner hidden turmoil (which she significantly describes as a *physical symptom*): "Another example in the film occurs in the scene when Wanda goes to the factory to get some money and to get put back on the job. The factory boss turns her down, and she just thanks him... Many times when people give us terrible news or completely reject us... *our stomachs may be turning over*, but we don't show it... Wanda... has been numbed by her experiences, and she protects herself by behaving passively and wandering through life hiding her emotions."[32]

Then Loden was informed that her cancer was "involving" her liver as well. "I looked at Barbara. No reaction, her face masked as ever, guarded. Later she told me she [had been told] that her problem was the liver, not her breast... 'Yes,' she said to me, 'all my anger is stored there'."[33] Kazan adds that Loden died angry, crying out "Shit! Shit! Shit!" when her liver gave out.[34]

Barbara Loden was born in Marion, Ohio, in 1932, and had a difficult childhood. "She was white trash... from the wrong side of the tracks. Her father left her and she lived with her grandparents. The boys were after her at a very young age."[35] Kazan describes her as "working class. Her father and brothers carry pistols when they go out to drink at night. She's self-educated – and smart. Had to be to survive."[36] At 17, she came to New York, and danced for a while at the Copacabana. "Her first husband [Larry Joachim] met her on 42nd street. She had come with some musician... Larry asked her why she had come to New York, and she said 'I want to be famous...' So she married him – he was a nice guy and took care of her."[37] Proferes thinks that it is Joachim who introduced her to Kazan; this happened when she was 23, that is, in 1955. Kazan eventually married her in 1967. In the meantime, Loden gave birth to her first son, Leo, and, later, to Joachim's child, Marco.

Even after she had reached notoriety as an actress, Loden took acting classes with her mentor, Paul Mann. At 25, she was cast in her first Broadway play, *Compulsion* (1957). She became a member of the Lincoln Centre Repertory

Company, and won a Tony award for her "stunning performance" in Arthur
Miller's *After the Fall* (1964, as "Maggie, the sexy, popular entertainer who ines-
capably [was] equated with [Miller's second wife], Marilyn Monroe".[38] Kazan,
who had directed the play, was sure that Loden "fitted the role" because he
"knew her past in detail, and ... knew Marilyn's personal history as well.
They'd both been 'floaters' and come out of almost identical childhood experiences, which had left them neurotic, often desperate, and in passion difficult to
control."[39]

In 1960, Kazan cashed in on Loden's 'hillbilly' origin and gave her a small
part opposite Montgomery Clift in WILD RIVER. [40] A year later, he cast her as
Warren Beatty's promiscuous and self-destructive sister in SPLENDOR IN THE
GRASS. Her performance is feisty, amusing, fiery, tragic, over-dramatic, and
she makes the best of her baby-blue eyes, porcelain skin and perfect legs. Yet
the part is conceived as a foil for the good-girl-tormented-by-the-flesh played
by Nathalie Wood, and foil it was doomed to remain. If anything, it confirms
how Loden stood in Kazan's sexual fantasies: she was bad, she was "trash",
she was sexy and a lot of fun, but she was the one *who knows*. In SPLENDOR, she
tells her weak brother that he is destroying his life by being obedient to their
over-masculine father. In the novel *The Arrangement*, the character of Gwen
bluntly explains to Eddie Anderson that his life is a bore and he should stop
writing ad campaigns for cigarettes.[41] In Kazan's life, Loden was instrumental
in helping him give up theatre and write his own screenplays. Such women, in
Kazan's worldview, are in the position of Lacan's "subject supposed to know"
– the position of the Absolute Other. Yet their knowledge is limited: it only concerns the male protagonist's pitfalls, which they help to heal. Their "knowledge" is instinctual, rather than rational. They can only hint at the truth. It is
the man's role to analyse, dissect, understand, draw conclusions. Moreover,
they have no knowledge of *themselves*; they are creatures of passion and act im-
pulsively, with the supreme wisdom of the madwoman (or the unfathomable
wisdom of the Mother), and it is the man in their lives, who, having tamed the
shrew, will recount their stories.

And so Kazan did with *The Arrangement*, which "was essentially an autobiographical study of him and his wife".[42] When he signed a contract with
Warner Brothers to turn the book into a movie, Loden was going to play "her
own" part, opposite Marlon Brando's Eddie Anderson. When Brando eventually refused the part, it went to Kirk Douglas. That meant keeping Loden out of
the picture, for "the studio said 'Kirk Douglas and Barbara Loden, nobody's
going to see that'. So they got Faye Dunaway."[43] According to Kazan, "Barbara
never forgave [him]".[44] She should also have been wary of the way she was
portrayed in the book. While Anderson is given a complex, albeit unbearably
self-centred, internal monologue, Gwen is denied interiority, and her identity

and self-worth are entirely defined by the way she looks: "Gwen didn't need an analyst to build her self-esteem. All she needed was a mirror."[45] One is reminded of the character of Jenny in Yvonne Rainer's PRIVILEGE (1990), who discovers the sexism of her partner when he says: "You can always tell how a woman feels about herself by looking at her legs."[46] Yet, as Rainer notices, Jenny didn't mind then, because she was sexually attracted to the man. Kazan recognised that his Gwen loved Eddie to distraction, and how patient Loden had been – for years she was his secret mistress as well as supportive mate and companion – but the question of female desire eludes him, as proven when, after her death, he tries to understand Loden: "Like many pretty girls I've known, she felt worthless, felt that the only thing that gave her any value was a man's desire for her."[47] Except making WANDA.

A Film of One's Own

> How inarticulate Tonka was! She could neither talk nor weep. But how is one to define something that neither can speak nor is spoken of, something that dumbly merges with the anonymous mass of mankind, something that is like a little line scratched on the tablets of history?
>
> Robert Musil[48]

The idea of the film started when Loden read a newspaper article about "a girl [Wanda Goranski] who had been an accomplice to a bank robbery and was sentenced to 20 years in prison... When the judge sentenced her, she thanked him."[49] Due to Loden's insecurity, it took her a while before coming to terms with her own desire to direct. She wanted "to be an artist... to justify her own existence... [But she] was very self-effacing, and never intended the film for release... This was a way to take the pressure off – the pressure to produce a work of art – if it didn't turn out half-way decently."[50]

It took about six years to raise the money,[51] and it eventually came from Harry Shuster (credited as producer in the film), who was "just a friend... they met in Africa... I don't think he was even in film."[52] Kazan and Loden set out to find a suitable collaborator. Through a common friend, who had started to work as an executive producer for WANDA, but later dropped out (and hence received no credit), Proferes was introduced to the couple, so they could use his screening room to look at the work of potential candidates. Then, Proferes recalls, "[my friend] said 'I want to show them one of your films, to give them [more] possibilities.' And they picked *me*. I was very reluctant. I had never shot any feature... Also, working with a woman, an actress - [that] didn't seem a good idea, or even an interesting idea. I don't know what made me do it."[53]

Born in 1936 in rural upstate New York, Proferes moved to New York when he was 25, and met D.A. Pennebaker through a friend. Pennebaker's producer, Robert Drew, was running a company in which Richard Leacock and the Maysles Brothers were also involved, and had received a significant sum of money from *Time/Life* to do a series of cinema-verité documentaries. Proferes was hired as an apprentice editor, and later learnt to shoot: "With Leacock, there was no distinction. We were just filmmakers, and we did everything."[54] Starting with Leacock's PRIMARY (1960), Drew Associates produced landmark cinema-verité films.[55] "They were going to create almost like a dramatic narrative to take over Hollywood. So it was very exciting, it was a very heady time."[56] Proferes eventually started his own company and made FREE AT LAST, a film on Martin Luther King (who was shot while Proferes was following him throughout the United States) which won the Best Documentary Award at the 1969 Venice Film Festival.

Loden's decision to shoot in 16mm was motivated by the need to keep the costs down; it also allowed her to explore new ways of combining fiction and documentary, and to question the impulse that had been behind the conception of WANDA. Loden found her initial project "somewhat old-fashioned in that it [told] a story".[57] During the making of WANDA, she came to realise that a traditional narrative might not be the ideal form to express what she had in mind: "Now I know why people make those so-called avant-garde films that jump around from one thing to another without any connection or purpose. Because it's much easier."[58]

Carney reads the influence of WANDA's novel approach to narrative in some of Cassavetes's films: "Loden's film pointed the way for the much more important stylistic breakthrough of the new kinds of editing and sound work Cassavetes would employ in MINNIE AND MOSKOWITZ. [WANDA]... uses an extraordinarily full and layered soundtrack to create a world of extreme density and complexity around the central characters, and uses certain kinds of editorial ellipses to jump rapidly and unpredictably between scenes to create a feeling of extreme rush and haste."[59]

However, Carney's analysis eschews any consideration of sexual politics; it even turns WANDA into a love story,[60] thus failing to concentrate on Wanda's solitude. While Minnie ends up with a man and a retinue of children, Wanda leaves her children behind and ends up, boozing and smoking, her silent depression lost amidst the boisterous merriment that surrounds her. Loden's new style of filmmaking had taken her into the opaque, ambiguous territory of unspoken repression that has so often defined the condition of women – a territory only glanced at occasionally, *from the outside*, by generous male writers

Barbara Loden in/as WANDA

like Musil. What makes Loden a pioneer female filmmaker is that she viewed filmic experimentation as a way to express the "unspoken of". As the African-American poet Audré Lord noted, the master's house cannot be destroyed with the master's tools. Wanda's historical importance lies precisely at this junction: Loden wanted to suggest, *from the vantage point of her own experience*, what it meant to be a damaged, alienated woman – not to fashion a "new woman" or a "positive heroine".

WANDA was shot over a period of ten weeks in Connecticut and Pennsylvania, with a small crew of four people, composed of Loden and Proferes, who "did everything, [even] the costumes",[61] a lighting/sound technician (Lars Hedman) and an assistant (Christopher Cromin). Michael Higgins recalls that, when they were shooting near the Kazans' residence in Connecticut, Loden would cook for the cast and crew.[62] While stressing "WANDA was Barbara's film," Proferes explains that "it was really co-directed... Once in a while, she would look through the viewfinder. But most of the time she trusted me... I was responsible for the framing and the composition of 99% of the shots. Then we would look at the dailies together."[63] Yet Loden alone supervised the performances, including her own splendid rendering of the heroine.

The film was shot in 16mm reversal, to make it easier to blow it up to 35mm. Proferes was used to reversal: with "Ricky [Leacock] and all these people we were shooting on reversal, and would go to internegative to get off the A and B roll".[64] The film was shot documentary-style, with a hand-held camera and without much additional lighting: Proferes had to "push" the ASA, which contributed to the grainy quality of the image. When Wanda seeks shelter in the auditorium of a Hispanic movie theatre, the sequence was pushed to 1000 ASA. There was no storyboard, no rehearsals, and a high shooting ratio – the original footage amounted to "15 or 20 hours".[65] The filmmakers took advantage of unexpected situations, and the scenes were improvised in front of the camera.[66] Higgins, who once told Proferes "he never had before and never had since experienced such freedom",[67] also credits the latter's fluid, competent camerawork for making this freedom possible: "In the scene where I go around the cars stealing clothes, Nick just told me: 'You do what you have to do, and I'll follow you.' I set the clothes and the shoes in the various cars, and I just took off quickly... Nick is greatly responsible for the movement of that picture. There are very few directors who do that. Of course, with a 35mm camera, you can't do it."[68]

Some of WANDA's strongest moments came from chance encounters. As Higgins recalls: "On the other side of the open field, there was a man with his son, playing with a toy plane guided by remote control. And Barbara said 'Can you do something with that?' I loved the idea and said 'Yes, I can.' So, while it was flying around, I was saying 'Come back,' waving my hand at the plane. Then I jumped on the [top of the] car, and raised my arms toward the sky."[69] This sequence also shows some of the rare moments of real, albeit unspoken, tenderness between the two protagonists. On a late, lazy afternoon, Wanda and Mr. Dennis are eating and drinking beer in an empty field. Mr. Dennis wanders off and comes back to the car and to Wanda, takes off his jacket and puts it on her shoulders. While she remarks that "the sun's going down," he goes behind her, looking intently at her hair. His gaze, his attitude, are those of an obsessive lover, in contradiction with his harsh words: "Your hair looks terrible." Wanda doesn't look very concerned, but when Mr. Dennis suggests she could cover it with a hat, she tells him that she has no money to buy one. He calls her "stupid", and expounds what he thinks about money (the bitter wisdom of a man who never had any): "If you don't have money, you are nothing." Wanda, apparently, doesn't mind being "nothing", which makes Mr. Dennis angry. As the protagonists have revealed to each other their points of utmost vulnerability, the irritating noise of the toy plane invades the filmic space, till Mr. Dennis climbs on the top of the car, gesturing and screaming at it. The scene ends with him casting one look at Wanda and asking her "Why don't you get a hat?" For Loden, this sequence was "a Don Quixote image where Mr. Dennis is flailing at imaginary things against him or reaching for something unattainable".[70] In this moment of cinematic grace, Loden grants us a rare glimpse into Mr. Dennis's quest for human dignity and the hidden romanticism of her two misfits.

The prize received in Venice "completely changed [Loden]. She became a director in her own mind. She had this validation."[71] However, Kazan who had helped Loden in many stages of the preparation of the film, to "protect [her]",[72] wasn't altogether happy: "When I first met her, she had little choice but to depend on her sexual appeal. But after WANDA she no longer needed to be that way, no longer wore clothes that dramatised her lure, no longer came on as a frail, uncertain woman who depended on men who had the power... I realised I was losing her, but I was also losing interest in her struggle... She was careless about managing the house, let it fall apart, and I am an old-fashioned man."[73] (Interestingly, those last reproaches are similar to the grievances aired by Wanda's husband while he's waiting for her in court.) Though flattered by the attention his beautiful wife had received from the paparazzi in Venice, Kazan was quite dismissive of Loden's efforts to make another movie: "I didn't really believe she had the equipment to be an independent filmmaker, but she and Nick were a good combination."[74] How difficult, writes Virginia Woolf, it is to be "deaf to that persistent voice, now grumbling, now patronising, now grieved, now shocked, now avuncular, that voice that cannot let women alone, but must be at them, like some too conscientious governess...".[75] Eventually, because "she had succeeded completely in making a life independent"[76] of him, Kazan convinced Loden (as Goranski had Wanda) to agree to a divorce. Shortly after, she discovered the lump in her breast. In mainstream cinema, the master owns the tool factory, and the tool store as well. The gaps open in the master discourse are promptly closed. Loden never made another film.

Yet she had spent the last ten years of her life struggling and trying. Exploring her study after her death, Kazan found "three piles of xeroxed manuscripts, completed screenplays she'd written with Nick Proferes. I'd watched how hard she and Nick had worked, month after month."[77] Proferes recalls one particular project about an alcoholic star for which he was to direct Loden: "We did a lot of improvisation. We were writing the script, and then improving it."[78] These screenplays may have been "dramatically weak", but "like WANDA, there was an honesty about them," he adds. Yet, "nobody was really interested in Barbara directing these little movies. They still didn't treat her – or me – with any kind of respect. The only reason we'd get to see people, maybe, was because of Kazan."[79] However, Proferes's career benefited from his work on WANDA: Kazan hired him as cameraman, editor and producer for THE VISITORS (1972), the film he produced independently and with non-union help.[80]

After Venice, and right until her death, Loden taught an acting class of about 12 students who "regarded her as a saint",[81] and directed a number of theatre productions, often in collaboration with Proferes. Higgins, who saw most of Loden's theatre productions and worked with her when she was preparing Wedekind's *Pandora's Box* (a never-realised project), was impressed by the way she was communicating with actors, using "very few words... that came from the heart."[82] Proferes confirms that "she was very good with actors (most of them came from her acting class)" and that, in spite of the difficult financial conditions of Off-Off-Broadway, her productions had "really brilliant moments".[83] A few months before her death, she co-directed with David Heefner *Come Back to the Five and Dime, Jimmy Dean, Jimmy Dean*, in which she also gave "a glowing performance", although "the play got a cold reception from the critics".[84] Meanwhile, Milos Forman, unaware she had been diagnosed with cancer, had offered her a job in the Film Department of Columbia University. She gracefully suggested Proferes in her stead. This turned out to be the gift of a lifetime: he still teaches there.[85]

The Wand-erer

A film that traces no counter and delimits no form.
A film that is comfortable with readings that float.
A film that both attracts spectators and allows them no place to rest.
A film where the prefilmic proves to be hopeful rather than accurate.
A film that is elated at being a particle, a sprout, an unfinished song
Teshome Gabriel [86]

WANDA's theme is elegantly revealed in its first few minutes: we have a woman who simply doesn't fit within her environment, doesn't belong anywhere (she's *never* shown as having a home of her own), and whose very presence, more often than not, is an eyesore to the men around her (which doesn't prevent her from being a sex object). The film starts with an extreme long shot [1] panning from right to left in a coal field: slag-heaps, a crane in the distance, the repetitive noise of coal extraction. In [2] we cut to a long shot of two dump trucks excavating from the heaps; [3] takes us to the corner of a cheap house. In [4], we are inside the house, where a grandmother sits absorbed in solitary needlework. [5]: through a glass door, a little kid is seen walking, then heard crying. [6] takes us on the other side of the glass door, with a medium shot of a reddish-blonde woman seen from the back, in a white night-gown. A tighter shot [7] shows the baby crying on the bed.

The next two shots are characteristic of Proferes's documentary style. In [8] the woman walks toward the fridge with the baby in her arms, opens it and then walks to the stove; the camera leaves her to pan back to the right and frames a man, wearing a T-shirt, entering the kitchen door, while picking up his jacket from the wall and looking sourly in the direction of the woman, not off-screen; the camera pans back toward the woman, leaving the man who then exits our field of vision on the right side of the screen, while the woman offers him some coffee. [9] shows the man exiting the front door without a word; the camera then pans right and downward, revealing a woman lying on a couch, entirely covered by a sheet (except for a naked leg that sticks out). This is followed by a series of reverse-angle shots: a medium close-up of the woman holding the baby [10]; a shot of the woman on the couch (Wanda), stirring up under the sheet, revealing a mass of blonde hair, while the baby cries off-screen [11]; a medium close-up of the woman with the baby [12]; a tighter shot of Wanda raising her head and saying "He hates me because I'm here." [13]; the camera then alternates between the first woman [14] and Wanda, who raises her head again and looks ahead [15]. The next shot shows us what she sees through the window: two dump trucks, making the appropriate noises, while, inside, the baby cries [16]. Then we go back to Wanda on the couch, who begins to get up, revealing a black bra [17].

One of the ellipses admired by Carney, the next shot [18] displays the same bleak coalfields, and we expect it to be, like shot [16], what Wanda sees. In fact, as we'll realise later, quite a bit of time has elapsed since the previous shot, and Wanda is no longer *looking at* the landscape, she *is in* it. Shot [18], held longer than usual (about 2 minutes), starts with an extremely large view, then slowly zooms toward a tiny, white, almost incandescent figure, lost amongst the grey-ness. When the zoom stops, we are still far enough from the figure to distinguish it clearly, so it remains mysterious and quasi-magical; then the camera starts panning to follow the figure who walks from left to right. An invisible dog is heard barking.

The next cut starts a new sequence: a car driving under a bridge [19]; the car arriving in front of an industrial building [20]; a medium shot of the car, with two children inside, two adults in the back, and a man (Goranski) getting out [21]; a tighter shot of Goranski screaming to a man off-screen (Steve) that he has to go to court [22]; a long shot of Steve standing in a loading dock [23]; a reverse angle of Goranski waving at Steve and re-entering the car [24].

We cut back to the space of shot [18]: in the landscape darkened by coal dust, the camera pans to the right to follow a truck, revealing the same white figure, still in a distance, walking [25]. [26] is the long shot of an old man picking up coal. [27] shows him at a closer angle, while a female voice greets him; the camera pans to the right, until the "figure" appears, now closer and recognisable: it is Wanda, wearing clear coloured slacks and blouse, her hair in curlers under a white scarf. We pan back to the old man, then follow him as he walks toward Wanda, until the two of them are in the frame together. Then Wanda asks him "Could you lend me a little bit of money?"

Wanda's first two lines frame her relationship to men. Her brother-in-law "hates her" simply because she is there. She must have gone to her sister's to find a place to stay after leaving her husband. Later in court, Goranski accuses her of having "deserted" him and the children. He seems impatient to get married as soon as possible with the young lady who "helps [him] take care of the kids". Silenced by his accusations, she says: "Listen, judge, if he wants a divorce, just give it to him." What is at stake in this court is Goranski's desire, not hers. What does she want? Not her husband: when the camera frames them together in the courtroom, she doesn't look at him once. Nor her children: in a master coup – while lesser filmmakers would not have resisted a bit of sentimentalism – Proferes keeps the children off-screen while Wanda is in the courtroom, and Loden does not allow herself a single stolen glance in their direction.

The long shot showing Wanda as a frail, lost figure in the grey landscape also goes against the grain of traditional Hollywood narratives. Kazan's films, even if they show a man in transit (like Stavros in AMERICA, AMERICA [1963]) or leaving his old life behind (Eddie in THE ARRANGEMENT), stage the protagonist as firmly rooted in a land, a home. When he leaves it, this decision is "heroic" or "ethical". In any case, the man dominates his surroundings. Likewise, in a standard "road movie", the protagonist may be a drifter, but he commands attention, the never-ending space is structured around a vanishing point determined by his will, his desire and his gaze. It doesn't compare with the loneliness, the desolation suggested by the quasi-surrealistic walk of Wanda-the-waif who never quite manages to occupy the centre of the long shot (the camera movement duplicates her own hesitating gait), who seems swallowed by her environment, "overwhelmingly ugly and destructive".[87]

In films directed by men, women are often associated with the home in which they reside, pining for the protagonist and welcoming him back like Penelope. So, even though some isolated voices such as African-American film historian Teshome H. Gabriel claim that "the nomadic epic at its best, is truly a woman's epic",[88] there is very little tradition about the female wanderer (the "bad woman", the "drifter" is a commodity, not a full-blown character) unless, as in the Bonny and Clyde fantasies, she is companion to a man. Drawing his inspiration from Deleuze and Guattari's *A Thousand Plateaus*,[89] Gabriel is fairly ambiguous about the role played by women within nomadic aesthetics, reducing them to mythical figures. Similarly, in spite of their brilliant analysis of Virginia Woolf's position on women's writing,[90] Deleuze and Guattari eschew sexual politics when they discuss their famous distinction between "smooth" (or nomadic) and striated space. Maybe the opposition between the non-partitioned space of cultivation and animal-raising and the partitioned, closed space of the city-dweller and sedentary cultivator[91] has more to do with a war among the sexes than a war among tribes, as Gabriel himself acknowledges, quoting an ancient Mauritanian sheik: "It is the women who make us live in the desert. They say the desert brings health and happiness, to themselves and the children."[92] The archaeology of religions seems to confirm this hypothesis: it is with the development of sedentary agriculture that the archaic female goddesses became displaced by male gods.[93]

Gabriel was interested in using the concept of "nomadic art" in his "research for an alternative aesthetic of black independent cinema" (as an extension of his prior, seminal work on "Third cinema"), since nomads and blacks are "both marginalised and (de)territorialised people".[94] Like Deleuze and Guattari, he reads the "nomadic space" as an alternative to the state apparatus of Western capitalism, but nothing can prevent us from deciphering it as a subterranean counter-space offsetting the striated order of patriarchy.[95] Indeed, Gabriel's description of nomadic cinema fits WANDA like a glove: "The journey is the link(age); without it there is no film. There is no film in and of itself. A film by itself is therefore meaningless – it conveys nothing. Film exists so that the journey may exist, and vice versa."[96] For him, nomadic aesthetics unfold "liberated spaces outside Hollywood and oppositional cinema [in which] a new, newly born cinema is emerging, a cinema not-yet-here but no-longer-there, a travelling cinema – nomadic cinema".[97]

WANDA's nomadic sensibility is apparent first in its narrative structure: Michael Higgins stresses that, from the Pennsylvania coal fields to the Connecticut highways, from Waterbury where Mr. Dennis meets his father to Scranton where the robbery is performed, the protagonists keep going in circles and "not going anywhere" (interview, Higgins). As *Plateaus* notices, "*nomads do not move. They are nomads by dint of not moving, not migrating*".[98] To use an American idiomatic phrase, Wanda does *not* "go places", she's not socially mobile, and her story is non-directional: at the end, she is no less in the lurch (alone, without money, drifting) than she was at the beginning. Moreover, the diegetic space of the film is structured without a vanishing point and its architecture of reverse-angle shots does not follow the rules of classical narrative filmmaking. According to Lacanian analysis, the vanishing point within a representational image is precisely what marks the place of the subject.[99] This, in turn, is not contradictory with Deleuze and Guattari's understanding of the striated space (that also implies a certain positioning of the subject) as "defined by the requirement of long-distance vision: constancy of orientation, invariance of distance through an interchange of inertial points of reference, interlinkage by immersion in an ambient milieu, constitution of a central perspective".[100] The striated space seems a perfect example not only of classical painting, but also of the classical Hollywood *mise en scène*, which WANDA subverts. Mentioning "the absence of point-of-view and shot-reverse shots" in the film, Carney quotes Loden as replying to an interviewer that she always "saw [Wanda] *in* something, surrounded by something",[101] which seems very close to the definition of a Deleuzian smooth space. Moreover, Proferes's *cinéma-verité* mode of handling the camera, of following his subjects (even when they are at a distance) with an almost tactile approach, of integrating foreground and background, is a good example of the *close-vision-haptic space* which *A Thousand Plateaus* assigns to nomadic aesthetics. In the case of WANDA, this closeness is not purely aesthetic but reflects an inner sympathy – rather than a judgmental or purely scopophilic stance – on the part of the filmmakers for their heroine. As Loden shamelessly admitted: "In my opinion Wanda is right and everyone around her is wrong."[102] Yet the smooth and the striated keep overlapping and transforming into each other; in this case, Proferes's editing, by "cutting" and shaping the material, projected it onto another "plateau", thus reaching a fragile, graceful and splendid synthesis between the two spaces.

Yet, even with Proferes's invaluable contribution, Loden was alone, as alone as these 19th century female writers described by Virginia Woolf: "Whatever effect discouragement and criticism had upon their writing... that was unimportant compared with the other difficulty that faced them... when they came to set their thoughts on paper – that is that they had no tradition behind them, or one so short and partial that it was of little help."[103] A pioneer female filmmaker, Loden was working without a net, without role models, without a network of female collaborators ('sisterhood' was not invented then), in a void. Of her lonely fight, we know practically nothing, for she was shy and found it difficult to express herself, especially in public and in interviews. What we know of her life has been recounted by her male collaborators, so it is in the fictions she wrote we must look for her true voice. Apart from the difficult-to-see WANDA, her work has disappeared or is not available. No wonder women's lives are often no more than "a little line scratched on the tablets of history". So it is to WANDA that I'll turn again, as a story of the sentimental education of a woman, who, despite the differences of name, age, class or ethnic background, could be Barbara Loden, or you, or me.

When Wanda has lost everything: her shelter in her sister's house, her husband, her children, her job, whatever self-respect she had left when the travel-

ling salesman dumped her, and finally her last dollars stolen in the movie theatre – when she has nothing to lose, this is the moment she meets Mr. Dennis.

It has been noted that the pace of the film and its formal strategies were altered with the arrival of Michael Higgins. Lack of budget, but also the search
for people who would be "real" led Loden to cast "ordinary people living in
the area"[104] for the minor characters. On the other hand, Higgins was a seasoned professional actor, with a long track record in theatre. Loden had met
him on the set of *The Arrangement*, in which he was playing the part of Kirk
Douglas's brother. In his background and sensibility, Higgins was very close to
Loden and Proferes. This Brooklyn kid, who "had this ambition of doing
something big",[105] joined a local Shakespearian company when he was 17, and
stayed there four years: "I did everything, including the costumes."[106] Severely
wounded during WW II, he was the first student admitted at the American
Theatre, "the professional training program for actors and directors after they
got out of the army. And while I was a student, I was working on Broadway."[107]

When Higgins arrived on location, he had done his homework, and prepared the character of Mr. Dennis. "This is a man who has been in prison for
some years. Which led me to think of what kind of a guy he was, what kind of
things he wore, his haircut, and of course, his suspicious attitude. Barbara suggested the dark sunglasses. We also used some of Kazan's old clothes (he never
threw anything away), and I decided to put the scar on my forehead. We didn't
have anybody doing make-up. So I had to put the scar on me every day of the
shoot. There was a certain amount of funny quality about this guy. He was not
a good crook. He knew he was going to get in deep trouble."[108]

Zombiique or defiant, Wanda's relationship to Mr. Dennis is far from being a
passive one. Going deeper and deeper into the truth of the character, Loden
gave up as "phoney" her original "Pygmalion theme where the man builds the
girl up and makes her into something"[109]. In the sequence of shots that describes Wanda's first encounter with Mr. Dennis, she is the one who imposes
her presence onto him, and not he who "picks her up".[110] When she enters the
bar, he first tries to get rid of her by saying "we are closed". She physically
struggles with him to gain access, demanding to use the bathroom. Her stubbornness is different from the desperate way in which she was trying to
"cling" to the travelling salesman. This is the first time we see Wanda expressing her desire and acting on it. Initially, this desire seems devoid of erotic components. Then it becomes clear that Wanda has, consciously or not, chosen Mr.
Dennis as a partner. The rest of the scene shows her positioning herself within
the gaze of the man, so as to evolve from object of irritation to object of desire.
This is articulated through a series of demands. Coming back from the bathroom, she first asks for a towel - which she does not get: the camera pans down
from Mr. Dennis's face to the only towel in the joint. It has been used to gag the

bartender who lies tied up behind the counter, invisible to Wanda. In this single shot, Wanda's desire becomes intricately linked with Mr. Dennis's narrative. It is because he is in the process of a petty robbery that Mr. Dennis cannot respond to Wanda's demand. So, being unable to give her the towel *she* wants, he proceeds to get what *he* wants: the money from the cash register. Mr. Dennis's non-fulfillment of Wanda's demand opens up a space in which her desire will be articulated.

Before, Wanda's relationship to men was lived under the sign of demand and necessity. And she was getting, more or less, what she asked for: a little bit of money, a job, a beer. Yet, she was always short-changed: less money than she had hoped, a job that lasted only two days, a beer for a short ride and a quick fuck. Because Mr. Dennis does not even give her the scraps she was used to receiving from men, she is prompted to ask for more. She shamelessly starts eating the potato chips on the counter, then asks for something to drink – he pours beer from the tap for her – and then something she never had before: attention when she speaks. She flatly tells him "somebody stole all [her] money". Then she requests something personal, almost intimate from the man: "a comb or something". He obliges reluctantly and pulls a comb out of his breast pocket.

Wanda's single-minded stubbornness reminded me of the third part of JE TU IL ELLE (1974), in which we see the protagonist (also played by the director of the film, Chantal Akerman) literally forcing her way into the home of a former lover she is still obsessed with. Akerman's problem is to find a way to spend the night (and eventually have sex) with a woman who is determined to make her leave. Instead of saying "I want you to love me", Akerman bluntly says "I am hungry," and the other woman has no other choice but to feed her. "More," she says. And then, having eaten ravenously, she adds: "I am thirsty." In the next scene, the two women are having sex.[111]

By uttering this series of demands, Wanda turns Mr. Dennis into a partner. He understands this, for the next time he talks to her, he refers to them as "us": "Let's go!" In the next scene, they already behave like an old couple: He's taken Wanda to dinner, they're eating spaghetti, and he criticises her "sloppiness". He is this kind of man, an "emotional cripple" who, unable to say something nice to his partners, keeps criticising them as a way of paying attention to them. The scene ends with a medium shot of Mr. Dennis casting a desiring look in the direction of Wanda off-screen. There is no reaction shot, but the next cut shows them in bed, where Wanda's misguided (but rather aggressive) efforts to have a conversation with Mr. Dennis, or even simply to touch him, irritate him, and he orders her to go and buy three hamburgers, in the middle of the night.

At this moment Mr. Dennis's point of view is constructed to coincide with that of the spectator, and he fails to read the articulation of Wanda's desire:

when he sends her off to get food, he gives her "too much money", and she protests (this is NOT money she wants from him). Later, hearing police sirens, he looks through the window and sees Wanda talking to a man and leaving with him. Visually, this image is similar to Wanda's long walk in the coalfield, during which the audience could not identify her: she is a small white figure lost in the darkness around her. Mr. Dennis shrugs, closes the window, turns off the light, locks his door and goes to bed: she is this kind of girl, you give her some money, and she's off with some other guy. Things change when Wanda returns and he slaps her: by her absence she has entered his space, he's no longer a spectator but involved in something very close to passion – jealousy.

Yet Wanda is not a love story. When the heroine loses Mr. Dennis, this is not pure 'bad luck', it was structurally inscribed in the dynamics of their relationship. In the poignant scene with his father, we see Mr. Dennis as a man to whom the simple dignity of being a good son has been denied (his father refuses his money) due to a lifetime of petty crime and failure. This is the inner urgency that prompts him to design, against all odds, the bank job. Yet he's doomed, and he knows it. And then Wanda becomes "Wanda" to him, for a short time: only when he urges her to become his accomplice does he use her first name, instead of calling her "stupid". Yes, he wants to use her, but this is also a drowning man uttering a word of love. "Listen to me. Wanda. Maybe you never did anything before. Maybe you never did. But you're going to do this." At this moment, Mr. Dennis is standing behind Wanda, holding her by the shoulders, and he speaks to her in a low voice, almost into her ear. A reverse angle shot reveals they are in front of a mirror, and, like in Lacan's mirror stage, Mr. Dennis gets a confirmation of his own existence, his own identity, by looking at his reflection with Wanda. Even at the moment of their strongest bond, he's not really talking about her, he's talking about him. A prisoner of the sexual impasse that defines us all, he thought he could establish a true partnership with a woman if he asked her (begged her, convinced her, forced her) to do with him what he wants to do. As a poignant aside, we'll notice that, when Mr. Dennis prepares the robbery with Wanda, he behaves like a director with a reluctant actress, telling her to dress like a pregnant woman, and giving her a 'script' she should memorise. Obviously, Loden was commenting about her own experience as an actress (and the fact that Higgins was wearing Kazan's suit only confirms this interpretation). Wanda also comments on how women are constantly forced to play a part within the 'script' written by the men who desire them, so as to play up to this desire and have a chance of being loved. As Mr. Dennis reveals more of himself, Wanda's desire, once emerging, is eclipsed again. Yes she wants this man. But she doesn't want money. He never gave her a chance to know *his* first name. Maybe she would have wanted to say it, once, just once.

And, as most women would, she blames herself for her loss. She "did good" in the first part of the robbery, but she spoiled everything when she was stopped by the policeman. *We* know (but *she* doesn't) that Mr. Dennis's death is due to his own mistake (he had planned the caper a few minutes too early) and suicidal stubbornness (he'd rather be shot than go back to jail). She wasted time, her getaway car was late, she'll never forgive herself. She'll never understand that, even with Mr. Dennis, she was betrayed from the beginning. And so, in this final freeze frame influenced by Truffaut's 400 BLOWS [112] she might as well say, like Anne in Carl Dreyer's DAY OF WRATH (1943), betrayed by her lover and promised to the stake: "I see you through my tears, but nobody comes to wipe them away."

Special thanks to Thom Andersen, Margie Hanft and the staff of the California Institute of the Arts Library, Michael Higgins, Alex Horwath, Kent Jones, Nick Proferes and, for their inspirational work, Chantal Akerman, Nina Menkes, Yvonne Rainer and Virginia Woolf.

Notes

1. *New York Times*, September 6, 1980, 261.
2. Interview with Nicholas T. Proferes, February 12, 1995, hereafter referred to as "Proferes".
3. Elia Kazan, *A Life*, Alfred Knopf, New York, 1988, 807.
4. *Ibid*, 809.
5. *New York Times*, March 21, 1971, Section II, 1.
6. *New York Times*, March 1, 1971, 22.
7. *New York Times*, April 25, 1971, Section II, 11.
8. The film was much better received in continental Europe. A few months before her death, Loden was the object of a long interview by a German television station (Kazan, p. 807). Among the articles written in Europe about the film are an interview by Michel Ciment (*Positif*, No 168, April 1975, 34-39); a review by Joel Magny (*Téléciné*, No 198, April 1975, 23); a text by Jean-Loup Passek (*Cinéma*, No 196, March 1975, 133-35); a short review by Claude Beylie (*Ecran*, No 34, March 1975, 70); a review in *Positif* (No 168, April 1975, 31-33); a very interesting conversation between Marguerite Duras and Elia Kazan (*Cahiers du cinéma*, No 318, December 1980, 5-7); a text by Ebert Jürgen in *Filmkritik* (Vol XXV No 3, March 1981, 120-130); a text by Yann Lardeau (*Cahiers du cinéma*, No 342, Dec 1982, 49-50); a text by Jacqueline Nacache (*Cinéma*, No 288, Dec 1982, 66-67); a short text in *Cinématographe* (No 84, December 1982, 51); a short article by Helena van der Meulen (*Skrien* No 148, Summer 1986, 21); a review in the TV magazine *Télérama* (No 2301, Feb 16, 1994). Among the texts written in America that I have managed to dig out since

first writing this article in 1995 is a short review in *Take One* (Vol III, No 2, February 1972, 3); "Barbara Loden Revisited", in which Loden discusses WANDA with the Madison Women's Media Collective (*Women and Film*, Vol 5-6, 1974, 67-70); and a text by Chuck Kleinhans, "WANDA; Marilyn times five; seeing through cinema vérité" – in which he compares WANDA to a film by Bruce Conner that also "deals with women as victims" (*Jump Cut*, May-June 1974, 14-15). WANDA is being re-released in France (July 2003), and more texts are being written, which hopefully will re-open the discussion on the film.

9. Ruby Melton, "An environment that is overwhelmingly ugly and destructive: an interview with Barbara Loden," *The Film Journal*, Vol I, No 2, Summer 1971, 10-15.

10. Molly Haskell, *From Reverence to Rape*, Penguin Books, Baltimore, 1974, 18.

11. *Ibid*, 366.

12. Andrew Sarris, *The American Cinema: Directors and Directions 1928-1968*, E.P. Dutton & Co. New York, 1968. (The irony is that the book is dedicated to Sarris's wife, Molly Haskell.)

13. *Women and the Cinema: A Critical Anthology*, Karyn Kay and Gerald Peary ed., E.P. Dutton, New York, 1977, 385.

14. Raymond Carney, *American Dreaming: The Films of John Cassavetes and the American Experience*, University of California Press, Berkeley, 1985, and *The Films of John Cassavetes*, Cambridge University Press, Cambridge, 1994.

15. Carney, 1994, 146-7.

16. *Ibid*, 271.

17. Fritz Lang's YOU ONLY LIVE ONCE (1937) is a dark tale in which, in spite of their youth, love and ultimate innocence, the protagonists (Sylvia Sidney and Henry Fonda) are manipulated to their doom by forces of society beyond their control. Nicholas Ray's THEY LIVE BY NIGHT (1948, with Farley Granger and Cathy O'Donnell), more loosely inspired by the original story, is a tale of *amour fou* gone wrong. Joseph H. Lewis's GUN CRAZY (1950) casts two not-too-smart loser victims of the Depression (John Dahl and Peggy Cummings) who have to use guns simply to survive.

18. One of the few exceptions to this trend has been another independent feature, Leonard Castle's THE HONEYMOON KILLERS (1969), also the work of a one-time director, in which an overweight nurse and a flashy gigolo team up to con and murder lonely women. Like WANDA, the film has gained cult status in Europe.

19. Melton, 11.

20. Carney, 1994, 307, Note 220.

21. Carney, 1985, 152.

22. The film was eventually acquired by Castle Hill Productions in New York. Asked by phone and by fax when the film was bought, whether it existed in 35mm, 16mm or video, where the negative was kept, and if the film was available for rental for classroom or research use, the company declined to answer. However, they replied positively to an enquiry put forward by the conference "Women and Madness" that took place in Vienna in 1998 (sentence added in 2002).

23. *Women in Film: An International Guide*, Annette Kuhn and Susannah Radstone ed., Fawcett Columbine Books, New York, 1990, p.82-83 (initially published in Great Britain as *The Women's Companion to International Film* in 1990 by Virago Limited).

Since then, I have leant that Cinemien is *no longer* distributing WANDA (sentence added in 2002).

24. Annette Kuhn, *Women's Pictures. Feminism and Cinema*, Routledge and Kegan Paul, London, 1982, 135.
25. *Ibid*, 174-5.
26. Kazan, 1988, 571-2.
27. Kazan, 1988, 587.
28. Kazan, 1988, 558-9, italics mine.
29. Kazan reports how he saw Kelman as an obstacle when he tried breaking off with Barbara rather than marrying her, after the death of his first wife, Molly. "[Barbara] says the same thing, that bitch, that you say about me, that I'm an *emotional cripple* [italics mine]... I get mad at her, but I respect her because she hides nothing. Imagine telling me every boyfriend she ever had... Anyway, I don't want to be tied to a damn actress, do I?... I'm going to break off with her, no matter what you say... One more minute. Please. Tell me. Why do I keep going back to her? 'You stay with her because she's like you,' he said, 'the victim who victimises. She gets back at those who hurt her by hurting them whenever she has the power and the chance. That's what you do. Revenge. Poor Molly.' 'Bullshit', I said. He ... said 'Poor Barbara', turned and left the room... I got up and went home, where I wrote her a letter telling her I wasn't going to see her anymore... I wrote another letter, this one to Dr Kelman, informing him I wasn't going to see him anymore and asking him to please send me his bill." (Kazan, 1988, 723-4).
30. Kazan, 1988, 795.
31. Melton, 14.
32. Melton, 11, italics mine.
33. Kazan, 1988, 801-2.
34. Kazan, 1988, 793.
35. "Proferes".
36. Kazan, 1988, 723.
37. "Proferes".
38. *New York Times*, January 24, 1964, 18.
39. Kazan, 1988, 668.
40. *Ibid.*, 559-600: "A 'hillbilly' from the back-country of North Carolina, Barbara had a side to her character – to go with her great sensitivity – that was defiantly tough... Barbara was as wild as the river I was making about."
41. Kazan credits Loden as having inspired the character of Gwen, both by her presence in his life, and by the conversations he had with her (Kazan, 1988, 736 and 738).
42. Interview with Michael Higgins, February 19, 1995, hereafter referred to as "Higgins".
43. "Proferes". Dunaway had been Loden's understudy when she played Maggie in Arthur Miller's *After the Fall*.
44. Kazan, 1988, 754.
45. Elia Kazan, *The Arrangement*, Stein and Day, New York, 1967, 53.
46. Quoted in Scott McDonald, *Screenwriting, Scripts and Texts by Independent Filmmakers*, University of California Press, Berkeley, 1995, 230.
47. Kazan, 1988, 793-4.

48. Robert Musil, *Five Women*, Godine Publisher, Boston, New York, 1986, p.84.
49. Melton, 11.
50. "Proferes".
51. Kazan, Loden and Proferes quote slightly different figures for the cost of the film: $200,000 for Kazan (Kazan, p.793); between $80,000 (the original budget) and $115,000 (the money actually spent) for Loden (Melton, p.12); and $75,000 for Proferes.
52. "Proferes".
53. "Proferes". Maybe he accepted because of a memory. In 1957, Proferes was in the Navy, and during a period of R&R, was offered a ticket to his first Broadway show: it was *Compulsion*. "I was up in the balcony... and down below there was a blonde girl in a red dress doing the Charleston. I carried this image with me for years. It was Barbara..."
54. "Proferes".
55. One must mention Richard (Ricky) Leacock's Eddie Sachs in Indianapolis (1961), Football (1962), The Chair (1963), Happy Mother's Day (1963, in collaboration with Joyce Chopra), Igor Stravinsky, a portrait (1966), Albert and David Maysles's What's Happening!, The Beatles in the USA (1964) and Salesman (1969), Pennebaker's Don't Look Back (1966) and Monterey Pop (1967), and the Maysles-Charlotte Zwerin collaboration, Gimme Shelter (1970).
56. "Proferes".
57. Melton, 12.
58. *Ibid.*
59. Carney, 1985, 152.
60. "Both films [Wanda and Minnie and Moskowitz] are about the interaction of personal style and hostile environment, and, further, about the interaction of the different senses of timing, and their different styles of acting... Both films are, in short, about the possibilities of productive synchronisation and creative counterpoint of personal styles and timings that might be said to be one possible definition of a loving relationship." *Ibid.*
61. "Proferes".
62. "Higgins".
63. "Proferes".
64. "Proferes".
65. "Proferes".
66. This is a major difference with John Cassavetes's work, which, contrary to some rumors that have circulated, "*looks* improvised, but was entirely scripted... [At the time he directed Shadows] John had an acting class, and the theme of Shadows was the result of improvisational exercises by his students. It is the only film in his entire career that was improvisational... He loved actors. He rehearsed quite a bit while shooting, and he followed the actors' suggestions, changing the dialogues, or even the storyline, if they found something better to do. For Faces, we had three weeks of rehearsals, then we shot about 150 hours of footage." (Al Ruban, longtime collaborator of Cassavetes, interviewed and quoted by Bérénice Reynaud in "Al Ruban: Tout, plus le reste," *Cahiers du cinéma*, No.417, March 1989, 23-24.)
67. "Proferes".
68. "Higgins".

69. "Higgins".
70. Melton, 14.
71. "Proferes".
72. "Higgins".
73. Kazan, 1988, 794.
74. Kazan, 1988, 794.
75. Virginia Woolf, *A Room of One's Own*, Harcourt Brace Janovitz, New York, 1989, 75.
76. Kazan, 1988, 794.
77. Kazan, 1988, 815.
78. "Proferes".
79. "Proferes," who adds that the only other filmwork that Loden and he were offered was when the Learning Corporation of America asked them to direct "a couple of one half-hour dramatic films, some sorts of moral tales," which they shot in the same conditions as WANDA. Apparently there are videocassettes of these films (sentence added 2002).
80. Kazan, 1988, 754-6.
81. "Proferes".
82. "Higgins".
83. "Proferes".
84. Kazan, 1988, 806-7.
85. "Proferes". This information was received in 1995. In September 2002, Nick Proferes was still teaching at Columbia.
86. Teshome H. Gabriel, "Thoughts on Nomadic Aesthetics and the Black Independent Cinema: Traces of a Journey", in *Blackframes: Critical Perspectives on Black Independent Cinema*, Mbye B. Cham and Claire Watkins, ed., MIT Press, Cambridge, 1988, 76.
87. Melton, 10.
88. Gabriel, 76.
89. Gilles Deleuze and Felix Guattari, *A Thousand Plateaus – Capitalism and Schizophrenia,* Brian Massumi trans. University of Minnesota Press; Minneapolis, 1987.
90. "When Virginia Woolf was questioned about a specifically women's writing, she was appalled at the idea of writing 'as a woman.' Rather, writing should produce a becoming-woman as atoms of womanhood capable of crossing and impregnating an entire social field." *Ibid,* 276.
91. *Ibid.,* 497.
92. Gabriel, 67.
93. *Genesis* gives a strange homosexual version to this passage: the feminine figure of Abel, the shepherd, is sacrificed by Cain, the farmer. Abel dies without progeny or legacy, while it is Cain, even though "marked"/striated by his fault, who carries the law of a male, monotheist and "jealous" God.
94. Gabriel, 70.
95. This in itself would grant a much longer development. I can only mention, as fellow travellers in the exploration of this space, filmmakers Nina Menkes (THE GREAT SADNESS OF ZOHARA, MAGDALENA VIRAGA, QUEEN OF DIAMONDS), Leslie Thornton (especially ADYNATA and THERE WAS AN UNSEEN CLOUD MOVING) and Trinh T. Minh-ha (who is also an essayist and whose writing on women and "the interstice" have been particularly inspiring).

96. Gabriel, 72.
97. Gabriel, 73. Gabriel continues as follows: "It is only in open free spaces that a new cinema can both deconstruct and construct this cinema. It is only through work of nomadic sensibility that black cinema, independent, feminist, exile and Third World cinema will capture its axis."
98. Deleuze and Guattari, 482.
99. See Jacques Lacan, "The Line and the Light," in *The Four Fundamental Concepts of Psycho-analysis*, Alan Sheridan trad., Norton, New York, 1977, 91-102.
100. Deleuze and Guattari, 494.
101. Carney, 1985, 130.
102. Melton, 11.
103. Woolf, 76.
104. Melton, 13.
105. "Higgins".
106. "Higgins".
107. "Higgins".
108. "Higgins".
109. Melton, 11.
110. Or "kidnaps her", as written in a misinformed summary of the film.
111. Strangely, even though the narrative and the formal means to express it are different, JE TU IL ELLE and WANDA also have a very similar structure: the depression in an enclosed space (in WANDA this part is barely shown), the 'wandering' on the road, assorted with a brief sexual encounter, in which what is at stake is more the jouissance of the man than of the woman (although Akerman's trucker is shown with more tenderness than Loden's travelling salesman), and finally, a relationship of desire with a reluctant partner (in WANDA this part occupies most of the film, while in JE TU IL ELLE it is neatly confined to the last third). In both cases, this relationship is shown as short-lived – Akerman has to leave the next morning, and Mr Dennis is killed – but both women have found a way of articulating their desire. It is probably no accident that this articulation is done through the stubborn assertion of the physical presence of the filmmaker's body on screen, as if to say "I am here to stay". Even though Akerman had directed a number of short films before, and both JE TU IL ELLE and WANDA are the directors' first features, and both had difficulties getting recognition – JE TU IL ELLE, shot in a grainy 16mm black and white, with a cast of unknowns (the truck driver, Niels Asterup, was a stage actor at the time) was distributed *only after* the art house success of JEANNE DIELMAN (shot in 35mm and graced by the presence of a movie star, Delphine Seyrig). My insistence to compare Loden's and Akerman's work in the seventies comes from the fact that I think they both strove to articulate some important elements of a female subjectivity that was barely being uncovered at the time. None of the works are 'pious', and even less 'politically correct'. Also, I consider that, while Akerman, maybe one of the ten most important filmmakers of the last 25 years, fully deserves the critical and theoretical attention she received, the lack of a similar attention bestowed on Loden is unfair.
112. Melton, 12.

Everybody Knows This Is Nowhere

The Uneasy Ride of Hollywood and Rock

Howard Hampton

> Remember all the movies, Terry, we'd go and see /
> Tryin' to learn how to walk like the heroes we thought we had to be
> Bruce Springsteen, "Backstreets", 1975

From its beginning, Martin Scorsese's 1973 MEAN STREETS is the most seductive union of movies and rock imaginable: a prowling, claustrophobic fever dream where the images and music are locked in an interpenetrating embrace, each intensifying, elaborating, and undermining the meanings of the other. We first see Harvey Keitel's Charlie abruptly waking from a nightmare – what looks like a nightly ritual, a subconscious form of penance. But the nightmare stays with him, clinging like a caul. Going to the darkened mirror, the reflection he sees there could be his double looking back at him from the confessional or the grave: a stillborn twin. Charlie returns to the empty bed, and his head falls to the pillow in trance-like slow motion. The suspended drum beats of a song seem to come from his pounding chest rather than the soundtrack. Time stands still, and then, as the wave of yearning that is "Be My Baby" washes over the screen, turns back on itself. The Ronettes song, produced in 1963 by Phil Spector ("a one-man millennium", as Nik Cohn tenderly described him)[1] distilled young love into a utopia of self-fulfilling desire, where to wish for something is to make it so. As embodied by the teenage Veronica Bennett's aching soul-kiss of a voice, it's the reflection of everything Charlie's self-cancelling life is not.

As the opening titles roll, "Be My Baby" orchestrates the home movies we see projected above the neatly lettered credits, like a guilt-ridden Catholic version of Kenneth Anger's SCORPIO RISING. Its aria of longing sucks the viewer into Charlie's penny-ante world of duty and crime: an upwardly mobile low-life, he's an altar boy in the Mafia's hierarchy of corruption. "I'll make you so proud of me," the future Mrs. Spector sings, Ronnie's unsteady teenage voice bursting with so much passion it infuses the 8mm memories on screen with a radioactive intimacy. At the same time, we feel a suffocating undercurrent as

Spector's "wall of sound" closes in, breathless grandeur taken to the breaking point, loss covertly written into the promise of total gratification. (Spector's music presents itself as an all-encompassing conspiracy against silence.) In Hal Blaine's double-edged drumming – the most fated beat anyone in rock has found – there's both tremendous exhilaration and terrible finality. It's the cadence of a lover's plea and a priest giving last rites rolled into one. Behind the tenderness of "Be My Baby" lies the inexorable pull of dread, and that is the bittersweet, doubt-haunted rhythm MEAN STREETS moves to – the steady pulse of impending chaos, the rapt trance of waiting damnation.

MEAN STREETS was the first movie narrative to truly integrate rock into a dramatic *sensibility*, transfiguring the blasphemous, iconographic abstractions of SCORPIO RISING (where Anger's cheeky, experimental homoerotics simultaneously bordered on Camp and Porn) into a new form of heightened, pop-operatic naturalism. Scorsese reached across several eras of rock to mix the music of the Ronettes, Derek and the Dominos, the Marvelettes, the Miracles, Johnny Ace, and the Rolling Stones together to map those streets, much as Bruce Springsteen's 1973 album *The Wild, the Innocent, and the E-Street Shuffle* fused a similar range of styles with echoes of the same post-Brando bravado. The music seemed to grow out of the story and vice-versa, even if Scorsese's real inspirations for the characters and milieu came from the pre-Spector/Motown/Beatles era, the Little Italy where Dion and the Belmonts' doowop ruled supreme. He turned the manic smile of the Marvelettes' "Please Mr. Postman" inside out by scoring a wild, Keystone Thugs brawl to it in real time, as a kind of slapstick cinema vérité. (Putting a lithe, high-kicking Robert De Niro on a pool table, Scorsese turned him into a hoodlum Iggy Stooge: the first punk Rockette.) The doomsday purr of "Jumpin' Jack Flash" served as a Greek chorus for a barroom Hades, while the Russian-roulette romance of the late Johnny Ace's "Pledging My Love" and the crazed jive of "Mickey's Monkey" by Smokey Robinson's Miracles foreshadowed looming disaster. But "Be My Baby" established the tone of what was to come – graffiti scrawled in the blood from Charlie's wet dream, the one he recounts to his mortified girlfriend where he ejaculates it all over the place. Charlie's a real piece of repressed work, as tortured by intimations of heaven as by those of hell.

Phil Spector had been the first rock auteur, conceiving his productions as three-minute epics. He worked in aural *CinemaScope*, blowing teenage home movies up into wide-screen passion plays. Early hits like "To Know Him Is to Love Him", "Spanish Harlem", "Uptown", the scandalous "He Hit Me (It Felt Like a Kiss)" and "He's a Rebel" were nothing less than Spector's version of WEST SIDE STORY. Only he stripped away the Broadway respectability, the virtuous social conscience, all the corny Hollywood bromides, and went for something wilder and more elusive: the place where fantasy dissolves all the barriers reality throws in its way. Paying homage to Spector and the fabulous Veronica (a black Lolita in bouffant hair and a mini-skirt), Scorsese was also alluding to something cinema hadn't really acknowledged: the feeling that rock had replaced Hollywood as the primary source of America's most resonant, deeply felt representations of itself. MEAN STREETS used rock songs themselves as its jumping-off point, an entrance into an undiscovered country of funk. Its music defined a terrain of defiance and repression, freedom and betrayal: a secret cinema playing inside Scorsese's characters. The death-dance of Keitel's Charlie and Robert De Niro's punk prankster Johnny-Boy found the tragic dimension latent in Spector's pop hallucinations, in the Miracles' and the Stones' jigsaw cool, in the sign language of unattainable grace and carnal pleasures that only exacerbate the pain of eternal suffering.

Scorsese's vision was of what had been left out of American movies in the wake of rock, the upheaval Hollywood hadn't come to terms with: the new synthesis of the mythic and the quotidian ushered in in the wake of Elvis Presley and Spector, the new style of poetic license fashioned by Bob Dylan and the Rolling Stones. The hybrid quality of MEAN STREETS drew on neo-realism and film noir (on each as a version of the other) as well as rock, and it layered Godard-Bresson after-effects in between the pop juice, but ultimately had more in common with *Let It Bleed* than Elia Kazan (let alone THE GODFATHER). Much as the Rolling Stones drew on blues, soul, and early rock to invent a language of pop rebellion that spoke directly to American experiences and fantasies (to America's penchant for experiencing its fantasies as revelation), Scorsese filtered new European cinema through a uniquely American perspective. Here, reinventing film in terms of rock, he was closest of all to Springsteen, who at the same time was re-imagining rock in terms of Kazan, James Dean, and Marlon Brando. In Springsteen's thrilling, poignantly fetishistic cosmology, it was as if WEST SIDE STORY had mutated a heterosexual SCORPIO RISING: "Backstreets" itself was a virtual answer record to Scorsese. It merged Keitel's Charlie with Steiger's ON THE WATERFRONT role, and Brando's Terry donned De Niro's delinquent clothes, ghosts moving through the back streets of Bob Dylan's "Like a Rolling Stone" as it might have sounded with Spector producing.

From the Fifties onwards, Hollywood had always kept rock at arm's length even as it sought to jump on the bandwagon: it tried to cash in on the youth cult explosion while muffling it with the wet blanket of show-business-as-usual. THE GIRL CAN'T HELP IT (1956) turned rock into baggy-pants burlesque – inspired burlesque, true, but Little Richard's monumental racial-sexual weirdness was reduced to novelty-act status, effaced by Edmund O'Brian's jowls and Jayne Mansfield's breasts. Later, youth revolt would be given the sociological-sensational treatment epitomised by Stanley Kramer's 1970 R.P.M.

(campus "revolution" effaced by Anthony Quinn's jowls and Ann-Margaret's breasts: Hollywood's idea of progress.) The entertainment industry was determined to assimilate rock if it couldn't replace it, so it exploited the latest craze even as it sought to replace it or give it a wholesome Pat Boone overhaul. Thus a new genre was born, 'the Elvis movie', which epitomised Hollywood's contempt for rock. Early on, with the casually insolent JAILHOUSE ROCK (1957), it seemed like Presley might become the natural successor to Dean or Brando or Mitchum – that his rockabilly menace and carnality could be translated to film, and he might be able to bring the wild unseen side of America to the movies. Yet for all his swagger in JAILHOUSE ROCK, Presley's line readings will suddenly go flat, his expression blanking out, the lithe body growing wooden and unsure of itself. Conviction deserts him, his sneer replaced by the obliging death-mask he would wear through countless travesties to come: almost presaging the glad-handing self-sabotage of MEAN STREETS' Charlie (albeit unintentionally, as a perverse form of careerism).

There would be no THUNDER ROAD for Elvis: the history of rock in Hollywood is mostly a history of travesty, or a history of what might have been. In the Fifties, an icon gap had opened up in American movies. THE WILD ONE and REBEL WITHOUT A CAUSE anticipated youth's new archetypes, but within a sonic vaccuum. Brando's poly-Orpheus scorn and Dean's charismatic anguish seemed anomalous, harbingers strangely cut off from the upheavals they heralded. But as rock took over and elaborated their gestures, the movies lagged behind, attempting to smooth the cracks in the facade. Hollywood offered Rock Hudson and Tony Curtis – a sexless sex symbol and a proletarian pin-up, old stereotypes upholstered in rugged, durable plastic. There's no better illustration of the mentality at work here than RIO BRAVO, which served up emasculated would-be rocker Ricky Nelson as a sop to 'the kids' (he just about oozed sincerity and clean-living), but made him comically subordinate to the real men in the picture. Dean Martin embodied the industry's prevailing notion of entertainment: so casual and agreeable he makes indifference signify as the height of show business mastery. (His assured Vegas-cowboy guise – the hipsterism of the unhip – is precisely what Elvis will emulate so disastrously in dozens of films.) And standing for manhood itself, none other than John Wayne – that most enduring icon of the America that wished to be purged of rock and rebellion alike.

RIO BRAVO's audience is meant to identify with the likes of Martin and Wayne: they represent what teens are supposed to embrace once the young outgrow rock and become productive members of society. The story goes that Nelson endured a classic Hollywood baptism at the hands of Martin and Wayne, who threw the pretty boy into a heap of steer manure on his 18th birthday. This is the primal scene Elvis will be asked to symbolically re-enact in one film after another, each more tedious than the one before, drowning in an excremental boredom that lent new meaning to the phrase "up shit creek". But to see what was truly absent here, and what was really at stake, imagine an alternate movie universe where instead of G.I. BLUES, he had been cast opposite Sinatra in THE MANCHURIAN CANDIDATE. Here is a film that captured the secret, encrypted side of Presleyan myth: the shell-shocked, brainwashed soldier-assassin as a version of the post-Army Elvis, even as the belief that rock'-n'roll was a communist plot would fit snugly into the movie's conspiratorial milieu. And surely Angela Lansbury's ruthless character suggests a deliciously malign composite of Presley's manager Col Tom Parker and his adored mother Gladys – totalitarian love, a military-industrial Oedipus complex. Operating in the shadow of Sinatra, this Manchurian Elvis could have given us a taste of the real one's tangled double-agency, at once pawn and King, culture hero and dupe, emblem of liberation and of the all-American craving to just follow orders. (Like an America getting ready to declare war on itself, there was no way to tell which side Elvis was really on.) From there it isn't hard to see him restored to his feral, greasy Memphis self, riding off into A FISTFUL OF DOLLARS or playing the noble astronaut-savage in PLANET OF THE APES, finally apotheosising his career in the Seventies with the role of a washed-up lifetime – FAT CITY.

Candy Clark in FAT CITY

Coinciding with the emergence of rock, a quality of suffocating dislocation entered the movies: by turns borderline hysterical (Douglas Sirk) and sanctimonious (Stanley Kramer), sometimes both at once (EAST OF EDEN), it gave off the hothouse air of a society on the verge of a nervous breakdown, steeped in denial and repression. Yet Kramer's terminally well-meaning 1958 THE DEFIANT ONES is oblivious to the fact its story was already being acted out to far more compelling effect by Elvis and Chuck Berry. Their odyssey across the racial barriers of American culture – this Huck-and-Jim pair bound together in the public imagination by nothing more than a shared desire to escape the shackles of their birth – was no plea for brotherhood, equality, 'a better world'. (Understood as the brotherhood of conformists, the equality of the assembly line, a world of drones.) "Jailhouse Rock" and Berry's "The Promised Land" drew on the divisive polarities of American life and the wish to smash through them: integration's secret promise and threat were to not only make the country finally live up to its professed ideals, but to replace a slave world with a free one. For their trouble and defiance, as a couple of entirely inadvertent civil rights workers, each earned stiff sentences: Berry's to be served in a real jailhouse and Presley's in the barely metaphorical one of KISSIN' COUSINS, SPINOUT, and CLAMBAKE.

Hollywood's resistance to this wayward new strain of mass culture often took the form of vague, self-conflicted anxiety. In the 1958 A FACE IN THE CROWD, a folk-singer rises to rabble-rousing prominence as a hybrid of Elvis and Joe McCarthy. The story is played straight as a grimly cautionary fable; even its pulpy undercurrent of panic is encrusted in a vertiginous respectability. Ten years later, AIP's WILD IN THE STREETS will do away with all that sanctimony and turn the spectre of bubblegum fascism into acidhead comedy. There the teen-idol demagogue becomes President, imposes martial law, sends everyone over thirty to concentration camps, all as prophesied in the irresistible rise of the President's hit single up the charts: "The Shape of Things to Come". (One might have substituted a garage-band version of the contemporaneous "Springtime for Hitler".) But located between these poles of self-important adult melodrama and trashy youth-exploitation fodder, THE MANCHURIAN CANDIDATE treated politics as pop culture and paranoid fantasy as the shape of politics to come, it leapfrogged right over the prevailing American archetypes (Elvis, JFK) to anticipate the real and symbolic violence that will befall them (Kennedy's assassination, Elvis's disintegration). It found a knowing, implacable tone for such material, a tightrope between absurdist humour, bitter put-on, and sardonic dread – the tone Bob Dylan will make his own on his mid-1960s records. THE MANCHURIAN CANDIDATE prefigured the carnivalesque undertow of Dylan's "Ballad of a Thin Man", with its sneering, pitiless refrain: "You know something is happening/ But you don't know what it is/ Do you, Mr. Jones?" It may offer a clue to Mr Jones' allusive origin as well, unobtrusively tucked away inside George Axelrod's screenplay, where Axelrod sets the garden club brainwashing scene like this: *Marco sits on the end of the line at stage right, in the Mr. Bones position (as in an old time minstrel show).*[2] Soon a lot of people would feel like Marco, like they too had assumed the Mr. Bones – or Jones – position in some great, newfangled mass-media minstrel show.

While it's been suggested the phenomenal rise of the Beatles in America amounted to a palliative for the first Kennedy assassination, A HARD DAY'S NIGHT offers more than reason enough in itself. The first rock movie to display a sensibility equal to the music itself had to be British, for the Beatles and director Richard Lester were in a position to bypass the Hollywood tendency to equate pop with pap. Borrowing from the freewheeling innovations of A BOUT DE SOUFFLE and BANDE À PART, A HARD DAY'S NIGHT epitomised a playfully irreverent style (actually, its wit and quicksilver nonsense is a little ahead of the music – the Beatles' songs will never quite catch up with the jump-cutting, wisecracking bliss presented here) that captured the joy and irony of pop life while evoking their evanescence. What Lester took from Godard was offhand technique and speed, a means of expressing the rhythms of an unfolding epoch – one composed of fleeting moments, fragments of possibility that vanished almost before their existence was registered.

It was a style that was as easy to imitate as its core sensibility was elusive. Within a year, HELP! showed Lester's mod devices had already become part of the accepted commercial lexicon; "Can't Buy Me Love" had opened the door for the marketing revolution that would culminate in MTV. It also revealed that much of what seemed so daring and original in the Beatles' personalities harked back to the knockabout, self-satirising Hope-Crosby ROAD pictures. Only HELP! was more of a 'Road to Nowhere' – overdetermined, underinspired, a lot of gesticulation substituting for any sense of purpose, an exercise in sped-up ennui. In America, that road led directly to the cloned-for-TV series *The Monkees*, which from 1966 to 1968 shamelessly churned out frantic sweatshop knockoffs of the Lester/Beatles-formula. But there was a weird New Hollywood twist to the Monkees' tale: they would stumble on to make the flop movie HEAD, whose chief distinction (apart from that false-advertising title) was as a stepping stone in the careers of its screenwriters, Jack Nicholson and Bob Rafelson (with Rafelson making his directorial debut there). Going from the counterculture kitsch of HEAD to the heavy-duty alienation of FIVE EASY PIECES, Nicholson and Rafelson enacted their own artwardly-mobile allegory: they raised themselves up from a chintzy little basement of hell to bigger and barer realist circles.

Belatedly inaugurating the 'New Hollywood' in 1967, BONNIE AND CLYDE took just the elements of A BOUT DE SOUFFLE et al. Lester had omitted from a A HARD DAY'S NIGHT: the mixed emotions of random violence, the romance of sudden death. Set in the Depression, with charmingly dated and/or timeless bluegrass music on the soundtrack, its attitudes were nonetheless pure Sixties. Its killers were depicted as instant pop stars, groovy outlaws living – and perishing – beyond the pale of law-abiding society. Their estrangement and faintly ridiculous fatalism gave off a tenderly erotic glow: the dying light of the beautiful – and impotent – damned. Presented in tragicomic pop terms, Bonnie Parker and Clyde Barrow were natural precursors of the rock-stars-as-outlaws (and as casualties-of-war) mythology that sprang up around Jim Morrison and Janis Joplin, Jimi Hendrix and Brian Jones. BONNIE AND CLYDE provoked the same alarm in the Establishment press the Rolling Stones did: "We rob banks," answered in advance Mick Jagger's mocking "What can a poor boy do?" The movie's amorality and violence seemed like an incitement, one all the more unnerving for being so unspecified. It made antisocial behaviour seem like fun, and spasmodic death look like romantic fulfilment. The film conveyed a sense that a bit of fun – some laughter at the expense of social conventions, some affront to upright values – might at any second erupt into gunplay, blood in the streets, an epidemic of anarchy. The bullet-riddled past BONNIE AND CLYDE seemed to blaze a trail into the future, as though in the mythic profiles of its stars one could already see the chalk outlines of Baader and Meinhof.

Those dumb rednecks who blow away Billy and Captain America at the end of EASY RIDER are the descendants of the posse that finally guns down Bonnie and Clyde in Arthur Penn's film. EASY RIDER is the counterculture's breakthrough movie: the rock soundtrack was as integral to it as the dialogue and images those songs accompanied (maybe more so). The fact that the movie (or for that matter the music) isn't much good is beside the point: everything that's desultory, crude, and obvious about EASY RIDER merely serves to authenticate it as the genuine article. Stoned on their own innocence, its hippie-martyrs are consumed with nostalgia for paradise lost. "We blew it, man," mourns Peter Fonda's stoic Captain America shortly before he's killed – the bikers are sacrificial lambs taking gleaming custom motorcycles to the slaughter. Yet EASY RIDER's retrospective present appears far more remote than BONNIE AND CLYDE's flippant Depression. Fonda, Dennis Hopper, and Jack Nicholson are served up on a hash house platter, cocaine-toting, reefer-toking refugees from the social-injustice movies of the 1930s, their persecution used sentimentally to induce audience sympathy.

"This used to be a hell of a good country", sighs Nicholson not long before *he* is beaten to death by some Southern goons. (In the movie, the young are

Arlo Guthrie in ALICE'S RESTAURANT

viewed with a benign, non-judgmental gaze, but the good-old-boy yahoos are held up as examples of innate, subhuman viciousness.) EASY RIDER deservedly made Nicholson a star and he articulates the movie's appeal when George drawls to Billy and the Captain, "They're not scared ah you. They scared of what you represent to 'em... What you represent to them is freedom." The characters in the movie are abstractions, bucolic conventions in new costumes: psychedelic Zen outlaws, spaced-out cowhands (cowheads?) chasing after the ghost of the Old West/Native America, all to the anthemic tune of Steppenwolf's "Born to Be Wild".

Many years later, Albert Brooks will parody this sequence in LOST IN AMERICA: the elephantine motorhome heading "out on the highway" to the sound of Steppenwolf's as-lumbering-as-ever "heavy metal thunder". But the true punchline comes when the leviathan is eventually pulled over by a Terminator-like motorcycle cop who wears the glint of fascism like a second badge. Told by the occupants they're trying to drop out in emulation of EASY RIDER, that death's-head face suddenly breaks into a delighted grin. "That's my favourite movie of all time", he gushes, caught up in the brotherhood of mutual identification. Here on an empty blacktop, lost in the America of indivisible simulation, an ad executive and a cop bond on the basis of a shared chimera. Each has "based his life on EASY RIDER": on representations of freedom that are already frozen into empty peace symbols. The incongruous pair are what the dope-dealing bikers might have become if they'd survived into middle-age ("Dennis Hopper wouldn't give Peter Fonda a ticket, would he?"). It turns out the real destination of the bikers must have been the grateful funeral of THE BIG CHILL – with Hopper and Fonda serving as their own pallbearers.

The music carries EASY RIDER, gives its long travelogue shots and staged *cinema verité* scenes a semblance of form. When Jimi Hendrix's snaking "If 6 Was 9" appears on the soundtrack, the cruising images take on the feel of a passage through a real time and place. But more typical are the Fraternity of Man and the Electric Prunes numbers – dreary, trite relics of erstwhile hipness (in its jocular and cosmic modes, respectively). Or else The Band's "The Weight," dragged down by the albatross of significance (a/k/a the bluebird of unhappiness). But the key to the movie is The Byrds' "Wasn't Born to Follow", which director Hopper likes so much he reprises it. A compendium of imitation Dylanisms and pleasantly ludicrous psychedelia, it's a marvel of blank self-righteousness. "In the end she will surely know I wasn't born to follow," bleats singer Roger McGuinn: another wee lamb lost in a big, bad country, on his holy-rolling way to being roadkill.

"Wasn't Born to Follow" was written by Gerry Goffin and Carole King, a team who had provided songs for Phil Spector as well as The Monkees. But when Spector himself turns up at the beginning of the film, wordlessly playing the dealers' dandified ferret of a buyer, it's something more than an inside joke of a cameo. For just an instant, there's a glimpse of the road not taken in EASY RIDER. Perhaps something more along the lines of SCORPIO RISING – moving to the rhythms of a secret society, a beat that could place the drug-dealing bikers' saga in ironic relief. Spector was an envoy from a pop world light years removed from hippie passivity (which by embracing both dope and Jesus got a double dose of mass-consumed opiates). His insistence on excess as the measure of all things doesn't connect with Peter Fonda's beatific space cowboy, but rather with the majestic dimensions (and dementia) of Henry Fonda's brutalist killer in ONCE UPON A TIME IN THE WEST or Jane Fonda's intrepid sex machine in BARBARELLA. European invocations of American iconography, Leone's grandiose meditation on the gunfighter myth and Vadim's homage to sci-fi cheesecake would ring bizarrely illuminating changes on their source material. Leone photographing his actors in widescreen close-up to resemble Monument Valley rock formations come to life, while Jane Fonda's demure orgiast could have been the futuristic sister to Spector's teen Valkyries like the Crystals and Ronettes.

Writing of Creedence Clearwater Revival's 1969 *Green River*, Greil Marcus might have been describing a Leone version of EASY RIDER by way of Mark Twain: "Stuck in the suburbs of San Francisco and dreaming of the Mississippi, John Fogerty crafted a timeless vision of America: a white boy (Fogerty) and a black man (Fogerty's heroes: Howlin' Wolf, Little Richard) sharing a raft, drifting south, finding friendship, defeat, fear, and salvation." There was everything Hopper and company missed, ignored, or trivialised – the paradoxes of race and the uneasy allure of a country where freedom and violence were chronically intertwined. "In other words," Marcus wrote of this music, "Elvis's Sun singles, without their innocence".[3] Leone did much the same with John Ford's westerns, stripping them down to skeletal archetypes. But he draped his walking skulls in the baggage of extremity, brute force, and empty appetite, which Leone then proceeded to poeticise, giving a human face (of beauty at least) to that death-wish.

In songs like "Tombstone Shadow", "Bad Moon Rising", "Effigy", "Graveyard Train", "Don't Look Now", "Sinister Purpose", "Run Through the Jungle", "Commotion", and "Who'll Stop the Rain", Creedence Clearwater Revival showed an America pinned down by its own crossfire. "Caught inside the fable," Fogerty sang, where assassination merged with folklore, good times were shot through with intimations of Judgement Day. That fable was history ("Once upon a time in America..." every song might easily have begun). "The true picture of the past flits by," Walter Benjamin had once declared, its images flashing out of the darkness in the cinema of time. "The tradition of the oppressed teaches us," he noted with patient irony, "that the 'state of emergency' in which we live is not the exception but the rule."[4] Such was the storm blowing through "Who'll Stop the Rain" (a promised future "wrapped in golden chains"), the fire that spreads outward from "Effigy" to consume the countryside.

Creedence's music instinctively cast its lot with the tradition of class rather than youth conflict, the tumult of collective forces not the Messianic aura of idols. In "Who'll Stop the Rain", the Messianic makes itself felt through absence, in the lack of any saviour to redeem the era's state of emergency. Invoking memory as a means of grasping their own time, Creedence's sound was the avatar of Bruce Springsteen's allusive, fatalist populism: it used the mnemonic power of the blues and country and early rock to place the present in the context of eternal struggle, the cyclical nature of bad-moon-risings. That context might be said to stand for all the movies, which will not be made in the wake of EASY RIDER.

As the film's final helicopter shot takes its leave of Billy and Captain America, they've conveniently died for their country's sins. But on closer inspection, the imaginary cross they're hoisted upon looks suspiciously like part of the

Hollywood Sign. Their celluloid martyrdom has less in common with the "Bad Moon Rising" over CCR's *Green River* than the buddy-buddy constellation in the box office sky of 1969. Like those other phoney outlaws in BUTCH CASSIDY AND THE SUNDANCE KID, their fate dovetailed with MIDNIGHT COWBOY's down-and-out sentimentality, lending Joe Buck/Sundance/Captain America and Ratso Rizzo/Butch/Billy a wholly specious, artificially inseminated humanity. (MIDNIGHT COWBOY's hustlers and rustlers were a far cry indeed from the polymorphous perversity of Andy Warhol, Lou Reed, and the Velvet Underground – Russ Meyer's ludicrous rock-themed breast-fest BEYOND THE VALLEY OF THE DOLLS at least recognised the camp-value of its sexual histrionics.) It's easy to forget that Butch and Ratso's sagas spawned much bigger hit songs than EASY RIDER: the insidious treacle of B.J. Thomas' "Raindrops Keep Fallin' On My Head" and the dolorous folk-schlock of Fred Neil's "Everybody's Talkin'". This is the prism of middle-of-the-road hegemony through which pop music was still seen by Hollywood, which viewed EASY RIDER as a wedge into the youth market far more than a subversion of any 'Establishment'. It was in the truest sense a fashion statement: slap some indiscriminate rock, long hair, and love beads on that hegemony and presto, it would become 'far-out', daring, radical.

Here was a sure-fire studio formula that would promptly bring forth disasters like THE STRAWBERRY STATEMENT and ZABRISKIE POINT. (Raging youth preferred LOVE STORY – old-fashioned craven pathos, a respite from the new, aggressive style of alienated banality.) With the imminent deaths of Jim Morrison and Jimi Hendrix about to seal their apotheosis as Butch-and-Sundance rock demigods (good-looking corpses entering the backdoor of myth), ZABRISKIE POINT's opportunistic vision of America-as-Death-Valley was already passé when the movie came out. MGM had imported Michelangelo Antonioni to do his BLOW-UP number on the materialism of Los Angeles and the student revolutionaries who were presumably waging war on it. ZABRISKIE POINT was a glossy picture postcard from the end of civilisation: having a miserable time, it said, wish you were here. Its big set-pieces – a teen orgy in the desert that might have come straight from the pages of *Playboy* and a swank orgy of destruction that sold apocalypse the way Madison Avenue did affluence – were paeans to anonymity, the finish of bourgeois individualism. But while Antonioni slapped the communal noodlings of Pink Floyd and the Grateful Dead over his images of pristine nothingness, rock had entered a new phase: the white, lumpen-teen wail of heavy metal, with groups like Black Sabbath offering a cruder, less refined form of snake-oil oblivion.

The one film that really connected with EASY RIDER's audience was Tom Laughlin's self-financed BILLY JACK (1971), which he directed, co-scripted, and starred in. Like Peter Fonda, Laughlin came out of biker-exploitation films: in

1967, he had made the trashy, fervid THE BORN LOSERS, which introduced the character of the halfbreed Billy Jack (he single-handedly took on a psychotic neo-Nazi motorcycle gang there). The premise of BILLY JACK was at base EASY RIDER if the hippies had fought back against the rednecks. Or had someone to fight back for them – Billy Jack was the champion of children, Native Americans, and women against the bigots who want to drive them out or keep them down. Laughlin's mystical, taciturn martial-arts-expert was the resurrection of Gary Cooper for the Age of Aquarius – a vigilante for peace and brotherhood, a real Captain America. The movie was so old-fashioned it felt brand-new to young people: Tom Mix lives!

This two-fisted moralism won out over ZABRISKIE POINT's vainglorious intellectual tourism, a mode that perfectly anticipates Jean Baudrillard's *Amérique*. "Show business kids making movies of themselves", Steely Dan sang of Hollywood's young Antonioni impersonators. "You know, they don' t give a fuck about anybody else." *Countdown to Ecstasy* was what the band called the 1973 album those lines appeared on: an ecstasy of negation which savaged all that was most problematic and compromised about the lust for youth, art, and radical chic in the aftermath of THE LAST MOVIE, GETTING STRAIGHT, and ALEX IN WONDERLAND. With a name lifted from William Burroughs and an attitude of malice toward all, Steely Dan drove nail upon nail into the coffin of counterculture illusions. Musical auteurs Walter Becker and Donald Eagen displayed a sensibility somewhere between Leopold & Loeb and the Coen Brothers. With the title song of *Pretzel Logic*, they anticipated BARTON FINK by way of remaking JAILHOUSE ROCK: Elvis as both a face in the crowd and the 'minstrel-show' face of show-biz fascism. The insurrection of "Blue Suede Shoes" is "gone forever/Over a long time ago". Mr. Bones lives as well.

Despite this dissenting view, the shift to pop nostalgia was by then underway, epitomised by George Lucas's AMERICAN GRAFFITI (1973), which looked back fondly to pre-Vietnam/Kennedy-assassination times. It used Fifties hits as a locus of the quaint and innocuous (much as Elton John's insipid "Crocodile Rock" did) – the embodiment, as the title of the hugely successful TV series it helped inspire had it, of *Happy Days*. In doing this, AMERICAN GRAFFITI turned the moral panic over early rock and the Fifties cinema of juvenile delinquency on its head: the explosive rebel-without-a-cause was replaced with a gang of meek, ingratiating Andy Hardys. The antic demystification of Brian De Palma's 1974 PHANTOM OF THE PARADISE bombed: it revelled in everything that was shady, underhanded, and debauched in the pop milieu. If PHANTOM OF THE PARADISE's score had been by someone like Randy Newman, it might have been a slapstick masterpiece. As it was, Paul Williams's hack songs were functional, though as the diabolical Swan of Death Records he was ideal. A fiendish gnome drawn from the legends of both Phil Spector and Dick Clark (the Dorian Gray-like mogul who hosted TV's *American Bandstand* for decades, seemingly in league with the devil or the FBI or both). Much of PHANTOM's parodistic horror-movie-musical tone was recycled – and blandly defanged – in that ultimate cult film THE ROCKY HORROR PICTURE SHOW (1975). The retro-camp treatment of glitter rock and monster-movie clichés there was like a Disney makeover of Warhol and the New York Dolls. Under the mascara and mock-outrage, a kinky wholesomeness prevailed – a BEACH PARTY movie in gothic drag.

But at least the sublime immolation of the school gym and senior class at the end of De Palma's CARRIE realises one of rock's primal fantasies: the bottomless pit of teen anomie made into macabre comedy, the ultimate eroto-destructive distillation of Alice Cooper's "Eighteen" and "School's Out" ("... *Forever*," insisted the latter's blithe, zero-for-conduct chorus). With CARRIE De Palma seemed to be saying, "You want a rocky horror picture show? I'll give you one, all right". The image of a prom-queen antichrist's hand reaching out from the grave definitely has more to do with rock's place in the Western cultural-unconscious than Tim Curry camping it up in drag queen hand-me-downs. There's more of the music's frisson in De Palma's jarring, tactile images than in official rock documentaries such as WOODSTOCK and GIMME SHELTER too. Those films are souvenirs of the music – keepsakes. (In GIMME SHELTER's case, a memento mori.) What's missing is a talismanic quality, the engine of fetish and imagination that separated the Rolling Stones from, say, Country Joe and the Fish. On screen, Carrie White's let-it-bleed catharsis conveys what most concert films elide: the invasion of the normal by the uncanny. Robert Frank's Rolling Stones tour movie COCKSUCKER BLUES doesn't have that either, just the druggy, futile entropy of the road. Which is why the band had the film suppressed, less that it sullied their public image than because the staged scenes of the Stones' junkie parasite entourage confirmed it all too well. COCKSUCKER BLUES has a fine eye for the rancid underside of pop life. It provides the reality behind the greasepainted gags of PHANTOM OF THE PARADISE, the devil wallowing in the tedious details of celebrity.

The appearance of SUPERFLY announced the opening of another Hollywood beachhead – the black community. Set against the sweetly ominous commentary of Curtis Mayfield songs like "Pusherman", the movie's story of a cocaine dealer who wants to escape the life after one last big score pegs it immediately as the black EASY RIDER. If anything, SUPERFLY's influence was even more pervasive and certainly more lasting, ushering in the low-budget blaxploitation genre (THE MACK, SLAUGHTER's BIG RIP-OFF, FOXY BROWN, et al.) as well as laying the whole foundation for the gangsta-rap movement almost two decades away. What SUPERFLY lacked was the conviction of its own music: it was a

shaky monotone poem to the longings and blocked avenues of black life. THE
HARDER THEY COME (1972) from Jamaica and starring the raw, charismatic reg-
gae singer Jimmy Cliff pointed to a far richer vein of pop cultural cross-polli-
nation. The movie's soundtrack – merely the best one ever assembled, much of
it performed by the lead himself – was overflowing with echoes of spaghetti
westerns, gangster sagas, and JAILHOUSE ROCK. All of which culminated in
Desmond Dekker's startling "007 (Shanty Town)", which placed Kingston's
self-styled outlaws in the context of James Bond's lethal Third World tourism
and (even more amazingly) the Sinatra-Martin-etc. vehicle OCEAN'S ELEVEN
(making the surreal yet inevitable connection between Jamaican Rude Boys
and the Las Vegas Rat Pack).

The cocaine dealer in SUPERFLY is a distant cousin of the superstud
moonshiner Robert Mitchum played in THUNDER ROAD (1958). And since
Mitchum then dabbled in pop music – as a Calypso singer no less – there's
even a trace of family resemblance in THE HARDER THEY COME: the crude,
lively pseudo-folkloric tone makes Mitchum's Tennessee backwoods the
rockabilly antecedent of Jimmy Cliff's Trenchtown (steeped in white lightning
instead of ganja). The movie also provided the title for "Thunder Road", the
first song on Bruce Springsteen's BORN TO RUN – an album that's drenched in
movie imagery and rock allusions, recasting cinematic mythology in rock
terms as intensely as MEAN STREETS recapitulated rock history in narrative
terms of violence, despair, and guilt. (The scene where Johnny-Boy does a
crazy, taunting dance to the Miracles' "Mickey's Monkey" while Charlie
watches from the getaway car is like a precis of Springsteen's first three albums, just as they in turn refract it a few dozen different ways.) When "Thunder Road" resurrects James Dean (in place of Mitchum) and Springsteen sings
"You're graduation gown lies in rags at their feet", the listener will be forgiven
if she mistakes the "Mary" of the song for "Carrie". His music of the time is a
call-and-response dialogue with a vast array of sources – movies old and new,
the histories of rock and soul music, the American experience as seen through
the warp of pop mythology. Beyond "Thunder Road", there would not only be
titles taken from movies ("Badlands") but movies themselves inspired by
Springsteen songs (Walter Hill's wondrous mock-operatic urban western
STREETS OF FIRE). There were songs that sounded like forgotten movies ("Incident at 57th Street") and ones that were basically movie remakes ("Adam
Raised a Cain" as an updated but no less fraught EAST OF EDEN). There was
"Born to Run", which encompassed seemingly every inch of cop-rebel geography under the postwar sun, and in return there would be Richard Gere's fasci-
nating homage to Springsteen (or just about his every stage mannerism) in the
American remake of BREATHLESS. Maybe the most convoluted example of the
whole process would be Meat Loaf's 1978 album *Bat Out of Hell* – an insanely

bombastic transformation of Springsteen's style into B-movie operetta (com-
poser-producer Jim Steinman as the Leonard Bernstein of drive-in schlock),
performed by a ROCKY HORROR PICTURE SHOW cast member who had derived
his bigger (and dumber) than life persona from Gerrit Graham's Beef in PHAN-
TOM OF THE PARADISE.

"I could walk like Brando right into the sun," Springsteen boasted in "It's
Hard to be a Saint in the City". But in "Backstreets" he made it stick: the song
takes in MEAN STREETS the same way Scorsese's picture played off of "Be My
Baby", as both touchstone and point of departure. "Backstreets" is just as rav-
aged, and ravishing – swallowing in addition ON THE WATERFRONT and "Like
a Rolling Stone" – a vision of identification and betrayal forever joined, where
the glimpsed freedom in Brando's walk or Dylan's tone winds up shattered,
crawling from the wreckage at the end of MEAN STREETS. It's a love song to
phantoms who haunt themselves: fugitives who've taken refuge in the movies, only to find there's no escaping their own lives. When Springsteen sings to
"Terry", he's calling out to Terry Malloy as surely as he assumes the burden of
Rod Steiger's Charlie, merging with Harvel Keitel's Charlie. It's the dream of
guilt and the guilt of hijacked dreams. As Brando and Steiger in the back of a
cab dissolve into childhood buddies De Niro and Keitel sharing a bed in Little
Italy, "Backstreets" is caught up in how a certain kind of history is made – emotional history. It's about how myth is transmitted and then lived out, as the
connecting fabric beneath everyday existence. "You don't make up for your
sins in the church," Keitel mutters to us, "you do it in the streets...". Those
streets of fire exist only in the imagination, in the Biblical chapter-and-verse of
movies and records: "I coulda been a contender. I coulda been somebody..."

We may be born to run, but what if there's nowhere to hide from the en-
croachment of society? That was the lament of Sam Peckinpah's PAT GARRETT
AND BILLY THE KID, which formulated the end of the counterculture in murder-
ously elegiac fashion. With Kris Kristofferson's Billy representing the dying
breed of rock outlaws, it offered a sepia-toned twilight of the idle idols. There's
even Bob Dylan himself as the self-effacing, incoherent Alias, who seems to
have wandered in from the fringes of McCABE AND MRS. MILLER – much like
Dylan's mournful acoustic score. Not a trace remained of the former "Like a
Rolling Stone" wordslinger, unless it's to be found in the tinny echo of
Kristofferson's toast to James Coburn's burnt-out Garrett, "How does it feel?"
"It feels," answers the old renegade-turned-lawman, "like times have
changed." The movie is swamped by world-weariness. "Jesus, don't you get
stale around here, Bill?" Garrett asks incredulously. Billy and his commune of
ragtag followers come off as narrow and as hidebound as the law they reject.
The poetic dementia of Peckinpah's BRING ME THE HEAD OF ALFREDO GARCIA
gets far closer to the dissipation which turned the Sixties' quest for existential

authenticity into the cocaine self-deception of the Seventies. That makes PAT GARRETT AND BILLY THE KID a way station on the road to the Eagles' *Hotel California*, where it turns out casualties Jim Morrison and Gram Parsons had more in common with Fred C. Dobbs than Jesus H. Christ.

In the space between BONNIE AND CLYDE and MEAN STREETS, an era took shape – a rapprochement less between movies and rock as such than the ideal of freedom rock represented, but was snuffed out almost as soon as it was born. THE MISSOURI BREAKS (1975) simultaneously marked its last gasp and heralded the new age of the package deal. Here we had director Arthur Penn, ultrahip writer Tom McGuane, Jack Nicholson with the full force of his post-EASY RIDER cachet intact, even Marlon Brando to lend the whole thing the lustre of immortality. But the movie's frontier parable of cattle baron imperialism vs. proletarian thieves came true in its making: THE MISSOURI BREAKS wasn't filmed so much as brokered among all cutthroat parties involved. Nicholson wound up adrift in the morass while Brando was acting up a storm – busy entertaining himself to keep boredom at bay, like an aging rock star on one last tour bus, trying on different masks and groupies for size. (Like an extroverted version Dylan's Alias, this performance might have served as the oblique inspiration for Dylan's own whiteface-minstrel feature RENALDO AND CLARA.) Under all that authentic looking blood and dung, rust had set in – a preview of a future where capital never sleeps, and HEAVEN'S GATE is just a mortician's kiss away.

In the dream-Western Neil Young had been piecing together since his days with Buffalo Springfield, this would not be a news flash. "When the first shot hit the dock," he sang in "Powderfinger", "I saw it comin'". A chiming death-knell reverie, the song had the open, desperate feel of a lost Anthony Mann eulogy, THE FAR COUNTRY given a foretaste of APOCALYPSE NOW: "Look out, mama, there's a white boat comin' up the river." The future had arrived and everyone's number was up ("It don't look like they're here to deliver the mail" was a bit of perfect Jimmy Stewart understatement). This was circa 1975, though like "Pocahontas" (originally titled "Marlon Brando, Pocahontas, and Me") it would be a few years till Young got around to issuing them on record. For "Pocahontas", Young even pictured himself getting chummy with Brando, chewing the fatted calf around the campfire: "We'll sit and talk of Hollywood and the good things there for hire." Out to pasture or up a creek without a paddle, he had said much the same in 1969, with his band Crazy Horse behind him, on an album that was as unforgiving as it was seductive: "Everybody knows this is nowhere."

Notes

1.   Nic Cohn, "Phil Spector," *The Rolling Stone Illustrated History of Rock & Roll*, 153 [1980 edition], edited by Jim Miller.

2.   George Axelrod, *The Manchurian Candidate* screenplay, Los Angeles: ScreenPress, 1987, 15.

3.   Greil Marcus, *Stranded*, New York: Knopf, 1979, 264.

4.   Walter Benjamin, *Illuminations*, "Theses on the Philosophy of History," New York: Schocken, 1968, 255, 257.

Auteurism and War-teurism

Terrence Malick's War Movie

Dana Polan

> If this were a movie, this would be the end of the show and something would be
> decided. In a movie or a novel they would dramatise and build to the climax of
> the attack. When the attack came in the film or novel, it would be satisfying, it
> would decide something. It would have a semblance of meaning and a semblance
> of an emotion. And immediately after, it would be over. The audience could go
> home and think about the semblance of the meaning and feel the semblance of the
> emotion. Even if the hero got killed, it would still make sense. Art, [Private] Bell
> decided, creative art – was shit.
> James Jones, *The Thin Red Line*

At one point in Terrence Malick's THE THIN RED LINE, just before a battle we
see a shot of a natural world followed by a shot of Colonel Tall (Nick Nolte)
who intones a phrase in Greek and then tells his soldiers that it's the "rosy-fin-
gered dawn" phrase from Homer's *Odyssey*. With this reference, THE THIN RED
LINE does two slightly different things – things that suggest the complicated
situation of the war film in today's culture. On the one hand, THE THIN RED
LINE clearly wants to take up identity as an epic of war – a film of vast sweep
with great means and great pretence. On the other hand, the use of an explicit
'citation' to 'declare' the film's lineage to an epic antecedent seems a resolutely
postmodern gesture: like all major war films today, THE THIN RED LINE is an
ersatz work, aware of fictionality, aware of tradition, only able to make itself
seem traditionally a war film by fictionally declaring itself to be so. Like a
speech-act which brings about a state of affairs by announcing that it is bringing about that state of affairs, THE THIN RED LINE isn't naturally an epic but
constructs itself as one. Indeed, is it accidental that so many big war films of recent years emphasise the cost and effort that went into their production as if to
reiterate the extent to which they build up narrative worlds and also build up
the world views they subtend? Not naturally, but through immense creative
human effort, they bring their war fiction into being. Even as eventually traditional a film as SAVING PRIVATE RYAN – applauded by middle-brow America as

a realist work that breaks through conventions to achieve Truth – seems in many respects to be about fictionality: from its play with the rules of genre (for example, the coward who in this case never finds the courage to become a hero) to the very ways it only gradually discovers narrativity out of an experimental opening battle that seems to go on and on, SAVING PRIVATE RYAN, too, is in large part about the war film as a construction, rather than a direct and innocent and natural expression of a national will about war.

Experiments in the revision of established, codified genres (such as the war film) probably have either (or both) of two intents. On the one hand, the attempt to alter the rules of genre can have to do with issues of content, with a sense that the ways the genre typically structures meaning blocks certain world views from achieving representation. A modification of the genre, it is hoped, will enable new experiences, new voices, new realities to come into existence. To take just one example, the shift from classic British detective fiction to American hard-boiled fiction was famously lauded by Raymond Chandler (in his "The Simple Art of Murder") as the replacement of the limited unreality of the British aristocratic view of the world by a modern, bluntly real, experientially authentic one, more attuned to the nature of contemporary urban existence.

On the other hand, experiments in genre can also have as their intent to revise form, to play with it, to uncover its ludic possibilities – to see codes as formal structures that future examples in the genre enact productive permutations upon. Here, again, we can cite the example of British detective fiction. So generally fixed is the moral universe of this fiction (a sedentary world of privilege into which crime comes as a disturbing stain, an upset that must be put aright) that only a revolutionary shift of the sort Chandler announces could change its meaning; before that revolutionary shift then, the internal history of the British detective story is one of authors engaging in gamelike formal variations (let's make the narrator the murderer, let's make all the suspects the murderer, let's make a totally incidental character the murderer; let's have the detective be a priest, a ...) that leave the moral universe itself untouched but create new generic delights for aficionados.

We might grasp the evolution of the combat film as the history of a genre in which experiments in form and in content are both at work, pushing individual works to say new things about the experience of war and to find new forms in which to say that. Traditionally, the combat film was a highly codified genre with set structure and set meaning. As outlined by Jeanine Basinger in its Second World War paradigm (*The World War II combat film: anatomy of a genre*, Columbia University Press, 1986), the model for the combat film deals with a team of soldiers from diverse civilian backgrounds who go off on a mission (for example, SAVING PRIVATE RYAN, to quote the title of a more recent World War II film) and, along the way, encounter conflicts both external (fights with the enemy) and internal (for example, outbreaks of cowardice that threaten group cohesion). For the soldiers, the mission can become the occasion for emotional growth and self-discovery but, in the ideology of the World War II film, one discovers what was really there all along – the meaningfulness of nation and national mission, the rightness of one's place, the justification of cause. There indeed can be internal division in the World War II combat film, but, as I argue in my study of Forties films *(Power and Paranoia: History, Narrative, and the American Cinema, 1940-1950,* Columbia University Press, 1985), the wartime film admits dissension only insofar as such dissension can be tamed, co-opted, converted. Indeed, "conversion" is, as I suggest in *Power and Paranoia,* a central narrative structure and strategy for the wartime film: for a war in which soldiers were told "there are no atheists in the foxholes", conversion to the mission of the combat team – and beyond that to the war effort as an organic whole – takes on directly religious meaning (see, for instance, Hawks's SERGEANT YORK where the pacifist title character converts after a weekend spent reading both the Bible and the U.S. Constitution and Bill of Rights). Moreover, conversion works here by suggesting not that the meanings of engagement are imposed onto the subject from without but that they exist rather as an inner spark that needs to be rekindled, a core of commitment that had been forgotten through cowardice or cynicism (as the opening title of the 1942 CHINA GIRL tells us, an American will fight for three things – money, a girl, his country – and the central character of the film is said to be fighting for two of these as the story begins). Conversion then brings back into the organic unity of nationhood those individuals who never really left, who had simply forgotten their national being and belonging (not for nothing does CASABLANCA tell us that Rick had a past as a freedom fighter; he does not convert to something new but rediscovers a buried part of himself).

For the wartime World War II combat film, meaning was natural: there was a mission (both the literal mission faced by the soldiers and the national mission of the war effort) and its purpose was evident, inevitable. Hence, the importance of conversion, for in its suggestion that one doesn't learn new things, that commitment isn't imposed on the subject from without but wells up from within, the narrative of conversion makes growth into commitment natural, logical, ordinary. Although as I suggest in *Power and Paranoia,* the moment of war sows seeds for the dismantling of the classical Hollywood narrative – insofar as the narrative of conversion to war commitment requires a disavowal of a commitment to the private realm of the romantic couple so central to classical Hollywood narrative – and thereby prepares the way for disunified postwar genres of battles of the sexes like film noir and the woman's gothic film, it is also important to understand the World War II combat film as one of the last perfections or accomplishments of the classical Hollywood cinema. Here is a genre where ease of style, naturalness of narrativity, matches an ease of world view, a naturalness of mission and meaning – a genre whose philosophy is pre-given (pre-given to the filmic form, pre-given to the characters in the narrative, pre-given to the target audience).

But in the recent combat film, unity – unity of form and content, unity of mission and meaning, unity of character and moral purpose – frequently comes undone. As cultural theorist Marita Sturken shows in her chapter on Vietnam and post-Vietnam variants of the combat narrative structure in her *Tangled Memories: The Vietnam War, the AIDS Epidemic and the Politics of Remembering* (University of California Press, 1997), the manifestations of the genre in these later historical moments both adhere to initial meanings of the genre (the mission as process of self-education and accomplishment) while suggesting that the original organic unity of the genre is no longer easily or readily to be had.

Without a coherent ideology to shore it up, the war film becomes directly in-coherent : for example, images that are overfilled and chaotically unreadable (the psychedelia of APOCALYPSE NOW), narrative trajectories that fragment into monadic bits (FULL METAL JACKET with its two major segments and its numerous set pieces), a visuality of baroque tangle (the tunnels of CASUALTIES OF WAR, the labyrinthine camera movements of FULL METAL JACKET), an experimentational fascination with a sheer temporality in which pure duration comes to substitute for the progress of narrative (the seeming endlessness of the opening battle in SAVING PRIVATE RYAN, the excruciating torture of the training sequence in FULL METAL JACKET, the temporally vast minimalism of the assault on the hillside in THE THIN RED LINE).

As Sturken notes, the political divisions of the Vietnam War have bequeathed to the representations of war a legacy of confusion, contradiction, struggles over meaning rather than assurances of natural meaningfulness. Indeed, if in the classic war conversion, we are passive participants in observing a meaningfulness that is naturally and easily recovered – conversion as the light of awareness that grows and glows across the face as the cynic realises his true mission, by contrast a number of recent war films show meanings being constructed, being tested, offered up as so many tentative hypotheses.

Hence, the sheer sense of discussion or didacticism in the recent war film: meaning does not pre-exist the characters and instead has experimentally to be built up for and by them. Thus, to take one example, PLATOON presents itself as a veritable debate – war as a battle for the souls of men (with the young innocent, Taylor, caught between the evil Barnes and the christological Elias). The allegorical weightiness of the film derives no doubt in large part from director Oliver Stone's sledgehammer conception of cinema as emphatic education (as is even more evident in BORN ON THE FOURTH OF JULY where scenes like that of the two vets in the Mexican desert become shouting matches of political position). But it is also necessary to see that this concern with cinema as imposed and obvious instruction or interrogation into the meanings of war seems to be the case of so many recent war films. Thus, to take an example that is often opposed to PLATOON, FULL METAL JACKET is a film of visual bravura, but it is also a film of constant debate and discussion: at many moments, the swirl of war (the emphatic sweeps of the camera matched by the frenetic rock music of the 1960s) gives way to intensely static shots in which figures face off against each other and enounce positions (for example, the meeting of the war correspondents with their commander, filmed as so many close-ups of talking heads; the scene of Joker facing off against the General who mechanically intones clichés of war patriotism; the scene of the men being filmed by a TV crew and expressing their often-cynical views of the war). Where FULL METAL JACKET differs from PLATOON in this respect is not in its sense that meaning is a construction – since both films argue that – but in its radical, and less reassuring, sense that the construction of meanings has no end, that there is no morality that is natural, even at the end of a journey of discovery. Where PLATOON's Taylor learns of the bifurcation of morality, of the essential and essentially conflictual Nature of Good and Evil, it is not clear that Joker learns anything at all (how much lack of irony, or not, is there, for instance, in his final declaration that he is not afraid, enounced to the background chant of Mickey Mouse?). One shot in FULL METAL JACKET is emblematic of its postmodern refusal of answers: as Sergeant Hartman slaps Private Pyle around once again, we cut to a shot of Private Cowboy watching but the look on the face offers no clue of moral perspective, of narrational point-of-view.

Given this context, we would easily anticipate that the newest and most ambitious of war films, Malick's THE THIN RED LINE, would readily come off as an incoherent work, but one in which incoherence is less an aesthetic failing than an aesthetic and 'political' inevitability for a film in this cultural moment. To be sure, there is in Malick a romanticism that seeks to posit a coherent authenticity of nature beyond all subterfuge, beyond all the incoherencies of human conflict. THE THIN RED LINE seems to imagine incoherence as only a contingent situation that one is in danger of falling into rather than a fundamental condition that one inevitably is always already in: hence, the opening of the film which portrays a timelessness of nature and native into which narrative gradually arrives (a white soldier appears, a naval boat appears). But in our postmodern age, such romanticism itself can only appear ersatz, a derivative cliché (and Malick's use of natives to portray lost innocence is certainly politically problematic and not at all itself innocent, just as is his similar use of femininity as memory-trace of a joy lost in the ravages of war – the intercut shots of a woman, especially of her breasts, that posit her as an essential purity outside the fall into war/culture – seems awkwardly out of time; as a friend of mine says, "Where has Malick been for the last twenty years? In a cave somewhere?!?"). Not for nothing do so many later reminders in the film of the purity of nature come as reminders precisely – obtrusions that arise from shock editing (cuts to animals, jumps into flashbacks of femininity) that turn into emphatic declarations by means of the mechanical art of montage enacted upon a realm of the supposedly natural.

In this respect, it is important to note that for many moviegoers, THE THIN RED LINE will be viewed as the film of an auteur, its images of nature not naturally and spontaneously arising before us but seen to be enounced for us by a strong creative voice, the images brought into being by his authoring of a cinematic universe (the stories of the time it took Malick to come back to filmmaking parallel in this way the stories of the complicated production histories behind so many recent war films, reminding us of their constructed nature).

Now, auteurism certainly has long had a bad reputation in the critical study of film, and my own intent in talking of Malick's authorial presence is not to revive mythologies of creative genius. Quite differently (and with an emphasis on the hypothetical and tentative nature of this), I would want to posit contemporary auteurism as one of the effects of the same political climate that led to the incoherencies of the contemporary Vietnam film. Authorial voice is a product of its time. The classic auteurs – the auteurs of the Hollywood studio system – may have had personal voices but increasingly we see how many of them were pure Hollywood Professionals (to use the title of a series of books on the classic auteurs), their own coherence as filmmakers merging easily and logically and, dare we say, naturally with the organic world of Hollywood narrative. A good Howard Hawks film, for instance, is generally good both as a Hawks film and as a Hollywood film. But as the organicity of American consensus disappears in the 1960s – along with the coherence of the studio system – a new auteurism, more contemporaneously American in nature (Andrew Sarris, writing on American film for the experimental journal *Film Culture* is the key figure here), arises, and by the end of the 1960s, it is about the isolation of lone creative voices that spring up against the bland conformity of establishment and system. Not for nothing does a book at the very cusp of the end of the 1960s encapsulate in its title the notion of authorial voice as personal vision – Joseph Gelmis's *The Film Director as Superstar* – and the late years of the Vietnam War will also be the years of a rampant auteurism, a Hollywood renaissance that so many cinephiles still think back on with deep fondness.

The point to make in an analysis of such auteurism is not that it is somehow a force of creativity that arises magically against the social and political conditions of the nation, but that it is itself a force generated by those conditions, personal creativity becoming one of the ways the 1970s and after live out issues of constraint and conformity. Not for nothing, then, are so many Vietnam films auteur films, not so much films about the war but about this or that director's take on

Martin Sheen in BADLANDS

the experience of war and, more often, on the experience of filming war –
Coppola's Vietnam, Kubrick's, De Palma's, and perhaps Stone's, and now definitely Malick's. In this respect, there is little possibility of reading the natural images of THE THIN RED LINE naturally; they come to us as voiced, as authored. To
take just one example, how when an auteur has not made a film for twenty
years, is it possible to read just the nature in the new film's opening shot (an alli-
gator that immerses itself in murky swamp water up to its eyes) and not also
read for authorial voice, visual talent, this director's take on the war movie?

Indeed, for all its romanticism for an Eden before the human fall, before the
inscription of the human onto the surface of the world (as ostensibly is the case
in the opening shot), THE THIN RED LINE is also very strongly a writerly film, a
film of voice and narration and inscription, a film whose processes of construction are rendered manifest. As with other auteur Vietnam films, THE THIN RED
LINE is a film of discussion and debate: there are numerous set pieces of verbal
sparring, such as that between Welsh and Witt (for example, in the film's second scene, after its romantic opening), between Tall and Staros, between Tall
and Quintard, and for all of the film's modernist emphasis elsewhere on private voices (men caught in their own agony, men given in to personal obses-

sion), it is also very much a film about conversation and interchange, albeit one in which no closure of position is brought to the debate.

Indeed, cutting between the social world of public communication and the private world of personal obsession or fantasy, there runs through the film the experimentalism of its voice-over narration. Reviews just after the film's release tended to treat this narration – which moves around various characters – as an expression of inner thought but the actual functioning of the narration seems more complicated (more incoherent) than that for it is in no easy way a direct expression of character thought. Like the infamous *style indirect libre* of Gustave Flaubert's *Madame Bovary* which offers both the character's perception and an intelligent comment on her perception that Emma herself could never have had, the narration in THE THIN RED LINE both originates in various characters and goes beyond them, creating a floating perspective in keeping both with the film's epic pretence and its poetic ambition to represent unities of the human and of the natural beyond all artificial divisions. Not only does the narration say things we do not necessarily imagine the particular characters to be capable of saying, but it also seems to waft beyond any particular character's perception, becoming a virtually pan-individual disquisition on war and existence. Indeed, many reviewers have noted, and criticised, the fact that several characters resemble each other and have similar styles of narration, but what for the reviewers is generally a failure of the film can also be read as part of the film's ambition, one of the things it is impelled to do as contemporary war fiction by an auteur.

But if intellectualising is one of the things we can expect auteurist cinema to quest after, a very different experimental goal of such cinema has to do with its desire to achieve what we might term a pure experience, an experience outside debate and discussion. What I mean by this is not that experience 'of war' that certain films try to offer up as their achievement of realism, their claim to Truth. That mythology has been pinpointed by Sturken who talks of the ways PLATOON's claim to "'experience' was contingent on its following certain codes of cinematic realism – portraying the details of a patrol, the boredom, the confusion of combat, the presence of the jungle. Heightened 'naturalised' sound of the jungle at night, rapidly edited combat scenes, and on-location shooting..." (p. 99). Beyond that documentary realism that claims to capture Experience, there is in the works of several Vietnam auteurs the glimpsing of experientiality itself, a pure immersion in temporality, in a duration that only vaguely adds up to either meaningfulness or anything resembling realism. I think, for instance, of the opening of FULL METAL JACKET where narrativity only eventually emerges to give some sense to an experience at the limits of tolerability, a cinema of cruelty not unlike extremes of theatrical experiment (in the enclosed space of the barracks, the shaven-head men seem to come from some ritual theatre laboratory on the edge of being, à la Artaud or Peter Brook or Jerzy Grotowski). Similarly, though its fall into narrative is all the more traditional, the battle sequence at the beginning of SAVING PRIVATE RYAN also catches some of the experience of a temporality outside of narrativity, a viscerality that only partially has to do with the horrific content within individual images.

In this respect, one of the most ambitious experiments in THE THIN RED LINE has to do with its rendition of its central battle – a set piece that takes on epic lengths (depending on how one segments it, it goes on for more than an hour) but that is only ambiguously epic in meaning. Strangely, for all its violence and explosions and action, the battle is also intensely minimalist, moving toward that sparse cinema, that cinema of silence, that also captivates Vietnam auteurs (see, for instance, the influence of Bresson on Paul Schrader). The legacy of the new war film comes not only from earlier forms of the genre but also from other Sixties forms, such as the structural cinema of Warhol or Michael Snow. As in the excruciating beginnings of FULL METAL JACKET and SAVING PRIVATE RYAN (discounting the latter film's kitsch prologue at a war cemetery), much happens but little happens, and action is emptied out to give way to blockage, repetition (the training that goes on and on in FULL METAL JACKET, the assaults that keep happening with new troops endlessly replacing the wounded and the dead in SAVING PRIVATE RYAN and THE THIN RED LINE) noncumulative explosions of violence that lead nowhere and mean nothing. And where SAVING PRIVATE RYAN portrays battle as a messy chaos (the beach cluttered with war paraphernalia, the focus that blurs backgrounds against Tom Hanks), THE THIN RED LINE renders action sparse even in its look: the long waves of grass so beloved by Malick (see his fetish for wheat fields in DAYS OF HEAVEN) become here a pure space of experience as we see nothing but endless fields with no advance, no logic, no fixities of point of view.

Like the narration that can go anywhere but never adds up to a final meaning, the field of battle in THE THIN RED LINE is a space of floating, of meaningless violence that can come from anywhere, but also of the effect of just waiting, of living with non-action. One might want to imagine that this is the experience of war, but it is also an experience of cinema, a comment on modern cinema's narration, its rediscovery of what Gilles Deleuze famously termed the "time-image", a confirmation of modern cinema's ambitious and auspicious inability to find a clear way to recount war today.

Author's Note (2003): This short reflection was written for an imminent deadline in the days that immediately followed the release of THE THIN RED LINE (1999). The time constraints meant that it could involve no research on the film. The piece was not revised for this present publication.

Part Four
Critical Debates

The Pathos of Failure: American Films in the 1970s

Notes on the Unmotivated Hero [1975]

Thomas Elsaesser

Looking at THIEVES LIKE US and remembering THEY LIVE BY NIGHT, wanting to compare JEREMIAH JOHNSON with RUN OF THE ARROW, or thinking of THE NAKED SPUR when watching DELIVERANCE may simply be the typical pastime of someone who has seen too many movies; nonetheless the similarities are also another reminder of how faithful the classical American cinema is to its basic themes and forms. One can safely venture, for instance, that the new Hollywood of Robert Altman, Sidney Pollack and Alan J. Pakula, or of Bob Rafelson, Monte Hellman and Hal Ashby is as fond of mapping out journeys as were the films of Nicholas Ray, Sam Fuller or Anthony Mann in the 1950s. And yet, it is equally evident that this motif has nowadays less of a thematic or dynamic function: journeys are no longer the same drive- and goal-oriented moral trajectories they once were. And although still serving as an oblique metaphor of the archetypal American experience, they now foreground themselves and assume the blander status of a narrative device, sometimes a picaresque support for individual scenes, situations and set-pieces, at other times the ironically admitted pretext to keep the film moving. One wonders whether TWO-LANE BLACKTOP, FIVE EASY PIECES, THE LAST DETAIL, CALIFORNIA SPLIT (to name but a few) will come to be seen as apt examples of a shift, no doubt historically significant, that makes the existential themes of one generation of filmmakers no more than reference points to be quoted by the next – and to be used perhaps in order to scaffold a cautious, but differently constructed architecture of film narrative.

For if the themes remain the same, the attitudes and thereby the forms could not be more different, and there is evidence that in the films just mentioned an aspect of experimentation and meta-cinema is hidden, of the kind familiar only from the masters of classical *mise-en-scène* and from cinematically self-conscious European directors. What follows is an attempt to speculate in what sense some mainstream American films of the 1970s might be considered 'experimental', in the sense of reflecting on the meaning and ideology of forms, especially where these forms are so embedded in a tradition – that of classical Hollywood – as to be self-evident and invisible.

Admittedly, my choice of films is selective, and my argument may be regarded as self-contradictory, in that it both asserts a seamless continuity with this classical tradition and posits a break, the latter by fastening on an element that seems excessively esoteric in the context of this American cinema of the 1970s, whose virtues are its down-to-earth realism, its unostentatious detachment, while still managing to convey the customary accuracy of observation, the palpable physical presence and emotional resonance of setting, spectacle and action. My claim is that the break occurs at another level: the significant feature of this new cinema is that it makes an issue of the motives – or lack of them – in its heroes. My second claim is that this has implications for the narrative form and thereby for how one sees these films, both in relation to classical Hollywood cinema and to its apparent opposite, the European cinema of the 1960s. The contradiction – or tension – lies in the combination of the unmotivated hero and the motif of the journey, that is, the recourse on the one hand to a motivation, ready-made, highly conventionalised and brought to the film from outside, and on the other, the lack of corresponding motivation on the inside, on the part of the protagonist's inner drive or palpable conflict. On the part of the director (or the community he represents), this discrepancy would appear to correspond to a kind of malaise already frequently alluded to in relation to the European cinema: the fading confidence in being able to tell a story, with a beginning, a middle and an ending. But is the unmotivated hero of American Cinema in fact the same phenomenon as the self-conscious awareness of the status of narrative and fiction so noticeable in Claude Chabrol or Luis Buñuel, Jean Luc Godard or Michelangelo Antonioni?

To put the problem in perspective: it will be remembered that the so-called classical narrative was essentially based on a dramaturgy of intrigue and strongly accentuated plot, which managed to transform spatial and temporal sequence into consequence, into a continuum of cause and effect. The image or scene not only pointed forward and backward to what had been and what was to come, but also helped to develop a motivational logic that functioned as an implicit causality, enveloping the hero and connecting him to his world. Whether Hitchcock thriller or Hawks comedy, one was secure in the knowledge that the scenes fitted into each other like cogs in a clockwork, and that all visual information was purposive, inflected towards a plenitude of significance, saturated with clues that explained motivation and character. Out of conflict, contradiction and contingency the narrative generated order, linearity, and articulated energy. Obviously, at a deeper level, such a practice implied an ideology: of progress, of forging in the shape of the plot the outlines of a cultural message, understood and endorsed by Hollywood's audiences as the lineaments of a pragmatism in matters moral as well as metaphysical. The dramaturgy on the other hand posited figures who were psychologically or emotionally motivated: they had a case to investigate, a name to clear, a woman (or man) to love, a goal to reach. Ideological critics therefore detected in the classical cinema a fundamentally affirmative attitude to the world it depicts, a kind of a-priori optimism located in the very structure of the narrative about the usefulness of positive action. Contradictions were resolved and obstacles overcome by having them played out in dramatic-dynamic terms or by personal initiative: whatever the problem, one could do something about it, and even eventually solve it.

Such implicit confidence is less easy to find in the films of the 1970s that pick up the motif of the journey. On the contrary, the off-hand way it is usually introduced specifically neutralises goal-directedness and warns one not to expect an affirmation of purposes and meanings. Taking to the road comes to stand for the very quality of contingency, and a film like Two-Lane Blacktop is symptomatic in this respect: there is only the merest shadow of an intrigue, the action provocatively avoids the interpersonal conflicts potentially inherent both in the triangular relationship and in the challenge personified by the Warren Oates character, and finally, the film toys with goals (the race to Washington) in an almost gratuitous, ostentatiously offhand way. On this level, Hellman has made, and doubtless intended, an anti-action film, deliberately playing down an intrigue that might goad the spectator into involvement or a plot that could generate a psychologically motivated causal web of action and romance.

Hellman is not alone in this. The change I think one can detect is that the affirmative-consequential model of narrative is gradually being replaced by another, whose precise shape is yet to crystallise. This is why the films I am here interested in have a transitional status. Their liberal outlook, their unsentimental approach to American society makes them reject personal initiative and purposive affirmation on the level of ideology, a rejection which has rendered problematic the dramaturgy and film-language developed by classical Hollywood within the context of a can-do culture. But the changes have also something to do with the altered conditions of production. Television has not only affected the economic structures of film-making, it has also brought ideologically less representative groups into the cinemas, notably the young who now see the cinema as an escape from television, rather than as its natural predecessor. And since independent producers and directors are now under pressure to tailor their films to the ideological assumptions of prospective audiences, more relentlessly than in the days when a studio could cushion even a string of failures by a production schedule planned on an annual basis, it is not surprising to find that films reflect stances of dissent typical among minority groups, such as the young or college-educated spectators. Compared with the 1940s and 1950s, the commercial cinema has such a tenuous economic hold over its audiences that it is in practice forced to seek them out, capture them either by an intensity of emotional involvement that is unavailable to television – a dramaturgy of suspense, spectacle and violence – or by an anticipation of favoured emotional anti-stances, such as world-wise cynicism, or the detached cool of a certain machismo. Cop-thrillers or disaster-movies cater for the first type, road-movies with rebels and outsiders are a useful outlet for the second.

The problem that emerges from seeing recent American films is that directors seem unsure of how to objectify into plot, or articulate into narrative the mood of indifference, the post-rebellious lassitude which they, rightly or wrongly, assume to predominate in their audiences. The trend, where it is not towards the defiantly asserted lack of direction and purpose, as in the road-movies just named, manifests itself in stories that do not have a linear plot structure, and in situations that live from a kind of negative, self-demolishing dynamic. For in one sense, the American cinema still understands itself as governed by a realism of place and setting, while elaborating this setting metaphorically. The give-and-take between the documentary texture of a location, and the existential allegory it may have to carry is as strong as ever in Hollywood, and a film that is not simply feeding off the television genres of the 1950s often manages to convey (like much of the best American fiction) a central image that powerfully reverberates as an icon standing for the present state of America. Thus, one finds recent films favour locations that intentionally carry such emblematic overtones: the open prison in SUGARLAND EXPRESS or THE MEAN MACHINE, the dance hall on an ocean pier of THEY SHOOT HORSES, DON'T THEY, the movie house of THE LAST PICTURE SHOW. What the heroes bring to such films is an almost physical sense of inconsequential action, of pointlessness and uselessness: stances which are not only interpretable psychologically, but speak of a radical scepticism about American virtues of ambition, vision, drive: themselves the unacknowledged, because firmly underpinning architecture of the classical Hollywood action genres.

This becomes all the more evident when one looks at what might be called the conservative or 'Republican' films of the 1970s – the cop-thriller or vigilante film, for instance, which now presents a desublimated version of the moralised violence typical of the drive-orientated hero that used to feature in the films from the 1930s to the 1950s. The neurotic streak in this tradition, such as the Cagney characters of PUBLIC ENEMY or WHITE HEAT, the Hawks characters in overdrive (SCARFACE, HIS GIRL FRIDAY, ONLY ANGELS HAVE WINGS) or the Fuller and Ray heroes blemished by uncontrollable violence (SHOCK CORRIDOR, THE STEEL HELMET, ON DANGEROUS GROUND, IN A LONELY PLACE) possessed either anarchic grace in their romantic hubris or a moral complexity of compulsion and motivation that made them symbolic of the contradiction in the American ideal of self-fulfillment. By contrast, a Clint Eastwood in DIRTY HARRY or a Charles Bronson in DEATH WISH, both so purposive and determined, so firm and single-minded, nonetheless appear powered above all by the negative energy of resentment, frustration, and spite, seeking to vent its destructive rage under the guise of a law-and-order morality. These coldly determined heroes featured in excessive, violent plots are the reverse side of the unmotivated heroes in the liberal films: both typify the predicament of mainstream cinema, when it is attempting to represent in narrative-dramatic form the contradictions in American society, while having as its language only the behaviourist code of direct action and raw emotion, devised for an altogether different philosophy of life or masculine ideal. But if violence, whether physical or emotional, is the defensive gesture of the self-alienated male in a society he does not understand and over which he has no control, then the affirmative mode of the cop thriller, and all other forms of strongly dramatised narratives, is evidently also a subjective, compensatory reflex, responding to a felt lack, a gap and an absence. The image of the non-committed hero, on the other hand, the one who keeps his cool (who seems at first wholly depoliticised and subjective) might well be the vehicle of a perspective from which American society, in its present state of crisis and self-doubt, can be seen more analytically and less hysterically.

One finds such an attempt to create an objective realism in the type of hero depicted by actors like Jack Nicholson (FIVE EASY PIECES), James Taylor (TWO-LANE BLACKTOP), Warren Beatty (THE PARALLAX VIEW) or Elliot Gould (CALIFORNIA SPLIT). But a cinema that could be considered progressive in this context would have to be more than symptomatic: one would be looking for signs that the director had thematised in the very structure of the narrative an awareness of the problem he is facing. The question comes down to how the scepticism about motives and justification in the hero, and the doubt about an experience of social and political life where reality is pasted over by ideological fictions, are translated into a formal search for a film narrative free from the parasitic and synthetic causality of a dramaturgy of external conflict. On the other hand, is there a mode of representation that validates (social) reality without encasing it in the categories of symbolism and the spectacular? In other words, one is asking for a mise-en-scène that can take a critical stance. What evidence is there today that the liberal film is finding an appropriate mise-en-scène of differentiation?

Among the directors whose involvement with the dynamic-affirmative model dates back to the 1950s and early 1960s, it is Robert Aldrich and Sam Peckinpah (both of whom have a more than casual interest in 'violence') who show most clearly that they are affected by the crisis of motivation. BRING ME

THE HEAD OF ALFREDO GARCIA is an interesting study (within the now familiar Peckinpah thematic) of a hero who has no past to romanticise (as in THE WILD BUNCH, or JUNIOR BONNER) and who is thus more radically unmotivated than any previous Peckinpah character. When he does find a cause, it is made clear that the use of violence comes to Benny (Warren Oates) almost as a form of moral rearmament, highly ambiguous and yet devoutly desired as such violence always is in Peckinpah (cf. STRAW DOGS). However, in ALFREDO GARCIA Peckinpah is fascinated by a zero-degree of motivation and nonetheless too attached to the apocalypse to conceive of any narrative other than a cathartic one.

Lack of motivation is even more explicitly the subject of Aldrich's THE MEAN MACHINE, a movie whose complex narrative conception appears in the realisation more awkward than elegant. It is as if Aldrich, as much in desperation as disgust, had broken his film into several disjointed pieces, and one can unscramble at least three strands pushed into each other. In the first, the Burt Reynolds character gets out of bed, savagely mauls his girl, drives her sportscar across a half-opened bridge-leaf, dumps it in the river and then stands at the bar waiting for the cops to pick him up. The violence is excessive, the motivation nonexistent. One feels that neither movie nor hero can go in any direction whatsoever, and one wonders whether one has seen the last 15 minutes of the previous film, or the pre-credit scene to a flashback movie that never follows. What does follow is another film, which superficially belongs to the time-honoured genre of the prison film, where the hero rehabilitates himself by organising the sports team, turning anti-social convicts into loyal teammates. Aldrich twists the genre out of shape, and the rehabilitation does not mean release, but converts the sentence into an indefinite one. However, the real twist is that inside the second film is a third one, which by rights is not a movie at all, but a Saturday-afternoon TV-baseball game complete with commentator and cheerleaders. The suspense is wholly predictable, and one suspects that Aldrich is giving (by default?) an object lesson about the impossibility of making dramatic films: unmotivated heroes, morally bogus genres, puerile audiences – three times he is showing us drama without consequence, three variations on one theme. A stretch of dialogue midway through the film verbalises the situation once more: we know there is something obscure in the hero's past that concerns his motivation. His friend keeps asking "why did you do it?" Finally, Burt Reynolds gives an explanation, a sob-story belonging to the conventions of the rehabilitation genre, but before we have recovered from its painful pathos, Reynolds starts to grin and admits that he has been having his friends on, and that he just doesn't know why he "did it" – maybe just for the money.

Clearly, in Aldrich's film, the salient fact is that whatever was important to his hero, the determining events happened long ago, and this in itself is a telling metaphor of the film's motivational predicament: if characters have no moral history that can plausibly explain their behaviour, action is the spectacle of gratuitousness. (What makes certain disaster movies archaic and naive is their assumption the catastrophe is yet to happen, and that all one needs to be prepared is to rehearse it.)

A more familiar form of self-consciousness than that practised by Aldrich is to resort to adaptation, parody, pastiche: Bogdanovich, Altman, Polanski. CHINATOWN, a poker-faced pastiche of the film noir is nonetheless as dismissive of its hero's motives as is Altman in THE LONG GOODBYE, except that Polanski's lack of respect for his hero appeases itself in the meticulous craftsmanship of the reconstruction of his moral demise. Altman's parodies (THE LONG GOODBYE) and reprises (THIEVES LIKE US) would appear to mark him out as the director with the most 'European' sense of fictional impasses, reminiscent in fact of the Godard and Truffaut films of the mid-1960s. In THIEVES LIKE US, the heroes listen as compulsively to radio-shows and want to read about themselves in the newspapers as avidly as the heroes of BAND À PART or BAISERS VOLÉS were caught in the seductively narcissistic mirror of the mass media or cheap romances. Altman, possibly taking his cue from Penn's BONNIE AND CLYDE, develops the mytho-poetic magic of the American cinema's own past through the double mytho-mania of newspaper and radio-serial, but then, choosing a 1930s setting, is he not himself helping to build up the myth of the Thirties? I don't think so: the movie wants to impress by its unromantic, anti-glamorising sobriety, and it is as much anti-BONNIE AND CLYDE as in another way it is anti-THEY LIVE BY NIGHT.

Paradoxically, this distance is the result of pastiche, the replication of the object in the gesture of citation. Altman is one of the few modern directors who still occasionally employ a symbolic language that clearly belongs to the epoch of the classical *mise-en-scène*: the symbolisation of objects through thematic use in the narrative. One would have thought that it belongs too obviously to a cinema of purposive development and positive meanings to be of use in any other form than as quotations, and yet, in THIEVES LIKE US a patchwork quilt is given all the grand rhetorical orchestration that Shirley McLaine's 'sweetheart' pillow had in Minnelli's SOME CAME RUNNING (a film whose symbolic objects Godard remembers in both LE MÉPRIS and PIERROT LE FOU). Kechie's patchwork quilt is symbolically charged in an early scene when she covers the injured Bowie and then slips under it herself when they make love for the first time. The importance of the quilt is then emphasised when she explains that it was made by her grandmother and is her sole personal possession and memory of her family. It then reappears when the two have their decisive quarrel

and it attains its thematic apotheosis when Bowie, now a corpse riddled by police bullets, is wrapped up in it and dumped, mud- and blood-spattered, into a
puddle. The price Altman pays for using such obvious dramatic symbolism is
a stylized poignancy possibly too overt not to disrupt the sombre, unemphatic
ending, but it is in line with other formal devices (the repetition of the line from
Romeo and Juliet, for instance), where Altman seems unsure just how self-
consciously he can treat the genre he has chosen to pastiche, while retaining its
pathos.

The penchant for pathos, however, goes deeper. "We blew it": one remembers the resigned and melancholy admission of Captain America. For all its
traditionalist plot elements and stylistic uncertainties, EASY RIDER still functions along with BONNIE AND CLYDE as the only popular and successful alternative to the affirmative stance. Not just because it is a film about heroes without a goal, who take 'drive' out of the Freudian psyche and onto the road, and
who take 'trip' off the road and into the mind. The film is also a paradigm of
the open-ended, loose-structured narrative, so often imitated since. The heroes
are still motivated, though, for thematically EASY RIDER revives the ever-pres-
ent Huck Finn motif in American culture, about the male couple ganging up to
escape civilisation and women. In fact, the double male lead still predominates
(from MIDNIGHT COWBOY, BUTCH CASSIDY AND THE SUNDANCE KID, THE STING
down to CALIFORNIA SPLIT and THUNDERBOLT AND LIGHTFOOT) and has become a genre for both conformist and dropout attitudes. The permutations
reach from Ashby's THE LAST DETAIL to Spielberg's SUGARLAND EXPRESS, the
latter particularly interesting, because a BONNIE AND CLYDE type story ends up
as the sentimental love-story of the all-male couple, when the young policeman taken hostage befriends and is in turn befriended by the boy whom we
know from the start to be a very reluctant accomplice in his wife's hijack trip to
recover her baby.

Over all the movies that take to the road on quests that are escapes and escapes that are quests, there hangs like a haze the sweet poignancy of defeat. At
the end, when they face the law, the rednecks, the mean-mouthed farmers and
hick gas-stop attendants, the scowling women and bragging middle-aged men
with fast cars and high-powered rifles – all those who were already there before the heroes came on the scene and who win out and survive, as they invariably do – then the characters' wry self-abandonment and lassitude register
with the particular pathos reserved for 'beautiful losers'. And the cool mock-
ery, the detached satire, which such films direct against the America of the silent majority, fades out on a wave of self-pity.

If one sees this simply in thematic or ideological terms, the new American
cinema here shows its weakest side. For it appears that directors opt for a kind
of realism of sentiment that tries to be faithful to the negative experiences of re-

cent American history (and the movies reflect the moral and emotional gestures of a defeated generation), but this strategy – since it is concerned neither
with cause nor historical circumstances – gives both heroes and the world that
dooms them a mystification and starkness of contrast which must finally affect
the intelligence of the observation and therefore the value of this new realism
of understatement. The narrowness of the emotional response at the climax of
THIEVES LIKE US is counteracted by a kind of emotionally flat coda, and it is noticeable that a lot of the so-called nostalgia pictures have such an epilogue
(AMERICAN GRAFFITI): it neutralises the dramatic charge, but the irony of
hindsight rings hollow. By foregoing the dramaturgy of interpersonal conflict,
suspense, intrigue or the self-alienated aggressiveness of emotional frustration, the films are somehow led to stylising despair or helplessness into the pathos of failure. On the other hand, it answers the pressing problem of how to
end an indeterminate narrative: pathos provides the emotional closure to an
open-ended structure and retrieves affective contact with the audience.

Thus, if one feels uncomfortable about the unqualified emotional sympathy
enjoyed by the heroes of THIEVES LIKE US, SUGARLAND EXPRESS or AMERICAN
GRAFFITI, one needs to bear in mind that under cover of such a relatively simple but effective hold over the spectator's involvement and identification a
new type of popular film narrative is trying to cope with the technical problem
of how to depict the unmotivated hero. European directors – from Jean Marie
Straub to Jacques Rivette, from Luis Buñuel to Alain Tanner – have long been
conducting experiments into the nature of a narrative not generated by any of
the conventional dramatic supports such as melodrama, quest, investigation,
journey (though as his recent films indicate, Buñuel is more than ever committed to the picaresque mode). But while they can work at purely situational narratives (as in Rivette's CÉLINE ET JULIE S'EN VONT EN BATEAU) in the comforting
knowledge of an appreciative intellectual audience, the pressures on such experimentation in Hollywood mainstream cinema are obviously different.
Where French directors in particular like to allow the fictional substance of
their films to whittle itself out of existence through an ever-more sophisticated
play of multiple fictional strands and fragments, such possibilities are not
open to an American director faced with a similar dilemma of representational
realism: his remains an audience-orientated cinema that permits no explicitly
intellectual or meta-narrative construction. Consequently, the innovatory line
in the American cinema can be seen to progress not via conceptual abstraction
but by shifting and modifying traditional genres and themes, while never
quite shedding their support, be it to facilitate recognition or for structuring
the narrative. In search of a new realism, Altman or Hellman after periods of
experiment with less commercial subjects (BREWSTER MCCLOUD, THE SHOOT-
ING) can now be seen to return to the realm of the thematic material that is, as it

were, culturally coded and already cinematically sanctioned. One can see them in their recent films tread the narrow path between locating a new image of America, and the need to keep in touch with the visual and emotional rhetoric of their culture, and thereby keep open the lines of communication with a mass public. The price of relevance to the historical moment seems to be an acknowledgement of the reigning ideology, and the condition of realism in this situation is the emotional stance of defeat.

Given this dilemma, it follows that the much-maligned cycle of nostalgia movies should perhaps be regarded under a double aspect. Certainly, PAPER MOON, AMERICAN GRAFFITI are testimony to a symptomatic search for an affirmative, innocent past, free from guilt and responsibility. But the quest for a lost national Eden (perhaps more overtly apologetic in films like SUMMER OF '42 or THE WAY WE WERE in which a pointedly a-political apprehension of reality is rather shamefacedly celebrated against the background of a highly politicised period) in the first instance communicates a direct thematisation of the absence of consequence and history, which, I have tried to suggest, is one of the structurally and ideologically determined features of the American cinema today. Yet it also gives directors the opportunity to scan a historical and geographical American landscape – notably the Depression era, the early 1950s, small-town rural communities – for clues towards what one might call a new verisimilitude of the American image. It is not a question of a pristine visual experience, nor of a documentary objectivity, more the depiction of a gestural and physical world that connotes historicity as an effect of both distance and proximity. Culturally resonant without being overtly symbolic, this other America is in contrast to the perfected glamour, the aesthetic closure of beauty as has been attributed to Hollywood itself, and which critics refer to as the fetishism of the cinematic illusion (believing in it and not believing in it at the same time). How else is one to understand the assiduous work, say, of Altman who seems bent on emotionally charging the rough, the squalid, the unattractive and plain, the imperfect and incomplete in McCABE AND MRS MILLER, THIEVES LIKE US, THE LONG GOODBYE, CALIFORNIA SPLIT? Particularly in his genre movies Altman uses this pathos of historical patina and nostalgia to transform objects and decor – from mining town to Coke bottle and heart-shaped purse – into signs, at once saturated and empty. Not symbols to be used in another kind of discourse (this is why the patchwork quilt in THIEVES LIKE US is so exceptional, for it points in the other direction, that of the classical mise-en-scène, in which objects and decor are truths of a higher reality), but to refer to themselves, while raising expectations of a pay-off on the level of positive meanings which never quite constitutes itself, except as tender or ironic pastiche.

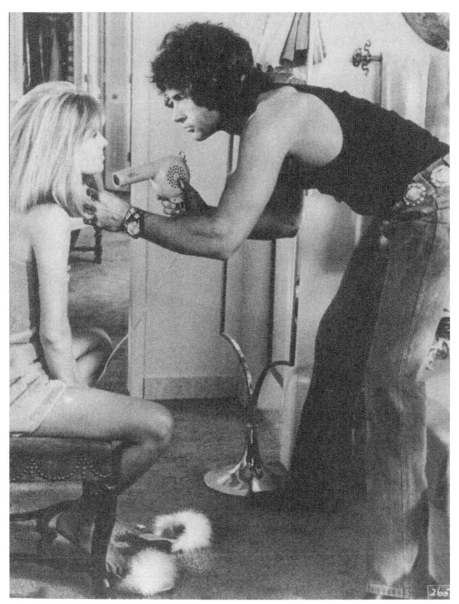

Julie Christie and Warren Beatty in SHAMPOO

In his experimentation with a reality both falsely innocent and knowingly oblivious to the symbolic accretions that have made so much of the American urban and rural landscape into dramatic clichés, Altman seems to admit the status of the image as inescapable sign, but its sign character can be exploited by focusing emotional resonance on its palpable facticity and materiality. Genre conventions, objects and even the intrigue henceforth function in an inverse sense; instead of providing the elements of first-level verisimilitude and causal logic that guarantee the coherence of the secondary level of meaning, they become mere vehicles of phatic communicative contact, where discrete visual moments are underscored, tableau-like, but voided of any specific moral significance. In the absence of positive motivation of either hero or plot, the fabric of narrative shows through, and the pathos of failure becomes the zero-degree of the moralised emotions, which the dynamics of affect, eros and violence once supplied to the classical narrative.

Similar tendencies can be observed elsewhere, since they extend beyond the nostalgia and genre films. In a sense, it is easier to test the possibilities of such a non-metaphoric realism in the context of historical reconstruction or the pre-formulated expectation of the genre, for they give the narrative a provisional structure of empathy and recognition. Yet films with a contemporary setting, such as FIVE EASY PIECES or TWO-LANE BLACKTOP, are generated out of the same desire for an image of America that becomes palpable not because of the interplay between moral symbolism and an ideological plot structure, but because of its solid specificity, its realised physical presence, whatever the degree of dramatic intensification may be, which such films employ in order to make this realism acceptable. And again we find the same tautological pathos that charges the image with emotion while neutralising its moral energy.

Significantly, Rafelson, Hellman, Spielberg and others choose a 'rural' America, recognisable by its stretches of barren roadside, its drive-ins, petrol stations and hick-town main streets – the kind of scenery precisely nowhere and everywhere in America, and therefore furnishing an important element of abstraction without being itself the least bit abstract. It is a scenery that obviously has the sanction and precedent of the *film noir*, that other high period of an almost documentary realism in the American cinema. This time, however, it is without the black romanticism of mood, nor the heavy machinery of fate and destiny that used to knit together character and incident. Comparable movies today are low-keyed, de-dramatised, but ultimately not so different in their insistence on the emotional stance appropriate to American realism – negativity, a stand-off cool, the somewhat sentimental gestures of defeat. One way of looking at it is to say that the new realism is itself a defensive stance. Is not the focus on rural America conveying something of an ethnographic perspective on an America, where nothing ever seems to happen, where time has stood still and where a people survives that apparently has no history? One remembers the encounter of the heroes in DELIVERANCE with the banjo-playing boy. In the very understatement of the scene is hidden an anxious wariness for clues to what it was that made the United States of the 1960s so appallingly what it is today, as if only the secluded places, the gaps and silences could give an explanation for the violence, the paranoia that was to follow. As if, finally, only rural hamlets could explain urban ghettos and suburban hysteria. A favourite image, put to good effect in THIEVES LIKE Us, is to show a fine silence at dawn in an idyllic landscape suddenly torn apart by a furious exchange of gunfire (also found in SUGARLAND EXPRESS).

Faced with such symbolic re-enactments of morning raids on the Black Panthers or Kent State shootings, one wonders how long directors can go on codifying the experience of a rebellion whose impulse towards change aborted, and which (where it does not lead to a pure sense of loss) is now somehow transfixed in stunned moments of inconsequentiality, such as that of George Segal piling up his chips at the end of CALIFORNIA SPLIT, or Gene Hackman sitting in his demolished room at the end of THE CONVERSATION. Today's heroes are waiting for the end, convinced that it is too late for action, as if too many contradictions had cancelled the impulse towards meaning and purpose. In TWO-LANE BLACKTOP everything goal-directed appears simply neurotic, uncool, a compensation for frustration, like the fantasies that GTO, the Warren Oates character, tells to himself more than to his passengers. In AMERICAN GRAFFITI the action, the constant stream of cars circling the town's main street, revolves around an 'empty' centre: the mythical DJ whose disembodied 'Wolfman' persona is nothing more mysterious than a lonely man sitting amongst a lot of technology in his radio-mast sucking popsicles. Clearly in a period of historical stasis, these movies reflect a significant ideological moment in American culture. One might call them films that dramatise the end of history, for what is a story, a motivated narrative (which such movies refuse to employ) other than an implicit recognition of the existence of history, at least in its formal dimension – of driving forces and determinants, of causes, conflicts, consequence, and interaction?

Finally, there is another point: if one considers, as I have suggested, the pervasive pessimism of the American cinema in the 1970s less as a personal statement of their authors and more as the limiting constraint of a new, modern realism, the price this cinema pays for being exploratory and tentative, then the strength of a film like TWO-LANE BLACKTOP lies in the way that, sheltered by the structure of the journey motif, it quietly steers towards a level of abstraction, a documentary minimalism unknown in the Hollywood canon except perhaps in the work of Jacques Tourneur. Released from the strong fable and from the need to engineer the narrative into didactic shape, the images develop an energy that charges representation with something other than symbolic overtones or metaphoric substitutes. One is, naturally, reminded of the studied literalness in Paul Morissey's films for Andy Warhol, but Monte Hellman's film is free from the claustrophobia so carefully controlled in FLESH or TRASH (though no stranger to their fear of utter meaninglessness). Whether the cancellation of the melodramatic impulse and the search for narrational rhythms now taken from the novel will suggest less problematic downbeat endings is difficult to say: the freeze-frame may connote no more than the indecisiveness of the director on just this point. In TWO-LANE BLACKTOP, by its own logic, the drive, and thus the film, could go on indefinitely: that is its beauty as a composition of pure movement. The ending – in order to work – quite clearly must have the status of a 'device': Hellman motivates his hero, the James Taylor character, rather conventionally when underneath his cool he reveals an obsession with the girl. This impulse is allowed to live itself out, albeit destructively – he takes risks and finally meets his nemesis. But cinematically, the ending is aptly 'formal': Hellman lets the image burn itself out in the projector in extreme slow-motion, clearly a metaphor both for the hero's obsession and the film's obsession with itself.

The fact that this ending is borrowed from Jerzy Skolimowski's LE DÉPART, also a film about racing and impossible quests, throws an interesting sidelight on the no doubt complex interchange between European and American filmmaking today. Tentatively, however, one might assume that both, aware of essentially similar problems, proceed along different routes. Against multiple fictions and the double diegetic worlds in Rivette or Buñuel, the American directors prefer to literalise their cinematic language, de-dramatise their narratives, and strengthen the inner dynamism of their scenes: the momentum of action gives way to the moment of gesture and the body. A new form of mise-en-scène seems in the making that could mean a revaluation of physical reality on the far side of either fetishistic fixation on the image or conceptual abstraction of the form. In that case, the unmotivated hero and the pathos of failure will be the two negatives that result in a positive.

Trapped in the Affection Image

Hollywood's Post-traumatic Cycle (1970-1976)

Christian Keathley

It has long been commonplace to talk about many American films of the late 1960s and early 1970s as being about or in response to the Vietnam experience. Even during those years, this seemed to be the case. Asked in a 1972 interview about the curious absence of any films about the Vietnam war, Pauline Kael replied, "Vietnam we experience indirectly in just about every movie we go to. It's one of the reasons we've had so little romance or comedy – because we're all tied up in knots about that rotten war." [1] Though any number of films from this period may be discussed in relation to Vietnam, I would like to focus here on a group of deeply pessimistic Hollywood films from the first half of the 1970s – a group that may be dubbed the 'post-traumatic cycle', a term I will explain shortly. This cycle includes (but is not limited to): MIDNIGHT COWBOY, FIVE EASY PIECES, MCCABE & MRS MILLER, THE CANDIDATE, DELIVERANCE, MEAN STREETS, THE SUGARLAND EXPRESS, THE CONVERSATION, CHINATOWN, THE PARALLAX VIEW, CALIFORNIA SPLIT, NIGHT MOVES, DOG DAY AFTERNOON, and SHAMPOO. It is this cycle, I want to suggest, that stands most clearly as America's first round of Vietnam films. Although none is set in and only a few make explicit reference to that war, these films represent and replay, in a displaced fashion, the Vietnam war's defining experience: the onset of trauma resulting from a realisation of powerlessness in the face of a world whose systems of organisation – both moral and political – have broken down. Or, to use a different set of terms, this cycle of films exemplifies what Gilles Deleuze has described as a "crisis of the action-image".

The Crisis of the Action Image

In his two volume study – *Cinema 1: The Movement-Image* and *Cinema 2: The Time-Image* – Deleuze borrows the concepts of movement and time articulated by Henri Bergson in *Matter and Memory* and applies them to the history of cinema, developing as he does a typology of images and signs. [2] From this typology, he concludes that, for the first half of its existence (and in most of its product since), cinema has been content to reproduce human perception of movement, and its plots have largely been driven by movement's corollary: *action*. But, Deleuze argues, at certain points in history, the schema for perception processing was thrown into a state of crisis – thus producing a crisis in cinematic representation. To understand the nature of this crisis, it is necessary to review what Deleuze (via Bergson) defined as the three primary image components of the sensory motor schema: the perception-image, the affection-image, and the action-image. Though it is perhaps something of an oversimplification, one can understand these three components as roughly analogous to the shot sequence in Kuleshovian montage: 1) we see a person looking; 2) we see what he or she is looking at (perception-image); 3) we see his or her reaction (affection-image); and this reaction leads him or her to take some action (action-image). Though he is quick to point out that an individual film shot may include two or even three of these different "images," Deleuze emphasised that the classical American cinema, which was above all a cinema of action, operated primarily according to the three alternating components of this schema, tightly linking character, narrative, and film form into a standardised sequence. Deleuze summarised the emergence of the crisis in cinema's representation of this perceptual schema in the following way:

> The cinema of action depicts sensory-motor situations: there are characters, in a certain situation, who act ... according to how they perceive the situation. Actions are linked to perceptions, and perceptions develop into actions. Now, suppose a character finds himself in a situation, however ordinary or extraordinary, that's beyond any possible action, or to which he can't react. It's too powerful, or too painful, or too beautiful. The sensory motor link is broken.[3]

It is not that the above described three-shot sequence disappears in post-action-image cinema (though it may indeed become more rare), but rather that the active cause-and-effect chain it implies is disrupted. Broadly speaking, the cinema practice that emerged from the first of these crises was post-WWII European art cinema. As Deleuze explains, for the filmmakers of Italian neo-realism and for many others who followed, the crisis of the action-image marked an opportunity that they saw and exploited for an alternative concept of the image. In both style and narrative, post-war European art cinema opened the interval between perception and action – what Bergson referred to as the "interval of thought" – to explore a cinema predicated not on action, but on the possibilities inherent in the interval *between* perception and action. That is, art cinema privileges, expands, and explores the affection-image.

David Bordwell has grouped the formal and narrative characteristics of art cinema under two broad headings: *realism* and *authorial expressivity*.[4] The characteristics of realism include: characters who lack clearly defined goals and thus slide passively from one situation to another; a cause-and-effect narrative structure whose looseness opens space for digressions into "contingent daily reality" or the "subjective reality" of the film's complex characters; and a pre-occupation with the conditions – moral and philosophical – of modern life.[5] Authorial expressivity refers to this film practice's "recurrent violations of the classical norm" of Hollywood filmmaking – that is, the use of formal strategies that call the viewer's attention to the fact that there is a guiding subjectivity be-hind the construction and arrangement of what they are watching.[6] One film that was crucial in initiating the strong realist strain in post-war filmmaking is Roberto Rossellini's GERMANY YEAR ZERO (1947). Set in the rubble of that re-cently defeated nation, the film centres on a young boy, Edmund, who strug-gles to survive in miserable conditions along with his ailing father, his older sister, and an older brother, a former Nazi who is unable to provide for the family's needs. Edmund, doing whatever he can to help his family, is ulti-mately led by the advice of his former Nazi schoolteacher into poisoning his father. The final act of the film, during which Edmund realises the enormity of his act, consists of the boy wandering the streets and abandoned buildings of the city; finally, Edmund throws himself out a window and is killed. Deleuze, echoing Bazin, focuses on the "dispersive, elliptical, errant" quality of the film's narrative, especially this final section, which consists of "deliberately weak connections and floating events".[7] He further characterises Rossellini's immediate post-war films as representative of the crisis of the action-image, as well as pointing to its beyond: "This is a cinema of the seer and no longer of the agent."[8]

Though it is commonly the norm against which art cinema is defined, Hol-lywood, too, enjoyed a brief period when a surprising number of its films in-corporated, in a somewhat diluted form, the formal and thematic characteris-tics of art cinema. The cultural circumstances of that moment – the late 1960s and early 1970s – further identify Hollywood's art cinema practice as being a response to crisis. Deleuze argues that, in its initial appearance, the crisis of the action-image was precipitated by the host nation's recent *historical* crisis – spe-cifically, the traumatic experience of war. After World War II, Deleuze ex-plains, Italy found itself in a unique situation: as neither victor nor van-quished, that nation saw clearly defining extremes such as those fall away in the face of deep ambiguity. This crisis provoked an interrogation of the estab-lished ways of conceiving of and representing the world, especially in the cin-ema. It was the historical trauma of the Vietnam war that, along with other fac-tors but more so than any of them, provoked American cinema's encounter with a crisis of the action-image.[9]

There is, however, an important distinction to be made between the European and American filmic expressions of this crisis. While Hollywood cinema could face the crisis of the action-image, it could never fully engage with the alternative practice that European cinema did. Indeed, in the six pages of *Cinema 1* in which Deleuze defines the crisis of the action-image, he cites over a dozen films, all but a couple of which are American films from these years. The point here is that, for Deleuze, much American cinema of this period exemplifies the crisis of the action-image without also exemplifying the alternative that European art cinema discovered. Instead, Hollywood represented the opening up of the interval between perception and action as a traumatic event. Further, the perception to which the characters in these films are unable to respond is always the same, for the films of the post-traumatic cycle repeatedly lead their protagonists to the same end: the realisation of their total powerlessness.

The Post-traumatic Cycle

In spite of their status as reasonably budgeted, studio-backed films featuring major stars of the period (Jack Nicholson, Warren Beatty, Gene Hackman) and intended for mainstream distribution and exhibition, the movies of the post-traumatic cycle evince what Robin Wood has called a "major defining factor of Hollywood cinema of the late 1960s and 1970s": the "breakdown of ideological confidence in American culture and values."[10] This breakdown of confidence, however, was reflected in the cinema of this period in two stages. As David Thomson explains, many of the "naive and liberal revolutionary notions" that had focused the optimistic energy of the counter-culture movement of the 1960s were, in the first half of the 1970s, "confounded by actual experiences" that revealed "the moral bankruptcy of the established order".[11] Along with numerous other "actual experiences," but more powerfully than any of them, America's lengthy involvement in the war in Vietnam and the impingement of that experience on the national consciousness served as the focus point for this breakdown of confidence. While in the 1960s, the heady energy of college campus protest had been reflected in the counter-culture cycle, by the early 1970s, the trauma suffered by soldiers in Vietnam, then by the nation as a whole, was reflected in this second cycle of films whose heroes, like the heroes of Vietnam, are manipulated, exploited, and left paralysed by the realisation of their powerlessness in the face of a corrupt system. The overwhelming feelings of disaffection, alienation, and demoralisation that permeate these films are, in a sense, a displaced repetition of the intense trauma suffered by the Vietnam generation.

While there is no neat match between this cycle and any given genre, or any given director's entire output during the period, Robert Altman's films during these years come closest to exemplifying this trend. Robin Wood's description of the "most consistent and recurrent pattern in Altman's films" serves also to describe most films of the post-traumatic cycle: "The protagonist embarks on an undertaking he is confident he can control; the sense of control is progressively revealed as illusory; the protagonist is trapped in a course of events that culminate in disaster (frequently death)."[12] In fact, while the counter-culture films of the late 1960s regularly ended with their protagonists' martyrdom (think of BONNIE AND CLYDE, EASY RIDER, etc.), these films often leave their protagonists not dead, but rather wounded and helpless, disconnected from their surroundings, often muttering to themselves in a catatonic, traumatised state. In Deleuze's schema, this traumatic realisation registers as each of the characters finds himself trapped between perception and action in the affection-image. That is, as the accompanying film stills show, each film concludes with its protagonist literally trapped in a reaction shot that shows not only his devastation at what he has perceived, but also his paralysis as he is unable to respond to it. "The situation [that the protagonist] is in outstrips his motor capacities on all sides, and makes him see and hear what is no longer subject to the rules of a response or an action," Deleuze writes. "He records rather than reacts."[13] As the affection-image finds its purest expression in the face,[14] so it is that these films end on a close-up of the protagonist as he registers the full horror of what he is perceiving and of the realisation of his own inability to act in response. Two examples:

In THE CANDIDATE, Bill McKay, an idealistic young lawyer, is encouraged to run for Senator against an unbeatable conservative incumbent. Because he has no chance of winning, McKay is told by his advisors that he needn't follow traditional political standards; he can say whatever he wants, thus bringing attention to the issues he feels need it. As the campaign continues and McKay's popularity grows, he gradually loses this autonomy and begins to succumb to the political system he sought to challenge. Confirmation of this loss of power comes at the film's end when, having scored an upset victory, McKay retreats to a hotel room with his campaign manager and appeals in a stunned voice, "What do we do now?"

In CHINATOWN, private detective Jake Gittes wants to find out not only who killed waterworks engineer Hollis Mulwray, but also who paid a woman to pose as Mulwray's wife and hire Gittes, thus initiating the events that led to Mulwray's death. At the film's conclusion, Jake not only sees his mistress and client, the fragile Evelyn Mulwray, gunned down by police; he is also (again) forced to confront the fact that, in spite of his best and most honourable intentions, he is powerless to help the innocent or bring the guilty to justice. The film's title refers not only to the protagonist's past and his haunted state of mind, but to a world in which 'order' is determined by the rich and powerful, regardless of how corrupt they may be. Jake's blank stare and barely audible muttering ("as little as possible") remind us of the warnings that he has repeatedly received: that his power and authority are limited, and that any attempt to exercise what he has inappropriately, especially on moral grounds, will result in complete emasculation.

I am using the term 'post-traumatic' here not only because it accurately describes the experience reflected in this cycle of films, but because it was through research and work with mentally and emotionally scarred Vietnam veterans that psychologists came to a more complex and subtle understanding of the condition that had traditionally been called 'shell shock'. The resulting diagnostic term, 'post-traumatic stress disorder' (PTSD), was soon applied not only to those who had experienced battle, but was also used to describe the clinical condition suffered by anyone who exhibits a specific set of symptoms as the result of some intense experience outside normal life patterns (e.g., child or spousal abuse, rape, natural disasters, accidents resulting in serious injury or death). Such a traumatic event might be generally understood as a sudden and violent disruption of the order that defines regular experience of the world and, more importantly, the values (ethical, moral, political) that are taken for granted to lie firmly at the basis of this order.[15] This clinical description of PTSD divides trauma into two categories: the first has to do with a traumatic event that might be described as arbitrary – a random, 'act of God' event such as a natural disaster or sudden death; the second and often more serious kind of trauma results from betrayal by persons or institutions in positions of authority – that is, those with whom the rules of order are generally associated.

Furthermore, Judith Lewis Herman, a psychiatrist who has conducted comprehensive work on the effects of trauma, has argued that the experience of trauma is not limited to individuals; indeed, entire cultures and societies can suffer this tragedy. But if, as Lévi-Strauss has put it, a culture's ideological conflicts regularly find expression and resolution in its myths, the films of the post-traumatic cycle are a unique exception, for they refuse to offer the reassurance of such reconciliation; in this way, they work a complex variation on classical Hollywood cinema's dominant thematic paradigm – a paradigm that, as Robert Ray has argued, seeks to conceal the necessity for choice as a prerequisite to action.[16] Instead, Andrew Britton has argued that, reflecting the Vietnam experience as they do, films of this period "give evidence of the meaninglessness and ineffectuality of choice".[17] That is, these films first foreground the apparent necessity of choice or feature protagonists who believe in the existential responsibility an individual has to make choices (especially moral choices); but they then undercut this notion, showing instead that the privileging of choice implies the opportunity of the individual to gain power and self-deter-mination - something these films reveal to be an impossibility. In THE CONVER-SATION, wire-tapper Harry Caul acts initially as a pure professional, interested only in getting a perfect surreptitious recording; but when he suspects that his recording will result in the murder of two people, he takes a stand, refusing to hand over the secret tapes to his client, a wealthy and secretive businessman. This resolve costs Harry, and the tables are turned: a murder is committed (not the one he expected), and he becomes the victim of a surveillance that shatters his closely guarded and controlled privacy.

An important characteristic of these films is that their heroes exist in a mid-dle position between the 'official hero' and 'outlaw hero' favoured by classical cinema.[18] While the films of the counter-culture cycle favoured outlaw heroes (BONNIE AND CLYDE, BUTCH CASSIDY AND THE SUNDANCE KID, etc.), the protag-onists of the post-traumatic cycle films are usually marginal establishment fig-ures. For example, although McCabe in McCABE AND MRS. MILLER and Char-lie in MEAN STREETS trade in vice and/or have connections to organised crime, both consider themselves businessmen, as are, in a more legitimate way, the men in DELIVERANCE. Buddusky in THE LAST DETAIL is an unambitious career Navy man; Bobby Dupea in FIVE EASY PIECES is an oil worker. But the repre-sentative figure here is the private investigator, of which there are several in the post-traumatic cycle: Jake Gittes in CHINATOWN, Philip Marlowe in THE LONG GOODBYE, Harry Moseby in NIGHT MOVES, Joe Frady in THE PARALLAX VIEW. As unofficial lawman, the investigator identifies himself as being com-mitted to upholding the law, while at the same time residing outside of, and of-ten having a somewhat antagonistic relationship with, its official institutions. While most of these figures do not directly challenge the established system as the figures of the counter-culture cycle did, all are at least partly alienated from it. Nevertheless, each pays this established order – and, more importantly, the values that order represents – a measure of respect, and he assumes that it will do the same for him. This faith is the basis of each man's downfall. Each na-ively assumes that the combination of his own competence and the larger moral order will not permit any real harm to come to him or those close to him.

Just as these films' narrative, character, and thematic similarities can be un-derstood in terms of art cinema's preoccupation with realism and the condi-tions of modern life, many of these films also possess certain similar formal and stylistic characteristics that can be understood as authorial expressivity. Rather than employing classic Hollywood's "invisible style", these films use overt stylistic and technical devices – telephoto lenses, zooms, unmotivated pans, oblique camera set-ups, complex editing patterns of both image and sound – all to create a look which is simultaneously more naturalistic and more stylised than dominant cinema's norm. That is, on the one hand, the films often employ the formal codes associated with documentary filmmaking that were disseminated largely by television news; at the time, these codes functioned quite powerfully to evoke an almost wholly unmediated representation of reality, much like Americans encountered in nightly news coverage of Vietnam. On the other hand, the films often also reflect the complex, contradictory, fragmented nature of accounts of trauma regularly offered by those who have suffered it.[19] The opening of THE PARALLAX VIEW is a clear example. The cluttered, uncentred shots showing an Independence Day parade, the arrival of a political candidate (who will soon be assassinated), and his interview by a television reporter combine the documentary qualities of television reporting with the formal rigor and complexity of a formalist art cinema. This formal approach is used to comment on the complex nature of perception, particularly in a world where the moral and political landscape that once was so clear has turned opaque, and any misperception can be fatal. Perhaps more than any group of films in Hollywood's history, these films demand a measure of work from the audience; that is, crucial plot and character information is not always underscored, but is rather hidden in an ambiguous world that the viewer, like the protagonists themselves, must attend to with great effort and care.

For the most part, recent film historians have downplayed whatever differences exist between these films of the early 1970s and the films of Hollywood's classical period. For example, in their mammoth study, *Classical Hollywood Cinema: Film Style and Mode of Production*, Bordwell, Thompson, and Staiger describe the period since 1960 as marking "the persistence of a mode of film practice" that is commonly called "classical".[20] Similarly, in *A Certain Tendency of the Hollywood Cinema, 1930-1980*, Robert B. Ray writes that "the majority of American movies of the 1970s were remarkably similar to those of the 1930s".[21] One exception to this position can be found in Thomas Elsaesser's 1975 essay, "The Pathos of Failure: American Films in the 1970s".[22] What is remarkable about this too-little-known piece is not only its perceptive analysis of films in the historical moment, so to speak, but also the way it anticipates, in extraordinary ways, Deleuze's discussion of the crisis of the action-image.

In attempting to specify the difference of so many films of this period from their classical predecessors, Elsaesser begins by defining the primary narrative and thematic characteristic of classical cinema. He, like Deleuze, notes that those films, marked by an "implicit causality, were essentially based on a drama of intrigue and strongly accentuated plot, which managed to transform spatial and temporal sequence into consequence, a continuum of cause and effect. [. . .] Out of conflict, contradiction and contingency the narrative generated order, linearity, and articulated energy. [. . .] Contradictions were resolved and obstacles overcome by having them played out in dramatic-dynamic

PARALLAX VIEW

terms or by personal initiative: whatever the problem, one can *do* something about it."[23]

This schema, which Elsaesser dubs "the affirmative-consequential model", runs into problems by the late 1960s, and by the early 1970s, its inversion is underway. Instead of sure, active characters, we get characters who are motiveless or have their motives taken from them and revealed as folly; further, the presentation of the plots in which these characters find themselves "neutral-ises goal-directedness and warns one not to expect an affirmation of purposes and meanings".[24] The result is films that, when considered within the history of mainstream or dominant cinema, reveal a certain "experimental" quality.[25] Like Deleuze, Elsaesser links the tone and mood of these films to the cultural crisis of the period. Directors of this era, he writes "opt for a kind of realism of sentiment that tries to be faithful to the negative experiences of [then] recent American history, and the movies reflect the moral and emotional gestures of a defeated generation",[26] foregrounding as they do "the pathos of failure".[27]

The fragmented, often oblique style of these films – which Elsaesser sees as symptoms of a "fading confidence in being able to tell a story"[28] can be linked to trauma in an important way. In "The Modernist Event", Hayden White ar-gues that certain of this century's key events – the Holocaust, the Kennedy as-sassination, the Vietnam experience – are traumatic occurrences that outstrip the representational capacities of classical or 'realist' historiographic practice.[29] Those events "bear little similarity to what earlier historians took as their ob-jects of study and do not, therefore, lend themselves to understanding by the commonsensical techniques utilised in conventional historiographic inquiry nor even to the representation by the techniques of writing typically favoured by [...] traditional humanistic historiography."[30] Such events mark the limits and the beyond of the realist discourse that relies on continuity, cause-and-effect, and agency to emplot the events of history. Instead, White argues, such traumatic historical events demand a modernist style of representation, for the formal strategies of fragmentation, discontinuity, chance, and incoherence that are common to modernism are also the characteristics that mark one's experi-ence of a traumatic event. The filmmakers of the post-traumatic cycle seem to have intuited this necessity, for although on the one hand their films reside well within the limits of a realist storytelling practice, on the other hand, they employ modernist formal devices to show that realist practice as strained to the breaking point in even its most sincere attempts to contain the stories of trauma that they offer.

The tragedy of the protagonists of the post-traumatic cycle is, again, that they fail to see this state of affairs that everyone else seems to ignore or already take for granted. Repeatedly, the protagonists are warned that their actions are determined by an archaic set of codes, and that continuing will be fruitless. When, in The Parallax View, conspiracy theorist Joe Frady assures the cam-paign manager of a recently assassinated politician that he "knows the story", the man rebukes him, "Fella, you don't know what this story means". A simi-lar warning is given to Jake Gittes in Chinatown: "You may think you know what you're dealing with," Noah Cross tells the private detective, "but believe me, you don't." What the protagonist does not see is that the power of the perpetrator is so great that he alone has the ability to determine what counts as reality, and he can easily discredit any implicating evidence the protagonist might offer.[31] Inevitably, the protagonists ignore the warnings, and their stubborn insistence leads them to that horrible moment when they are faced with the tragic results of their own actions. Refusing as they do to return their characters to the state of quiescence with which they began, the films of the post-traumatic cycle instead leave their characters trapped between perception and action in what Deleuze also called "the centre of indetermination".[32]

A Series of Cycles

To more fully define the characteristics of the films of the post-traumatic cycle, it is helpful to see them in relation to the cycles of films that cluster around them. Various scholars have discussed Hollywood films of this period as being marked by broad 'right' and 'left' cycles that reflect the ideological polarisation that existed in culture at large. Following the counter-culture films of the late 1960s, the post-traumatic cycle clearly stands as the second movement of a key group of left-oriented films.[33]

On the right, both the Nostalgia & Disaster cycles sought to offer the ideological reassurance typical of classical Hollywood by featuring films that were either literally or figuratively set before the period of crisis. AMERICAN GRAFFITI, a film that provoked an extraordinary wave of 1950s nostalgia in the U.S., is set during the earliest days of America's involvement in Vietnam, but it makes no mention of that conflict, save for a cameo at the film's end explaining that one of its protagonists later perished there. Perhaps more than any other in the movie, that closing moment underscores the film's longing for a supposedly simpler time, one associated not only with adolescence, but also one whose future would be bright and fulfilling rather than needlessly wasted. Other nostalgia films offered reassurance by evoking not a historical past so much as a movie past. For example, at a time when films like THE WILD BUNCH and BUTCH CASSIDY were interrogating that most cherished of American myths, the story of the old west, TRUE GRIT offered cinema's most recognised and respected cowboy, John Wayne, in his most famous recurring role: as a lawman looking out for respectable folks (Kim Darby as a girl hunting her father's killer) and punishing society's disrespectful, disruptive element (among others, Dennis Hopper, who had starred in and directed EASY RIDER that same year). In films like THE TOWERING INFERNO, the Disaster cycle also acknowledged society's disruptive element, but did so indirectly, displacing it onto nature; further, those films functioned as a sort of reassuring public service announcements, for they suggested that the crisis was still to come and that, if we worked together and prepared, it could all be managed or even averted.[34]

The Fascist Cop films were those right cycle films that most explicitly staged the ideological conflict in American culture at the time. Like the left cycle films of this period, DEATH WISH and DIRTY HARRY diagnosed American society as diseased and corrupt, but saw radical liberalism as the problem. What is foregrounded in these films is not a system that is controlled capriciously by a powerful, privileged few, but one that is undone by the legal restrictions placed on law enforcement to protect society, thus rendering the police impotent and the criminals empowered. As the inverse of the counterculture cycle of films, the Fascist Cop movies, too, suggest that the only position of agency available is one outside of existing institutions; but they further show that any such actions are limited in time and scope, for they lack the societal support that would allow them to be extended and to have lasting impact. These films can also be read as Vietnam allegories, for they portray the political right's exasperation at a military involvement marked at every turn by rules and regulations of engagement which implicitly restrict the possibility of success.

The exceptional quality of the films of the post-traumatic cycle becomes even clearer when they are contrasted with the two major film cycles which follow: the Vietnam and Blockbuster cycles. If the post-traumatic cycle replays the loss of confidence in American culture and values precipitated by our involvement in Vietnam, then the Vietnam and Blockbuster cycles represent a rebuilding, in very different ways, of this lost confidence. Around 1978, the first films to explicitly address the subject of Vietnam began to appear. In films such as THE DEER HUNTER and COMING HOME, Hollywood began to directly explore the experience of the Vietnam soldier, both in combat and upon his difficult re-entry into American life and culture. While the post-traumatic films can be said to be a replaying or recollection of the process *leading to* the traumatic event, these films represent a more obvious *working through* of the Vietnam trauma. Also, while the post-traumatic films end at the point of trauma, many of the Vietnam films dramatise and attempt to formally represent the symptoms that result from such a trauma: flashbacks, sleeplessness, feelings of guilt, hyper-alertness and hyper-vigilance, memory and concentration problems, and so on.[35]

Around this same time, a group of blockbuster films began to emerge that represented a denial of the trauma the nation had suffered. In fact, these films are in many ways a direct inversion of the post-traumatic films. Rather than heroes who are competent and confident, blockbuster films such as ROCKY and STAR WARS feature protagonists who are, at the outset, ambitious but uncertain of their abilities; but as the film goes on and they are challenged, they learn that they are indeed competent and able to effect some positive change – that is, to take some decisive, productive *action* in response to what they perceive. The film which is the most obvious turning point into this trend is JAWS, a movie which is one of the versions of what Robert Torry calls "therapeutic narrative": an attempt to "diagnose and propose a remedy for the national trauma of the Vietnam era". [36] JAWS begins like a post-traumatic film, featuring a protagonist who is, though morally strong, naive with regard to the forces that would seek to control him and determine his actions. When the waters off the small Long Island resort town of Amity are set on by a killer shark, the first instincts of its Sheriff Brody are to protect his citizenry by closing the beaches until the shark is caught. But the mayor and the town council, representing the business interests of the town who are concerned about losing crucial summertime revenue, thwart Brody's honourable efforts at every turn. Ultimately, however, the blockbuster mentality takes over: the deaths continue, the townspeople rebel, and the once sea-fearing sheriff is able to gather his wits and defeat the menace.

As Andrew Britton notes, following the pessimism of the post-traumatic cycle as it does, "JAWS might best be described, perhaps, as a rite – a communal exorcism, a ceremony for the restoration of ideological confidence". [37] This move is part of a larger movement in the history of Hollywood cinema that Britton has dubbed "Reaganite entertainment" – a reactionary, conservative cycle of films whose primary functions are repression and reassurance. [38] Further, the films of the blockbuster cycle return to the dominant formal style of Hollywood, underscoring all-important narrative components via lighting, camera placement, sound, and editing. These movies present a Manichean world in which good and evil, dangers and safety are always clear, and whatever moral or ethical ambiguities exist are ultimately sorted out.

Though the blockbuster mentality came to dominate Hollywood filmmaking in the late 1970s and beyond, the post-traumatic cycle enjoyed a brief, if commercially disastrous, reprise in the early 1980s. BLOW OUT and WINTER KILLS, for example, replay some of the post-traumatic cycle's primary themes, but it is Michael Cimino's HEAVEN'S GATE that stands most obviously as the cycle's coda. It seems likely that much of the negative press that greeted HEAVEN'S GATE on its release was due, in part, to the fact that the film revisited themes that many viewers and critics simply no longer wanted to face. The blockbuster cycle was well underway, and there was every initial indication that Cimino's film would participate in the cultural rebuilding of American ideological confidence. First of all, Cimino had already directed the most honoured of the Vietnam films, THE DEER HUNTER, and HEAVEN'S GATE's reclaiming of the Western, a genre crucial to the American cinematic mythos but for some time in disrepute, seemed to signal that Cimino's film would be a re-building of lost confidence. Further, although THE DEER HUNTER possessed some of the characteristics of the post-traumatic cycle, its ending, in which a group of surviving Vietnam veterans and their loved ones sit around a table at their local bar and sing a fragile, tear-stained version of "God Bless America", was ambiguous enough (controversially so) to provide its audience with a measure of reassurance.

But it is hard to imagine a less reassuring Hollywood film than HEAVEN'S GATE. Indeed, the story replays the pessimistic theme of the darkest films of the post-traumatic cycle. Set in Johnson County, Wyoming, in the late 1800s, where starving immigrants are forced to steal cattle in order to feed their fami-lies, HEAVEN'S GATE focuses on the efforts of the local marshall, Jim Averill (Kris Kristofferson), to protect these settlers from the cattle baron Canton (Sam Waterston), who, with the approval of the state government, has drawn up a 'death list' bearing the names of suspected rustlers whom his bounty hunters will kill. Averill's efforts are, of course, unsuccessful, not only because the gov-ernment was so thoroughly sided with the interests of big business, but also because of the failure of the members of the threatened community to come to-gether to protect themselves. Instead, they mimic the forces threatening them and concern themselves primarily with individual, rather than collective, self-interest.

In an eloquent and convincing defence of the film, Robin Wood writes that, like the earlier films of the post-traumatic cycle, "HEAVEN'S GATE is an epic about failure and catastrophe. [. . .] It shows the destruction of a possible alter-native America (one located in the historic past, but bearing in its values strik-ing resemblance to the radical movement of the 1960s and 1970s)."[39] Further, Wood notes that the hostile reaction to the film took two forms: "the objection was that the narrative was so muddled that it verged on the incomprehensible, and a vague, troubled murmur about Marxist content (liberal anxiety being by no means aroused exclusively by the right wing)".[40] These are, indeed, two of the key characteristics of the films of the post-traumatic cycle: complex narra-tive/representational strategies and a thematic discontent with the dominant order that could best be described as leftist. Further, the film has the standard post-traumatic ending: for the epilogue, the film moves forward some twenty years to a scene in which the wealthy, ageing protagonist – the former Wyo-ming lawman – sits aboard his yacht. He is distant, disengaged, morose, lost in a haze – still trapped between perception and action, still traumatised by his inability to act.

Notes

1. Leo Lerman, "Pauline Kael Talks About Violence, Sex, Eroticism and Women & Men in the Movies." *Conversations with Pauline Kael*, ed. Will Brantley (Jackson: University Press of Mississippi, 1996), 36. For a discussion of the curious absence of Vietnam films during the years of the war, see Julian Smith, *Looking Away: Hollywood and Vietnam* (New York: Scribner's, 1975), and Gilbert Adair, *Hollywood's Vietnam* (London: Heinemann, 1989).

2. Gilles Deleuze, *Cinema 1: The Movement-Image*, trans. Hugh Tomlinson and Barbara Habberjam (Minneapolis: University of Minnesota Press, 1986); *Cinema 2: The Time-Image*, trans. Hugh Tomlinson and Barbara Habberjam (Minneapolis: University of Minnesota Press, 1989).

3. Gilles Deleuze, "On The Movement-Image." *Negotiations 1972-1990* trans. Martin Youghin (New York: Columbia University Press, 1995), 59.

4. David Bordwell, "The Art Cinemas as a Mode of Film Practice," *Film Criticism* Vol. IV, No. 1 (1979).

5. Ibid., 58-59.

6. Ibid., 59-60.

7. Deleuze, *Cinema 2*, 1.

8. Ibid., 2.

9. Deleuze acknowledges that the crisis "depended on many factors, ... some of which were social, economic, political, moral and others more internal to art, to literature, and to the cinema in particular. We might mention, in no particular order," he writes, "the unsteadiness of the American Dream in all its aspects, the new consciousness of minorities, the rise and inflation of images both in the external world and in people's minds, the influence on the cinema of the new modes of narrative with which literature had experimented, the crisis of Hollywood and its old genres...". 206.

10. Robin Wood, *Hollywood from Vietnam to Reagan* (New York: Columbia University Press, 1986), 23.

11. David Thomson, "The Decade When Movies Mattered." *Movieline* (August 1993, 42-47, 80), 45, in this volume.

12. Ibid., 31.

13. Gilles Deleuze, *Cinema 2*, 3.

14. Gilles Deleuze, *Cinema 1*, 66.

15. A fine general study of trauma is to be found in Judith Lewis Herman, *Trauma and Recovery* (New York: Basic Books, 1992). Studies focused more specifically on trauma and the Vietnam war include William E. Kelly, Ed., *Post-Traumatic Stress Disorder and the War Veteran Patient* (New York: Brunner/Mazel Publishers, 1985), and Richard A. Kulka, et al., *Trauma and the Vietnam War Generation* (New York: Brunner/Mazel Publishers, 1990).

16. Robert B. Ray, *A Certain Tendency of the Hollywood Cinema, 1930-1980* (Princeton: Princeton University Press, 1985).

17. Andrew Britton, "Sideshows: Hollywood in Vietnam." *Movie* 27/28, 2-23.

18. Robert B. Ray, *A Certain Tendency*, 58-59.

19. Judith Lewis Herman, *Trauma and Recovery*, 1.
20. Bordwell, David, and Kristin Thompson and Janet Staiger, *Classical Hollywood Cinema: Film Style and Mode of Production* (New York: Columbia University Press, 1985).
21. Ray, 68.
22. Thomas Elsaesser, "The Pathos of Failure: American Films in the 70s," *Monogram* 6 (October 1975), 13-19 in this volume.
23. Ibid., 13-14.
24. Ibid., 14.
25. Ibid., 13.
26. Ibid., 17.
27. Ibid., 18.
28. Ibid., 13.
29. Hayden White, "The Modernist Event," in *The Persistence of History*, ed. Vivian Sobchack (New York: Routledge, 1996).
30. Ibid., 21.
31. See Judith Lewis Herman, *Trauma and Recovery*, 8.
32. Gilles Deleuze, *Cinema 1*, 65.
33. Ray, *A Certain Tendency*.
34. An excellent discussion of the Disaster Film cycle can be found in Nick Roddick, "Only the Stars Survive: Disaster Movies in the Seventies," in *Performance and Politics in Popular Drama*, ed. David Brandby, Louis James, and Bernard Sharratt (New York: Cambridge University Press, 1980).
35. For a more detailed description of the most common symptoms of PTSD, see Richard A. Kulka, *Trauma and the Vietnam War Generation*, 31-32.
36. Robert Torry, "Therapeutic Narrative: The Wild Bunch, Jaws, and Vietnam," *The Velvet Light Trap* 31 (Spring 1993, 27-38), 27.
37. Andrew Britton, "Jaws." *Movie* 23 (27-32), 27.
38. Andrew Britton, "Blissing Out: The Politics of Reaganite Entertainment." *Movie* 31/32, 1-42.
39. Robin Wood, *Hollywood from Vietnam to Reagan*, 316.
40. Ibid., 299-300.

Grim Fascination

FINGERS, James Toback, and 1970s American Cinema

Adrian Martin

> During FINGERS' ninety minutes, [Keitel] rapes two women (one, pointedly, only
> after insisting she remove her diaphragm), terrorises two others, observes two
> women's heads being smacked together by another man (and feels humiliated by
> this performance because he's not man enough to have engaged in such behav-
> iour!), endures further 'humiliation' as his prostate is examined by a doctor, and
> prematurely ejaculates several times. And he's the film's hero!
> Ken Eisen, "The Young Misogynists of American Cinema"[1]

Last Chant for a Slow Dance

A room, a piano, a man. The camera dollies in. Expansive construction of a
sonic space: the fugue from J. S. Bach's *E Minor Toccata* flows, performed by
Jimmy Angelelli (Harvey Keitel), ostentatiously expressive at the piano in the
manner of Glenn Gould. This is a picture of Jimmy's interior world. But there is
also an exterior world, which exists only insofar as it is framed by a window
and made neatly available to the man's gaze. Hence the second phase of this
opening scene: having finished the piece, Jimmy rests, rises, looks out the window; the camera lifts with him. As if willed by his gaze or seduced by his music, a woman – Carol (Tisa Farrow) – stands outside. A shot/reverse-shot vol-
ley ensues, with Jimmy's second POV shot slowly zooming in on her as she
turns away. A jump cut hurls us headlong into Jimmy's breathless pursuit of
the object of his desire. He has been drawn out into the larger world. A moment's confusion shows Jimmy looking this way and that. At last spying
Carol, Jimmy's sound output renews itself – he switches on a large portable
tape recorder blaring out "Summertime, Summertime" by The Jamies – and
expands to fill both the exterior environment and the film's soundtrack. A
dolly shot stands in for his forward moving POV, bearing down on Carol.

In its opening moments FINGERS (1978), the debut feature written and directed by James Toback, lays its cards on the table in a strange and disquieting

manner. It is a perfectly classical premise, for cinema and cinema theory alike: a steely artist-hero in control of space, action, sound and the look. Yet there's a neurotic quality to the film's exposition: too rushed, abstracted, diagrammatic, non-psychological. None of the usual filling-out is happening; it's as if we are already in the register – unannounced – of fantasy and hallucination. Toback is wise to the abrupt chilliness of the fantasy scenarios he likes to depict: "It's almost as though one gears the enactment of desire, if and when the opportunity comes, to recapitulate as precisely as possible what the fantasy was (...) [to see] it from the outside while in the midst of it."[2] The result is less a passive, complicit reflection of social codes of masculinity than a strained and tense will-to-masculinity. Not a hero, but the difficult, pained effort to conjure one.

What is so far implicit in the inauguration of FINGERS soon becomes completely explicit. As the film continues on the street, Carol turns and Jimmy jumps back slightly, already losing face and control. And this is only the beginning of his long, slow fall. If Jimmy incarnates the painful dissolution of the "whole sensory-motor continuity" which forms, for Gilles Deleuze, the "essential nature of the action-image",[3] Toback's film reveals that this break-up relates above all to the wavering tenability of a functional male hero.

In this regard, as Deleuze suggests, Alfred Hitchcock may have sown the seed of destruction in the very cinematic system which he perfected. By insisting on a structure of character vision – a long, lingering series of looks – inside the chain of exterior actions which constitute a plot, Hitchcock introduced an increasingly reflective pause or gap. This vision slows down and absorbs the action, placing it at a contemplative distance, rendering it ghostly and intangible, cutting it to the measure of a frustrated desire. What we arrive at, especially in VERTIGO (1958) – to nuance what Laura Mulvey first made of Hitchcock's look in her seminal 1970s essay "Visual Pleasure and Narrative Cinema"[4] – is not the apogee of masculine power, possession, privilege and penetration, but one of the first historic signs of its paralysis.

Hitchcock ushered in a realm of cinematic fiction centred on obsession, rather than action, and the 1970s was the era in which this temptation truly took grip. Recall all those tales of the period about guys relentlessly pursuing some dream-ideal – a woman first conjured through a tantalising photograph, a fleeting glimpse, a tempestuous hallucination, an unrequited memory, even the figure of a mannequin in a shop window – in films including AMERICAN GRAFFITI (George Lucas, 1973), 10 (Blake Edwards, 1979), BAD TIMING (Nicolas Roeg, 1980) and OBSESSION (Brian De Palma, 1976). This is a model of obsession with a total and often savage inward turn.[5] Obsession is all-consuming for these troubled heroes, and also all-encompassing in that it tends to shrink the entire world down to the co-ordinates of the obsessive scenario. But, unlike the unfussy apartments shared by mutually obsessed lovers in films of the LAST

Harvey Keitel in FINGERS

TANGO IN PARIS (1973) ilk, with their creation of a "world apart", the solitary
world of an obsessive man is mobile – a pure projection along his lines of sight
and movement. It is the world he observes, explores, carves out, brings into being through his Schopenhauerean will.[6]

Such is the *mise-en-scène* of the obsessive pursuit: its pleasures for the protagonist and the audience are in those processes prior to action – the stealthy
watching, planning, staging (as in Scorsese's TAXI DRIVER, 1976) – and sometimes afterwards, in its endless replaying in memory or on some audiovisual
screen. The obsessed hero is consumed by the vocation of 'show-making' (to
use Dennis Giles's suggestive term from another classic 1970s text),[7] anticipating and preparing the final, delicious outcome of his pursuit. He transforms
his life into a kind of theatre.

It is a special legacy of the 1970s that, today, obsession is rarely glorified in
movies of any persuasion. Even supposedly pure, sublime, romantic obsession tends to look creepy these days, as in Paul Schrader's FOREVER MINE
(2000). Desire, separate from the action of its fulfillment, often registers as a
form of disease. Hitchcock's decisive move, within the matrix of popular genres, was to take the figure of the disabled, reflective, melancholic male hero
from the 'women's weepie' (like PORTRAIT OF JENNIE, 1948) where he had been
safely cordoned, and place him at the heart of action plots in the 1950s; the
crisis of the action-image reverberates from there. Action becomes less and less
possible as obsession moves in. The lost, burnt-out heroes of the 1970s – like
James Taylor in Monte Hellman's TWO-LANE BLACKTOP (1971) or Gene Hackman in Arthur Penn's NIGHT MOVES (1975) – mutate, in the 1980s and beyond,
into various types: the frenzied investigators who lose their way and their self
in 'hysterical texts' such as CRUISING (William Friedkin, 1980); the tragic,
Faulknerian figures twisting in a labyrinth of deceptive memories, like Robert
De Niro in ONCE UPON A TIME IN AMERICA (Sergio Leone, 1984); and the
Scorsesean heroes who grab and lose the whole world in an inevitable, crashing arc (GOODFELLAS [1990], CASINO [1996]).

Already, by the end of the 1970s, there is a spectacle of masculine failure in
which both hero and film wallow; the severest and most radical expression of
this comes from the experimental sector, Jon Jost's micro-budget feature LAST
CHANTS FOR A SLOW DANCE (1977) inspired by the Gary Gilmore case and inaugurating a bleak trilogy of movies featuring actor Tom Blair in which atro-
cious violence is steadily turned away from the Other and in on the family
(SURE FIRE, 1990) and eventually the self (THE BED YOU SLEEP IN, 1993). Those
American heroes in this 1970s vein are paranoiacally consumed to the point of
losing their career and their family (Scorsese's RAGING BULL, 1980); or so
dreamily stupid that everyone else takes them for a ride (De Palma's BODY
DOUBLE [1984]). If obsession signifies an immersion in a pleasure or fantasy
principle then, at another moment or level of the film, a reality principle comes
in hard for the kill (comically so in 10). Obsessive pursuit becomes something
dogged, haunted; the inward turn no longer signals a crowning moment of
selfhood but a dead end.[8] Fifteen years on from RAGING BULL, Todd Haynes (a

keen scholar of 1970s cinema) will, in SAFE (1995), at once offer the final laurel on this tomb of the self and democratise its traditional gendering by portraying a cosmically allergic woman (Julianne Moore) whose pursuit of the phantom of her own health and well-being renders her rather less than human.

Crude but Fascinating

James Toback is eerily sensitive to this new mood as it emerges in 1970s American cinema. A Jewish New Yorker and Harvard literary graduate, he began writing in 1966 for publications including *Commentary*, *Dissent*, *Esquire*, *Harper's* and *The Village Voice*; his first piece was titled "Norman Mailer Today". Later, he contributed a chapter to a sociological anthology titled *Violence: Causes and Solutions*, celebrating the controversial emergence of such milestones as BONNIE AND CLYDE (Penn, 1967) and John Boorman's POINT BLANK (1967), coining an aesthetical-ethical catchphrase reminiscent of *Cahiers du cinéma* in its auteurist 1950s: "style as morality".[9] His next step was to immerse himself in the participatory New Journalism of the period, moving in with the black sports star Jim Brown (eventually cast prominently in FINGERS) in order to write a "self-centred memoir" titled JIM (1971) which records how he and his subject "got to the bottom of all sexual possibilities".[10] Putting all that together, it is easy to see how, still today, Toback is routinely reduced to the stereotype of the libertarian "white Negro".[11]

Toback's first important work in cinema was the script for THE GAMBLER (1974), an unjustly overlooked film that is more notable in retrospect than it seemed to commentators at the time. Its unique collision of topics, drawing from many genres but following the template of no single genre – criminality, sexuality, sport, gambling, family melodrama, high culture – sets the distinctive pattern for all future Toback projects, including the documentary 'happening' THE BIG BANG (1990). The fledgling auteur, in and around THE GAMBLER, was already talking up his big, existential themes: loss of control, uncertainty of self, reckless risk, erotic ecstasy, magnificent obsession, the continuum of the artist and the gangster ("Acting imitates crime; encourages it, deplores it, glorifies it, rechannels it – is obsessed by it"[12]), and defiance of the mainstream system (in the 1990s, he called studio executives "pathetic, dull, cowardly, hypocritical, vapid presences ... I don't just mean artistically, I mean financially pathetic, too"[13]). Even the briefest glimpse into the Toback mosaic of scripts, films, writings and interviews uncovers patent psycho-autobiographical echoes from one text to another: for instance, a line uttered by Jimmy's father, Ben (Michael V. Gazzo), echoes the words of Chaim Weizmann which Toback encountered through his grandfather: "If you will it, you will have it."[14]

Karel Reisz's direction of THE GAMBLER makes for an instructive benchmark against which to measure Toback's own subsequent style. Resembling the method of Sidney Lumet at his best and anticipating Paul Thomas Anderson's HARD EIGHT (1997), Reisz blends neo-classical precision-control with the legacy of the Nouvelle Vague: each scene presents itself as a block of finely observed and performed detail (James Caan at the gambling table, for instance). Only a long way down the chain of scenes are we able to piece together all the pertinent character relations and retroactively see the narrative set-ups so casually planted within the flow of gesture and atmosphere. Toback astutely noted Reisz's "extremely successful creation of tightness, tension, movement, and dramatic force" within a stylistic framework that, at the same time, is characterised by "a kind of leisurely and graceful fluidity".[15]

But Toback himself, as a director, is not 'into' control. There is a phenomenon of semantic contamination in his work – a restless contagion of metaphors and associations that is closer to the irrepressible zaniness of Larry Cohen (THE PRIVATE FILES OF J. EDGAR HOOVER, 1977) than either the opportunistic conceits of Mike Figgis (LIEBESTRAUM, 1991) or the baroque edifices of Richard Rush (THE STUNT MAN, 1980). It begins with the title: FINGERS evokes all at once Jimmy's activity and his passivity, the criminal role he plays for his father, music and sex, and an especially memorable medical examination. Toback is eloquent on this manner of working: "I like movies that speed by, that one has to grab at with the eye and the mind, and that are scene-for-scene and shot-for-shot gone as soon as you do grab them (...) there is a point [in the editing process] when you just realise that you're in the rapids, and the most you can do is kind of guide it around rocks."[16] Toback takes as a personal motto the words of Jean Cocteau that François Truffaut cited in praise of FINGERS: "Whatever isn't raw is merely decorative."[17] Even those critics temperamentally ill at ease with the cinema of John Cassavetes (or later the Dogme movement) found something gripping in Toback's initial display of rawness: Leonard Maltin, for example, rates FINGERS highly as a "crude but fascinating melodrama".[18] And the reference to melodrama is apt: "What I really like to do is stretch things to their limit of credibility, and then really get into those extreme situations which reveal the core."[19]

Toback's films present themselves as messy and impulsive – even more so lately, in TWO GIRLS AND A GUY (1998) and BLACK AND WHITE (2000), which place enormous faith in the psychodramatic improvisations of their game casts. His work, taken as a whole, is undoubtedly less skilful, less artful than that of Scorsese, and less dynamic and inventive on a fine-grain level than that of Abel Ferrara – to name his closest, contemporary neighbours in the American chapter of the cinema of obsession and madness. Toback is better at the broad strokes of a scene – concept, casting, location, musical accompaniment – than its shot-to-shot sculpting.

But what makes Toback a figure of central significance is that his work is compelling and confounding in equal measure. It is hard to determine where his films stand on the many, hot issues (of gender, race, power, identity ...) that they so vividly raise and dramatise. Like Ferrara or Larry Clark (who emerges as a major American filmmaker in the mid 1990s), Toback seeks a mode of heightened, tabloid reportage (the Sam Fuller heritage) that is also, without self-censorship, a projection of the artist's murkiest and most disquieting phantasms. Such work – profoundly ambiguous in its meaning and generative of equally profound ambivalence in its spectators – poses a big challenge to any critical tradition which aims to draw a clean line between films that are progressive and those that are reactionary, or between those which explore the contradictions of their content and those which merely reflect such problems symptomatically (an example of such a model is Robin Wood's distinction between coherent and incoherent texts).[20] Merely labelling the outrageous and troublesome elements of Toback's cinema 'problematic' – for the past two decades the favourite word of disapproval in cultural studies – is a sorry cop-out.

Toback belongs to a critically undervalued 'cinema of sensation'. A sometimes queasy sense of amorality is the honour-badge of this cinema: the most extreme situations are to be gazed upon, by filmmaker and spectator alike, not only with curiosity but also active fascination.[21] The only distance from ideological givens is arrived at through excess, through immersion, through a laying bare or overexposure that is at once lucid and savage. To truly enter into the spirit and peculiar complexity of movies like FINGERS, Ferrara's THE BLACKOUT (1997) or Clark's BULLY (2001), one must be prepared to surrender to their sticky embrace.

Is the ultimate fault-line in the discussion of these films the value we place on *despair*? Since the dawn of the 1970s, much independently minded American cinema, from Hellman to Haynes and David Lynch via LAST EXIT TO BROOKLYN (Uli Edel, 1989) and most of Altman's oeuvre, has generated its most intense powers from nihilism and fatalism, the overwhelming sense that everything is doomed to end badly or tragically. Some critical schools judge this tendency harshly as defeatism or, worse, quiescence to the status quo. Of course, American breast-beating over a vague, amorphous malaise is too often merely facile (as in P. T. Anderson, or Sam Mendes' AMERICAN BEAUTY [1999]). But there is, paradoxically, something bracing and vital about works in which, as Ross Gibson said of Lynch's BLUE VELVET (1986) and Paul Morrissey's MIXED BLOOD (1984), "[v]alues exist as sentimental residues, as vestiges of a society in moral twilight, or as clay pigeons to be blasted by the films' cynical armouries".[22] It is precisely the "provocative absence of virtue" which gives these films their power as social critique, even if the exact terms of that critique are not spelt out or embodied within the fiction itself (as a classically inclined commentator would demand). The amoral cinema of sensation shifts the burden of interpretation, and of moral judgement, back onto the viewer.

Like his characters, Toback has relentlessly pursued, across two and a half decades, the realisation of deeply personal projects dreamt up near the beginning of his film career: especially THE PICK-UP ARTIST (1987), eventually watered down from its original incest-fantasy scenario, and HARVARD MAN (2002), which recreates a momentous LSD trip from his 1960s youth (and which, throughout the 1990s, was to have starred Leonardo DiCaprio). Like his characters, Toback has regularly been accompanied – and sometimes usurped – by more powerful players in the industry, ego ideals who are masters of aesthetic control and/or Hollywood spin: Reisz, Warren Beatty, Barry Levinson, big men who either get to direct Toback's scripts (as in the case of Levinson's fine film of BUGSY [1991]) or rework his early contributions to their own projects (as with Levinson's JIMMY HOLLYWOOD [1994] and Beatty's BULWORTH [1998]).

And, once more like his characters, Toback is not only driven but haunted – spooked by the artistic and critical (if not commercial) success of FINGERS, which Dusan Makavajev warned him he would probably never again equal. That prophecy has, so far, proved substantially correct, with even such faithful champions as David Thomson driven to point out the fact: every Toback film is intriguing on one plane or another, but FINGERS remains his only masterpiece to date. That is partly a happy accident arising from a volatile combination of elements – including Keitel at his most comprehensively inventive as an actor, Matthew Chapman's hard-edge cinematography and a certain, bracing minimalism in Robert Lawrence's editing that may well have come from Toback's first-timer unfamiliarity with extensive scene coverage coupled with budget restrictions and a tight shoot – but it is also surely a matter of historic context.

Toback finds himself today hailed by the likes of the popular *Movieline* magazine as someone "whose roots go back to the most extraordinary stint of originality-tolerance that modern Hollywood's seen", making films that prove that "the 1970s weren't for nothing"[23] – partly because of his ongoing association with Robert Downey Jr., who has his own family tie to those glory days via his father, Robert Downey (director of PUTNEY SWOPE, 1969). But this is a relatively recent accolade, a veritable re-invention of the public persona. During the 1980s Toback slipped into semi-obscurity as he tried uneasily to negotiate trends like the teen movie (in THE PICK-UP ARTIST) and international co-production (EXPOSED, 1983). In the 1990s he scratched out a sideline between script commissions as an acerbic, roving commentator, becoming better known (and sometimes derided) for his appearances in the pages of *Interview* or on the TV series *E! Hollywood True Stories* – not to mention the infamous exposé performed on his private life in *Spy* – than for his film work. But, simultaneously, the booming script-advice industry, with its how-to manuals, professional journals and world-wide events of the 1990s, has helped reboot Toback's serious reputation – as has happened for many longstanding writer-directors who began their careers in the 1960s and 1970s, like Robert Towne of CHINATOWN (1974) fame. These days, Toback is as likely to be called upon for battle stories from an 'indie' prehistory or hip wisdom into present trends by *Scenario* magazine as by UK's *Projections* annual or *Positif*.[24]

FINGERS, of course, arrived almost too late to ride on the coat-tails of the now rather mythic and overly romanticised Altman-Coppola-Bodganovich 1970s parade of free cinema. JAWS (1975) and STAR WARS (1977) had already re-oriented the production landscape decisively and irrevocably towards the blockbuster era that has dominated the market ever since. It was no longer possible, in 1978, for Toback's maverick vision to be the beneficiary of any off-studio privileges; his film was eccentrically financed (via Fabergé impresario George Barrie), poorly distributed, and subject to slight censorship problems in many countries to which it travelled (for its spectacular castration and re-venge-murder scene). In the press, its initial reception was mixed. Thomson followed Pauline Kael in giving it high-profile critical support – although the latter's enthusiasm for Toback's "true moviemaking fever" was balanced against her sense that "because he doesn't censor his masculine racial fantasies, his foolishness and his terrible ideas pour out freely";[25] and *Film Comment* gave it decent space – tellingly, not as a stand-alone event, but within a dossier on screen acting.[26]

However, a wave of commentators with different ideological priorities and new theoretical agendas, in *Cineaste*, *Jump Cut* and elsewhere, were all set to denounce what they (rather too hastily, in my view) judged as the passé, macho-countercultural posturings of Toback and several of his contemporaries, including Schrader and De Palma, pegged as relics of the dead, deluded 1960s. Ken Eisen, for example, waxed polemical: "With Toback, as with his fellow misogynists, there's never any question of ambiguity or possibility of criticism entailed in their narratives."[27] LOVE AND MONEY (1980, released 1982), Toback's subsequent and weakest film, did nothing to maintain any career momentum. It is not exactly surprising that when, in the mid 1980s, we reach the sophisticated political and aesthetic critiques of Wood in *Hollywood from Vietnam to Reagan* and his colleagues at *Cineaction* and *Movie*, Toback is entirely overlooked as a figure bearing any radical or populist-progressive potential.[28]

If FINGERS can strike us today as a final, defiant gasp of the 'grand exception' of American cinema in the 1970s, that is doubtless because it gathers so many elements, themes and tropes from the better-respected classics of the decade: Coppola's interpenetration of gangsterism and family life; the Pyrrhic victories in Schrader's revenge-quest tales; Penn's sense of a modern hero lost in a labyrinth; Bob Rafelson's men split between high culture and nomadism. Scorsese's MEAN STREETS (1973) must have been a particularly significant event for Toback, since he borrows from it Keitel as the iconic, divided Italo-American, the grinding clash of social cultivation and streetwise experience, and the insistently ironic use of popular music in stark contradiction to the actions it accompanies. But, at the same time, FINGERS separates itself from this illustrious company and announces a new tone for a different, coming era.

Like TWO-LANE BLACKTOP at the beginning of the decade, FINGERS at its end is a severe film which does not trade in the slightest vestige of sentimental rhetoric, in the way that the works of Coppola, John Milius, Clint Eastwood, Michael Cimino, Oliver Stone, Scorsese or even the militantly radical Robert Kramer invariably do. It is not surprising that certain French critics of the time (notably Pascal Bonitzer in *Cahiers*) hailed Hellman's landmark film for offering a terse, astringent, almost Lacanian kind of post-humanism, untainted by romantic illusions.[29] Likewise Toback's film, by pushing so much of the 1970s cinema ethos of spontaneous transgression (ultra-violence, verbal obscenity, sexuality revealed at the heart of every character neurosis) into brutal hyperdrive, opens a door to the dizzy, analytic logics of postmodernism that would emerge in the 1980s. The modern individual as portrayed by Toback doesn't "break on through to the other side" (as The Doors sang), but beats his or her way into a hellish, asphyxiating hall of mirrors where self and other enter a fatal feedback loop – allowing, as this auteur described his formative drug experience, "the knowledge that my entire repertoire of communication – words, movements, gestures – belonged to someone else; that I didn't exist. That 'he' was playing 'me'."[30]

Now Is Forever

After its introductory sequence, FINGERS moves on to Carol and Jimmy in his car. It quickly becomes clear that Jimmy's initial performance at the piano is his only 'act' that will ever go smoothly or well. As the film extends the performance motif – into driving, sexual prowess, verbal skill, clothing, gangster stand-over tactics, and the "presentation of self in everyday life" (as sociologist Erving Goffman termed it[31]) – Jimmy's act increasingly erodes, blocks, fails. His first major moment of physical failure already compounds several performance problems. "I'm a terrific driver, this car's part of my body, it's an extension of my d ..." – and then he crashes into the back of another car.

"A whole upsurge of sensory-motor disturbances", indeed.[32] The message from the head to the body and then to its tools (a car, a gun, a piano) gets lost every time ("My hands don't work right and my mind starts interfering"). Jimmy's body-ego draws itself inward and then puffs itself up. It maintains itself through tension, nerves – reminding any 1970s buff of James Taylor's brusque rejection of a neck massage in Two-Lane Blacktop, because he prefers to have a muscle "jumping around" back there. In Fingers the male body-ego dreams it is still young and perfect, and projects this dream onto others – Ben says of his fiancée Anita (Georgette Muir) that "she's got a body that won't stop". There is a similar aura of invincibility encasing Jimmy's extended, sensory 'personal space' – which is allowed, through criminal privilege, to function oblivious to its surrounding reality, as in the restaurant scene. But such equilibrium is a delusion; meanwhile, the actual, mortal body is breaking down. This is particularly evident in Ben. He is a spectacle of pathetic masculine decay – fat, coughing, wheezing, collapsing in the street. The emission from his vocal chords – always harsh and constricted – is a true sound for the stressed-out 1970s, poised between the drone of Alpha 60 in Godard's Alphaville (1965) and the microphone-assisted emanation from the damaged throat of an old gangster in Cimino's Year of the Dragon (1985). Ben tries his best to pass off a lifetime of dissipation and excess as virile vitality; in Toback's galaxy of character types, he is the grotesque flip side of Bugsy Siegel, the archetypal gangster-star for whom glamour is a mask to be fastidiously applied and maintained, even in the midst of the most violent acts.

By contrast, simply to look at Jimmy in repose or dressed to kill or lost in the rapture of music, one would conclude that he is naturally much closer to the ideal of youthful glamour to which Bugsy aspired. But the genius of Keitel's performance lies in its embodiment of a neurotic condition of twitching extremities. Nervous energy doesn't come near describing it: the fingers which always drill rhythms; a posture which is so easily thrown off-balance by any external element, from the very first moment that Carol turns to face him; the painfully awkward sexual positions; the fragile bodily parts – especially those extremities – susceptible to sudden injury at every turn (as in the truly frightening incident in the stuck elevator when Jimmy hurts his finger on the buttons); the outbursts of violence that lurch excessively out of control (his debt collection performance; the restaurant blow-up; the final revenge against Riccamonza [Anthony Sirico]). The opening shot of an early scene is classic: Jimmy singing distractedly off-key and out of sync to The Chiffons' "One Fine

Day", while his hands mime extravagant piano arpeggios that bear no relation to the music.

FINGERS portrays a man in desperate search of his identity via the "motivating" links of cause and effect – a classical narrative identity. Jimmy is endlessly trying to force connections, to add up a trajectory which could make him a hero in control of his own story. But his life keeps falling apart – either into disconnected scenes in which he spasmodically and inconsequentially exercises his will upon the world (such as when he raves to Esther [Jane Elder] on the street); or into separate threads (his musical career, his affair with Carol, the relationships with his split parents), each of which reach a brutal impasse. A crisis in any one of these areas leads to the effort to force a compensatory link in some other area. So, his desire for Carol only seems to come in a rush in moments of desperation that originate elsewhere, such as the failed audition, rejection from his mother, Ruth (Marian Seldes), or Ben's homosexual taunts.

In FINGERS, Jimmy's interior identity is a mad makeshift comprised, in no discernible hierarchy or sequence, from bits of his familial and cultural environment. This goes beyond an Oedipal split between (as Richard Combs put it) fatherly money, aggression and violence versus motherly culture, sensitivity and virtuosity.[33] If the chief index of that split is the two associated types of music (the mother's past classical music career, Ben's Jerry Vale tape), then what complicates the binary arrangement is a cultural sign more obviously contemporary with Jimmy's formative years – the 1950s and 1960s pop music that accompanies him at all times.

The primary function of the music (which appears in ten out of the film's twenty-five sequences) is to foreground a dynamic of the moment, an eternal present, displacing any deeply rooted pathology stemming from childhood trauma. Toback's collage of found music stresses a certain, sticky sensuousness: the songs are highly affective, syrupy kitsch, pulling the situations they accompany in often incongruous directions. This might seem a standard device of narrational irony (and a rather heavy handed one at that, as when Merrilee Rush and The Turnabouts' "Angel of the Morning" accompanies Jimmy's strong-arming of Luchino [Lenny Montana], or when Vale's "Now is Forever" plays over the spectacle of Ben's corpse), but its effect is more visceral, testifying essentially to the notion that events are always flying apart (Toback: "I like, at least in one other way, pulling a scene in its opposite direction"[34]) and that the individual lives within these competing, tearingly incommensurate frames of reference. But Toback understands well that while pop music can mark a strategy of insistent disjunction for the alert spectator, it also acts as a social and ideological clue in the world of these characters (and by extrapolation, in the real world beyond it): it transforms violence into fun spectacle (as Stanley Kubrick first intuited in A CLOCKWORK ORANGE [1971]) and enhances the imaginary adoption of a "white negro" hipsterism, a fantasy in which even the most painful discombobulations can register (Mick Jagger style) as a macho funkiness.

The formal construction of the film reflects on every level this conception of forces that are out of sync and phasing strangely. Jimmy's pop music tape obeys few diegetic rules, playing continuously over ellipses and rarely altering its volume according to the norms of sound perspective ruling shot changes. Jimmy's question in one scene ("what's your name?") is answered weirdly at the end of the next scene ("Carol"). The *découpage* insistently disarticulates the diversely framed spaces in a scene, rarely allowed to 'add up' in a clear or conventional manner. The first restaurant scene is exemplary. Without an establishing shot, we first see Jimmy in a collapsed telephoto frame, entirely self-absorbed. Then, having shifted 180 degrees to film the facing spatial plane, the camera reveals at last the presence of Ben (only the edge of the tape recorder overlaps these two frames). With the next shot on Jimmy, Ben is given an off-screen line of dialogue which is an incomprehensible explosion of rasping, guttural noise. Once a clear dramaturgical line of force has been laid for a conventional shot-reverse shot dialogue exchange – with, eventually, a traditional establishing shot – this eye-line is broken up by off-frame distractions (the gay men here functioning formally like the little girl in a later park scene).

The sense of an eternal present is secured by the peculiar quality of scene transitions and their non-cumulative value. The film's hallucinatory, even nightmarish quality derives from the way in which its narrative organisation sticks close to Jimmy's apprehension of events – even as he loses grip of them. This headlong trajectory introduces key expository elements abruptly and often quite late (such as Dr Fry [Murray Moston], and Ruth), and just as disconcertingly leaves them immediately behind (Anita is never mentioned beyond the restaurant scene, and Jimmy's musicianship is abruptly dropped from proceedings once he has failed his audition). The plot also veers wildly off into pure, unstitched digressions (such as the appearance of Esther) and plants clear narrative set-ups which don't appear to pay off (does Julie [Tanya Roberts] tell Riccamonza that Jimmy had sex with her?). Jimmy's pathetic attempt to superimpose an intelligible and morally freighted time-frame on these cascading events, "What do you want to do with the baby we made last night?", is met by an indifferent "What do *you* wanna do with it?" from Carol.

The classical narrative system which (as Raymond Bellour has demonstrated)[35] builds its sense of volume through the careful repetition and development of motifs gets well and truly amputated here. There is a deliberately attenuated mimicry of this system in the cyclical return of certain situations and places, such as Jimmy at his piano (four times in all). This thread is emblematic of the gradual dissociation and emptying-out which is at the heart of the film: it moves from the initial scene of fullness and presence, to an image-and-sound trick whereby Jimmy seems to be playing but is in fact miming to a tape, to the final dissociation of elements wherein the piano music exists only on the soundtrack while Jimmy appears beyond consciousness.

A Dumb Fuck

FINGERS investigates subjective and intersubjective levels of experience. Intersubjective relations carry the weight of a reality principle in this tale; it is effectively only Jimmy who believes in, and attempts to live, a pristine ego-subjectivity – which he suffers for, and eventually loses (this is also the path for Scorsese's and Ferrara's heroes). It is in the intersubjective field that the workings of power, the dynamics of conflict and control, occur. Toback establishes an elaborate, highly systematic logic for intersubjective exchange.

Exchange implies a contract, an agreement of wills. Taking up ideas offered by Geoffrey Nowell-Smith and Thomas Elsaesser in their respective discussions of 1970s European cinema,[36] exchange can be conceptualised in two distinct forms. There is an exchange of like-for-like (as in a friendship struck up on a mirroring basis) or an exchange of two commodities that are different in kind (e.g. money for sexual favour). A third form of exchange can also be posited: a reciprocal form of personal relation beyond strict codes of barter, a give-and-take without accounting. This relation might be empathy, affection, or love. FINGERS forecloses, through its jet-black humour, even the possibility of such reciprocity. Jimmy is always conjuring moments of reciprocity (to Carol: "Don't you understand what's here, what's there between us?") and empathy ("I'm going to bring you into your dreams of yourself"). His biggest (and maddest) *faux pas* is to blurt that Carol "loves" Dreems. And the film's bitterest irony is contained in the empathetic words of musical maestro Arthur Fox (Dominic Chianese) preceding Jimmy's catastrophic audition: "I have a good feeling about today."

The simplest kind of exchange in FINGERS is brutally physical coercion, of the kind Jimmy carries out on behalf of Ben: if the client doesn't cough up money, he gets bashed, as in the pizzeria stand-over. But such coercion is the least effective and the most easily undermined form of exchange, for it inevitably invites and meets resistance. Truly binding exchange happens at an emotional-psychological level.

Jimmy falls foul of repeatedly attempted like-for-like exchanges, which are badly judged or blankly refused. He desperately seeks mirror-figures to shore up his failing self-image, and never finds one. This becomes the index of his foolishness, his desperation and his crisis. With Carol, from the word go, he keeps throwing mirror-cues (questions such as "you like all kinds of music, huh?") which he then has to pick up himself and confirm, after the pause in which she remains stonily silent ("So do I"). When Carol does speak, she flatly contradicts him (He: "You're as crazy as I am"; She: "You're not crazy, you're just scared"). A key part of the film's micro-texture is an almost screwball series of flat refusals, like after Jimmy gets out of jail: "Can I use your phone?" – "No". Jimmy's most extravagant attempt to secure a mirror identification, with a cop (Zack Norman), on the bases of race, lifestyle and culture – "We're brothers, we're twins ... you're a sensitive guy, you should be out on the street listening to Shostakovich, Gesualdo and The Drifters ... the fucking Arabs are looking to bury us, the French are looking to bury us ... we gotta take care of each other!" – lands him instantly in jail.

The dominant and most successful form of intersubjective exchange in FINGERS involves the submission of one will to another, of a Self to its Other. The basic survival law of this jungle is: dominate or let yourself be dominated. This is once again a pragmatic matter; there is no option outside the rules of this exchange-game. There are those who know their place in the game (Carol "wanted to" have sex with Jimmy, but forbids herself) or are explicitly reminded of it (Dreems to Carol: "Don't ever cross me"; Riccamonza to Julie: "I'll break your face"). And then there are suckers like Jimmy who are easily tricked, bound into an unspoken intersubjective domination.

Jimmy's parents are dominators, masters of the deadly psychological ploy of the double bind.[37] They hold out to their son the promise of a selfhood, while all the time obligating him into submission. Thus the irony of Ben's platitude to Jimmy – "If you know you can do it, you'll do it" – which encourages a Self but issues a command from an Other. (Ben offers a complicit smile and immediately adds: "It's just like collecting.") Ben consistently exploits Jimmy's need to please his Big Daddy Other in order to receive self-confirmation. He obligates his son through phrases like "I got nobody, I got you", "Ever since you were a kid, did I break my word to you? ... So you can't blame me if I expect the same from you, can you?" When Jimmy tries to halt this obligation, or fails to live up to it, Ben savagely erases his identity: "I should have strangled you in your crib." This is topped only by Ruth who doesn't even wait for a report before she rejects Jimmy – "I don't want to hear it ... Whatever it is you plan to hurt me with" – and who, in an unforgettable gesture, blots out her son's face with her hands. Like Ben, she psychologically (and literally) pulls Jimmy close and pushes him away in consecutive split seconds; her opening line is immediately followed an exhortation ("Don't I get a kiss?") and then an admonition ("You call *that* a kiss?").

Such familial double binds construct a fraught subject position for Jimmy. When he goes into a compensatory act in a sphere not overshadowed by the edict of his parents – all that's really left is the sphere of sexuality – he miscomprehends and confuses all the rules of exchange. In the toilet scene, Jimmy chats up Julie (a way to transgress Riccamonza) with a sexual come-on – "I love your ... pussy. Your silk pussy". After one of the quickest and most uncomfortable-looking sex acts in movie history, he informs her of his motivation ("Tell him I did this"). But then, in an effort to affirm *both* the indifferent exploitation *and* the sexual intimacy attached to his action, he adds: "It's nothing against you, you *are* silk" – which leaves her just hurt, exasperated and confused, because she has been made an object of exchange in two ways at once, both as a means and as an end.

There is a similarly confused psychological dynamic in the scene where Jimmy confronts Carol in her apartment. He is out of his mind at this point with frustrated desire, mixed with an increasing dread of impotence in other spheres of his life. But he doesn't force himself on her. He wins a voluntary gesture of reciprocity – "I need you to want me. If you don't want me, I just can't do anything" – which he can also take as an admission of her desire (as distinct from a simple submission to his will). But having been granted this much, he then plays macho master by ordering her to take out her diaphragm – as if to stipulate that *she* can only have sex with *him* if reproduction is a possibility.

Given Jimmy's hyper-nervous way of inhabiting his body – his trigger-edge tension, his inability to manage its bloated or damaged extremities – having sex is inevitably a nightmare. He suffers from premature ejaculation and prostate pain. But, even more crucially, the film shows sex to be a matter of exchange – and a problem for Jimmy because he doesn't ever understand this. The urological examination scene (a one-take wonder unique in the annals of American cinema) establishes this theme with characteristically risible directness. Jimmy grimly endures Dr Fry's rectal examination but obviously regards it as an aberrant homosexual violation of his manhood – he enquires in a panic as to why Fry's surgical glove extends to the elbow. This priceless dialogue follows:

Doctor:	The golden rule of urology: if you get an erection, you come; and if you don't get an erection, you walk.
Jimmy:	Yeah ... What about heroic fucks?
Doctor:	What's that?
Jimmy:	You're ready to come and you're in love and the girl needs more. She's gonna cry inside if you shoot it all out, so you do your razor blade fantasies and you hold back.

Doctor: That's not a heroic fuck, that's a dumb fuck – You're straining your prostate gland, you're congesting it. Jimmy, you gotta make up your mind. Whose penis are we talking about here, yours or hers?

The scene drolly evokes, in its own terms, Lacan's famous dictum that there is no sexual relation possible between men and women, providing a succinct statement of the story's intersubjective dilemmas. Beyond being unable to conceptualise sex only, or primarily, as a matter of penis power, Jimmy doublebinds himself twice over. Firstly, in trying to please the other in the only way he can imagine, he has to breach the limit of his own capacity, thus hurting himself. Secondly, in attempting to give his all physically, he assumes that he gets the same back emotionally; he is certain, in his own inimitably confused way, that love is at stake in all this. He has no access to the idea of a contract or a negotiation based solely in the realm of the physical. Fry, for his part, certainly has no interest in fathoming the sexual relation: he reduces both genders to the same physical model ("whose penis – yours or hers?") as a way of counselling Jimmy to simply concentrate on the bodily mechanism of his own pleasure. But Jimmy – like the central characters in Barbara Turner's remarkable scripts for GEORGIA (Ulu Grosbard, 1995) and POLLOCK (Ed Harris, 2000) – does not have a sure enough sense of Self to do anything so uncomplicated. Heroism is also at stake in this urology scene. To be a hero is – in Jimmy's terms – to possess extraordinary powers of empathy and understanding in relation to all others, and to be able to translate those mental powers into actions like the "heroic fuck". But that kind of heroism is – as the doctor says – just dumb.

There is a ghostly shimmer of like-for-like exchange in FINGERS. Logically, it can never actually take place – and never does – since proliferating difference is the principal characteristic of its postmodern world. But those who dominate can *assert* that it is taking place, and bask in the ensuing illusion of camaraderie without fear of being contradicted. This is true of Ben who, rather ludicrously, likes to see Jimmy as his mirror, and offers him the services of his tailor; it is particularly true of Dreems who, in classic jive talk, introduces Jimmy to others as his "main man". Jimmy, of course, is unable to disagree with either of these principal ego-ideals.

However, exchange can also break down. This occurs either when its terms are defied (as by Luchino), or when the difference of the Other suddenly becomes nonnegotiable. The anticipation of the Other's violence within the nervous Self results in a 'first strike' violent act which then precipitates escalating warfare. Between men, the act of marking and declaring a non-negotiable difference means casting it in an aberrant sexual form, wholly and sickeningly Other. Thus, anyone with whom an exchange cannot or will not be negotiated is immediately a "cocksucker" (Luchino's defiance: "Suck my cock ... double suck"), a "motherfucker", or a "cunt" (which is Jimmy's most extreme epithet): in other words, a faggot, a pervert, or a woman. Actual women are a different matter and pose a separate problem for these men: although they are eminently buyable, they nonetheless carry the inextinguishable aura of castrating threat, as is clear from Ben's speech (coming, significantly, just before the introduction of his fiancée Anita): "Of course your dick keeps hurting you, it's a conspiracy ... women bust your balls ... the moment they lose their virginity, they're all whores."

An expanded model of such fraught and violent exchange – covering attributions of race, status and even hygiene as well as sexuality – is hilariously sketched in the prison scene. Formally, this scene resumes most of the film's parameters and strategies: incommensurate segments of space which are not immediately established in the *découpage* (one side of the jail with Jimmy and an Italian prisoner [Tom Signorelli], the other with black prisoners [Pembrose Dean and Arthur French]); a verbal monologue (the joke) which never reaches its end-point; Jimmy's complete obliviousness to events and his nervy introversion, mentally practising his musical piece while others try to speak to him; a gaggle of people in the same, enclosed, aquarium-like space, all at cross purposes, scarcely seeing or hearing each other; and the hero's totally misjudged attempt at show-making, trying to peacefully unify the situation by going into his act, but only atomising it further (the scene ends abruptly with Jimmy's weird gesture of centring himself). But it is in the dialogue that the micro-action of the scene, with its second-by-second twists and turns, really happens:

Italian Prisoner:	There's three guys in the desert, you see. An Italian, an Irishman and a Polak. The Italian's got a hunk of gorgonzola cheese, the Mick's got a can of beer, and the Polak's carrying a ... a car door under his arm. So they run into this Arab in the middle of the desert ...
Black Prisoner 1:	Hey man, why don't you shut your ass and go to sleep?
Italian Prisoner:	Who's talking to you, asshole?
Black Prisoner 1:	I'm talkin' to you, sucker.
Italian Prisoner:	Bullshit, all you're doin' is sittin' around in your dry piss.
Black Prisoner 1:	Whose dry piss?
Italian Prisoner:	I don't see anybody else sittin' here.
Black Prisoner 2:	And what about me? You don't see me?
Italian Prisoner:	You a human being? You're a fuckin' animal!

Black Prisoner 2:	Maybe I kick your little white wop ass you see me, huh?
Italian Prisoner:	You couldn't kick my sister's ass. And she's in a fuckin' wheelchair in Daytona.
Black Prisoner 2:	You got a sister in Daytona?
Italian Prisoner:	Yeah. What about it? You wanna make something of it?
Black Prisoner 2:	No. I got a sister in Daytona too.
Italian Prisoner:	Yeah. No shit.
Black Prisoner 2:	You bet your Jew ass I do.
Italian Prisoner:	I ain't a Jew, what do you keep calling me a Jew, you cross-eyed motherfucker ...
Jimmy:	Hey listen, listen ... Instead of you guys talking all this philosophy, why don't you, er, let me sing, ah, the Bach, the Fugue from the *E Minor Toccata* for you, alright?

Problematic Men

FINGERS shows masculinity as a shared, internalised, lived social code performed, deformed and reformed in the rituals of intersubjective exchange. Consider again the dynamic of the father-son relation – a particularly vicious and closed masculine circuit. Any problem internal to either man, or endemic to their relationship, is denied: projected onto others (Jimmy's prostate problem is due to castrating women), or reciprocally cancelled. In the restaurant, Jimmy suggests to his father that he give up smoking. Ben's answer affirms male stereotypes with chilling force, in the same moment as it evades the problem which is killing him: "I'll stop smoking when you stop fucking." Not only is this an injunction from father to son to *keep* fucking; it also rests on the assumption that his son cannot possibly have any problems in that department.

Masculinity in FINGERS is indeed a fragile ensemble, haunted by that which it attempts to repress – most spectacularly, other sexual options. One thread in the film keeps confronting Jimmy with the ambivalently fascinating and horrifying spectre of his own potential gayness (the guys who distract his gaze in the restaurant; the rectal examination; the "cocksucker" obscenities which cast him in a gay position, particularly Ben's violent "stick your prick up my ass!"). Thomson mentions intriguingly that, due to Barrie's budget cuts, "Toback had to drop a handful of scenes, including a homosexual encounter."[38]

Doubtless the most fiercely problematic of Toback's men – and the aspect of FINGERS which stirred the greatest liberal anger at the time of its release – is the character of Dreems played by Jim Brown. His appearance instantly hikes the quasi-hallucinatory feel of the film up a few notches. Is he a figment of Jimmy's flipped-out imagination? The symbolic significance of his name is crushingly direct: Dreems is Jimmy's ideal guy, black, virile, powerful, in control, a man of few words. He is also emotionally coercive and physically violent. The film's freakiest moment, when Dreems bangs the heads of Carol and Christa (Carol Francis) together, was appropriated by Toback from a real-life incident that shortly followed the participatory research for JIM. In life, Brown was arrested for this, and the charges were later dropped; in the film, the recreation of that traumatic moment was performed for real, a "secret three-way actors' complicity", as Toback proudly described it.[39] A similar flare-up occurs between another black sports legend, Mike Tyson, and a fictional character played by Robert Downey Jr. in BLACK AND WHITE (1999). This was a fistful of psycho-drama – a conflation or confusion of reportage with fantasy projection – for which few journalists could forgive the filmmaker at the time.

Dreems is also a figure of great humour – a subterranean aspect of FINGERS that is often misrecognised. In a few key respects he is as "full of shit" as Jimmy – the sole difference being that no one is about to point that out to Dreems. He provides a point of exaggeration, a far-out parody, of Jimmy's conspicuously self-deluding heroism. For instance, Dreems's declarations of empathy with others easily outstrip Jimmy's in absurd grandiloquence. Concerning Carol, he advises Jimmy, "you don't understand her ass," immediately before once again abusing her. In a central scene of would-be, four-way, kinky sex, where Dreems eventually resorts to violence when the free-love tableau doesn't happen exactly as he wishes, he utters these immortal words (worthy of a Barry White song) to Christa: "Ain't gonna do nuthin' with you, or to you, that's not for you, baby."

This scene trains a cruel irony upon Jimmy's obsessive pursuit. Faced with the materialisation of his ultimate sexual fantasy, he becomes completely blocked. As Dreems half-heartedly exhorts Jimmy to "get his thing together", he tells the little story of a guy who can never get it up when the heat is on – "his dick ain't worth a shit". Jimmy, for his part, responds with a familiar repertoire of alienated gestures – from escape into taped music to frazzled implosion. The scene is another homage to catatonia and irresolution: Toback again snatches the scene away so abruptly that it's impossible to determine who exits with whom and when from this catastrophe.

Jimmy does get one other shot at a love scene. With Carol's loud encouragement, he finally manages to forego his arduous practice of the heroic fuck and ejaculates (it takes all of twenty-eight seconds). Then a fade to black – the only such moment of calm in the entire film. But the afterglow effect is deceptive. Suddenly there is a cut to Jimmy, alone on the bed the next morning, still half dressed and twitching like crazy at all his extremities. Carol enters the frame abruptly, already dressed and prepared for the day ahead. She asks Jimmy with complete indifference: "Bad dream?"[40]

What happens when Jimmy's everyday shoring up is no longer possible, when all escape routes either inward or outward are closed off definitively? The final, pitiless movement of FINGERS records Jimmy's brutal attempt to constitute himself as hero. This occurs, as for so many before him (Jimmy Stewart forcing Kim Novak up the door in VERTIGO) and after him (Willem Dafoe moving like a zombie in Schrader's LIGHT SLEEPER [1992]), through an act of revenge. Suddenly, and for the first time, Jimmy is one step ahead of what we know about him; he strides with purpose, crossing spaces and places with a mysterious but fixed destiny before him. It's as if, in tracking and annihilating Riccamonza, the one who first derailed his father's little empire, Jimmy can restore the chain of cause-and-effect to its pre-catastrophic starting point, and wipe out the nightmare of fraught intersubjectivity. And more: in castrating Riccamonza, he can take back into himself the lost power of masculinity.

FINGERS is a movie which is over before it starts; one of the first things we hear about Jimmy is that he "used to be" a great collector. He may go through the motions, but the *élan vital* of a once glorious man – and a once glorious gangster genre – is missing, played out. Jimmy's ultimate victory feels like no victory at all – it's too desperate, too excessive, it doesn't deliver a high to either the doer or its spectator. The action is emptied out, exhausted. At the end of his "last run" (a common figure in many melancholic male stories) the hero is not even delivered to death's door. Like Edward G. Robinson at the end of Fritz Lang's prophetic SCARLET STREET (1944), Jimmy becomes one of the living dead, paving the way for a veritable carnival of ghostly souls in action films of the 1980s and 1990s: De Niro in ONCE UPON A TIME IN AMERICA, Eastwood in PALE RIDER (1985), Christopher Walken in Ferrara's KING OF NEW YORK (1990), Johnny Depp in Jim Jarmusch's DEAD MAN (1995), Al Pacino in De Palma's CARLITO'S WAY (1993) ...

FINGERS ends, as do THE CONFORMIST (Bernardo Bertolucci, 1971), THE CONVERSATION (Coppola, 1974), BLOW OUT (De Palma, 1981) and CRUISING, with a blank, static, solitary hero – and like several of his fallen brothers, he stares with enigmatic finality into the camera. In a savage reversal of the opening image, Jimmy now sits at his piano – naked, reduced to animal status, as Keitel would again be fourteen years later in Ferrara's BAD LIEUTENANT (1992). His hand on the window expresses not yearning but withdrawal, an erasure of alterity, like the freeze-frame of a crazed fan's hand on a car window at the start of Scorsese's THE KING OF COMEDY (1983). Jimmy looks out for a moment before turning to us, but all the lines – sight lines, action trajectories, connections to other people – are blocked.

Thomson cryptically notes Toback's Big Question, the one that motivates his work: "Are you completely out yet?"[41] FINGERS presents the grim but fascinating spectacle of an expulsion from all orifices and by every means: shitting, fucking, spending, beating, shooting, going mad. The hero keeps nothing, wins nothing. His only real drive is to empty himself totally. When the hero is completely out, will he have the consciousness to even know it?

This chapter is an extensively revised and updated version of an essay which appeared in *Intervention* nos. 21-22, 1988.

Notes

1. Ken Eisen, "The Young Misogynists of American Cinema", *Cineaste* September 1983, 32.
2. Michael Dempsey, "Love and Money, Ecstasy and Death: A Conversation With James Toback", *Film Quarterly*, Winter 1980-81, 34.
3. Gilles Deleuze, *Cinema 1: The Movement-Image* (Minneapolis: University Of Minnesota Press, 1986), 213.
4. Laura Mulvey, *Visual and Other Pleasures* (Bloomington: Indiana University Press, 1989), 14-26.
5. Schematically, obsession can be considered to take two broad, essential forms, inward and outward turning. (I owe this distinction to Ross Harley.) An outward turning obsession is fixed on something outside oneself – some specific object of interest in the world. It is a little too easy to turn this into a moral distinction – narcissistic obsession is bad and sick, 'outgoing' obsessions are good and healthy. In reality the distinction between these modes of obsession often proves difficult to draw. David Cronenberg's CRASH (1996), for instance, presents a richly ambiguous case study in obsession – as does the phenomenon of cinephilia itself, or indeed any "collecting" mania.
6. Adrian Martin, "Will and Representation in Martin Scorsese", *Scripsi* vol. 8 no. 1, 1992, 146-159.
7. Dennis Giles, "Show-making", in Rick Altman (ed.), *Genre: The Musical* (London: Routledge & Kegan Paul, 1981), 85-101.
8. Adrian Martin, ONCE UPON A TIME IN AMERICA (London: British Film Institute, 1998); and "Mr Big", *Stuffing: Film: Genre* June 1987, 50-77.
9. James Toback, "BONNIE AND CLYDE, POINT BLANK: Style as Morality", in Renatus Hartogs and Eriz Artzt (eds.), *Violence: Causes and Solutions* (New York: Dell, 1970); cf. also Adrian Martin, "Pulp Affliction", *World Art* November 1994, 84-88.

10. David Thomson, *Overexposures: The Crisis in American Filmmaking* (New York: Quill, 1981), 262.

11. For recent critiques along this line, cf. Josh Kun, "The White Stuff", *Weekly Wire*, 24 April 2000, http://weeklywire.com/ww/04-24-00/boston_music_2.html; Dennis Harvey, "J.T. the Bigga Figga?", *sfbg.com*, 5 April 2000, http://www.sfbg.com/AandE/34/27/biggafigga.html; and Manohla Dargis, "Being James Toback", *LA Weekly*, 7-13 April 2000, http://www.laweekly.com/ink/00/20/film-dargis.php

12. James Toback, "Notes on Acting", *Film Comment* January-February 1978, 35.

13. Tod Lippy, "Writing *Vicky*: A Talk with James Toback", *Scenario* vol. 2 no. 2, Summer 1996, 200.

14. Thomson, *Overexposures*, 257.

15. Dempsey, "Love and Money, Ecstasy and Death", 27.

16. Ibid, 31.

17. Ibid, 35. But note Truffaut's rage as expressed in his *Correspondence 1945-1984* (New York: Noonday, 1990): "I obviously never said, or wrote, that FINGERS was one of the greatest American films of the sound period" (529).

18. Leonard Maltin, *Movie & Video Guide* (New York: Signet, 2001), 452-3.

19. Dempsey, "Love and Money, Ecstasy and Death", 30.

20. Robin Wood, *Hollywood from Vietnam to Reagan* (New York: Columbia University Press, 1986), 46-69; cf. also Adrian Martin, "The Wood and the Trees", *Filmnews*, September 1988, 16.

21. Adrian Martin, "A Larry Clark Portrait", in Peter Craven (ed.), *Best Australian Essays 2002* (Melbourne: Black Inc, 2002).

22. Ross Gibson, "BLUE VELVET", *Filmnews* February 1987, 12.

23. Editorial introduction to James Toback, "The Father of the Man", *Movieline* June 1997, 47.

24. Tod Lippy, "Writing *Vicky*"; James Toback, "Divisions and Dislocations: A Journal for 1994", in John Boorman and Walter Donohue (eds.), *Projections 4* (London: Faber and Faber, 1995); Laurent Vachaud, "De l'érection à la résurrection: entretien avec James Toback", *Positif* no. 397, March 1994, 29-36.

25. Pauline Kael, *5001 Nights at the Movies* (London: Zenith, 1984), 185-6.

26. "Midsection: Acting", *Film Comment* January-February 1978, includes Toback's "Notes on Acting" plus Stuart Byron, "The Keitel Method", 36-41, which contains an invaluable discussion with the actor about his role in FINGERS.

27. Eisen, "The Young Misogynists of American Cinema", 32.

28. An exception within this 'school' is Brad Stevens, "James Toback and *The Pick-up Artist*", *Screening the Past* no. 12, March 2001, http://www.latrobe.edu.au/screeningthepast/firstrelease/fr0301/bsfr12a.htm

29. Pascal Bonitzer, "Lignes et voies", *Cahiers du cinéma* no. 266-7, May 1976, 68-70. He suggests that, in comparison with Kramer's MILESTONES (1975), Hellman is "less duped by truth, intersubjective communication, tribal speech, and revolutionary messianism" (68).

30. Toback, "Notes on Acting", 35.

31. Erving Goffman, *The Presentation of Self in Everyday Life* (New York: Doubleday, 1959).

32. Deleuze, *Cinema 1*, 213.

33. Richard Combs, "ALICE IN THE CITY", *Sight and Sound*, Autumn 1980, 265.

34. Dempsey, "Love and Money, Ecstasy and Death", 32.

35. Raymond Bellour, *The Analysis of Film* (Bloomington: Indiana University Press, 2000).

36. Geoffrey Nowell-Smith, *"Radio On"*, *Screen* vol. 20, no. 3/4, Winter 1979-1980, 29-39; Thomas Elsaesser, *Fassbinder's Germany: History Identity Subject* (Amsterdam University Press, 1996).

37. Gregory Bateson, *Steps To An Ecology of Mind* (Frogmore: Paladin, 1973).

38. Thomson, *Overexposures*, 264.

39. Toback, "Notes on Acting", 35.

40. Larry Pryce's mind-boggling novelisation of *Fingers* (Los Angeles: Universal, 1978), while following the film virtually scene by scene, manages to completely re-heroise Jimmy; all signs of disturbance are missing. Pryce's version of the opening pursuit: "The song and the man appeared to be in complete harmony with each other as he approached her with a soft, almost cat-like walk" (7). Sex with Carol: "Slowly at first, and then with a growing urgency their bodies became one, as a wild heat overtook both of them and their rhythm of loving moved on into the long night" (96). Pryce is moved to add the ending of a bizarre and spectacular sui-cide gesture, doubtless in a desperate attempt to square plot and character: Jimmy jams razor blades under his fingernails and jumps out his window!

41. Thomson, *Overexposures*, 263.

Allegories of Post-Fordism in 1970s New Hollywood

Countercultural Combat Films, Conspiracy Thrillers as Genre Recycling

Drehli Robnik

This essay deals with some aspects of the New Hollywood cinema of the late 1960s and early 1970s, focusing on non-canonized works among the war movies and conspiracy thrillers of that period, and on some related diagnostic, critical and historiographic discourses. One concern is to ask how such accounts of New Hollywood, in the historically narrow sense of the term, can be related to our present media-cultural experience, and what meanings the films in question can be made to reveal in a retrospective, allegorizing approach – in short: how to remember New Hollywood circa 1970. The retrospective frameworks employed here are (fragments of) a genealogy of subjectivities and temporalities characteristic of post-Fordist social production (which is where issues of 'flexibility' and 'recycling' and arguments made by Michael Hardt and Antonio Negri will come in), and the pre-history of today's blockbuster-oriented American cinema – the one which we know as New Hollywood in a larger sense.

Hollywood's Crisis and the Countercultural Pressure: Redefining Purposeful Action

In 1971, *monogram* film magazine published a dossier on contemporary Hollywood in which the latter's overproduction crisis was interpreted as a crisis of its cultural, ethical and aesthetic presuppositions – of the conceptions of narrative orientation and meaningful action underlying its products. Peter Lloyd saw Hollywood as being in "crisis and transition" and as blindly grasping at trends in the youth market, largely due to "the gradual collapse of the efficacy of the heroic individual in the American cinema".[1] And Thomas Elsaesser pointed to massive differences between classical Hollywood's "central protagonist with a cause, a goal, a purpose – in short, a motivation for action" and the "unmotivated hero" in recent films like EASY RIDER (1969).[2] The "crisis of motivation" became a key term in Elsaesser's 1975 diagnosis of the "pathos of failure" in American cinema during its contemporary transition from an "affirmative-consequential" conception of narrative action to an as yet undetermined mode. Referring mainly to New Hollywood's youth and road movies like EASY RIDER and TWO-LANE BLACKTOP (1971), Elsaesser wrote: "What the heroes bring to such films is the almost physical sense of inconsequential action, of pointlessness and uselessness, a radical scepticism, in short, about the American virtues of ambition, vision, drive."[3]

New Hollywood's blocking of narrative goal-orientation was later summarised under the headlines negativity and nihilism by Chris Hugo. In his 1986 polemic retrospective view, EASY RIDER again serves as the chief example for "the fashion for the supposed 'New Hollywood Cinema'" and its "beautiful loser" protagonists "who became, for a short period, the chief youth picture audience identification figures. They were the opposite to those characters in classic Hollywood pictures who found themselves able to take positive action in the world, because they showed a belief in the essential correctness of the dominant values that classic Hollywood cinema embraced." – "In general, the most frequent narrative strategy in EASY RIDER could be summarised in terms of simply reversing the conventions of classic Hollywood from positive to negative. The central characters are passive, anti-social and goal-less."[4]

From a different perspective, Gilles Deleuze came to similar conclusions about 1970s New Hollywood (which he oddly subsumed under "post-war American cinema, outside Hollywood"). In 1983, he emphasized the failure of Hollywood's action-oriented cinema to extricate itself other than negatively from its classical tradition. In Deleuze's genealogics of modern cinema, New Hollywood appeared as a dead end: to him, Altman's "dispersive situations", the weak linkages between actions, perceptions and affects for instance in Scorsese, EASY RIDER's voyage form, detached from active and affective structures, or the no-win stories and loser heroes of Penn's and Peckinpah's neo-westerns were characteristic of a fundamental "crisis of the action-image" which coincided with the crisis of the "American Dream".[5]

In Deleuze's latter formulation, a larger historical context in which to situate New Hollywood is invoked rather passingly. Elsaesser's version of what one could call the "failure argument" indicates more specifically how to frame this critical moment of American cinema culturally and politically: to Elsaesser, the pathos of failure, as the predominant narrative stance of New Hollywood's youth movies, reflects "the moral and emotional gestures of a defeated generation" and "the experience of a rebellion whose impulse towards change aborted".[6] In the mid-1970s, New Hollywood's inability to offer a narratively and ethically efficient substitute for the goal-oriented narratives and heroic subjectivities it had broken with could be read as a symptom of the defeat of the 1960s countercultures. But in the same period, a less pessimistic picture of this relationship was also possible: In an article on "New Hollywood Cinema" which in parts responded to Elsaesser's critique of the pathos of failure, Steve Neale rated the impact of "the youth and students movement" and of "countercultures and ideologies generally" on Hollywood in more positive terms: "The very pressure of these groups and ideologies meant that the media had to 'give' at some point (even if this largely resulted in recuperation): Hollywood, certainly by the mid-1960s, was the weakest point."[7] While differing in their evaluations, both Elsaesser's and Neale's views imply that with Hollywood's short-lived orientation towards the (broadly) countercultural value-system of educated urban youth audiences, there is more at stake than just the marketing task of finding entertainment formulas for a preferred target group.

I want to address the question of social pragmatics and subjectivities underlying New Hollywood's images and narratives, i.e., the conception of purposeful action that gives cultural meaning to these movies and allows them to be placed in a larger historical framework. I suggest that by taking New Hollywood's countercultural dimension seriously, commodified as it may be, and by slightly shifting the film references to less canonized productions, the familiar "failure narrative" about New Hollywood can be reworked into a historical success story. To put it less teleologically, I attempt to revisit the crisis of Hollywood's action-image circa 1970 and to identify symptoms of the emergence of a new conceptualization of purposeful, productive action. What distinguishes American industrial cinema circa 1970 from earlier versions of a "new" or "post-classical" Hollywood is, to a large extent, its youth and countercultural orientation.[8] The latter's negative gestures of refusal – a refusal (or inability) to perpetuate classical Hollywood's affirmative-consequential narrative, generic and ethical norms of action, or a nihilism that "simply revers[es] the conventions of classic Hollywood practice from positive to negative", as Hugo put it[9] – can be seen as preconditions of a positive, innovative moment.

Some concepts and perspectives suited to this kind of re-evaluation can be found in the genealogy of post-Fordism contained in Michael Hardt's and Antonio Negri's political theory of *Empire*. Hardt and Negri highlight a historical success of the 1960s youth and countercultures, in that these movements' creativity in inventing new social subjectivities and standards of purposeful, productive action has been the driving force of capitalism's shift away from Fordist discipline: "[...] *The 'merely cultural' experimentation had very profound political and economic effects.* [...] The youth who refused the deadening repetition of the factory-society invented new forms of mobility and flexibility, new styles of living. [...] The indexes of the value of the movements – mobility, flexibility, knowledge, communication, cooperation, the affective – would define the transformation of capitalist production in the subsequent decades."[10]

What follows is neither an attempt to annex New Hollywood to a history of anti-disciplinary resistance nor a contribution to a theory of countercultures.[11] Rather, I will first of all employ flexibility and affectivity as key terms to highlight American cinema's role in an overall culture-driven redefinition of capitalist production – of what counts as purposeful active behavior productive of meaning and value, as well as of the social production of subjectivity in Hardt's and Negri's sense. My notion of a New Hollywood that explores these pragmatics and ethics is connected to the Benjaminian understanding of the cinema as a mass-cultural "rehearsal" of modernization, and to Jonathan Beller's provocative equation of cinema and capital as modes of producing and organising experience. As Beller claims in his Benjamin- and Deleuze-inflected argument, "cinema may be taken as a model for the many technologies which in effect take the machine off the assembly line and bring it to the body in order to mine it for labor power (value)." Cinema thus "functions as a kind of discipline and control akin to previous methods of socialization by either civil society or the labor process (e.g., Taylorization)"; it is "the potential cutting and splicing of all aspects of the world to meet the exigencies of flexible accumulation and to develop new affects."[12] The formation of Empire's post-Fordist regime of production – in which distinctions between economy and culture as well as between productive and unproductive labor become contingent[13] – emphasizes cinema's explorative role in processes of socialization as mediatization and capitalization. In Beller, "capital cinema" performs a "tapping of energies", a globalization of capital which is "less a geographical project and more a matter of *capturing* the interstitial activities and times between the already commodified endeavors of bodies. *Every movement and every gesture is potentially productive of value.*"[14]

The first half of this chapter suggests a (retrospective) look at New Hollywood's part in this redefinition and re-evaluation of productive action: along with the crisis and failures of motivated, goal-oriented and purposeful action, I demonstrate that the American cinema circa 1970 also reveals lines of flight pointing from disciplined pragmatics and subjectivities to flexible and affective ones. My examples come from a genre which usually makes one think of rigid discipline rather than of New Hollywood: the American war movie – rendered flexible in its encounter with the countercultures.

Hippies at War: Explorations of Flexibility in M*A*S*H, THE DIRTY DOZEN **and** KELLY'S HEROES

There is one American war movie which is generally considered to be a New Hollywood classic. Anticipating the noisy dispersiveness of situations and the crumbling of linear narratives in Robert Altman's later work, M*A*S*H (1969) seems to plainly confirm the failure argument put forward by Elsaesser, Hugo or Deleuze. However, it is only from the vantage point of disciplined storytelling and behavior that the narrative stuttering and idle motion in M*A*S*H, its protagonists' digressive escapades and extravagant self-fashioning appear as symptoms of nihilism or collapse. Pauline Kael's review of the film offered a different interpretation, in terms that seem to echo and reverse some of the later New Hollywood criticism in advance: "The movie isn't naive, but it isn't nihilistic, either." – "[I]t's hip but it isn't hopeless."[15] The soldier protagonists' "adolescent pride in skills and games – in mixing a Martini or in devising a fishing lure or in golfing", all those micro-actions which would be written off as meaningless, disturbing or at best ornamental within a classical narrative economy of the genre, were seen by Kael as manifesting a new pragmatic orientation: "People who are loose and profane and have some empathy – people who can joke about anything – can function, and maybe even do something useful, in what may appear to be insane circumstances."[16] In M*A*S*H, the possibility of useful, productive action and of a socially functioning sense of self depends on the protagonist's playful culturalization of work routine and undisciplined communication under conditions of industrialized warfare. *Sight and Sound*'s reviewer of M*A*S*H also hinted at the very usefulness of integrating jocularity and profanity into the military labor process and drew from the film a lesson in flexibilization: "[...] If there's one moral that can safely be drawn from the succession of gags and incidents which provide the film's sprawling narrative structure, it's that inflexible attitudes to war (chauvinistic, religious, bureaucratic or heroic) lead straight to the strait-jacket."[17]

Following Jeanine Basinger's historical "anatomy" of the American "World War II combat film", one can place M*A*S*H (a 'service comedy' set in the Korean War rather than an outright combat film) at the culmination point of the narrative abstractions, revisions and sometimes parodic inversions which Hollywood's war movie genre underwent in the late 1960s. Two of the films which Basinger subsumes under that period's revisionist 'dirty group movies' warrant a closer look in the context of my flexibilization argument in relation to New Hollywood. Seen from Basinger's genre-formalist point of view, Robert Aldrich's THE DIRTY DOZEN (1967) and Brian G. Hutton's KELLY'S HEROES (1970), the former a major box-office success, exemplify the popularity during the 1960s of the war movie's 'commando raid' variant which highlights attack missions carried out by small, specialized 'maverick units' in World War II.[18]

In THE DIRTY DOZEN, a US Army major (Lee Marvin) is ordered to train twelve soldiers, who have been sentenced to death or long prison terms as criminals, for a special mission: in exchange for suspension of their sentences, they are to raid a chateau used as a brothel by the German military and kill as many generals as they can. Basinger emphasizes the 'dirtiness' of these skilled combat workers and interprets their training process and the tricks they play on the US military establishment in terms which reflect, at the level of genre, the notion of Hollywood's action-image in crisis. Pointing to the negativity of the film's goal-orientation in contrast to traditional combat film ethics, she reads THE DIRTY DOZEN as being about criminal tendencies put to work inside the system, about fudging its rules and 'playing dirty'.[19] *Sight and Sound's* reviewer of THE DIRTY DOZEN saw the film as displaying many "surface elements of more honest war films, but without the accompanying moral justification. The effect is arguably less a broadening of scope for the entertainment film than a devaluation of useful currency."[20] These accounts are versions of the failure argument: they invoke the "devaluation" of genre's meaning-making capacities, or at best a "subversion" of the genre, which Basinger links to anti-Vietnam war sentiments strong among Hollywood's youth audiences, thus acknowledging the countercultural impact on late 1960s American cinema.

THE DIRTY DOZEN's disruption of the moral and disciplinary norms underlying the narrative motivation and orientation of action in classical war movies might, however, be seen as negative preconditions for an exploration of new use values with respect to purposeful, productive action. Such a perspective brings to the fore a *creative* (as opposed to merely "subversive") dimension of the film's address to – broadly defined – countercultural and anti-establishment audience positions. If, to quote once more from *Sight and Sound*'s review, in THE DIRTY DOZEN "no effort is spared in establishing this assortment of recalcitrants, morons and psychopaths as a bunch of likeable characters, and the more they work as a team the more likeable they become", then the important point about this "unholy teamwork" (as Basinger puts it) is just that it *is* teamwork.[21]

Much of the narrative goal-orientation of Aldrich's film as well as of its humorous and spectacular appeal is derived from the broadly displayed training process, especially its tactics of forging a team-identity alternative to the strategies of the military establishment.[22] The unusual training methods of Lee Marvin's character explore and mine the usefulness of subjectivities, energies and types of behaviour which would be wasted by the rationality of the Army's disciplinary labor regime. With its stress on unconventional (not just

THE DIRTY DOZEN

duty-based) motivation for the trainees and on their special, highly flexible skills at "project-oriented work", the concept of purposeful action underlying the film points towards a new, post-Fordist economy with its normalization of flexible social subjectivities.[23] What we can see anticipated in the film is the cohesive team-spirit and self-management of 'professional subcultures' in performing non-routine tasks (to use the language of the 'cultural turn' in post-1970 management theories), a system of production based on the 'social capital' of affective labor, tacit knowledge and undisciplined communication (to put it in terms of recent Marxist work on post-Fordism).[24]

Understood as an index of a new productivity and sociality, the very dirtyness of the dozen is an aspect of the culturalization of team labor as well as of the film's address to anti-establishment sensibilities within its audience. The key moment in the trainees' self and collective team differentiation is when they proudly refuse to wash and shave with cold water and prefer to remain dirty and grow beards instead. When one of Marvin's superiors threatens to have the dirty dozen bathed and shaved against their will, the scene is reminiscent of a late 1960s cliché (referenced, for instance, in EASY RIDER) about the way representatives of hegemonic culture and social discipline would want to treat hairy, filthy hippies if given the chance. With its display of the soldiers' rock-band type looks as a trademark of the film's spectacle-values, this scene is one of the moments which might situate THE DIRTY DOZEN in a closer connection to New Hollywood's early youth movies than its generic affiliation would seem to warrant.[25] While Ed Guerrero perceives a certain 'black power' sentiment expressed by a scene during the commando raid, in which African-American football-star turned actor Jim Brown scores high in throwing hand grenades into ventilator shafts to blow up German officers,[26] I think that THE DIRTY DOZEN addressed countercultural attitudes and aesthetic preferences mainly in rather general terms of an undisciplined pop lifestyle. This is also shown by the film's featurette OPERATION DIRTY DOZEN (1967), in which – according to descriptions on the Internet Movie Database – Aldrich's cast goes on another special mission, visiting Swinging London's pubs and dance clubs during a break in the film's shooting. "So we have this advertise-ment which emphasizes the mod scene of London," commented an IMDB user in 2001, "but this is most strange: essentially the Beatles and the new drug cul-ture (strictly anti-war) are being used to promote a pro-war film!" Already in 1967, the *Sight and Sound* reviewer of THE DIRTY DOZEN had been astonished by the fact that this war film "can appeal to hawks and doves alike".[27]

The latter formulation relies on what obviously was a trope widely used in critics' descriptions of the hybrid audience appeal of some New Hollywood war movies. Contemporary reviews of Franklin J. Schaffner's war movie-biopic PATTON – LUST FOR GLORY, a big box-office hit in 1970, describe the film as "a far-out movie passing as square", aimed at "hawks" and "doves" alike by a "Hollywood now firmly entreched behind the youth barricades".[28] Seen in this perspective, countercultural influences render a mass-market genre pro-duct flexible – instead of subverting it. And while Lloyd cited PATTON as one of the films in which "insanity" had replaced heroism in cinematic constructions of individual agency,[29] Hollywood's promotional discourse preferred to have such post-heroic insanity interpreted as a positive force of social innovation: "Patton was a rebel. Long before it became fashionable. He rebelled against the biggest. Eisenhower. Marshall. Montgomery. Against the establishment – and its ideas of warfare." To Robert B. Ray, this movie tagline exemplified a "free exchange of plots and motifs" between an ideologically conservative "Right cycle" and a counterculturally appealing "Left cycle" within what he retro-spectively called the "'New' American Cinema" of the late 1960s and early 1970s.[30]

In 1970, the flexible management of countercultural elements within the war film's generic framework allowed the ostentatious integration of hippie lifestyle into the narrative and spectacle values of a World War II combat film. Set in France in 1944, KELLY'S HEROES centers its overtly anachronistic toying with drop-out fashion and rhetorics on Oddball, the long-haired, bearded commander of a US Army tank unit, played by Donald Sutherland (who also featured among the Dirty Dozen and the socially skilled jokers of M*A*S*H).

The film stresses Oddball's penchant for taking things easy, his habit of calling disturbances "negative waves" and his comrades "maaan" or "baby", his unit's love for Oriental music, their commune life-style and souped-up tanks. In carnivalizing the US war machine, KELLY'S HEROES also draws on contemporary pop styles other than hippie: the Hell's Angels look which Oddball's men display wearing captured SS uniform parts at the end, or the spinning of a would-be pop hit by Lalo Schifrin (performed by The Mike Curb Congregation) in several versions throughout the film. Compared to a canonized counterculturally oriented film like EASY RIDER, these elements correspond to a rather broad, mainstream understanding of hippie and drop-out aesthetics: thus, ridiculing the long-haired in the eyes of the short-haired seems to be part of KELLY'S HEROES'audience address as much as is winking at the youth market. More importantly, the integration of countercultural elements into a combat film functions not just as a distraction from its narrative trajectory or as a subversion of the genre, but rather highlights the usefulness of playful creativity to the goal-orientation of its action. For instance, Oddball's unit achieves a triumphant victory by staging a surprise tank attack as a near-psychedelic multi-media performance, with loud country music and custom-made shells containing pink (instead of Jimi Hendrix's purple) haze fired at the Germans; the scene seems to anticipate the figuration of high-tech warfare as aesthetic spectacle in APOCALYPSE NOW (1979) – though with a reversed evaluation, stressing success by innovation rather than the insanity of war.[31]

A similar point can be made with respect to KELLY'S HEROES' relation to European genre (or rather: formula-based) cinema. In the context of New Hollywood's often noted susceptibility to influences from European cinema of the 1960s, THE WILD BUNCH (1969) has become the standard example for the impact of the Italian western on American movies. Whereas Peckinpah's western is usually held to intensify the violence and cynicism of spaghetti westerns to the point of insanity and self-destruction, KELLY'S HEROES feeds its even more overt stylistic and narrative borrowings from Sergio Leone into a success story. With its more or less dirty group of GIs going AWOL and advancing into enemy territory to steal a gold treasure from the Germans for personal gain, the film transfers the plot-motif of treasure-hunting between the front-lines from the Civil War setting of THE GOOD, THE BAD AND THE UGLY (1966) to World War II. While KELLY'S HEROES' heist-plot can be regarded as a generic hybrid of combat and caper movie, the film quite explicitly acknowledges its debts to Leone: the scene in which the central gold-seeker trio Sutherland, Savalas and Clint Eastwood march to their confrontation with a German tank is a coarse allusion to the showdown (and to Ennio Morricone's main-title theme) of THE GOOD, THE BAD AND THE UGLY – the film which had propelled Eastwood to worldwide stardom four years before.

Beyond Gung Ho! – War Movies as Allegories of Post-Fordist Production

The extent to which New Hollywood's war movies explore new pragmatics and subjectivities can be underscored by picking up a comparison suggested by Basinger as well as by Thomas Doherty in his study of Hollywood's relationship to World War II. Both authors consider the combat film Gung Ho! (Ray Enright, 1943) to be the model for the late 1960s 'dirty group' movies. Doherty writes: "However much the ante is upped in criminality, brutality, and irreverence, the rogues and rascals of The Dirty Dozen (1967), The Devil's Brigade (1968) and Kelly's Heroes (1970) are blood brothers to the misfits of Gung Ho! (1943)."[32] These accounts emphasize how in Hollywood films, the war machine makes use of destructive energies – the kind of rampage which is freqently referred to as cinematic "violence Gung Ho!-style". However, by positing a continuous link and family resemblance between Gung Ho! and New Hollywood's combat movies, they overlook important differences in the films' respective conceptions of violence as purposeful action and of its modes of socialization. With the US Marines accepting fanatics, a frustrated ex-boxer, a cut-throat and some aggressive 'no-good kids' from broken homes as volunteers for a special mission in the Pacific, Gung Ho! at first sight appears as innovative (and cynical) about productive teamwork as The Dirty Dozen. But Gung Ho!'s novel approach to combat efficiency – celebrated by numerous officers' speeches and by a semi-documentary training sequence with propagandistic voice-over commentary – still adheres to a logic of duty-based teamwork and thus amounts to a mere intensification of Taylorist discipline: it's all about "men fighting together with the precision of a machine", as the unit's commander (Randolph Scott) phrases it, before he goes on to explain his unit's training motto, which is also the film's title. According to Scott, "Gung Ho!" – a phrase nowadays synonymous with rampant bloodshed – is "Chinese" for "work in harmony".

In the relentless speeches to the soldiers and to its audience, Gung Ho! invokes the task of winning the war in the name of freedom and equality and, most of all, the notion of the combat team as informed by the self-image of the USA as social and ethnic melting pot. The meaning-making framework of the melting pot is typical of classical Hollywood's World War II (and Korean War) combat movies, and of the American action-image in general – or, to be exact, of its "large form" in Deleuze's sense.[33] Gung Ho!s underlying concepts of purposeful action and social subjectivity can also be considered in light of Deleuze's concept of the action-image's "small form". In this perspective, the notion of functionally defined, no longer organically founded groups (as

Deleuze detects them in Howard Hawks' westerns) becomes relevant.[34] Apart from its melting pot ideology, GUNG HO!'s "harmoniously working machine" draws on the technology-based functionalism of many wartime combat films for which Hawks' AIR FORCE (1943) established the paradigm. Instead of a people and its leaders (as in the films of the large form), these films show crews consisting of disciplined component parts and highlight the role of technology in forming them (social technologies such as the standardized division of labor; material technologies such as the submarine engulfing the Marines in GUNG HO! and the bomber plane in AIR FORCE).[35]

In any case, GUNG HO! defines its pragmatics of violent action within horizons of meaning very different from New Hollywood's war movies. The geopolitical mission of American democracy, the US Army as national melting pot, technology-based Fordist functionalism – all these encompassing meta-narratives are absent from the ethics and pragmatics of THE DIRTY DOZEN and KELLY'S HEROES.[36] And yet, these films' action-images of war are far from flirting with meaninglessness. In both films, the goal-orientation of the action-image depends not on fusing differences or reducing them to presupposed standards of efficiency, but on mining them for their use-values as potential productive forces. They are not about making misfits fit, but about misfits refitting and retooling the machinery. When in THE DIRTY DOZEN the Army psychologist supervising the training process describes Lee Marvin's team as "just about the most twisted anti-social bunch of psychopathic deformities I've ever run into", Marvin replies "Well, I can't think of a better way to fight a war". The cynicism that one might sense in this statement is merely the guise and the precondition of a positive conception of productivity capable of integrating, valuing and unfolding those potentials which a disciplinary rationality excluded as deviant. In the totality of post-Fordist social production, "it is thus no longer possible to identify a sign, a subject, a value, or a practice that is 'outside'," as Hardt and Negri write.[37] Similarly, when in KELLY'S HEROES the Telly Savalas character faces Oddball's hippie soldiers and shouts "That ain't an army, it's a circus!", this exclamation summarises the film's celebration of a "diversity management" of labor which is indeed closer to a circus than to Taylorist or military discipline. Or rather, the becoming-circus of the army-factory resembles the "increasing indistinguishability of economic and cultural phenomena" which Hardt and Negri see as an effect of the countercultural "attack on the disciplinary regime" of the "factory-society", driving the transition to the post-Fordist productive paradigm of cultural experimentation, affective labor, flexible communication and non-standardized knowledge.[38]

Finally, an affirmation of post-Fordist productivity becomes manifest in these two war movies if one reads them as "allegories of production" in the way in which David E. James interprets EASY RIDER. Exploring the metaphorical relation of EASY RIDER's plot to its production context (i.e., Hollywood's overproduction crisis and negotiation with youth audiences), James's version of the failure argument in relation to New Hollywood highlights how Dennis Hopper's "35mm ersatz underground film" is unable to remain loyal to and even "denigrat[es] the social alternatives represented by the counterculture that gives it market value."[39] According to James's critique, the film handles images of hippie-communal agrarianism or elements of avantgarde and psychedelic style as mere episodes and thus fails to present them as viable alternatives to technologized, capitalized cultural practices: "[...] We may read Captain America's remark 'We blew it' as an allegory of the film, of the failure of Hopper and Fonda to make a film adequate to the ideals of the counterculture [...]."[40] A clear case of "pathos of failure", to use Elsaesser's term. In contrast to this, the "professional subcultures" in THE DIRTY DOZEN and KELLY'S HEROES confront us with an overall "pathos of success". In order to read this stance as an allegory of production, one has to drop James's somewhat Platonic concern for the film industry's fidelity to countercultural ideals (or its lack thereof). Rather, the production context reflected in a self-congratulatory manner in THE DIRTY DOZEN and KELLY'S HEROES is the post-Fordization of American filmmaking – Hollywood's shift from the studio-based mass production of films to marketing fewer, more specialized films made independently and within transitory labor arrangements. This is the shift described as the adoption of the "package-unit system" of production after the mid-1950s by Janet Staiger.41 Hollywood's embracing of post-Fordist flexibility also involves a change in the consumer-cultural role of the industry's products, gradually replacing films' affiliations to the pre-established standards and genre disciplines of a studio's factory-system with the now familiar conception of big-budget films as singular events, multi-generic textures, and consumer-driven industries in and of themselves. The film conceived as a special mission and norm-defying event, carried out by a package-team of maverick experts with non-standardized skills and no institutional ties – this is the logic of flexible production that is allegorized by the successes of the undisciplined in New Hollywood's war movies.[42]

Mutation, Adaptation, Decline? The Two New Hollywoods – and How They Might Be Related

In my argument that New Hollywood explored a new pragmatic within the failure of an old one, I have so far emphasized its relationship to the earlier, classical period of American cinema. In the second half of this essay, I will focus on what followed the New Hollywood of the late 1960s and early 1970s. Murray Smith claims that "the sheer number of 'New Hollywoods' that one finds posited over the course of film history" recommends careful attention to Hollywood's constant "process of adjustment and adaptation to new circumstances [...]".[43] This "adaptation argument", as I would call it, is one way to resolve the inherent ambiguity of the term New Hollywood which becomes most urgent with respect to the question of how the American cinema of circa 1970 relates to that of today. In Smith's words: "The notion of the New Hollywood [...] underwent a strange mutation, ending up designating either something diametrically opposed to the American art film, or something inclusive of but much larger than it."[44]

We can see the latter, extended definition at work in Thomas Schatz's history of the New Hollywood, in which the term refers to the post-1945 genealogy of the blockbuster. According to Schatz, the "blockbuster hits are, for better or for worse, what the New Hollywood is about", and the establishment of this type of film, with its intermedia marketing potentials, as Hollywood's key product after 1975 marked "the studios' eventual coming-to-terms with an increasingly fragmented entertainment industry – with its demographics and target audiences, its diversified multimedia conglomerates, its global(ized) markets and new delivery systems".[45] To some degree, my rewriting of the failure argument into a success story of flexibilization is in line with Schatz's account, in that THE DIRTY DOZEN and KELLY'S HEROES can be situated among the many precursors of today's blockbusters; as such, they testify to the gradual reconceptualisation of Hollywood's main product in terms of a special event that replaces genre discipline with a playful, flexible, intertextual openness to a variety of cultural dynamics and viewing positions. However, in defining New Hollywood as a successful process of adaptation, Schatz downplays the creative, innovative aspect of Hollywood's flirtation with the countercultures: in his view, "[...] Hollywood's cultivation of the youth market and penchant for innovation in the late 1960s and early 1970s" mainly "reflected the studios' uncertainty and growing desperation".[46] The adaptation argument, which understands New Hollywood in a broad sense (the rise of the blockbuster), and the failure argument, which refers to New Hollywood in a narrow sense (centered on youth and road movies made around 1970), share the negative terms of disorientation and crisis in which they describe cinema's opening onto youth and countercultural value systems.

The other view which Smith hints at – New Hollywood turning from 'American art film' into its opposite – gives an emphatically positive judgement on Hollywood circa 1970 and ascribes to it some of the virtues usually associated with notions of 'art cinema'. In placing Hollywood's 'second golden age' in contrast to the industry's prevailing blockbuster orientation after 1975, this 'decline argument' reveals a certain cinephile melancholia, as for instance in an article by J. Hoberman from 1985: "The cultural upheavals of the late sixties spawned a cinema of genre criticism and directorial nonconformity; the retrenchment of the mid-seventies brought the waning days and ultimate reversal of the BONNIE AND CLYDE-EASY RIDER, small-and-weird-can-be-beautiful revolution. The past decade marked the decline and fall of the maverick genre revisionists (Robert Altman, Sam Peckinpah, Arthur Penn) [...]."[47] David A. Cook describes the decline of what he calls the "American auteur cinema" and its transformation into the blockbuster mode in particularly pessimist terms: "From the cinema of rebellion represented by films like BONNIE AND CLYDE, EASY RIDER, and MEDIUM COOL, America's youth transferred its allegiance to the 'personal' cinema of the seventies' auteurs without realizing how corporatist and impersonal it had become. And the auteurs themselves were transformed from *cinéastes* into high-rolling celebrity directors (many of them) with their own chauffeurs, Lear jets, and bodyguards [...] and recast their films as branded merchandise to be consumed along with T-shirts, action figures, Happy Meals [...]".[48]

A less moralizing thesis on the relationship of the two New Hollywoods was proposed in 1986 by Andrew Britton whose version of the decline argument is ideology-critical rather than cinephile. According to Britton, the "conservative reassurance in the contemporary Hollywood" has resulted in the "almost exclusive predominance of a type of film-making which, during the 'seventies, did not rule out the possibility of more interesting, contradictory and disturbing work. [...] It would have been difficult to feel certain in 1974 that THE TOWERING INFERNO, for all its phenomenal success, was about to become the main tradition. At the time, the disaster cycle seemed to be reactionary in a relatively simple sense: it was a desperate attempt [...] showing up a value-system which was obviously in ruins. What was less apparent was a potential cultural vitality. [...] In 1974, THE TOWERING INFERNO looked merely exhausted."[49]

The 1970s disaster movies are one point at which the discourses on New Hollywood part ways. From the viewpoint of adaptation, films like THE TOWERING INFERNO appear as (proto-)blockbusters and thus as examples of the larger New Hollywood; but, as Smith suggests, they can also be seen "in dialectical tension" with a New Hollywood which is either criticized for its pathos of failure or valued as "interesting, contradictory and disturbing".[50] If we are cinephile enough to regard New Hollywood as *The Last Great American Picture Show*, then THE TOWERING INFERNO is probably not a part of this *Last GAPS*, but rather represents *the last gasps* of the Old Hollywood – of "a value-system which was obviously in ruins", as Britton put it. But since there have been so many movies after 'THE LAST MOVIE'[51] – among them many more

American disaster films in the late 1990s – what interests me is Britton's notion of an "exhausted" cinema becoming the mainstream. The problem requires a look at Hollywood's changing ways of dealing with its past, using 1970s New Hollywood as a point of departure.

Westworld, Coma and the "Bio-politics of Recycling": from New Hollywood's Conspiracies to the Control Society's Blockbusters

While the early period of New Hollywood in the narrow sense – from the commercial success of BONNIE AND CLYDE (1967) to the box-office failure of TWO-LANE BLACKTOP (1971) – is marked by the film industry's relationship with countercultural values and audience positions, one trend discernible in the American cinema of the mid- and late 1970s is a cycle of conspiracy thrillers. These films (which have their equivalents in the Western European cinema of that period) approach the ruptures within American society from a different angle. Instead of exploring the new cultural visibility of what might lie outside the established order, they show attempts at investigating the order's hidden inside, emphasizing its systemic character, obstinacy and near invisibility. In some 1970s conspiracy thrillers, the young rebel protagonist of the earlier countercultural cycle seems to be displaced into the figure of the liberal investigator (often a not-so-young, but long-haired journalist) who either falls victim to the secret politics of surveillance and state power, like Warren Beatty in THE PARALLAX VIEW (Alan J. Pakula, 1974), or achieves a narrow victory, like Robert Redford in THREE DAYS OF THE CONDOR (Sidney Pollack, 1975), Dustin Hoffman and Robert Redford in ALL THE PRESIDENT'S MEN (Pakula, 1976), or Peter Fonda in FUTUREWORLD (Richard T. Heffron, 1976). In the latter film, a SciFi version of the trend, the Easy Rider turned journalist exposes a plot aimed at replacing politicians with remote-controlled cyborg doubles during their stay at a high-tech amusement park where humanoid robots serve the visitors' pleasure. Looking back on the 1970s conspiracy thriller, FUTURE-WORLD is of interest because it fuses elements of two better known films made by writer-director Michael Crichton. In his 'techno-thriller' WESTWORLD (1973), to which FUTUREWORLD is the low-budget sequel, the service robots of the same amusement park run out of control and attack the visitors of the Wild West, Ancient Rome and Middle Ages themed 'worlds'. And in Crichton's COMA (1978), the conspiracy that turns living people into technologically controlled bodies is transferred to a hospital where patients are secretly sent into

COMA

coma and kept alive in a computer-controlled storage space to provide organ transplants for sale on an international market.

COMA's terrifying images of technologically reified life almost literalize some points of Fredric Jameson's interpretation of the conspiracy motif as an allegorical figuration of contemporary capitalism's invisible, systemic totality. In Jameson, the "hermeneutic content" of Pakula's and other 1970s conspiracy thrillers – the promise of a "deeper inside view" into society's "hidden abode of production" – points towards the "new world system" of capitalism "whose study is now our true ontology".[52] The bizarre clinic in *Coma*, both life support system and stock exchange, offers a paranoid, ontological, allegorical glimpse into existence pervaded by capital; or rather, existence immersed in a mode of capital power to which Hardt's and Negri's concept of "biopolitical production" or "biopower" (derived from Foucault) applies: "Biopower is a form of power that regulates social life from its interior, following it, interpreting it, absorbing it, and rearticulating it. [...] The highest function of this power is to invest life through and through, [...] the production and reproduction of life itself."[53] What the hermeneutics of New Hollywood's conspiracy thrillers aim at is the new world system of capital's globalization – globalization not just in the sense of transnational markets, but rather as the "real subsumption" of social life under capital: the intensive, biopolitical "working through" of an already formally subsumed social terrain, up to the point at which "capital has become a world."[54]

In "Westworld", "Roman World" and "Medieval World" it is the accumulated symbolic capital of classical Hollywood genres that has become a world. In Crichton's theme park, the western and two versions of the historical epic have been cybernetically reworked into experiential environments, spectacles to be travelled and lived in by tourists. The conspiracy motif implicit in WESTWORLD – or rather, its suggestion of two conspiracies: that of the park's invisible control system, and that of the robotic gunslingers, knights and gladiators who suddenly massacre the visitors – exemplifies the critical "consciousness of clichés" and the "condemnation of the plot", two of Deleuze's characteristics of the American action-image in its crisis. In Deleuze, the plot which New Hollywood critically confronts is ultimately a global conspiracy of omnipresent media clichés which penetrate public spheres and minds. "But how can the cinema attack the dark organisation of clichés," Deleuze asks, "when it participates in their fabrication and propagation, as much as magazines or television?"[55] In some moments of the 1970s conspiracy cycle, the critical orientation of the action-image in crisis becomes self-reflexive: it shows the conspiracy as cinema, as in the psycho-killer test screening in THE PARALLAX VIEW, and the cinema as conspiracy – the conspiracy of outdated Hollywood genres whose clichés become dangerously alive in WESTWORLD.

The horror of a WESTWORLD fully subsumed under the capital of generic recognition value; the paranoia in Pakula's thrillers, caused by the persistence of the system and by the infinity of secret state power; and also Britton's critical dismay over the cultural vitality of a seemingly exhausted cinema, over the blockbusters that grew out of the ruins of THE TOWERING INFERNO: certain images and definitions of 1970s New Hollywood converge in an "epistemology of uneasiness" about the fact that something which should be dead is – still, again, or in as yet unknown ways – alive.[56] In these accounts of how the past, the already known, continues to rule over the present, the conspiracy metaphor figures prominently. According to Britton's critique of Hollywood after 1975, the self-referentiality of cinema's clichés turns entertainment into a solipsistic totality of knowingness, and the community-building role of genres is replaced by "a cosy conspiracy of self-congratulation and spurious familiarity".[57] Deleuze on the other hand, in his critique of American cinema's inescapable entanglement in its own tradition, employs metaphors which become literalized in disaster and horror movie images: Hollywood's genres "collapse and yet maintain their empty frame," he writes, and: "maltreated, mutilated, destroyed, a cliché is not slow to be reborn from its ashes."[58] Along these lines, Crichton's two films can be read as allegories of a cinema unable to rid itself of its past. The movie clichés – the ones which New Hollywood's shifting, critical

revision, and occasional mutilation of genres rather innovated and perpetuated than destroyed – literally stalk their audience in the form of Yul Brynner's
robot-gunslinger. In WESTWORLD's history-land of Hollywood's past, the
stereotype is a zombie who refuses to acknowledge his death and stubbornly
walks on; in COMA, it is a stiff body kept alive, serving as a reservoir for spare
parts, and the film's clinic presents itself as showroom for spectacular lighting
effects and as storage space for frozen lives, in short: as a cinema.

Such an interpretation, however, can only make sense within the discourse
on New Hollywood in the narrow, 1970s sense. Placed, however, in the context
of a larger New Hollywood – the one which gravitates towards the blockbuster and today defines the framework of mass-cultural encounters with the
movies on a global scale – the allegories of WESTWORLD and COMA point to a
different relationship of Hollywood with its past. The terms of this relationship have shifted from a negative conception – the cinema as conspiracy of the
exhausted, as comatose body and empty frame – to an affirmative, bio-political working through of cinema's history, a rearticulation of its 'standing reserve' and recycling of its past. This is Hollywood's rebirth from its ashes
which Deleuze mentions only in passing; the action-image's phoenix-like
(technology-based) revival in the blockbuster mode is not the concern of his
cinema books. But it clearly is Crichton's, or rather: the name Crichton is now
one of the brand-names associated with Hollywood's vitality and its embracing of the high-tech theme park. The films in question are the three JURASSIC
PARK blockbusters (1993, 1997, 2001).[59]

In his review, Peter Wollen called the first of these films a hybrid of
WESTWORLD and JAWS (the Spielberg film whose 1975 success is usually regarded as a watershed in the genealogy of the contemporary blockbuster); and
he described JURASSIC PARK in terms reminiscent of Crichton's theme park
movie made twenty years earlier: "[...] The monsters have not just run out of
control, they have come back from the dead [...]."[60] Unlike WESTWORLD, however, the all-encompassing reach of JURASSIC PARK is not a paranoid fantasy,
but a positive consumer-cultural reality. What would be unimaginable with
the former's topography and monsters was key to the latter's mass-cultural
impact – the existence of a real Jurassic Park ride and of a great variety of dino-
saur toys (famously displayed in the film itself), of services and commodities
for consumers participating in one of those intermediatized long-term events
known as blockbusters. As a history-land of genre cinema's revived past (KING
KONG, THE LOST WORLD and other monster movies), JURASSIC PARK actualizes
the virtuality of WESTWORLD, i.e., a new conception of the theme park as inhabitable biotope and life-world to the cinema, and a temporality in which coming
back from the dead is part of Hollywood's bio-political production.[61] Rising
from the ashes applies to a cinematic life-cycle which is mirrored in the cul-

tural-economic cycle of each big film – in the "multimedia reincarnation" of the blockbuster, of a "cultural commodity that might be regenerated in any number of media forms", as Schatz writes in his New Hollywood success story.[62] The near inexhaustibility of haunting clichés, which the New Hollywood of the 1970s glimpsed allegorically in images of conspiracy and horror, is fully explored as a life-affirming, future-oriented potential in the larger New Hollywood which thrives on the vitality of the blockbuster.

Steven Spielberg – whose career began within the New Hollywood of youth and road movies – is an even more famous brand-name for the larger New Hollywood's vitality and productivity. The latter are based on recycling. The distant pasts of one's own childhood, of genre cinema history and of traumatic modernity, and also the near pasts of theatrical viewing experiences are "worked through" – re-told in rescue narratives, remembered in rides and merchandise. "Something has survived!" is the tagline of Spielberg's therapeutic realism of real subsumption: time, history, and what is lost to them – THE LOST WORLD – are re-appropriated, re-interpreted, really subsumed under the self-revitalizing "capital cinema" of the blockbuster.[63] Hollywood's bio-political vitalism seems capable of bringing everything, including its generic past, back from the dead. "Life finds a way", as a geneticist in JURASSIC PARK puts it, and: "Bio-technology, like the cinema, makes it possible for us to engage in a kind of time travel," as Wollen writes about that film.[64] Generally, today's blockbusters act as media-cultural "time machines"; this is Elsaesser's name for the temporal logic of a Hollywood whose newness his recent articles frame as post-classical.[65] While Wollen compares Spielberg's dinosaurs which haunt the present to vampires, Elsaesser makes the vampire into a full-blown allegory of cinema's post-classical afterlife. "The very theme of the undead lies at the heart of the cinema's power and cultural presence," he writes; Hollywood affirmatively folds around its die-hard clichés, exerting its vampirist powers of infection-through-fascination, metamorphosis and revitalization.[66] Reading *Fantasy Island* (1978-1984), a TV series reminiscent of Crichton's Hollywood genres turned into worlds, as an allegory of its production, Elsaesser conceptualizes cinema's position in today's media-cultural temporality in terms of bio-power – in terms of cinema's "self-referentiality, repetition, revamping of genres, reiteration of formulas" as a "natural cycle", of movie history as a "natural history" to be rearticulated by television and the digital media.[67]

Hollywood's self-transmuting life-cycle and some other aspects of the above discussion can, finally, be grasped with a concept proposed by Deleuze. The term "control society" appears not in Deleuze's cinema books, but in his essays on contemporary media and modes of social power (with conceptual links to his logics of film that remain implicit, virtual). Historically, the control society is the vanishing point of capitalism's move from the rigid standards of Fordist discipline to a logic of flexible and dispersed power. Exploring this concept, Hardt and Negri see the formation of control societies as an outcome of the anti-disciplinary resistance and creativity of 1960s countercultures: with the production of hybrid social subjectivities, with institutions continually redefined according to the movements and temporal rhythms of the "multitude", capital power adapts to, integrates, normalizes and profits from the new pragmatic of flexibility and affective labor.[68] While disciplinary society's "confinements" acted as social "molds", Deleuze writes, "controls are a *modulation*, like a self-transmuting molding continually changing from one moment to the next [...]."[69] In this definition, Deleuze falls back upon the terms of his description of the cinematic "movement-image" as it captures the ever changing duration of the material world: the film-image is a "modulation" which "constantly modifies the mold, constitutes a variable, continuous, temporal mold."[70] When controls modulate society like film modulates reality, "the world itself 'turns to film'", as Deleuze remarks on the pervasiveness of television as a technology of control.[71] The world turns to film as capital becomes a world, to the extent that "capital cinema" – cinema as a rehearsal ground and agent of socialization – is itself rendered flexible, entirely mediatised, pervaded by electronic technologies. Giving film-images unprecedented global reach, connectivity and cultural penetration, the contemporary blockbuster best warrants Beller's notion of "capital cinema" and its place "at the heart of the society of control", as Patricia Pisters puts it.[72] In its blockbuster mode, cinema is deeply immersed in and at the same time rehearses the temporal logic of control societies, in which, according to Deleuze, "you never finish anything".[73] Life-long learning and continuous self-control, the flexible redefinition and working through of identities – these ethics and subjectivities are turned into consumer-cultural experiences by the cinema of the blockbuster, which is cinema as time machine and hardly ever finished event. Blockbusters exceed the molds of genre and narrative closure; they rework (movie) history and consumer biographies, and modulate between markets and media, anticipations and memories, trailers and DVDs, novelty and nostalgia.[74]

The formation process of the control society offers a framework for reconsidering the genealogy of New Hollywood and some ambiguities surrounding the term. In this perspective, the relationship between the New Hollywood of disciplinary crisis and countercultural experimentation, and the New Hollywood of the blockbuster is less one of opposition, than one of virtualities that are actualized. In other words, THE DIRTY DOZEN and KELLY'S HEROES, WESTWORLD and COMA become meaningful as symptoms and anticipations of media-cultural, hence social, experiences which are flexible, affective, undisciplined – and controlled. Hollywood has displaced and reworked the

WESTWORLD into the JURASSIC PARK, and one can also see a kind of legacy of THE DIRTY DOZEN in contemporary blockbusters: from the obvious example of ARMAGEDDON (1998) – with its rock band-like team of misfits and jokers on a special NASA mission, and with the DIRTY DOZEN-comparison circulated by promotional discourses and reviews of the film[75] – to TWISTER (1996) or XXX (2002), which contrast the productivity of affective labor and subcultural 'tacit knowledge' with the failures of disciplined action.

But of course, the (virtual) flexibility explored in the American cinema circa 1970 and the (actual) flexibility rehearsed in today's cinema of the blockbuster are not one and the same thing. A genealogical approach to our present global media culture probably has to consider processes of re-evaluation which have gradually turned flexibility and affectivity from indices of anti-disciplinary resistance into driving forces of today's creative industries, lifestyle economies and experience cultures. This point (which demands further inquiry) can be illustrated by a last visit to a theme park running on movie software, with a detour through the contemporary diagnostics of late 1960s New Hollywood. In 1971, Elsaesser contrasted classical Hollywood's motivation and goal-orientation of action with recent films like THE WILD BUNCH whose emotionally dislocated heroes "laugh uncontrollably for no apparent reason, only suddenly to break into outbursts of unmotivated and wholly irrational violence".[76] In 2002, Warner Bros. Movie World at Bottrop, Germany, opened – next to the LETHAL WEAPON, ERASER and WILD WILD WEST roller coasters, the BATMAN flight simulator, "Rick's Café Américain" and DIRTY HARRY's BBQ diner – a "free-fall ride" tower named after Peckinpah's western to end all westerns.[77] Advertised by the Movie World management as the worthy namesake of a "brutal and immoral" western's "anti-heroes", and with the subtitle of the film's German dubbed version added to its name, THE WILD BUNCH – *Sie kannten kein Gesetz* (literally *They Knew No Law*) now shoots up (or rather down) lawless theme park consumers who laugh uncontrollably under technologically controlled outbursts of violence. One New Hollywood's crisis of motivation has become the name of another New Hollywood's experience culture.

Notes

1.   Peter Lloyd: "The American Cinema: An Outlook", *monogram* 1, 1971, 12.
2.   Thomas Elsaesser: "The American Cinema: Why Hollywood", *monogram* 1, 1971, 9f.
3.   Thomas Elsaesser: "The Pathos of Failure", *monogram* 6, 1975, (15) in this volume.
4.   Chris Hugo: "Easy Rider and Hollywood in the '70s", *Movie* 31/32, 1986, 67, 69, 71.

5.   Gilles Deleuze: *The Movement-Image. Cinema 1*. [1983] Minneapolis: U of Minnesota P 1986, 167f, 207-210.

6.   Elsaesser: "The Pathos of Failure" (p. 17f), in this volume.

7.   Steve Neale: "'New Hollywood Cinema'", *Screen* 17, 2, 1976, 119.

8.   On historical usages and different meanings of the terms "New Hollywood" and "post-classical Hollywood" see Peter Kramer: "Post-classical Hollywood", in: John Hill, Pamela Church Gibson (eds.): The Oxford Guide to Film Studies. Oxford: Oxford UP 1998.

9.   Hugo: "Easy Rider and Hollywood in the '70s", 71.

10.   Michael Hardt, Antonio Negri: *Empire*. Cambridge, London: Harvard UP 2000, 274f.

11.   My rather loose usage of this latter term aims to interpret film-industrial practices and images at a historical conjuncture when, in the West, youth-culture and counter-culture are congruent to a higher degree than ever before or since. Regrettably, my approach here does not take feminist and African-American struggles within this counter-cultural context into account.

12.   Jonathan L. Beller: "Cinema, Capital of the Twentieth Century", Postmodern Culture 4, 3, 1994; web publication: http://www.iath.virginia.edu/pmc/text-only/issue.594/beller.594, paragraphs 10, 7, 59.

13.   Cf Hardt, Negri: *Empire*, 275, 402.

14.   Beller: "Cinema, Capital of the Twentieth Century", paragraph 6.

15.   Pauline Kael: "Blessed Profanity" [1970], in: *Deeper into Movies*. Boston, Toronto: Little Brown & Co. 1973, 93, 95.

16.   Ibid., 94.

17.   Jan Dawson: review of M*A*S*H, *Sight and Sound* 39, 3, 1970, 161.

18.   Jeanine Basinger: *The World War II Combat Film. Anatomy of a Genre*. New York: Columbia UP 1986, 202f.

19.   Ibid., 205ff, 201.

20.   Philip French: review of The Dirty Dozen, *Sight and Sound* 36, 4, 1967, 201.

21.   Ibid.

22.   Thus, one can see the film's self-positioning as a war movie-novelty – opening up an old genre to young audiences – as being allegorically reflected in its narrative stressing of innovation and inventiveness.

23.   Interestingly, among the few non-road movies to which Elsaesser referred in his "Pathos of Failure" essay is another Robert Aldrich film, The Mean Machine a.k.a. The Longest Yard (1974), with a prison plot focusing on the Burt Reynolds hero "turning anti-social convicts into loyal team-mates" at football. Elsaesser's remarks on this film ("The Pathos of Failure", 16, in this volume) emphasize its narrative disintegration and cognitive unreliability, exposing its "motivational predicament: if characters have no moral history that can plausibly explain their behaviour, action is the spectacle of gratuitousness". Generally, the frequency (and obtrusiveness) of narratives of male bonding in Aldrich's work might be of interest to a more auteurist approach.

24.   Cf Hardt, Negri: *Empire*, 273-276, 290-292; see also Michael Hardt: "Affective labor", Boundary 2, 26(2), 1999, 89-100; web publication: http://www.aleph-arts.org/io_lavoro/textos/Hardt.doc, and Ronald E. Day: "Totality and Representation: A History of Knowledge Management Through European Documenta-

tion, Critical Modernity, and Post-Fordism", *Journal of the American Society for Information Science and Technology*, 52, 9, 2001, 724-735. web publication: http://www.lisp.wayne.edu/~ai2398/kmasis.htm. It should be noted that while my approach to the pragmatics of some combat movies of New Hollywood circa 1970 stresses the notion of teamwork, Hardt's and Negri's analysis of today's "digital capitalism" gives much more prominence to the concept of network production.

25. Latin-folk pop singer Trini Lopez played a minor character among the Dirty Dozen; admittedly, he was not a prototypical rebel-idol of late 1960s youth culture.

26. Ed Guerrero: "Black Violence as Cinema: From Cheap Thrills to Historical Agonies", in: J. David Slocum (ed.), *Violence and American Cinema*. New York, London: Routledge 2001, 213f.

27. French: review of THE DIRTY DOZEN, 201.

28. Kael: "The Man Who Loved War" [1970], in: *Deeper into Movies*, 99; David Wilson: review of PATTON – *Lust for Glory*, *Sight and Sound* 39, 3, 1970, 160.

29. Lloyd: "The American Cinema: An Outlook", 12.

30. Robert B. Ray: *A Certain Tendency of the Hollywood Cinema 1930-1980*. Princeton: Princeton UP 1985, 314f.

31. Of course, there are New Hollywood war movies contemporary to KELLY'S HEROES which strongly emphasize a notion of the insanity of war; one could mention the crumbling of action-trajectories and the EASY RIDER-style editing of Sidney Pollack's World War II combat film CASTLE KEEP (1969), or Mike Nichols's CATCH-22 (1970), a rather dark and nihilistic World War II military satire in the wake of M*A*S*H's success.

32. Basinger: *The World War II Combat Film*, 203f; Thomas Doherty: *Projections of War. Hollywood, American Culture, and World War II*. New York: Columbia UP 1993, 296. Interestingly, the focus on the violence of the actions in THE DIRTY DOZEN – rather than on their cooperative and productive aspects – seems to allow for a smooth integration of Aldrich's film within the established canon of New Hollywood classics. As Michael Hammond writes: "The Robert Aldrich film is notable for its violence and brutality at the moment when the new rating system replaced the old Production Code. The film acts as an important precursor to BONNIE AND CLYDE (1967), and later THE WILD BUNCH, of the new, violent tone the new system would foster." Michael Hammond: "Some Smothering Dreams: The Combat Film in Contemporary Hollywood", in: Steve Neale (ed.): *Genre and Contemporary Hollywood*. London: British Film Institute 2002, 64.

33. Cf Deleuze: *The Movement-Image*, 144, 148.

34. Ibid., 164ff.

35. On disciplined co-operation and functionalism in wartime combat movies, especially in *Air Force*, see Doherty: *Projections of War*, 103ff, 110ff.

36. This also goes for the historical greatness of military missions celebrated in several all-star war epics from the early 1960s to the mid-1970s.

37. Hardt, Negri: *Empire*, 385.

38. Ibid., 273, 275.

39. David E. James: Allegories of Cinema. American Film in the Sixties. Princeton: Princeton UP 1989, 14f.

40. Ibid., 17.

41. Janet Staiger: "The package-unit system: unit management after 1955", in: David Bordwell, Janet Staiger, Kristin Thompson: *The Classical Hollywood Cinema. Film Style and Mode of Production to 1960*. New York 1985.

42. The complete detachment of a professional subculture of treasure-hunters from the system's overall effort in KELLY'S HEROES – "We're just a private enterprise operation," as Eastwood explains his unit's mission – is interpreted as an allegory of independent film production by Paul Smith. The author points to Clint Eastwood's increased reliance on his Malpaso company (founded in 1968) after his dissatisfaction with a major studio's production of KELLY'S HEROES, a film "whose central contradiction is that its servicemen do not actually serve, even though they are heroic entrepreneurs". Paul Smith: *Clint Eastwood. A Cultural Production*. London: University College Press 1993, 198.

43. Murray Smith: "Theses on the philosophy of Hollywood history", in: Steve Neale, Murray Smith (eds.): *Contemporary Hollywood Cinema*. London, New York: Routledge 1998, 14.

44. Ibid., 11. Along with Janet Staiger, Murray Smith would probably object to a conceptual connection of classical Hollywood's production logic with Fordist discipline. However, Staiger's remark that "making a film [in the classical studio system, D.R.] was not working on a Ford moving assembly-line" (in: "The package-unit system: unit management after 1955", 336) and Smith's points on classical Hollywood's ""'non-Fordist' peculiarities" (in: "Theses on the philosophy of Hollywood history", 8) do not, in my view, radically invalidate that comparison.

45. Thomas Schatz: "The New Hollywood", in: Jim Collins, Hilary Radner, Ava Preacher Collins (eds.): *Film Theory Goes to the Movies*. New York, London: Routledge 1993, 9ff.

46. Ibid., 15.

47. J. Hoberman: "Ten years that shook the world", *American Film* 10, June 1985, 34.

48. David A. Cook: "Auteur Cinema and the 'Film Generation' in 1970s Hollywood", in: Jon Lewis (ed.): *The New American Cinema*. Durham & London: Duke UP 1998, 35.

49. Andrew Britton: "Blissing Out: The Politics of Reaganite Entertainment", *movie* 31/32, 1986, 2.

50. Smith: "Theses on the philosophy of Hollywood history", 10. In "The Pathos of Failure" (14; in this volume), Elsaesser suggested a Hollywood landscape divided between the emotional involvement and spectacle offered by cop thrillers and disaster movies on the one hand, and "emotional anti-stances" catered for by road movies with rebel heroes on the other.

51. THE LAST MOVIE was a commercially unsuccessful, self-reflexive road-movie essay on Hollywood film-making, directed by Dennis Hopper in 1971 in the wake of EASY RIDER's success.

52. Fredric Jameson: "Totality as Conspiracy", in: *The Geopolitical Aesthetic. Cinema and Space in the World System*. Bloomington, Indianapolis: Indiana UP 1992, 15, 82.

53. Hardt, Negri: *Empire*, 23f.

54. Ibid., 386; on real subsumption see also Ibid., 255, 272.

55. Deleuze: *The Movement-Image*, 210.

56. In a closer look at the amusement park as an allegorical location in mid-1970s "uneasy" Hollywood, one would encounter ROLLERCOASTER (1975), a hybrid of disas-

ter film and cop thriller, set in various amusement parks. As a companion film to WESTWORLD's and FUTUREWORLD's horror of Hollywood genres cybernetically revived as virtual realities, one could mention WELCOME TO BLOOD CITY (1976): this British-Canadian co-production stars Jack Palance and 2001's Keir Dullea in an artificial Wild West environment remote-controlled for training purposes by a conspiratory secret service.

57. Britton: "Blissing Out", 5.
58. Deleuze: *The Movement-Image*, 211.
59. Crichton contributed the novel and screenplay to JURASSIC PARK and the novel to THE LOST WORLD – JURASSIC PARK; JURASSIC PARK III uses characters created by Crichton. From an *auteurist* point of view, one could highlight this writer-director's ongoing fascination with technologically controlled, isolated spaces and with "imitations of life" – from his novel filmed as THE ANDROMEDA STRAIN (1971), through his SciFi thriller LOOKER (1981) to the TV series *ER* he created in 1994.
60. Peter Wollen: "Theme Park and Variations", Sight and Sound 7, 1993, 8.
61. Observations on the relations between cinematic and theme park temporalities and experiential modes can be found for instance in Scott Bukatman "There's Always Tomorrowland: Disney and the Hypercinematic Experience", *October*, no.57, Summer 1991, and (with regard to JURASSIC PARK in the light of post-Fordist production and consumption) in Constance Balides: "Jurassic post-Fordism: tall tales of economics in the theme park", *Screen* 41, 2, 2000, 139-160.
62. Schatz: "The New Hollywood", 31, 29.
63. "Something has survived!" was a promotional slogan of the second JURASSIC PARK film, entitled THE LOST WORLD.
64. Wollen: "Theme Park and Variations", p. 7
65. see Elsaesser: "Specularity and engulfment: Francis Ford Coppola and BRAM STOKER'S DRACULA", in: Steve Neale, Murray Smith (eds.): *Contemporary Hollywood Cinema*, 199, and "The Blockbuster. Everything Connects, but Not Everything Goes", in: Jon Lewis (ed.): *The End of Cinema as we know it. American Film in the Nineties*. New York: New York UP 2001, 21f.
66. Wollen: "Theme Park and Variations", 8; Elsaesser: "Specularity and engulfment", 197f.
67. Elsaesser: "Fantasy Island: Dream Logic as Production Logic", in: Thomas Elsaesser, Kay Hoffmann (eds.): *Cinema Futures: Cain, Abel or Cable? The Screen Arts in the Digital Age*. Amsterdam: Amsterdam UP 1998, 154f.
68. See Hardt, Negri: *Empire*, 268ff, 318, 331.
69. Deleuze: "Postscript on Control Societies" [1990], in: *Negotiations 1972-1990*. [1990], New York: Columbia UP 1995, 178f. On control societies in Deleuze, see also his conversation with Negri, "Control and Becoming" [1990], also in the *Negotiations* volume.
70. Deleuze: *The Movement-Image*, 24. Deleuze derives his distinction between photographic mold and cinematographic modulation from André Bazin.
71. Deleuze: "Letter to Serge Daney: Optimism, Pessimism, and Travel" [1986], in: *Negotiations 1972-1990*, 76.
72. Patricia Pisters: "Glamour and Glycerine: Surplus and Residual of the Network Society: from *Glamorama* to *Fight Club*", in: Pisters (ed.): *Micropolitics of Media Cul-*

ture. Reading the Rhizomes of Deleuze and Guattari. Amsterdam: Amsterdam UP 2001, 140.

73. Deleuze: "Postscript on Control Societies", 179.
74. See Elsaesser: "The Blockbuster", 21f.
75. For instance in Andy Richards' review in *Sight & Sound* 9, 1998, 39.
76. Elsaesser: "The American Cinema: Why Hollywood", 10.
77. See for instance the German website http://www.germancoaster.de/features-2002-03-warnerpressekonferenz.html.

Bibliography

Adair, Gilbert, *Hollywood's Vietnam, from The Green Berets to Apocalypse Now* (London: Proteus, 1981)

Allen, Robert C., 'Home Alone Together: Hollywood and the "Family Film",' in Melvyn Stokes and Richard Maltby, (ed.), *Identifying Hollywood's Audiences: Cultural Identity and the Movies* (London: BFI, 1999) 109-131

Alloway, Lawrence, *Violent America: the movies 1946-64* (New York: MOMA, 1971)

Amis, Martin, 'Acts of Violence', *The Observer*, July 3rd 1994, 20-24

Appel, Alfred, *Nabokov's Dark Cinema* (Oxford University Press, 1974)

Assayas, Olivier, 'Tarkovsky: Seeing is Believing' (A Conversation with Berenice Reynaud) in *Sight and Sound*, January 1997, vol.7/1

Atkins, T.R., *Sexuality in the Movies* (Indiana University Press, 1975)

Auster, Albert, and Leonard Quart, *How the War was Remembered* (New York: Praeger, 1988)

Balides, Constance, 'Jurassic post-Fordism: tall tales of economics in the theme park', *Screen* 41, 2, 2000, 139-160

Balio, Tino (ed.), *Hollywood in the Age of Television* (Boston: Unwin Hyman, 1990)

Bart, Peter, *Who Killed Hollywood? ... And Put the Tarnish on Tinseltown?* (Los Angeles: Renaissance Books, 1999)

Bart, Peter, *The Gross: The Hits, the Flops – the Summer that Ate Hollywood* (New York: St Martin's Press, 1999)

Barthes, Roland, 'Structural Analysis of Narrative', *Image Music Text* (New York: Noonday Press, 1977) 79-124

Basinger, Jeanine, *The World War II Combat Film. Anatomy of a Genre* (New York: Columbia University Press, 1986)

Bazin, André, *What is Cinema* trans. Hugh Grey (Berkeley and Los Angeles: University of California Press, 1985)

Beller, Jonathan L., 'Cinema, Capital of the Twentieth Century', *Postmodern Culture* 4, 3, 1994 (web publication: http://www.iath.virginia.edu/pmc/text-only/issue) 594

Bernardoni, James, *The New Hollywood: What the Movies Did with the New Freedom of the Seventies* (Jefferson, N.C.: McFarland and Co, 1991)

Bersani, Leo, *The Freudian Body: Psychoanalysis and Art* (Columbia University Press: 1986)

Biskind, Peter, *Easy Riders and Raging Bulls* (New York: Simon & Schuster, 1999)

Blumenberg H.C. et al., *New Hollywood* (München: Hanser, 1976)

Bonitzer, Pascal, 'Partial Vision' *Wide Angle*, vol. 4 no. 4, 1981, 56-63

Bordwell, David, *Narration and the Fiction Film* (Madison: Wisconsin University Press, 1985)

Bordwell, David, Janet Staiger and Kristin Thompson, 'Since 1960: the persistence of a mode of film practice,' in *The Classical Hollywood Cinema: Film Style & Mode of Production to 1960* (London: Routledge, 1985) 367-377

Britton, Andrew, 'Blissing Out: The Politics of Reaganite Entertainment,' *Movie* 31/32, 1986, 1-42

Bruce, Bryan, 'Martin Scorsese: Five Films' *Movie* 31/32, 1986, 88-94

Bryman, Alan, *Disney and his Worlds* (New York: Routledge, 1995)

Buckland, Warren, 'A Close Encounter with RAIDERS OF THE LOST ARK: notes on narrative aspects of the Hollywood Blockbuster' in Steve Neale and Murray Smith (eds.), *Contemporary Hollywood Cinema* (Routledge, 1998)

Bukatman, Scott, 'There's Always Tomorrowland: Disney and the Hypercinematic Experience', *October* 57, 1991, 55-78

Bullis, R.A., MEAN STREETS, PhD Dissertation, Wisconsin, 1977

Byron, Stuart, 'THE SEARCHERS: Cult Movie of the New Hollywood,' *New York Magazine*, March 5, 1979, 45-48

Cagin, Seth, and Philip Dray, *Hollywood Films of the Seventies: Sex, Drugs, Violence, Rock 'n' Roll, and Politics* (New York: Harper & Row, 1984)

Carroll, Noël, 'Back to the Basics,' in Philip S. Cook, Douglas Gomery and Lawrence W. Lichty (eds.), *American Media*, (Washington, D.C: The Wilson Centre Press, 1989)

Carroll, Noël, *The Philosophy of Horror, or, Paradoxes of the Heart* (London and New York: Routledge 1990)

Carroll, Noël, 'The Future of Allusion: Hollywood in the Seventies (and Beyond),' *October*, no. 20, 1982, 51-81

Carroll, Noël, 'Towards a Theory of Film Suspense', *Persistence of Vision*, no.1, 1984

Cawelti, John G., '*Chinatown* and Generic Transformation in Recent American Films' in G. Mast and M .Cohen (eds.), *Film Theory and Criticism* (New York: Oxford University Press, 1979)

Clarens, Carlos, and Foster Hirsch, *Crime Movies* (New York: Da Capo Press, 1997)

Clover, Carol, *Men, Women and Chainsaws* (London: Routledge, 1991)

Cohan, Steven, and Ina Rae Hark (eds.), *Screening the Male: Exploring Masculinities in Hollywood Cinema* (London and New York: Routledge, 1993)

Colker David and Jack Virrell, 'The *New* New Hollywood,' *Take One* 6, 10 August 1978, 19-23

Collins, Jim, Hilary Radner and Ava Preacher Collins (eds.), *Film Theory Goes to the Movies* (London: Routledge 1993)

Cones, John W., *Film Finance and Distribution: A Dictionary of Terms* (Los Angeles: Silman-James Press, 1992)

Cook, David A., 'Auteur Cinema and the 'Film Generation' in 1970s Hollywood', in Jon Lewis, (ed.), *The New American Cinema*, (Durham & London: Duke University Press, 1998) 11-37

Cook, David, *Lost Illusions: American cinema in the Shadow of Vietnam and Watergate 1970-1979* (Berkeley: University of California Press, 2002)

Cook, David A., 'The Seventies and Eighties: Colonies of the Mind and Heart,' in *A History of Narrative Film*, 2nd ed. (New York and London: W. W. Norton & Co., 1991), 822-906

Cook, Pam, 'David Cronenberg's *Dead Ringers*', *Monthly Film Bulletin*, March 1989

Corman, Roger, with Jim Jerome, *How I Made a Hundred Movies in Hollywood and Never Lost a Dime*, (Delta Books: New York, 1990)

Corrigan, Timothy, *A Cinema without Walls: Movies and Culture after Vietnam* (London: Routledge, 1992)

Coupland, Douglas, 'Harolding in West Vancouver,' in Coupland, *Postcards from the Dead* (London: Flamingo, 1996) 101-106

Crary, Jonathan, 'Psychopathways: Horror Movies and the Technology of Everyday Life', *Wedge*, no 2, 1983

Davies, Philip, and Brian Neve (eds.), *Cinema, Politics and Society in America* (Manchester: Manchester University Press, 1981)

Davis, Brian, *The Thriller: The Suspense Film from 1946* (London: Studio Vista/Dutton Picturebook, 1973)

Dawson, Jan, review of M*A*S*H, *Sight and Sound* 39, 3, 1970, 161f

Day, Ronald E., 'Totality and Representation: A History of Knowledge Management Through European Documentation, Critical Modernity, and Post-Fordism', *Journal of the American Society for Information Science and Technology*, 52, 9, 2001, 724-735

Deleuze, Gilles, 'Letter to Serge Daney: Optimism, Pessimism, and Travel' [1986], 'Control and Becoming' [1990], 'Postscript on Control Societies' [1990], in *Negotiations 1972-1990*, (New York: Columbia University Press, 1995) 68-79 and 169-182

Deleuze, Gilles, *The Movement-Image. Cinema 1.* [1983] (Minneapolis: University of Minnesota Press, 1986)

Denby, David, 'Can the Movies be Saved?,' *New York Magazine* 19, 28 (1986) 24-35

Denzin, Norman K., *Images of Postmodern Society: Social Theory and Contemporary Cinema* (London: Sage, 1991)

Dickstein, Morris, 'Beyond Good and Evil', *American Film* vol. 6 no. 4, July-Aug 81, 49-69

Di Lauro, Al and Gerald Rabkin, *Dirty Movies* (New York/London: Chelsea House, 1976)

Disney Project, *Inside the Mouse* (Durham: Duke University Press, 1995)

Doherty, Thomas, *Projections of War: Hollywood, American Culture, and World War II* (New York: Columbia University Press, 1993)

Donahue, Suzanne Mary, *American Film Distribution: The Changing Market Place* (Ann Arbor: UMI Research Press, 1987)

Douglass, Wayne J., 'The Criminal Psychopath as Hollywood Hero', *Journal of Popular Film and Television*, vol. 8 no. 4, Winter 1981

Dunne, John Gregory, *Monster: Living Off The Big Screen* (New York: Vintage, 1997)

Durgnat, R., 'Spies and Ideologies', *Cinema* (UK) no. 2, March 1954

Edelson, Edward, *Tough Guys and Gals in the Movies* (New York: Doubleday, 1978)

Ellis, John, *Visible Fictions: Cinema, Television, Video* (London and New York: Routledge, 1982)

Elsaesser, Thomas, 'Fantasy Island: Dream Logic as Production Logic', in Thomas Elsaesser, Kay Hoffmann (eds.), *Cinema Futures: Cain, Abel or Cable? The Screen Arts in the Digital Age*, (Amsterdam: Amsterdam University Press, 1998) 143-158

Elsaesser, Thomas, 'Hyper-, Retro- or Counter Cinema: European Cinema and Third Cinema Between Hollywood and Art Cinema,', in John King, Ana M. López, Manuel Alvarado (eds.), *Mediating Two Worlds: Cinematic Encounters in the Americas* (London: BFI Publishing, 1993) 119-135

Elsaesser, Thomas, 'The Pathos of Failure: Notes on the Unmotivated Hero', *Monogram* no. 6, 1975, 13-19

Elsaesser, Thomas, 'NASHVILLE and Putting on a Show', *Persistence of Vision* 1, 1982

Elsaesser, Thomas, 'Specularity and engulfment: Francis Ford Coppola and *Bram Stoker's Dracula*', in Steve Neale, Murray Smith (eds.), *Contemporary Hollywood Cinema* (London, New York: Routledge 1998) 191-208

Elsaesser, Thomas, 'The American Cinema: Why Hollywood', *monogram* 1, 1971, 4-10

Elsaesser, Thomas, 'The Blockbuster. Everything Connects, but Not Everything Goes', in Jon Lewis (ed.), *The End of Cinema as We Know It. American Film in the Nineties*, (New York: New York University Press, 2001) 11-22

Evans, Walter, 'Monster Movies: A Sexual Theory', *Journal of Popular Film*, Vol. 2, No. 4, 353-65

Everson, William K., *The Detective in Film*, (Citadel Press, 1972)

Everson, William K, *The Bad Guys*, (Citadel Press, 1964)

Fadiman, William, *Hollywood Now* (London: Thames & Hudson, 1972)

Finler, Joel W., *The Movie Directors Story* (New York: Crescent Books, 1985)

Fiske, John, *Understanding Popular Culture* (London: Routledge, 1989)

Fluck, Winfried (ed.), *New Hollywood* (Berlin: J.F. Kennedy Institute, 1978)

Fox, Terry Curtis (ed.), 'City Knights', *Film Comment*, vol. 20, no. 5, Sept-Oct 84, 30-49

French, Philip, review of *The Dirty Dozen*, *Sight and Sound* 36, 4, 1967, 201-203

Gabler, Neal, *An Empire of Their Own* (New York: Crown Publishers, 1988)

Gagne, Paul, *The Zombies That Ate Pittsburgh* (New York: Dodd, Mead & Company, 1987)

Gallagher, T., 'Abel Ferrara: Violence and Responsibility', *22nd Rotterdam Film Festival Guide*, 1993, 156-164

Gaut, Berys, 'The Paradox of Horror,' and 'The Enjoyment Theory of Horror: A Response to Carroll,' *British Journal of Aesthetics*, vol. 33, no. 4, (October 1993), 333-345 and vol. 35, no. 3 (July 1995), 284-289

Giles, Denis, 'The Outdoor Economy', *Journal of the University Film and Video Association*, vol. 35, no. 2, Spring 1983, 66-76

Godard, Jean-Luc, and Pauline Kael, 'The Economics of Film Criticism: A Debate,' *Camera Obscura* 8/9/10 (1982) 163-184

Goldman, William, *Adventures in the Screen Trade: A Personal View of Hollywood and Screenwriting* (New York: Warner Books, 1983)

Goldman, William, *Which Lie Did I Tell?: More Adventures in the Screen Trade* (New York: Vintage, 2001)

Goldman, William, *The Big Picture: Who Killed Hollywood?* (New York: Applause Books, 2000)

Gomery, Douglas, 'The American Film Industry of the 1970s: Stasis in the 'New Hollywood',' *Wide Angle*, vol. 5, no. 4, 1983, 52-59

Gomery, Douglas, 'Corporate Ownership and Control in the Contemporary US Film industry,' *Screen*, vol. 25, nos. 4-5, July – October, 1984, 60-69

Gomery, Douglas, 'Hollywood's Hold on the New Television Technologies,' *Screen*, vol. 29, no. 2, Spring 1988, 82-89

Gomery, Douglas, 'Hollywood's Movie Business,' in Michael C. Emery and Ted C. Smythe, (eds.), *Readings in Mass Communication* 7th edition (Dubuque, Iowa: Wm. C. Brown, 1989)

Gomery, Douglas, 'Television, Wide Screen, and Color', 'A Transformation in Hollywood Moviemaking,' and 'An Epilogue: Contemporary Film History' in Gomery, *Movie History: A Survey* (Belmont, California, Wadsworth Publishing Company, 1991) 279-308, 311-345 and 423-441

Gomery, Douglas, 'Vertical Integration, Horizontal Regulation – The Growth of Rupert Murdoch's Media Empire,' *Screen*, vol. 27, no. 4, May/August 1986, 78-87

Gordon, David, 'Why the movie majors are major', *Sight and Sound*, Autumn 1973, 194-196

Gow, Gordon, *Suspense in the Cinema*, (Barnes & Noble, 1968)

Guerrero, Ed, 'Black Violence as Cinema: From Cheap Thrills to Historical Agonies', in J. David Slocum (ed.), *Violence and American Cinema*, (New York, London: Routledge 2001) 211-225

Hammond, Lawrence, *Thriller Movies: Classic Films of Suspense and Mystery*, (London: Octopus, 1974)

Hammond, Michael, 'Some Smothering Dreams: The Combat Film in Contemporary Hollywood', in Steve Neale (ed.), *Genre and Contemporary Hollywood*, (London: British Film Institute, 2002) 62-76

Hardt, Michael, 'Affective labor', *Boundary* 2, 26(2), 1999, 89-100

Hardt, Michael, and Antonio Negri, *Empire* (Cambridge, London: Harvard University Press, 2000)

Haskell, Molly, *From Reverence to Rape: The Treatment of Women in the Movies* (University of Chicago Press, Second edition, 1987)

Heath, Stephen, 'JAWS, Ideology and Film Theory', *Framework*, (4) 25-27

Hillier, Jim, *The New Hollywood* (Studio Vista, 1993)

Hirsch, Foster, *The Dark Side of the Screen: Film noir* (New York: Da Capo Press, 1988)

Hoberman, J., *Dennis Hopper: From Method to Madness* (Minneapolis: Walker Art Centre, 1988)

Hoberman, Jim, and Jonathan Rosenbaum, *Midnight Movies* (New York: Harper & Row, 1983)

Hoberman, J., 'Ten years that shook the world', *American Film* 10, June 1985, 34-59

Hoberman, J., *The Dream Life. Movies, Media, and the Mythology of the Sixties* (New York: The New Press, 2003)

Holub, R., *Critical Theory: An Introduction* (Methuen, 1984)

Holub, R., *Crossing Borders* (Wisconsin 1992)

Horwath, Alexander (ed.), *Cool – Pop. Politik. Hollywood 1960-68* (Wien: Viennale, 1994)

Hugo, Chris, '*Easy Rider* and Hollywood in the '70s', *Movie* 31/32, 1986, 67-71

Jacobs, Diane, *Hollywood Renaissance: the New Generation of Filmmakers and Their Works* (New York: Delta, 1977/1980)

James, David E., *Allegories of Cinema. American Film in the Sixties* (Princeton: Princeton University Press, 1989)

Jameson, Fredric, 'Totality as Conspiracy', in Jameson, *The Geopolitical Aesthetic. Cinema and Space in the World System*, (Bloomington, Indianapolis: Indiana University Press, 1992) 9-84

Jansen, Peter W., and Wolfram Schütte (eds.), *New Hollywood* (München, Wien: Hanser, 1976)

Jeffords, Susan, *Hard Bodies: Hollywood Masculinity in the Reagan Era* (New Brunswick: Rutgers University Press, 1994)

Jeffords, Susan, 'The New Vietnam Films: Is the Movie Over?' *Journal of Popular Film and Television*, vol. 13, no. 4 (1986), 186-195

Kael, Pauline, 'After Innocence,' *The New Yorker*, October 1, 1973, 113-118

Kael, Pauline, 'Blessed Profanity' [1970], 'The Man Who Loved War' [1970], in *Deeper into Movies*, (Boston, Toronto: Little Brown & Co, 1973) 92-102

Kael, Pauline, 'Why are the movies so bad?: Or, the numbers,' in Kael, *Taking it All In* (New York: Holt, Rinehart and Winston, 1984)

Kaminsky, Stuart, *American Film Genres* (Dayton, Ohio 1974)

Kaplan, E. Ann (ed.), *Women in Film Noir* (London: British Film Institute, 1999)

Kehr, Dave, 'The New Male Melodrama,' *American Film* 8, 6 (April 1989) 43-47.

Kellner, Douglas, and Michael Ryan, *Camera Politica: The Politics and Ideology of Contemporary Hollywood Film* (Bloomington and Indianapolis: Indiana University Press, 1988)

Kerr, Paul, *The American Private Detective Film*, (MA Dissertation, 1977)

Kisch, John, and Edward Mapp, *A Separate Cinema* (New York: Farrar, Strauss and Giroux, 1992)

Kolker, Robert Phillip, *A Cinema of Loneliness: Penn, Kubrick, Coppola, Scorsese, Altman* (New York and Oxford: Oxford University Press, 1980). 2nd edition 1988

Kramer, Peter, 'Post-classical Hollywood', in John Hill, Pamela Church Gibson (eds.), *The Oxford Guide to Film Studies* (Oxford: Oxford University Press, 1998) 289-309

Lambert, Gavin, *The Dangerous Edge* (New York: Grossman Publishers/Viking, 1976)

Lehman, Peter, 'Don't Blame This On a Girl' in Ina Rae Hark (ed.), *Screening the Male*, (Routledge 1993) 103-116

Lev, Peter, *The Euro-American Cinema* (Austin: University of Texas Press, 1992)

Lev, Peter, *American Cinema in the 70s* (Austin: University of Texas Press, 2000)

Lewis, Jon, *Whom God Wishes to Destroy: Francis Coppola and the New Hollywood*, (Durham: Duke University Press, 1995)

Lewis, Jon, 'Introduction,' in Lewis (ed.), *The End of Cinema as We Know It: American Film in the Nineties* (New York: NYU Press, 2001) 1-10

Lloyd, Peter, 'The American Cinema: An Outlook', *monogram* 1, 1971, 11-13

Martin, Adrian, *Phantasms* (Melbourne: Penguin, 1994)

McArthur, Colin, *Underworld USA*, (London: Secker and Warburg, 1978)

McCarthy, Todd, and Charles Flynn (eds.), *Kings of the Bs: Working Within the Hollywood System* (New York: E.P. Dutton, 1975)

Mitchell, E., 'Apes and Essences', *Wide Angle*, Spring 1979, 18-23

Monaco, James, *American Film Now: The People, The Power, The Money, The Movies* (New York: Oxford University Press, 1979; 2nd ed.: New York: Zoetrope, 1984)

Mordden, Ethan, *Medium Cool: The Movies of the 1960s* (New York: Alfred A. Knopf, 1990)

Namidon, Stephen, 'Lost in Cyberspace,' *Sunday Times*, 17 July 1994, 9-10.

Neale, Steve, *Genre*, (London: British Film Institute, 1980)

Neale, Steve, 'Hollywood Corner: RAIDERS OF THE LOST ARK', *Framework* No 19, 1982, 37-39

Neale, Steve, 'Hollywood Strikes Back – special effects in recent American cinema', *Screen* vol. 21 no. 3

Neale, Steve, 'New Hollywood cinema,' *Screen*, vol. 17 no. 2 (Summer 1976)

Neale, Steve, 'Masculinity as Spectacle: Reflections on Men and Mainstream Cinema,' *Screen*, vol. 24, no. 6 (1986), 2-17 and in Steven Cohan, Ina Rae Hark, (eds.), *Screening the Male: Exploring Masculinities in Hollywood Cinema* (London and New York: Routledge, 1993), 9-20

Odin, R., 'Fictivisation and the Fictionalising Space' and 'For a Semio-Pragmatics of Film' in Warren Buckland (ed.) *Film Spectator: From Sign to Mind* (Amsterdam: Amsterdam Press, 1994)

Ottoson, Robert, *Reference Guide to the American film noir* (Metuchen, N.J., Scarecrow Press, 1981)

Palmer, R. Barton, 'Defining the Independent Text,' *Persistence of Vision* 6, June 1978, 5-19

Parish, James Robert, and George A. Hill, *Black Action Films* (Jefferson, NC: McFarland & Company, Inc. 1989)

Paul, William, 'Hollywood Harakiri,' *Film Comment* 13, 2 (1977) 40- 43, 56-61

Penley, Constance, 'Time Travel, Primal Scene, and the Critical Dystopia', *Camera Obscura*, no. 15, Fall, 1986, 66-85

Pennington, Ron, 'Telescoping Tomorrow,' *The Hollywood Reporter's 48th Annual*, 1977, 174

Phillips, Julia, *You'll Never Eat Lunch In This Town Again* (New York: Signet, 1991)

Pisters, Patricia, 'Glamour and Glycerine: Surplus and Residual of the Network Society: from GLAMORAMA to FIGHT CLUB', in Pisters (ed.), *Micropolitics of Media Culture. Reading the Rhizomes of Deleuze and Guattari* (Amsterdam: Amsterdam University Press, 2001) 125-141

Porfirio, Robert G., *Dark Age in American Film*, PhD Dissertation, Yale 1979

Pye, Michael, and Lynda Myles, *The Movie Brats: How The Film Generation Took over Hollywood* (New York: Holt & Rinehart 1979)

Rabkin, Eric, *Narrative Suspense*, (Ann Arbor: 1973)

Ray, Robert, *A certain tendency of the American Cinema, 1930-1980* (Princeton University Press, 1985)

Reid, Mark A., *Redefining Black Film* (Berkeley/Los Angeles/Oxford: University of California Press, 1993)

Reinicke, Stefan, *Hollywood Goes Vietnam: Der Vietnamkrieg im US-amerikanischen Film* (Marburg: Hitzeroth, 1993)

Richards, Andy, ARMAGEDDON, Sight & Sound 9, 1998, 38-40

Rogin, Michael *Ronald Reagan: The Movie* (Berkeley and Los Angeles: University of California Press, 1987)

Rosen, Marjorie, 'Hollywood's New Old Movies,' *Millimeter*, May 1976, 28-30

Rosenbaum, Jonathan, *Movie Wars: How Hollywood and the Media Conspire to Limit What Films We Can See* (Chicago: A Cappella Books, 2000)

Rosow, Eugene, *Born to Lose: The Gangster Film in America*, (New York: Oxford University Press, 1978)

Sarris, Andrew, 'After THE GRADUATE,' *American Film* 3, 9 (1978)

Schatz, Thomas, *Hollywood Genres* (New York: McGraw-Hill, 1988)

Schatz, Thomas, *Old Hollywood/New Hollywood: Ritual, Art and Industry* (Ann Arbor: UMI Research Press, 1983)

Schatz, Thomas, *The Genius of the System* (New York: Pantheon Books,1988)

Schatz, Thomas, 'The New Hollywood', in Jim Collins, Hilary Radner, Ava Preacher Collins (eds.), *Film Theory Goes to the Movies* (New York, London: Routledge, 1993) 8-36

Schickel, Richard, 'The Crisis in Movie Narrative,' *Gannett Center Journal* 3 (1989) 1-15

Selby, S., *Dark City*, (London: 1984)

Shadoian, Jack, *Dreams and Dead Ends: The American Gangster Film* (Cambridge, MA: MIT Press, 1977)

Shaviro, Steven, *The Cinematic Body* (University of Minnesota Press, 1994)

Silver, Alain (ed.), *Film Noir Reader* (San Francisco: Limelight Editions, 1996)

Silverman, Kaja, *Male Subjectivity at the Margins* (London and New York: Routledge, 1993)

Sklar, Robert, *Film: An International History of the Medium* (Englewood Cliffs, NJ and New York: Prentice Hall, Inc., and Harry N. Abrams, Inc. 1993)

Smith, Gavin, 'Bad Faith,' *Sight & Sound*, June 1992, 21-23.

Smith, Gavin, 'The Moon in the Gutter,' *Film Comment*, July 1990, 40-44

Smith, Murray, 'Theses on the philosophy of Hollywood history', in Steve Neale, Murray Smith (eds.), *Contemporary Hollywood Cinema* (London, New York: Routledge, 1998) 3-20

Smith, Paul, *Clint Eastwood: A Cultural Production* (London: University College Press, 1993)

Smoodin, Eric, *Disney Discourse: Producing the Magic Kingdom* (Routledge, 1994)

Sobchack, Vivian, *Screening Space* (New York: Ungar, 1985)

Solomon, Stanley, 'Beyond Formula: American Film Genres' in O. Boyd-Barrett and C. Newbold (eds.), *Approaches to Media: A Reader* (Arnold, 1995)

Staiger, Janet (ed.), *The Studio System* (New Brunswick, NJ: Rutgers University Press, 1995)

Staiger, Janet, 'The package-unit system: unit management after 1955', in David Bordwell, Janet Staiger, Kristin Thompson, *The Classical Hollywood Cinema. Film Style and Mode of Production to 1960* (London and New York: Routledge and Columbia University Press, 1985) 330-337

Stanbrook, Alan, 'Hollywood's crashing epics', *Sight and Sound*, vol. 50 no. 2 (Spring 1981)

Steinbrunner, Chris., *Encyclopedia of Mystery and Detection*, (new York: McGraw-Hill, 1976)

Strick, Philip, 'Future States,' *Monthly Film Bulletin* (March 1989)

Tasker, Yvonne, *Spectacular Bodies: Gender, Genre and the Action Cinema* (London: Routledge, 1993)

Taylor, John, *Storming the Magic Kingdom* (New York: Kopf, 1987)

Telotte, J.P., *The Cult Film Experience: Beyond All Reason* (Austin: University of Texas Press, 1991)

Thompson, Kristin, and David Bordwell, 'Hollywood's Fall and Rise: Since the 1960s,' in Bordwell and Thompson, *Film History: An Introduction* (New York: McGraw-Hill, Inc., 1994) 696-722

Thomson, David, *America in the Dark*, (London: Hutchinson, 1978)

Thomson, David, *Overexposures: The Crisis in American Filmmaking* (New York: Morrow, 1981)

Thomson, David, 'The Decade When Movies Mattered,' *Movieline*, August 1993, 43-47, 90

Thomson, David, 'Who Killed the Movies?' *Esquire*, December 1996, 56-60, 62-63.

Tilton, Robert, *Pocahontas: The Evolution of an American Narrative* (Cambridge: Cambridge University Press, 1994)

Todorov, Tsvetan, *The Poetics of Prose* (Cornell University Press, 1977)

Trainor, Richard, 'Major powers', *Sight and Sound*, vol. 57 no. 1, Winter 1987-88

Truffaut, François, *Hitchcock*, (New York 1967, Revised edition: Touchstone Books, 1985)

Turan, Kenneth, and Stephen F. Zito, *Sinema* (New York: New American Library, 1974)

Tuska, Jon, *Dark Cinema: American Film noir in Cultural Perspective*, (London: Greenwood Press, 1984)

Tuska, Jon, *The Detective in Hollywood*, (New York: Doubleday, 1978)

Udovich, Mim, 'Tarantino and Juliette,' *Details* , February 1996, 112-117

Walker, Martin, 'Clinton's Hollywood,' *Sight & Sound*, vol. 3, no. 9, September 1993, 12-14.

Wasko, Janet, *Hollywood in the Information Age: Beyond the Silver Screen* (Cambridge: Polity Press, 1994)

Wide-Angle 5, 4 (1983) special issue on 'The New Hollywood'

Will, David, and Peter Wollen (eds.), *Sam Fuller* (Edinburgh Film Festival, 1969)

Williams, Linda *Hard Core: Power, Pleasure and Perversion* (London: Methuen, 1989)

Wilmington, Mike, 'Roman Polanski's CHINATOWN', *The Velvet Light Trap*, no. 13, Fall 1974

Wilson, David, 'PATTON – LUST FOR GLORY', *Sight and Sound* vol. 39 no. 3, 1970, 160-161

Wolf, William, 'Toward Movies Without Studios,' *Cue*, April 28, 1975, pp.24-25.

Wolfenstein, M., and N.Leites, *Movies A Psychological Study* (Glencoe, IL: The Free Press, 1950)

Wollen, Peter, 'Theme Park and Variations', *Sight and Sound* 7, 1993, 7-10

Wood, Michael, *America at the Movies* (New York: Basic Books, 1975)

Wood, Robin, *Hollywood from Vietnam to Reagan* (New York: Columbia University Press, 1986)

Wood, Robin, 'An Introduction to the American Horror Film' in Bill Nichols (ed.), *Movies and Methods II*, (Berkeley, London: University of California Press, 1985) 195-220

Wood, Robin, 'The incoherent text: narrative in the '80s', *Movie* no. 27/28 (Winter 1980) 24-42

Wyatt, Justin, *High Concept: Movies and Marketing in Hollywood* (Austin: University of Texas Press, 1994)

Zizek, Slavoj, '"The Thing That Thinks": The Kantian Background of the Noir Subject', in Joan Copjec (ed.), *Shades of Noir: A Reader* (London, New York: Verso, 1993) 199-226

List of Contributors

Notes on Editors

Thomas Elsaesser is Professor in the Department of Media Studies at the University of Amsterdam and Chair of Research in Film and Television Studies. Among his recent books are *Fassbinder's Germany: History, Identity, Subject* (1996), *Weimar Cinema and After* (2000), *Metropolis* (2000), *Studying Contemporary American Film* (with Warren Buckland, 2002) and *Früher Film und Kinogeschichte* (2002).

Alexander Horwath is director of the Austrian Film Museum, Vienna. As freelance critic and curator of film and the visual arts, he has edited books on the films of Michael Haneke and on Austrian avant-garde film. In his capacity as director of the Vienna International Film Festival from 1992 to 1996, he edited *The Last Great American Picture Show* (1995), on which the present volume is based.

Noel King currently teaches film in the Department of Media at Macquarie University, Sydney, Australia. He has published on 'New Hollywood' in Pam Cook and Mieke Bernink (eds.), *The Cinema Book* (1999) and was a contributor to the *Australian Journal of Media and Culture*.

Notes on Contributors

Richard T. Jameson has been a film critic, university lecturer in film, art theatre manager and film society programmer, and film festival consultant. A member of the National Society of Film Critics since 1980, he edited the NSFC anthology *They Went Thataway: Redefining Film Genres* (1994), as well as the journals *Movietone News* (1971-81) and *Film Comment* (1990-2000).

Kent Jones is programmer for the Walter Reade Theater at Lincoln Center in New York. A regular contributor to *Film Comment* and *Cahiers du cinéma*, among other journals, he is co-author of a documentary on Italian cinema directed by Martin Scorsese.

Jian Hoberman is the senior film critic for the *Village Voice*, New York. His books include *Midnight Movies* (1983, with Jonathan Rosenbaum), a history of Yiddish-language cinema, *Bridge of Light* (1995), a monograph on Jack Smith's *Flaming Creatures*, *The Red Atlantis* (1998) and, most recently, *The Dream Life: Movies, Media and the Mythology of the '60s* (New Press, 2003).

Howard Hampton has written about music and movies for numerous publications, including *Film Comment*, *Artforum*, the *Village Voice*, the *LA Weekly*, and the *Boston Globe*. He is still writing *Badlands: A Psychogeography of the Reagan Era* for Harvard University Press and still resides in Apple Valley, California.

Christian Keathley is an Assistant Professor in the Film & Media Culture Program at Middlebury College, Vermont. His work has appeared in *Art Papers*, *Film Comment*, and *Framework*, as well as in the volumes *Citizen Sarris* and *Directed by Allen Smithee*.

Adrian Martin is the film critic for *The Age* (Melbourne, Australia). He is the author of *The Mad Max Movies* (Currency, 2003), *Once Upon a Time in America* (BFI, 1998) and *Phantasms* (Penguin, 1994), and co-editor (with Jonathan Rosenbaum) of *Movie Mutations* (BFI, 2003). He is currently completing books on Terrence Malick and Brian De Palma. He is the co-editor of *Rouge* (www.rouge.com) and a Doctoral candidate at Monash University Faculty of Art and Design.

Maitland McDonagh is senior movies editor of *TV Guide Online*. Born and raised in New York City, she received her undergraduate education at Hunter College, New York, earned her MFA in film History/Theory/Criticism from Columbia University. She is the author of *Broken Mirrors/Broken Minds: The Dark Dreams of Dario Argento* (1994, Citadel), *Filmmaking on the Fringe: The Good, the Bad and the Deviant Directors* (1995, Citadel), *The 50 Most Erotic Films of All Time* (1995, Citadel).

Dana Polan teaches film in the School of Cinema-TV at the University of Southern California. He is the author of several books on film and is currently writing a study on the emergence of cinema studies in the United States.

Bérénice Reynaud is the author of *Nouvelles Chines, nouveaux cinémas* (Paris, Cahiers du cinéma, 1999) and Hou Hsiao-hsien's *A City of Sadness* (London, BFI, 2002). Her work has been published in *Cahiers du cinéma*, *Libération*, *Sight & Sound*, *Screen*, *Film Comment*, *Senses of Cinema*, *Cinemascope*, *Afterimage*, *Meteor*, *Springerin*, *Nosferatu* and *Cinemaya*, the *Asian Film Quarterly*, among others. She teaches film history, theory and criticism in the School of Critical Studies and the School of Film/Video at the California Institute of the Arts.

Drehli Robnik is a PhD candidate in Film and TV studies at the University of Amsterdam. He lectures in film theory and history at the University of Vienna and works as a film critic and as a disk-jockey. He has published in *Meteor, Jump Cut, UmBau*, www.nachdemfilm.de and *Zeitgeschichte*. He has contributed a chapter on the phenomenology of film as bodily experience to Jürgen Felix (ed.), *Moderne Film Theorie* (Mainz: Bender 2002)

Jonathan Rosenbaum is film critic for the *Chicago Reader*. His books include *Moving Places, Placing Movies, Movies as Politics, Greed, Dead Man, Midnight Movies* (with J. Hoberman), and *Abbas Kiarostami* (with Mehrnaz Saeed-Vafa).

David Thomson's writings on film include biographies of David O. Selznick and Orson Welles; film-novels, such as *Suspects* and *Silver Light*; and *A Biographical Dictionary of Film* (now in its fourth edition).

Acknowledgements

The essays by Maitland McDonaugh, Jonathan Rosenbaum, Richard T. Jameson, Kent Jones, Jim Hoberman, Bérénice Reynaud and Howard Hampton were first published in a German translation in A. Horwath (ed.), *The Last Great American Picture Show* (Vienna: Wespennest, 1995), which, among others, also included Alexander Horwath's 'Introduction' and 'A Walking Contradiction', published as a single introductory essay.

The introductory chapters by Noel King and Thomas Elsaesser, and the essay by Drehli Robnik are original contributions, written for this volume.

The following essays were previously published in English:
David Thompson, 'The Decade When Movies Mattered' appeared originally in *Movieline*, August 1993, 42-47, 80.
Howard Hampton, 'Everybody Knows this is Nowhere' appeared adapted as 'Scorpio Descending: In Search of Rock Cinema' in *Film Comment*, March-April1997, 36-42.
Bérénice Reynaud, 'For Wanda' was also published in the on-line journal *Senses of Cinema*, http://www.sensesofcinema.com, 22 (October 2002).
Dana Polan, 'Auteurism as War-teurism' was first published in the Australian journal, *Metro* 119 (1999) 58-62.

Thomas Elsaesser, 'The Pathos of Failure: Notes on the Unmotivated Hero' was first published in *Monogram* 6 (October 1975) 13-19.

Adrian Martin, 'Grim Fascination' is an extensively revised and updated version of an essay which appeared in *Intervention* 21-22, 1988.

Christian Keathley 'Trapped in the Affection-Image' was first published in Anthony Enns and Christopher R. Smit (eds.) *Screening Disability* (Lanham, MD: University Press of America, 2001).

We would like to thank the authors and their publishers for their kind permission to reprint.

Noel King would like to thank Macquarie University for their financial assistance with the publication of this book, as well as acknowledge the financial support received from the University of Technology, Sydney at an earlier stage in the project.

Pictures (with credits)

Cover photo caption
Faye Dunaway in BONNIE AND CLYDE (© Warner Brothers/Seven Arts)

Alexander Horwath, *The Impure Cinema: New Hollywood 1967-1976*
Ben Johnson in THE LAST PICTURE SHOW (© Columbia Pictures)
Dustin Hoffman and Faye Dunaway in LITTLE BIG MAN (© United Artists)

Noel King, *'The Last Good Time We Ever Had': Remembering the New Hollywood Cinema*
Gene Hackman in THE CONVERSATION (© Paramount Pictures)
Randy Quaid, Jack Nicholson and Otis Young in THE LAST DETAIL (© Columbia Pictures)

Thomas Elsaesser, *American Auteur Cinema: The Last -or First- Great Picture Show*
Tim O'Kelly in TARGETS (© Paramount Pictures)
'Bruce' in JAWS (© MCA/Universal Pictures)

David Thomson, *The Decade When Movies Mattered*
Jack Nicholson in CHINATOWN (© Paramount Pictures)
Sterling Hayden and Nina Van Pallandt in THE LONG GOODBYE (© MGM/United Artists)

Alexander Horwarth, *A Walking Contradiction (Partly Truth and Partly Fiction)*
Gary Lockwood and Anouk Aimée in THE MODEL SHOP (© Columbia Pictures)
Dennis Hopper in TRACKS (© Paramount Pictures)

Maitland McDonagh, *The Exploitation Generation, or, How Marginal Movies Came in from the Cold*
Al Pacino in THE GODFATHER (© Paramount Pictures)

Jonathan Rosenbaum, *New Hollywood and the Sixties Melting Pot*
Dennis Hopper in THE LAST MOVIE (© Universal Pictures)

Richard T. Jameson, *Dinosaurs in the Age of the Cinemobile*
John Wayne in TRUE GRIT (© Paramount Pictures)
Candy Clark in FAT CITY (© Columbia Pictures)

Kent Jones, *'The Cylinders were whispering my name': The films of Monte Hellman*
James Taylor, Laurie Bird, Dennis Wilson in Two Lane Blacktop (© Universal Pictures)

J. Hoberman, Nashville *contra* Jaws, *or 'The Imagination of Disaster' Revisited*
Roy Scheider in Jaws (© MCA/Universal Pictures)

Bérénice Reynaud, *For* Wanda
Barbara Loden in/as Wanda (© Gemini Films)

Howard Hampton, *Everybody Knows this is Nowhere: The Uneasy Ride of Hollywood and Rock*
Arlo Guthrie in Alice's Restaurant (© United Artists)

Dana Polan, *Auteurism and War-teurism: Terrence Malick's War Movie*
Martin Sheen in Badlands (© Warner Brothers)

Thomas Elsaesser, *The Pathos of Failure: Notes on the Unmotivated Hero*
Julie Christie and Warren Beatty in Shampoo (© Columbia Pictures)

Christian Keathley, *Trapped in the Affection Image: Hollywood's Post-traumatic Cycle*
The Parallax View (© Paramount Pictures)

Adrian Martin, *Grim Fascination:* Fingers, *James Toback and* 1970s American Cinema
Harvey Keitel in Fingers (© Brut Productions)

Drehli Robnik, *Allegories of post-Fordism in* 1970s New Hollywood
The Dirty Dozen (© MGM)
Coma (© MGM)

Index of Film Titles

Film Culture in Transition
General Editor: *Thomas Elsaesser*

Double Trouble: Chiem van Houweninge on Writing and Filming
Thomas Elsaesser, Robert Kievit and Jan Simons (eds.)

Writing for the Medium: Television in Transition
Thomas Elsaesser, Jan Simons and Lucette Bronk (eds.)

Between Stage and Screen: Ingmar Bergman Directs
Egil Törnqvist

The Film Spectator: From Sign to Mind
Warren Buckland (ed.)

Film and the First World War
Karel Dibbets and Bert Hogenkamp (eds.)

A Second Life: German Cinema's First Decades
Thomas Elsaesser (ed.)

Fassbinder's Germany: History Identity Subject
Thomas Elsaesser

Cinema Futures: Cain, Abel or Cable? The Screen Arts in the Digital Age
Thomas Elsaesser and Kay Hoffmann (eds.)

Audiovisions: Cinema and Television as Entr'Actes in History
Siegfried Zielinski

Joris Ivens and the Documentary Context
Kees Bakker (ed.)

Ibsen, Strindberg and the Intimate Theatre: Studies in TV Presentation
Egil Törnqvist

The Cinema Alone: Essays on the Work of Jean-Luc Godard 1985-2000
Michael Temple and James S. Williams (eds.)

Micropolitics of Media Culture: Reading the Rhizomes of Deleuze and Guattari
Patricia Pisters and Catherine M. Lord (eds.)

Malaysian Cinema, Asian Film: Border Crossings and National Cultures
William van der Heide

Film Front Weimar: Representations of the First World War in German Films of the Weimar Period (1919-1933)
Bernadette Kester

Camera Obscura, Camera Lucida: Essays in Honor of Annette Michelson
Richard Allen and Malcolm Turvey (eds.)

Jean Desmet and the Early Dutch Film Trade
Ivo Blom

City of Darkness, City of Light: Émigré Filmmakers in Paris 1929-1939
Alastair Phillips

Printed in Great Britain
by Amazon

27284637R00218